Atomic Obsession

Atomic Obsession

Nuclear Alarmism from Hiroshima to Al-Qaeda

JOHN MUELLER

OXFORD
UNIVERSITY PRESS

OXFORD
UNIVERSITY PRESS

Oxford University Press, Inc., publishes works that further
Oxford University's objective of excellence
in research, scholarship, and education.

Oxford New York
Auckland Cape Town Dar es Salaam Hong Kong Karachi
Kuala Lumpur Madrid Melbourne Mexico City Nairobi
New Delhi Shanghai Taipei Toronto

With offices in
Argentina Austria Brazil Chile Czech Republic France Greece
Guatemala Hungary Italy Japan Poland Portugal Singapore
South Korea Switzerland Thailand Turkey Ukraine Vietnam

Copyright © 2010 by John Mueller

Published by Oxford University Press, Inc.
198 Madison Avenue, New York, NY 10016
www.oup.com

First issued as an Oxford University Press paperback, 2012.

Oxford is a registered trademark of Oxford University Press.

Library of Congress Cataloging-in-Publication Data
Mueller, John E.
Atomic obsession : nuclear alarmism from Hiroshima to al-Qaeda / John Mueller.
 p. cm.
Includes bibliographical references and index.
ISBN 978-0-19-538136-8 (hardcover); 978-0-19-983709-0 (paperback)
1. Hiroshima-shi (Japan)—History—Bombardment, 1945.
2. World War, 1939–1945—Japan—Hiroshima-shi.
3. Qaida (Organization) 4. War on Terrorism, 2001–
5. Nuclear weapons.
I. Title.
HV6433.85.M84 2009
355.02'17—dc22   2009012860

9 8 7 6 5 4 3 2 1

Printed in the United States of America
on acid-free paper

To Judy,
to Karl, Michelle, Karen, Erik, Susan, and Kraig,
to Timothy, Samuel, Clara, Kara, Malcolm, Atticus, and Lida,
to Lois and Phyllis
and to the memory of Robert H. Johnson

Contents

Preface

Over the lengthy history of publishing, quite a few books have proven to be fairly reliable remedies for insomnia. This one, however, may be the first where that effect is the author's main intention.

Drowsiness will not be induced, I hope, because the prose is enervatingly flaccid, dry, confused, convoluted, opaque, or turgid. Rather, the book could have its desired effect if it fulfills its central purpose. That is to put to rest, or at any rate to attenuate, an often overwhelming concern that has for decades very commonly kept policymakers and ordinary citizens from enjoying as deep and uninterrupted a slumber as they presumably deserve: excessive anxiety about nuclear weapons.

Ever since the 1945 bombing of Hiroshima ushered in what is often dubbed the "atomic age" or the "nuclear era," people have obsessed about the potential for massive, even civilization-ending, destruction seemingly inherent in the weapon exploded there. Over the decades this obsession has variously focused on an endless array of creative, if consistently unfulfilled, worst-case scenarios deriving from fears about the cold war arms race, nuclear apocalypse, and the proliferation of the weapons to unreliable states (or even to reliable ones).

For example, in 1960 we were told by a distinguished pundit that it was a "certainty" that several nuclear weapons would go off within ten years, and a top nuclear strategist declared it "most unlikely" that the world could live with an uncontrolled arms race for decades. In 1974, a scientist glumly suggested that we'd "have to live with the expectation that once every four or five years a nuclear explosion will take place and kill a lot of people." In 1979, a very prominent political scientist proclaimed the world to be moving ineluctably toward a third world war and added that nothing could be done to prevent it.[1] In the process, there has also often been wild extrapolation when envisioning the effects of nuclear weapons. The explosion of a single atomic bomb capable of destroying a few city blocks is taken to portend the demise of the entire city, the economy of the country, the country itself, the modern state system, civilization, the planet. Armageddon and apocalypse have continuously been found to be looming just over the horizon.

Disaster has also been envisioned as the inexorable result if more countries obtain nuclear weapons. Before China obtained its bomb, the director of the Central Intelligence Agency prophesied that, with that event, nuclear war would become "almost inevitable." Moreover, the rate at which new countries would obtain the weapons has almost always been wildly off the mark. It was in 1960, for example, that a presidential candidate insisted that there might be "ten, fifteen, twenty" countries with a nuclear capacity by 1964. In 1964 itself a high-level committee asserted that the world was fast approaching a point of no return on this. And for decades, prominent analysts have prophesied that Germany and Japan would necessarily soon get nuclear weapons.

Declamations like that very much continue to this day. If Iran or North Korea gets a nuclear weapon, we are repeatedly told, the result will be a proliferation cascade (or epidemic or wave or avalanche), and the result of that will be a nuclear war or, in the words of the esteemed, and imaginative, head of the International Atomic Energy Agency, "the beginning of the end of our civilization." There is, a recent think tank report suggests, "something approaching a consensus" among experts "both in and out of government" that we are "on the verge of a new nuclear age" where there will be more states with nuclear weapons and a much greater chance the weapons will be used. As a result, the continuously discredited "nightmare vision" of the 1960s, in the words of another alarmed analyst, "still holds."[2]

Following on this grand legacy of impending doom, there has been a particular fixation since the terrorist attacks of September 11, 2001, on the potential for a terrorist atomic bomb, and politicians of all stripes preach to an anxious, appreciative, and very numerous choir when they, like President

Barack Obama, alarmingly proclaim it "the most immediate and extreme threat to global security."[3]

Among those deeply concerned is Governor Thomas Kean, chair of the 9/11 Commission, who has confessed that what keeps him up at night is "the worry of a terrorist with a nuclear device in one of our major cities." Bill Keller of the New York Times has complained about a similar disorder: after finishing a long article about nuclear terrorism for that newspaper's magazine entitled "Nuclear Nightmares," he remained boldly determined not to evacuate Manhattan, but, he admitted, "neither am I sleeping quite as soundly." Like Kean and Keller, FBI Director Robert Mueller reportedly wakes up in the middle of the night worrying about an al-Qaeda nuclear strike. Indeed the affliction seems general. Defense Secretary Robert Gates maintains that, when asked what keeps them awake at night, every senior leader declares it to be "the thought of a terrorist ending up with a weapon of mass destruction, especially nuclear."[4]

In the case of the FBI director, there are other worrying symptoms as well: it is carefully reported that there are "dark circles under his eyes" from thinking about the prospect, and when he utters the words, "nuclear device," he "knits his brow and clenches his teeth" even as his left eyebrow lifts "like an arrow poised in midflight." Similarly, Rolf Mowatt-Larssen, formerly a top investigator at the CIA, ranks himself among the many who consider the atomic terrorist to be an "existential" threat, and he, too, reportedly can't sleep because he is convinced al-Qaeda is "looking for uranium," that it "could build a Hiroshima-size bomb," and that "we'd never see it coming." His anxiety on the issue is quite palpable to concerned observers: "He's going grim, sepulchral. He hasn't touched his corn muffin."[5]

This book examines the atomic bomb problem and concludes that, like earlier insomniacs in the atomic obsession tradition, Keller, Governor Kean, Director Mueller, and former spook Mowatt-Larssen—indeed, the entire senior leadership—should feel free to get some sleep. Perhaps eyebrows can even be lowered and muffins consumed.

Central to the argument is an assessment of the costs and consequences of the obsession with nuclear weapons over the seven decades of our "atomic age." Fears and anxieties about them, while understandable, have been excessive, and they have severely, detrimentally, and even absurdly distorted spending priorities while inspiring policies that have often been overwrought, ill conceived, counterproductive, and sometimes massively destructive. And they continue to do so.

THE ROAD AHEAD

The book consists of three parts corresponding to the dimensions of the atomic obsession sketched above. Each relates to the others, but each is also substantially independent.

The first part examines the effects of nuclear weapons and the influence they have had on history since their invention. That impact, it appears, has been rather modest: things would have turned out much the same had the weapons never been invented. They were not necessary to prevent World War III because, even without them, the leading countries would still have been deterred from a war with each other and would have had strong incentives to keep their differences and crises under control. The weapons' impact on other substantive historical events (or nonevents) seems to have been quite limited as well.

At the same time, however, they have had a truly massive influence on hawkish and dovish rhetoric, on exquisite theorizing (particularly on the creative spewing out of fanciful worst-case scenarios), and on defense expenditures. Indeed, during the course of the cold war, calculates one astronomer, the United States spent somewhere between 5.5 and 10 trillion dollars on nuclear weapons—enough to purchase everything in the country except for the land.[6] All this, primarily to confront, to deter, and to make glowering and menacing faces at, a perceived threat of direct military aggression that, essentially, didn't exist. Two decades after the cold war, the outlays continue to be laid out even though it is not clear what relevant dangers remain out there that could possibly justify such expenditures.

The second part of the book assesses the effects of the spread of nuclear weapons within and to states. A prevailing technological fixation has inspired a concomitant assumption, or assertion, that because the weapons exist, war must inevitably follow, that it is weapons and arms races, not people, that principally and inexorably cause war. This perspective has led to decades of intense, and mostly futile and unnecessary, anguish over arms control and disarmament issues—or gimmicks.

Moreover, despite endlessly repeated predictions, remarkably few countries have taken advantage of the opportunity to develop nuclear weapons, and the sporadic proliferation that has taken place has, contrary to urgent forecasts, been of very little consequence. A key reason for this is that the possession of such expensive armaments actually conveys in almost all cases rather little advantage to the possessor. In the main, they are difficult to obtain, militarily useless, and a spectacular waste of money and scientific talent.

Because of this, and contrary to the policy consensus, diffusion of the weapons is by no means inevitable, and nuclear proliferation, while not necessarily desirable, is unlikely to accelerate or prove to be a major danger. At the same time, anxious and ill-advised antiproliferation efforts have actually enhanced the appeal of—or the desperate desire for—nuclear weapons for some regimes, and the wars and extreme sanctions they have inspired have been a necessary cause of far more deaths than have been inflicted by all nuclear detonations in all of history.

The third part of the book examines the atomic terrorist nightmare that has become so pervasive since 9/11, an expression of the atomic obsession that has not only caused widespread sleep disorders but has also inspired protective and policing expenditures that are likely to prove substantially excessive. Actually, it is not all that clear that any terrorist groups really want the weapons or are remotely capable of obtaining them should the desire to do so take hold of them. If they try, there are a host of practical and organizational difficulties that make their likelihood of success vanishingly small.

Atomic Obsession

PART I

The Impact of Nuclear Weapons

1

Effects

Beyond doubt, nuclear weapons are the most effective devices ever fabricated for killing vast numbers of people in a short period of time. This does not mean, however, that the explosion of a nuclear bomb or two—or even quite a few of them—will necessarily justify characterizing the destruction wreaked as total annihilation, vaporization, or societal extinguishment. Accordingly, it is important at the outset to assess the effects—and the limits—of nuclear weapons.

To suggest that such limits exist is not to deny the awesome capacity of nuclear weapons to inflict damage and expunge life. However, ever since the world became impressed by the ghastly spectacle of Hiroshima, the damage nuclear weapons can inflict, both physically and in terms of their social and political impact, has very often been rendered in hyperbolic, indeed apocalyptic, terms. Then, to make matters worse, a new category has been created, "weapons of mass destruction," that puts far less damaging weapons in the same category as nuclear ones.

This chapter will assess the effects of the weapons; the next, the hyperbole.

NUCLEAR WEAPONS

Atomic bombs, like the ones dropped on Japan in 1945 and like the ones most likely to be acquired by, or fall into the hands of, less-developed states, may have an explosive capacity—a yield—in the range of the equivalent of perhaps 10,000 tons of TNT, or 10 kilotons (KT). Substate groups might be able to create weapons of that size, though, more likely, any they are able to fabricate would be smaller.[1] Thermonuclear, or hydrogen, bombs can easily become much larger—even upwards of the equivalent of 1,000,000 tons of TNT, or 1 megaton (MT).

It makes a considerable difference in assessing the likely impact of a bomb whether it is airburst—set off so that the bomb's fireball does not reach the surface—or groundburst—set off so that it does. Bombs that are groundburst scoop up considerable quantities of earth and debris and loft them into the air, where they gradually settle to the ground as radioactive fallout. Bombs that are airburst, like the ones dropped over Hiroshima and Nagasaki, produce far less fallout, but their explosive range is much wider.

Electromagnetic Pulse

The bomb would set off an electromagnetic wave that, although causing no deaths, would short out or burn out electrical components. This effect would be fairly short-range for groundburst weapons, but a large bomb exploded at altitudes above 19 miles could have an impact over hundreds or even thousands of miles.[2]

Direct Radiation and the Neutron Bomb

Natural background radiation varies from locality to locality, but for the United States it averages about 3 millisieverts (mSv) per year. A radiation dose sufficient to kill 50 percent of the people affected is 5,000 mSv.[3] At the site of a nuclear explosion, those close in would instantly receive a lethal dose of radiation. For large bombs, those killed this way would also be within the lethal range of other effects of the bomb. However, for smaller, Hiroshima-size bombs, direct radiation would kill some people who were able to survive the other effects.[4]

A neutron bomb makes use of this difference. Its yield would be quite small, 100 tons or 0.1 KT. If a bomb like that were exploded a few hundred yards above the ground, it would do little damage to buildings on the ground, but it would still deliver a lethal radiation dose over an area. It could, then, kill tankers in tanks while leaving the vehicles undamaged, or librarians in libraries while leaving the books intact.[5]

Thermal Pulse: Heat and Light

A nuclear explosion would also produce a blinding flash of heat and light lasting perhaps two seconds that would inflict burns on people who are in its direct path and are insufficiently clothed or otherwise unshielded. Depending on distance, some would receive first-degree burns, equivalent to a bad sunburn, on their exposed skin, or second- or third-degree burns that, if covering a quarter or more of their skin, would likely prove fatal if untreated. There might also be many cases of blindness among people who looked at the flash, but they would recover their sight after several minutes.

An important additional effect would be the setting of fires that, depending on the availability and distribution of combustible material in the area, could become extensive and intense.[6] Most fires would be of the "conflagration" type: the fire would expand outward depending on the supply of combustible material nearby. Less common would be "firestorms" in which the fire does not spread but burns itself out intensely in a fixed area, sucking in oxygen to the point where people who were not killed by other effects would die of suffocation.

Blast

The bomb would also produce a destructive blast of overpressure and wind that could crush objects, move or collapse buildings, and throw people through the air. The destructive radius of an airburst 1-MT bomb is much greater than that of an airburst 10-KT bomb, of course, but not as great as those numbers suggest. The radius of destruction is about six times greater for the larger bomb, not orders of magnitude greater, as the yield measures would imply.[7]

Fallout, Longer-Term Radiation, and "Dirty" Bombs

A nuclear explosion lofts irradiated particles into the air—in considerable amounts for groundburst weapons, but far less for airburst ones. Depending on winds and other weather conditions, these lofted particles would be spread in a plume anchored at the blast site and, over a period of days and weeks, would fall to the earth, decaying, but mostly still radioactive. Where such particles descend in sufficient concentrations within this plume, exposed people could become ill or die from the radiation. People who remain anywhere within the plume area would likely stand an enhanced risk of contracting cancer in later years. Radioactive material could also be sprayed over a small area by a conventional explosion, a device routinely labeled a "dirty bomb."

Although radiation levels within an area affected, or contaminated, by fallout or a dirty bomb would eventually become safe by peacetime standards, it could take from two to ten years to do so, a process that could be speeded up by active decontamination procedures. However, "peacetime standards" are set at extremely conservative levels. Agencies have extrapolated down in a linear fashion from high radiation dose levels known to be harmful without conclusive evidence that this procedure is justified. In fact, the General Accounting Office in 2000 concluded that standards administered to protect the public from low-level radiation exposure "do not have a conclusive scientific basis, despite decades of research."[8]

The Environmental Protection Agency has deemed any enhancement of radiation to be unacceptable—that is, to be considered "contamination"— if, following its controversial extrapolation down from levels known to be harmful, the radiation would in principle increase an individual's chances of getting cancer by one in 10,000 if that individual continued to live in the affected area nonstop for 40 years. Since one's chances of dying from cancer are something like 20 percent already, that would be the equivalent of raising the cancer rate for such a stationary individual from 20 percent to 20.01 percent. In general, a person developing cancer years or decades later from the effects of a nuclear explosion would likely not be able to determine whether the radiation was the cause of the cancer.[9]

As it happens, the levels conventionally deemed unacceptable are almost within the error range for determining background levels: estimates for the average background radiation routinely endured by people in the United States range from 3.00 to 3.60 mSv per year, and the comparable figure for the United Kingdom is 2.70 mSv per year. Yet in both places agencies have declared a rise of more than 1 mSv per year above background levels to be unacceptable. For comparison, moving to Denver from coastal areas increases radiation exposure by some 0.21 mSv per year due to increased exposure to cosmic radiation and by an additional 0.63 mSv per year due to increased radon in the soil, and the enhanced radiation level for the two-mile-high Colorado city of Leadville comes in at 1.43 mSv per year. Meanwhile, one region in China has a background level of 6.4 mSv per year, and some areas within that region register at 17.0 mSv per year. Nonetheless, as it happens, Denver does not seem to suffer elevated cancer rates; indeed scores of studies conducted around the world have found little or no evidence of increased cancer risks in areas with high background radiation levels.[10]

A rise of 1 mSv per year is comparable to moving from the seacoast to a mountain in Colorado. However, the accepted convention is that if levels in an area become elevated above that level by, for example, fallout, they must be cleaned up so that they register at only 0.15 mSv per year above background by the standards set forth by the EPA or 0.25 mSv per year by those promulgated by the only slightly less conservative Nuclear Regulatory Agency.[11]

Some analysts find such standards far too conservative and recommend raising the permissible levels by a factor of ten. Among the critics is physicist Wade Allison of Oxford University, who forcefully argues that biological cells have developed the capacity to repair damage caused by low radiation doses and therefore low-level radiation represents no hazard whatever. He advocates relaxing acceptable radiation standards by a factor of at least 500. Actually, some scientists think raising radiation levels slightly above background levels may be beneficial by activating natural coping mechanisms in the body—rather in the way exercise is healthier than sloth, or the moderate consumption of alcohol, a poison at high doses, is good for the health.[12]

Questions about the dangers of the kind of limited increases in radiation levels that would be caused by most fallout and almost all dirty bomb effects have been raised for years. For example, radiation from fallout killed none of the 23 Japanese fishermen inadvertently exposed to very large doses, about 2,000 to 6,000 mSv, after a nuclear test in 1954 (the lethal dose, again, is 5,000 mSv). Also important are the results of an exhaustive study by eight United Nations agencies, completed some 20 years after the event, of the effects of the 1986 Chernobyl nuclear reactor meltdown in the Soviet Union. The accident, which lofted a huge amount of radiation into the atmosphere, resulted in the deaths of less than 50 people, most of them underprotected emergency workers. Thyroid cancer rates among children were raised, but almost all were treated successfully, and only nine died. The UN study concludes that even in the longer term, cancer rates may rise among the affected population by less—possibly far less—than one percentage point. In addition, there was no spike in fertility problems or in birth defects.[13]

Indirect and Longer-Term Effects

Beyond the human destruction, a nuclear attack would obviously have a punishing impact in the bombed area on communications, sanitation and health facilities, agriculture, and the economy. Depending on the extent of the attack, these effects could also have widespread and longer-term consequences, potentially leading to famine, epidemics, and societal disruptions or even breakdown. In addition, some scientists have controversially argued that the smoke and debris lofted into the atmosphere by an attack with thousands of large bombs might well block the sun's rays for a considerable period of time, leading to a "nuclear winter" that would have devastating long-term consequences not only for the bombed country but for the world at large, or at least for the northern hemisphere.[14]

All-Out Thermonuclear War

To begin to approach a condition that can credibly justify applying such extreme characterizations as societal annihilation, a full-out attack with hundreds, probably thousands, of thermonuclear bombs would be required. Even in such extreme cases, the area actually devastated by the bombs' blast and thermal pulse effects would be limited: 2,000 1-MT explosions with a destructive radius of 5 miles each would directly demolish less than 5 percent of the territory of the United States, for example.

Obviously, if major population centers were targeted, this sort of attack could inflict massive casualties. Back in cold war days, when such devastating events sometimes seemed uncomfortably likely, a number of studies were conducted to estimate the consequences of massive thermonuclear attacks. One of the most prominent of these considered several possibilities. The most likely scenario—one that could be perhaps be considered at least to begin to approach the rational—was a "counterforce" strike in which well over 1,000 thermonuclear weapons would be targeted at America's ballistic missile silos, strategic airfields, and nuclear submarine bases in an effort to destroy the country's strategic ability to retaliate. Since the attack would not directly target population centers, most of the ensuing deaths would be from radioactive fallout, and the study estimates that from 2 to 20 million, depending mostly on wind, weather, and sheltering, would perish during the first month.[15]

That sort of damage, which would kill less than 10 percent of the population, might or might not be enough to trigger words like "annihilation."

However, the study's ultimate scenario undoubtedly would do so for just about everyone. It considered the impact of an attack in which thousands of thermonuclear warheads, most having yields of a megaton or more, were rained down not only on military targets but also on urban and industrial ones. In this extreme scenario, the study calculates—or, to use its word, speculates—that something like 20 to 55 million would likely perish in the lowest set of estimates, and between 155 and 165 million in the highest. And there would also be, needless to say, catastrophic negative societal aftereffects.[16]

The study concluded as well that under either attack scenario, there could be considerable ecological impact—including, potentially, a nuclear winter effect—that could conceivably be as devastating in the long run as the attacks themselves.[17]

Hiroshima and Nagasaki

An examination of the destruction wreaked by the atomic bombs that were exploded by airburst over the Japanese cities of Hiroshima and Nagasaki in the last days of World War II is particularly useful for present purposes. These are, of course, the only cases in which nuclear explosions have taken place on populated targets, and there is a considerable amount of information about both the short-term and long-term effects of the bombings. In addition, in many respects these are the kinds of weapons of greatest concern today. Although plenty of thermonuclear weapons still exist, particularly in the arsenals of the United States and Russia, any nuclear bombs fabricated by terrorists or set off by newly emerging nuclear states like Pakistan or North Korea are likely to have yields similar to, or perhaps quite a bit lower than, those exploded over Japan in 1945.

About 67,000 people were killed in the two cities on the first day, and another 36,000 died over the next four months. Many casualties were due to fires in these tinderbox cities filled with wooden houses, and they were high both because of the especially flammable nature of the building construction and because an unusually large number of people happened to be outside, were lightly clothed on those August mornings, and took no shelter. Only superficial wounds were received by those two and a half miles (4 km) away even when fully exposed, and the 400 people at Nagasaki who managed to be inside cavelike bomb shelters were uninjured even though they were close to ground zero. The physical damage inflicted in the bombings was also, of course, extensive, in part because of the exceptional vulnerability of most of the buildings with their thick tile roofs on light, flammable wooden frames. However, many modern buildings of steel and concrete survived the attack, even when they were close to the blast center; no nonwooden bridges were destroyed; and railroad tracks, streets, and underground water lines were largely undamaged. Electrical service was restored within one day, railroad and trolley service within two, telephone service within seven, and the debris was largely cleared up within two weeks.[18]

Because of this experience, some analysts in the early days were skeptical about the military value of the atomic bomb. If the atomic bomb couldn't destroy bridges, its potential military contribution was not entirely obvious; perhaps, they reasoned, the atomic bomb might be useful only to terrorize people or blast cities. In addition, the official estimate was that it would have taken 210 bomber sorties to inflict the same damage on Hiroshima and 120 for Nagasaki, something that would have been quite feasible at the time.[19]

Because both bombs were airburst, they produced little fallout except locally. Extensive long-range studies of the attacks find that while cancer rates among the survivors were somewhat elevated from radiation, the experience made little or no difference in mortality or in birth defect rates.[20]

The Effects of a Groundburst Hiroshima-Size Atomic Bomb or Device

An atomic explosion perpetrated by a terrorist group, it is widely assumed, would likely not be a "bomb" at all—that is to say, a weapon launched through the air by a bomber or missile. Rather, it would be a "device," an explosive transported to the site and then detonated on the ground. If it had a yield comparable to the Hiroshima bomb, however, its blast and thermal pulse effects would be considerably less extensive. Specifically, the area undergoing severe blast would extend less than a half mile out from the explosion, and the full range of such damage would extend out to less than a mile, compared to the up to two and a half–mile radius of destruction at Hiroshima—that is, the damage would cover about three square miles as opposed to Hiroshima's ten or twenty. The lethal range of direct radiation—the area in which half of those exposed could be expected to die from radiation disease within two months—would extend about eight-tenths of a mile out from ground zero.[21]

However, fallout effects would be much greater than at Hiroshima because the groundburst weapon would loft far more radioactive debris into the atmosphere. Estimates suggest that, if there were no wind, an area of from two to six miles out from the explosion could become lethally contaminated—that is, over half of those who remained in the area could be expected to die of radiation within two months.[22] Rather than spreading out evenly, of course, the fallout pattern would likely extend out in a plume determined by local winds and weather, potentially diluting the impact somewhat. Rain could also reduce the effect considerably.

As noted earlier, a terrorist nuclear bomb or device, including one of the "suitcase" variety, would probably be quite a bit smaller than the one dropped on Hiroshima—perhaps 1-KT, about the yield of those tested by North Korea in 2006 and 2009, or even less. The largest conventional bomb has a yield of 11 tons, so a bomb of 1,000 tons would be, of course, far more destructive and, if exploded in a populated area like New York's Times Square, would kill many people. But, to keep things in perspective, that same bomb exploded a few blocks away in the middle of Central Park would not be able to destroy any buildings on the park's periphery.[23]

THE WMD EXPANSION

A sort of bait and switch extrapolation emerged in the wake of the cold war. Perhaps because policy makers did not have enough to worry about at the time, the term, "weapons of mass destruction" came into vogue.[24] Although the phrase had been used earlier, it was often taken to be simply a dramatic synonym for nuclear weapons or to group nuclear weapons with weapons that might in the future be developed with similar destructive capacity.

According to one analysis, the phrase in various meanings came up at most a few dozen times a year in the *New York Times* through 1989. Since then, however, it has been used hundreds of times each year in that newspaper, and, more importantly, beginning in 1992, the phrase was explicitly codified into American law and determined to embrace not only nuclear weapons but chemical and biological ones, and then, in 1994, radiological ones as well. Nuclear weapons can indeed inflict massive destruction, but chemical, radiological, and most biological weapons simply do not belong in the same category of destructiveness.[25]

Chemical arms may have the potential, under appropriate circumstances, for panicking people; killing masses of them in open areas, however, is beyond their modest capabilities. Although they obviously can be hugely lethal when released in gas chambers, their effectiveness as weapons has been unimpressive, and their inclusion in the weapons of mass destruction category is highly dubious unless the concept is so diluted that bullets or machetes can also be included.

Thus, biologist Matthew Meselson calculates that it would take fully a ton of nerve gas or five tons of mustard gas to produce heavy casualties among unprotected people in an open area one kilometer square. Even for nerve gas this would take the concentrated delivery into a rather small area of about 300 heavy artillery shells or seven 500-pound bombs. This would usually require a considerable amount of time, allowing many people to evacuate the targeted area. A 1993 analysis by the Office of Technology Assessment of the U.S. Congress finds that a ton of sarin nerve gas perfectly delivered under absolutely ideal conditions over a heavily populated area against unprotected people could cause between 3,000 and 8,000 deaths. Under slightly less ideal circumstances—if there was a moderate wind or if the sun was out, for example—the death rate would be only one-tenth as great. Or as the Gilmore Commission, a presidential advisory panel, put it later, it would take a full ton of sarin gas released under favorable weather conditions for the destructive effects to become distinctly greater than could be achieved by conventional explosives.[26]

Properly developed and deployed, biological weapons could potentially, if thus far only in theory, kill hundreds of thousands, perhaps even millions, of people. The discussion remains theoretical because biological weapons have scarcely ever been used. For the most destructive results, they need to be dispersed in very low-altitude aerosol clouds. Since aerosols do not appreciably settle, pathogens like anthrax (which is not easy to spread or catch and is not contagious) would probably have to be sprayed near nose level. Moreover, 90 percent of the microorganisms are likely to die during the process of aerosolization, while their effectiveness could be reduced still further by sunlight, smog, humidity, and temperature changes. Explosive methods of dispersion may destroy the organisms, and, except for anthrax spores, long-term storage of lethal organisms in bombs or warheads is difficult: even if refrigerated, most of the organisms have a limited lifetime. Such weapons can take days or weeks to have full effect, during which time they can be countered with medical and civil defense measures. In the summary judgment of two careful analysts, delivering microbes and toxins over a wide area in the form most suitable for inflicting mass casualties—as an aerosol that could be inhaled—requires a delivery system of enormous sophistication, and even then effective dispersal could easily be disrupted by unfavorable environmental and meteorological conditions.[27]

Radiological weapons or "dirty bombs," in which radioactive materials are sprayed over an area by a conventional explosion, are often called "the poor man's nuclear weapon." However, unlike the rich man's version, they are incapable of inflicting much immediate damage at all. In fact, it would be almost impossible to disperse radioactive material from a dirty bomb explosion so that victims would absorb a lethal dose before being able to leave the area, and it is likely that few, if any, in the target area would be killed directly, become ill, or even have a measurably increased risk of cancer.[28]

Actually, most analysts consider radiological devices to be more nearly weapons of mass disruption than of mass destruction. This is because, although the sudden release of additional radiation into the environment by a nuclear device would kill few, if any, people outright (perhaps some who happen to be standing nearby would be killed by the explosion itself), it might engender panic or at least mass disorientation or overly hasty efforts at evasion. It could also raise radiation levels in an area into ranges officially considered unacceptable, thereby in principle requiring expensive evacuation and decontamination procedures made necessary by official radiation safely levels that are remarkably, and perhaps excessively, conservative.

Moreover, although a dirty bomb would be easier to assemble than a nuclear weapon, the construction and deployment of one is difficult and requires considerable skill.[29] Among other problems, the bombmakers would risk exposing themselves to doses of radiation so lethal that even suicidal operatives might not live long enough to deliver and set off the device.

Despite these inconvenient facts, distinctions between the weapons have often been blurred in alarmed discussion. In the process, the sometimes essentially absurd expansion of the WMD category has taken hold to the point where anguish over the possibility that a country might obtain chemical weapons can be almost as great as that inspired by its possible acquisition of nuclear ones, a phenomenon on view in the United States in the debate during the run-up to the 2003 war against Iraq.

WMD AND BATTLEFIELD MESSINESS

Although chemical, biological, and radiological weapons scarcely merit classification in the same category as nuclear ones by most standards, there is one interesting similarity between them: from the perspective of the battlefield, all are particularly messy.[30] And, although rarely remarked upon, this interesting characteristic has special relevance to some of the issues concerning nuclear proliferation.

In World War I, chemical weapons proved to be almost wholly ineffective against well-protected troops except as an inconvenience. Indeed, in the conclusion to the official British history of the war they are relegated to a footnote which asserts that gas "made war uncomfortable... to no purpose." Military distaste for the weapons was inspired not only because gas masks were awkward, heavy, and uncomfortable, but because the weapons complicate the battlefield enormously and present huge problems of logistics, training, and decontamination, all to little military benefit.[31]

Similarly, a central reason why biological weapons have never really been used stems from the fact that their impact is very difficult to predict, while in combat situations they, like gas, may spread back on the attacker. Moreover, there seems to be no certain way damage can be halted once it is set in motion.

Few radiological weapons make much battlefield sense either. Unless a lethal dose can be crisply administered (as with a neutron bomb perhaps), raising the level of radiation in an area makes little sense because, although it may increase cancer rates in the indefinite future, there is no immediate effect on the enemy's fighting capacity, and an area one might later hope to occupy would become complicatedly contaminated. And, as with biological weapons, the effects of the weapons would be difficult to predict, to plan for, and to control.

Unlike chemical, biological, and radiological weapons, nuclear weapons have, of course, been built into military planning. However, the bulk of this consideration has been concerned with deterrence, not with battlefield applications. When one considers the impact of nuclear weapons in combat situations, many of the military defects found with the other weapons placed (however questionably) in the WMD category obtain. Of special concern would be the messy problems presented by fallout and by radioactive contamination—particularly because many battlefield applications would require that the weapons be groundburst.

These issues do not hold as strongly for calculations by terrorists, who might simply seek to use such weapons to sow anxiety, fear, and uncertainty. However, when assessing the potential battlefield utility of nuclear weapons, state military planners have frequently been unable to see how, on balance, they are superior to conventional ones. In consequence, the military value of the weapons is, to that degree, contained, and enthusiasm for obtaining them can be similarly attenuated.

2

Overstating the Effects

Ever since Hiroshima there has been a tendency to overstate the likely impact of a single atomic explosion, and then, in further amplification, the impact of a single, smaller explosion has often been casually equated (or conflated) with the impact of a much larger one—or even with that of a series of larger ones. As historian Spencer Weart describes the process, "You say 'nuclear bomb' and everybody immediately thinks of the end of the world."[1] Imagery can lead to obsession and, although nuclear weapons are certainly exceptionally destructive, the common tendency to inflate their effects, sometimes to an absurd degree, can have undesirable intellectual and policy consequences.

OVERSTATING THE PHYSICAL EFFECTS

Exaggeration of the physical impact of the bomb goes back to the dawn of the atomic age. A year after the bombings in Japan, A-bomb maker J. Robert Oppenheimer maintained that three or four men with smuggled atomic bomb units could "blow up New York." This represents either a massive exaggeration of the capacity of the bombs of that era or a staggering underappreciation for the physical size of the city. Although expanding fires and fallout might increase the effective destructive radius, a groundburst Hiroshima-size device would "blow up" about 1 percent of the city's area. Oppenheimer also repeatedly recollected that, upon witnessing the first atomic test, he was reminded of a verse from the Bhagavad Gita, the mystic Hindu scripture he had been fascinated by for years, "Now I am become death, the destroyer of worlds." Obviously, Oppenheimer is entitled to savor any vivid literary allusions that happen to spring into his mind at emotional moments, but, taken literally, the atomic bombs he was so instrumental in fabricating scarcely had the capacity to become the destroyer of worlds. Hyperbole is also suggested in the title of one of the most important early books on the bomb: *The Absolute Weapon*.[2]

In the ensuing decades, massive exaggerations of the physical effects of nuclear weapons have been very much the rule. Words like "liquidate," "annihilate," and "vaporize," not to mention "Armageddon" and "apocalypse," have been commonly applied in scenarios where those sorts of extreme characterizations are simply not sound. As with Oppenheimer in 1946, it remains a massive overstatement to confidently insist, as the prominent foreign policy analyst Joseph Cirincione does today, that "a nuclear 9/11 would destroy an entire city," or to conclude with Robert Gallucci that a single terrorist atom bomb would be capable of "obliterating a large portion of a city." Nor is it correct to casually assert, as journalist Lawrence Scott Sheets does, that an atomic bomb of the size exploded at Hiroshima (or smaller) could, in the hands of terrorists, "kill millions of people."[3]

And defense analyst Brian Jenkins is (presumably knowingly) engaging in rather extravagant hyperbole when he says that America's "awesome nuclear arsenal" during the cold war could have "destroyed the planet." But his auditors are likely to take him literally, and they are likely to do so as well for Cirincione when he asserts that the world's remaining arsenal of 26,000 nuclear weapons is enough "to destroy the planet several times over." By contrast, as one physicist points out, "the largest bomb that has ever been exploded anywhere was sixty megatons, and that is one-thousandth the force of an earthquake, one-thousandth the force of a hurricane."[4]

The effects of radiation from nuclear explosions—particularly from fallout—have also frequently been inflated (and even more so for radiation emitted by a so-called dirty bomb). Nuclear radiation can make extensive areas technically uninhabitable but, as discussed in the previous chapter, in many cases this is because tolerance standards for radiation have been set at levels that are extremely conservative.

Particularly in the case of terrorism, there has been a persistent tendency to exaggerate the physical impact not only of atomic explosions, but also of conventional ones. Thus, in 1999 a man was intercepted crossing the Canadian border in a car with some 130 pounds of explosives and bomb-making material in his trunk. He was apparently planning to detonate his bomb at Los Angeles International Airport, and if he had been able to accomplish this mission, he could have visited considerable damage to the airport and might have killed dozens of people in the process. However, his mission has routinely been rendered as "a plot to blow up Los Angeles International Airport," a characterization that is a huge exaggeration: the amount of explosives he was transporting could not possibly have taken out that sprawling facility. By contrast, the truck bomb that ripped apart a single building in Oklahoma City in 1995 contained somewhere between 5,000 and 7,000 pounds of bomb material, and it delivered an explosion equivalent to 4,000 pounds of TNT.[5]

OVERSTATING THE SOCIAL AND POLITICAL EFFECTS

If there has been a tendency to overstate the physical destruction of nuclear weapons, particularly of atomic bombs, there has been a parallel drumbeat of hyperbole concerning their likely social and political impact. These consequences are, of course, not as calculable as those of the bombs' likely physical effects. However, even allowing considerably for uncertainty, people of all stripes have for decades massively exaggerated the likely response to the kind of nuclear explosion posited in their arguments.

As suggested in the previous chapter, there are nuclear attack scenarios that could visit damage to a society that can credibly be characterized as "existential." However, that extreme word has often been casually applied to ones in which the damage is likely, however tragic, to be vastly more limited. If it is absurd, reckless, and irresponsible to suggest that a single Hiroshima-size atomic bomb could kill millions of people, it is even more so to suggest that an attack with one or a few such weapons would cause a large country like the United States to cease to exist.

Nonetheless, such extreme, even hysterical, proclamations proliferate, and they have gone almost entirely unexamined and unrefuted, perhaps in part because potential examiners and refuters are wary of seeming to be callously trivializing the horrors of an atomic blast. But to maintain that one or a few atomic explosions are scarcely likely to spell the end of society is not to maintain that their effects would be trivial.

Postured exaggeration has become commonplace particularly in the wake of 9/11. Thus Senator Richard Lugar contends that terrorists armed with atomic weapons (or even of lesser "weapons of mass destruction") present an "existential" threat to the United States, and so does the CIA's alarmed Rolf Mowatt-Larssen, without, of course, bothering to explain how that "existential" thing actually plays out in practice. Meanwhile, political scientist Joshua Goldstein is convinced nuclear terrorists could "destroy our society." Two counterterrorism officials from the Clinton administration, Daniel Benjamin and Steven Simon, contend that a small atomic detonation would halt or even reverse globalization, "could be the defeat that precipitates America's decline," and would "trigger an existential crisis for the United States and its allies." When he was chairman of the Joint Chiefs of Staff, General Richard Myers calculated that if terrorists were able to kill 10,000 Americans in an attack, something quite possible with an atomic bomb, they would "do away with our way of life."[6]

Some have indulged in even grander nightmares. Graham Allison asserts that atomic terrorists could "destroy civilization as we know it," and Matthew Bunn and Anthony Wier contend that they threaten the "world's security." Michael Ignatieff becomes positively cosmic by warning alarmingly that atomic terrorists threaten "the ascendancy of the modern state." And legal scholar Philip Bobbitt, deeply alarmed that nuclear weapons are becoming "commodified," espies a "threat to mankind."[7]

The process by means of which one or a few atomic explosions would lead to the extinguishing of a country like the United States, much less of "civilization," "mankind," or the "modern state system," is rarely made clear in such extravagant proclamations—it is apparently taken to be self-evident. Thus, former Central Intelligence Agency Director George Tenet is confident that if terrorists "manage to set off a mushroom cloud," that would "destroy our economy," but he nowhere bothers to explain how the instant and tragic destruction of three square miles in, say, the middle of Ohio would lead inexorably to national economic annihilation.[8]

Others at least take a stab at it. Goldstein thinks it would take two terrorist bombs in cities to "destroy our economy and way of life." After the second blast, he suggests, "Not knowing what was coming next, Americans might stream out of the major cities (what would you do?) and bring the economy to a standstill." Charles Ferguson and William Potter speculate that the explosion of a crude nuclear weapon in the center of a city would cause Americans to live in fear that they would die in a future attack, a fear that would "erode public confidence in the government" with the result that "the tightly interconnected economies in the rest of the world could sink into a depression." Benjamin and Simon array more detail. If terrorists were able to detonate a "relatively small—ten kiloton—bomb" in lower Manhattan,

> the financial and cultural center of the United States would cease to exist. The metropolitan area would be uninhabitable, living only in the nation's imagination and in aerial footage of the blast zone. America's GDP would fall by 3 percent immediately, and one of its major ports would be closed indefinitely...Americans could lose confidence in their social and political institutions. The potential for a breakdown in public order would necessitate the suspension of civil liberties...Populations would desert major urban areas. The vast number of wounded and traumatized people from the New York region, and the shattered national sense of physical security, would precipitate an unprecedented and long-lasting public health crisis.

In like manner, General Tommy Franks, in an interview in *Cigar Aficionado*, opines that a "massive casualty-producing event somewhere in the western world" (not just one in the United States) could well cause the American population "to question our own Constitution and to begin to militarize our country," in the process losing "what it cherishes most, and that is freedom and liberty."[9]

Alarmist Ignatieff writes with impressive certainty that "inexorably, terrorism, like war itself, is moving beyond the conventional to the apocalyptic," but he does pause to explain how this will come about. Although Americans did graciously allow their leaders one fatal mistake in September 2001, he contends, they simply "will not forgive another one." If there are several large-scale attacks, particularly with "ultimate weapons," he confidently predicts that the trust that binds the people to its leadership and to each other will crumble, and the "cowed populace" will demand that tyranny be imposed upon it, and quite possibly break itself into a collection of rampaging lynch mobs devoted to killing "former neighbors" and "onetime friends." The solution, he thinks, is to crimp civil liberties now in a desperate effort to prevent the attacks he is so confident will necessarily impel us to commit societal, cultural, economic, and political self-immolation.[10]

As the subtext (or sometimes the text) of these vivid and imaginative warnings suggests, excessive political and social consequences of an atomic attack would arise not so much from what the terrorist bomb would do to us, but what we would do to ourselves in response. In Bobbitt's vision, when hit by a series of terrible attacks, America will transform itself into a "state of terror...We will confront this fate with repugnance at first, of course, and then with reluctance, then with desperation, and finally with resignation."[11]

But, although it is a speculative consideration, it seems rather unlikely that the United States would react to an atomic explosion by summarily and necessarily destroying itself. A nuclear explosion in the United States would be horrible of course, and judicious, cost-effective efforts to further reduce the already distant likelihood of such an event are certainly justified. But in all probability the country would prove to be resilient, and readily, if grimly, absorb even that kind of damage without instantly becoming a fascist state. In 1945, Japan weathered not only two nuclear attacks but intense nationwide conventional bombing, a horrific experience that nevertheless scarcely destroyed Japan as a society or even as an economy. Nor has persistent, albeit nonnuclear, terrorism in Israel caused that state to disappear—or to abandon democracy. Moreover, the notion that a terrorist attack would cause the people to lose confidence in the government is belied by the traumatic experience of 9/11, when the confidence expressed in America's leaders soared. And it further flies in the face of decades of disaster research, which repeatedly documents that socially responsible behavior increases under such conditions.[12]

General Myers' prediction that the sudden deaths from terrorism of 10,000 Americans would "do away with our way of life" might be assessed in this regard. As it happens, officials estimated for a while in 2005 that there would be 10,000 deaths from Hurricane Katrina. Although this, of course, was not a terrorist act, there were no indications whatever that such a disaster, while catastrophic for the hurricane victims themselves, would do away with the way of life of the rest of the nation. It is also easy to imagine scenarios in which 10,000 would have been killed on September 11—if the planes had hit the World Trade Center later in the day when more people were at work, for example—and indeed, early estimates at the time were much higher than 3,000.[13] Any death is tragic, but it is not at all obvious that a substantially higher loss on 9/11 would have necessarily triggered societal suicide—even if it had been accompanied by a mushroom cloud.

OVERSTATING THE IMPORTANCE OF THE EXISTENCE
OF NUCLEAR WEAPONS

In addition to the improvident and often cosmic inflation of the likely physical, social, and political impact of a nuclear explosion, there has been a consistent alarmed exaggeration of the impact of the weapon's mere existence.

Although no nuclear weapons have been exploded in a hostile manner since 1945, it has often been maintained that their existence means they must necessarily go off at some time—and usually soon. Perhaps the most dramatic example of this is novelist/scientist C.P. Snow's once-heralded alarmist broadside published a half century ago in which he claimed somehow to know that, unless a restriction was placed on nuclear armaments, "Within, at the most, ten years, some of those bombs are going off." He went on to insist that he was rendering a "certainty" and "saying this as responsibly as I can."[14]

Sober analysts also insist that the bombs by their very existence somehow automatically create a damaging "instability"—or sometimes, even more vaporously, "complexity"—in an area. Accordingly, one of them insists that if any one of a number of potential nuclear countries simply reduces the time required to acquire nuclear weapons, the development "would have a destabilizing impact" not only on regional, but also global security. And there have been perennial worries that, by their existence, nuclear weapons will cause wars. General Larry Welch voices concern about the likelihood that "highly destructive wars would increase as the number of actors armed with these weapons rises."[15]

The world has managed to live for two-thirds of a century with increasing numbers of nuclear weapons, now amounting to tens of thousands dispersed over several countries. Plenty have existed, but none have gone off. The notion that they automatically will somehow explode or cause major trouble could now use, one might think, some reexamination rather than empty, if alarming, repetition.

A NOT-SO-DISTANT MIRROR: CHEMICAL WEAPONS

World War I, called "the Great War" for two decades after it came to an end in 1918, is particularly remembered for a ghastly innovation: chemical warfare. However, although gas was used extensively, it actually accounted for less than one percent of the battle deaths, and on average it took well over a ton of gas to produce a single fatality. Only some 2 or 3 percent of those gassed on the Western front died; by contrast, wounds caused by traditional weapons were some 10 or 12 times more likely to prove fatal. Moreover, troops wounded by gas returned to combat more quickly than those wounded by bullets or shrapnel, and suffered less. Longer-range health effects also seem to have been quite limited.[16]

Nonetheless, quite a few people were soon embracing extreme visions of doomsday—some of them at least as extravagant as those spun out about nuclear weapons after the next world war. As one prominent politician recalled later, "We thought of air warfare in 1938 rather as people think of nuclear warfare today."[17]

It was maintained, for example, that Paris could be "annihilated" in an hour by 100 airplanes each carrying a ton of gas, and a former British War Ministry official told the House of Lords that 40 tons could "destroy the whole population of London." Others claimed that 20 large gas bombs could destroy Chicago or Berlin, or that "one air force group ... could completely paralyze all activities in a city the size of New York for any protracted period." Some military theorists, especially the influential Italian general Giulio Douhet, concluded from the experience of the Great War that any ground war would quickly and necessarily degenerate into a stalemate, while air power would determine the outcome. He calculated that 500 tons of bombs, mostly gas, could destroy a large city and its inhabitants. One report anticipated "that such permanent and serious damage would be done ... in the depopulation of large sections of the country, as to threaten, if not destroy, all that has been gained during the painful centuries of the past."[18]

Others envisioned even grander images of destruction. Winston Churchill concluded that war had now become "the potential destroyer of the human race. ... Mankind has never been in this position before. Without having improved appreciably in virtue or enjoying wiser guidance, it has got into its hands for the first time the tools by which it can unfailingly accomplish its own extermination." Psychoanalyst Sigmund Freud concluded his 1930 book *Civilization and Its Discontents* by expressing his own discontent with the way civilization had developed: "Men have brought their powers of subduing nature to such a pitch that by using them they could now very easily exterminate one another to the last man." British prime minister Stanley Baldwin was one of many who declared that in the next war European civilization would be "wiped out."[19] World War II did, of course, prove to be horrific, but civilization and mankind did survive the experience.

EXPLANATIONS FOR OVERSTATEMENT

In the 1936 motion picture *Things to Come,* with a screenplay by H. G. Wells, an English character observes on Christmas Day 1940, as a cataclysmic war employing the dreadful weapons of the time is about to break out, "If we don't end war, war will end us." More than two decades later, American president John F. Kennedy, with nuclear weapons in mind, insisted that "mankind must put an end to war or war will put an end to mankind."[20]

At least some of the reasons for such dire extrapolations are the same in both cases—though, of course, Kennedy's assertion is considerably more likely to be justified. To begin with, chemical and nuclear attacks are similar in that they have a peculiar horror about them that has attracted journalists and others who know well that ghoulish copy very commonly sells.

After World War I, a few people mused that gas was actually a comparatively humane weapon because, like bullets and shrapnel, it incapacitated the enemy in a militarily productive manner but did not actually kill nearly as many of those it incapacitated. Therefore, gas allowed battles to be decided with a minimal loss of life. For example, H.L. Gilchrist, the U.S. Army's leading expert on the medical effects of chemical warfare, concluded that gas "is the most humane method of warfare ever applied on the battle field," and the prominent British defense analyst Basil Liddell Hart speculated in 1925 that "gas may well prove the salvation of civilization from otherwise inevitable collapse in case of another world war." Nonetheless, most people found gas to be a repulsive form of warfare, perhaps because of the *way* it killed or because of the ghoulish images of men dehumanized by gas masks, though it is far from obvious why a soldier wearing a gas mask is held to be foolish, inhuman, and monstrous, but not one whose head is encased in a knight's helmet.[21]

The peculiar hostility to nuclear weapons is also not entirely clear. They can kill lots of people, but the casualties at Hiroshima and Nagasaki were quite a bit lower than those inflicted in earlier bombing raids conducted with conventional ordnance. Most of the most horrible pictures from the atomic bombings show charred bodies or survivors with disfiguring burns, but pictures like that could have been produced aplenty after the firestorm raids on Tokyo. It was novel in warfare to kill people by radiation, but that actually accounted for only a minority of deaths at Hiroshima and Nagasaki.

Nonetheless, as the poet didn't say, ugliness lies in the eye of the beholder. And journalists and essayists were ready to play to their audience after both world wars when the public quickly came to deem death by gas in one case, or by a nuclear explosion in the other, to be peculiarly repugnant.

Aiding in the process have been the exaggerations of those who, both before and after World War II, assiduously sought to make the next war seem supremely dreadful in hopes that the sheer horror of the images of things to come would frighten people into making sure wars didn't happen. Thus, in the wake of the atomic bombings, notes historian Paul Boyer, "atomic scientists, world-government advocates, and international-control advocates played upon the profound uneasiness pervading the nation." As a result, "America's airwaves, pulpits, and lecture halls were full of such frightening fare ... as the nation's atomic fears were manipulated and exacerbated by the media and by political activists."[22]

Consequently, atomic scientist Phillip Morrison mused, "We have a chance to build a working peace on the novelty and terror of the atomic bomb," and Albert Einstein expressed the hope that the bomb "would intimidate the human race into bringing order into its international affairs," even as another scientist insisted that "only one tactic is dependable—the preaching of doom." Meanwhile, *Bulletin of the Atomic Scientists* editor Eugene Rabinowitch indicated that a purpose of his publication was "to preserve civilization by scaring men into rationality," and J. Robert Oppenheimer said he returned "so insistently to the magnitude of the peril" because he espied "an opportunity unique and challenging" in "our one great hope" that the "vast threat" to "all the peoples of the earth" might generate a politically productive "terror." This "politicization of terror," notes Boyer, was decisive in shaping the cultural climate after Hiroshima. Indeed, "the strategy of manipulating fear to build support for political resolution of the atomic menace helped fix certain basic perceptions about the bomb into the American consciousness, and it set a precedent for activist strategy that would affect all later anti-nuclear crusades."[23]

However, the hype actually helped the hawks. Some commentators warned at the time that "no man or nation was ever frightened into real brotherhood or peace," and, concludes Boyer, the fearmongering of the doves "had the reverse effect, leading to an increased reliance on the bomb as the best source of security in a threatening world," especially after the Soviets tested their first atomic bomb in 1949.[24]

Concerns about this possibility had been voiced before. Baldwin may have exaggerated the likely consequences of another war in Europe, but he was aware of the dangers, from his point of view, in doing so. "Fear is a very dangerous thing," he warned. "It is quite true that it may act as a deterrent in people's minds against war, but it is much more likely to act to make them want to increase armaments to protect them against the terrors that they know may be launched against them."[25]

And indeed, during and after the cold war, both conservative and liberal hawks have used the horrors of nuclear weapons in the hands of actual or potential enemies to stoke support for increases in defense expenditures to defend and to deter.

Moreover, there may be interests that benefit in one way or another from the exaggeration.[26] Thus, in the wake of World War II, both the Japanese and the Americans had an incentive to inflate the importance and the destructiveness of the Hiroshima and Nagasaki bombings. For the Japanese, notes one historian, "the bomb offered a convenient explanation to soothe wounded Japanese pride: the defeat of Japan was not the result of leadership mistakes or lack of valor; it was the result of an unexpected advance in science by Japan's enemy." And the Americans, as the bomb's sole possessor, may have felt it would enhance their prestige and influence in the region.[27]

CONSEQUENCES OF OVERSTATEMENT

To repeat: it is certainly true that nuclear weapons can be massively destructive. Moreover, if thousands (or maybe hundreds) of the largest are launched, the results on society could be as calamitous as the alarmists insist—or nearly so. But because an all-out attack with thermonuclear weapons could be catastrophic, it does not follow that similar descriptors should unthinkingly and casually be applied to explosions that would do vastly less damage, however horrible the consequences of those explosions would be in their own right. Moreover, it obviously does not follow that because these weapons exist, they will necessarily and inevitably go off.

Nevertheless, because of the vivid, dramatic, and unforgettable impression left by the Hiroshima bombing, and in part perhaps because of the exertions in the postwar period by legions of alarmists from all corners of the political spectrum, nuclear fears have escalated to the point where simply lacing the weapons into the conversation often causes coherent thought to cease.

Concern about nuclear weapons and about their awesome destructive capacity is certainly justified. But routine exaggerations of that capacity, and the obsession with the weapons such exaggerations have inspired and enforced, have often led to international policies that have been unwise, wasteful, and destructive—sometimes even more destructive than the bombs themselves.

Thus, wars have been fought and devastating economic sanctions have been inflicted to prevent fully deterrable and containable countries from obtaining nuclear weapons. And the consummate horror that terrorists might be able to obtain an atomic bomb has inspired costly policies and exertions, often without any consideration about how likely dread consequences are to happen. Even many of those who do not consider the al-Qaeda terrorists to present much of a threat are nonetheless mesmerized by the fear of an atomic weapon in their hands. These considerations are central to the discussion in the remainder of this book.

3

Deterring World War III

Essential Irrelevance

Although many people concluded after Hiroshima that the continued existence of nuclear weapons promised eventual calamity, not to mention apocalypse, Armageddon, annihilation, and doomsday, others, in very distinct contrast, came to argue that the historical impact of the weapons could actually be supremely beneficial. This perspective is reflected in the confident assertion by a group of prominent foreign policy experts in 2007 that nuclear weapons proved to be "essential to maintaining international security during the cold war because they were a means of deterrence."[1]

Essentially embracing what can be called the "Churchill counterfactual," this proposition emphasizes the emergence after World War II of a "curious paradox" and a "sublime irony" whereby nuclear weapons vastly spread "the area of mortal danger," with the potential result that "safety will become the sturdy child of terror, and survival the twin brother of annihilation."[2]

Rendered in more pointed, if less eloquent, phraseology, the Churchill counterfactual holds that if, counter to fact, nuclear weapons had not been invented, disaster was pretty much inevitable. That is, the people running world affairs after 1945 were at base so incautious, so casual about the loss of human life, so conflagration-prone, so masochistic, so doom-eager, so incompetent, and/or simply so stupid that in all probability they could not have helped plunging or being swept into a major war if the worst they could have anticipated from the exercise was merely the kind of catastrophic destruction they had so recently experienced in World War II.

Following this line of thinking, defense analyst Edward Luttwak has argued that "we have lived since 1945 without another world war precisely because rational minds... extracted a durable peace from the very terror of nuclear weapons," while political scientists Robert Art and Kenneth Waltz contend that the probability of a world war is "practically nil precisely because the military planning and deployments of each, together with the fear of escalation to general nuclear war, keep it that way." Accordingly, those who abhor war should presumably take the advice of Waltz and "thank our nuclear blessings" or, as Elspeth Rostow proposes, bestow upon the atomic bomb the Nobel Peace Prize.[3]

To me, the opposite counterfactual seems more plausible. It suggests that if nuclear weapons had never been invented, another massive war would still have failed to come about, that the weapons were essentially irrelevant to the process.

Although there has been no world war since 1945 and although nuclear weapons have very consciously been developed and deployed in part to deter such a conflict, it does not follow that the weapons have prevented the war. In fact, stability has been overdetermined: even without nuclear weapons, the major nuclear countries would have been deterred from a war with each other. Or, to put it another way, while nuclear weapons may have been sufficient to prevent another world war, they have not been necessary to do so.[4]

It is possible to imagine hypothetical situations in which nuclear weapons could make, or could have made, a difference, and it is certainly true that nuclear weapons have, as will be discussed in chapter 5, substantially influenced political rhetoric, public discourse, and defense budgets and planning. But in the world we've actually inhabited, they do not seem to have been necessary either to deter world war or, more generally, to cause the major nuclear countries to behave cautiously in crisis situations.

DETERRENCE OF WORLD WAR

Those supporting the Churchill counterfactual have variously contended that nuclear weapons give "rational people pause," that they have "drastically reduced the probability" of war between "states that have them," that nuclear deterrence is "much more robust than conventional deterrence," that nuclear weapons can cause destruction that is "unimaginably enormous" to *both* sides and can do so extremely quickly, that "the vision of future war that Hiroshima burned into everyone's mind was vastly more frightening than any that had existed before," and that new technologies of war have "amplified the message of this century's war experiences by many decibels, and set it firmly in the minds of the wide public as well as those of political and military leaders."[5]

It is appropriate to compare probabilities and degrees of robustness, to note increased degrees of destructiveness, and to calibrate burning visions, rational pauses, and decibel levels. But it is important as well to consider what those levels were before they were enhanced. A jump from a 50th-story window is quite a bit more terrifying to think about than a jump from a 5th-story one, and quite a bit more destructive as well; but anyone who finds life even minimally satisfying is readily deterred from either adventure. Nuclear weapons may well have "reinforced an already declining propensity on the part of great powers to fight one another," as historian John Gaddis puts it.[6] But in my view, this was essentially similar to the way a $1,000 gift reinforces a millionaire's wealth or a straitjacket reinforces a Quaker's propensity to shun violence.

To contend that the ominous presence of nuclear weapons prevented a war, one must assume that there would have been a war had these weapons not existed. In the case of the nuclearized rivalry between the United States and the USSR, there were several important war-discouraging factors: the memory of World War II; the general postwar contentment of the victors; the cautious emphasis of Soviet ideology—the chief upsetting element in the postwar world—on lesser kinds of violence and warfare; and the fear of escalation.

The Memory of World War II

The people in charge of world affairs during the cold war were the same people or the direct intellectual heirs of the people who tried assiduously, frantically, desperately, and, as it turned out, ineffectually, to prevent World War II. They did so in part because they feared—correctly, it gave them no comfort to discover—that another major war would be even worse than World War I. I find it difficult to understand how people with those sorts of perceptions and with that vivid and horrifying experience behind them would eventually become at best incautious about, or at worst eager for, a repeat performance. But that, essentially, is what the Churchill counterfactual asks us to believe. On the face of it, to expect these countries somehow to allow themselves to tumble into anything resembling a repetition of that experience—whether embellished with nuclear weapons or not—seems almost bizarre.

It is true they could be expected to be even *more* hostile to a nuclear war, but neither side needed visions of mushroom clouds to conclude that a direct war between them was a really terrible idea. For them, nuclear weapons simply compound and dramatize a military reality that by 1945 had already become appalling: few with the experience of World War II behind them would contemplate a repetition with anything other than horror. As Secretary of State Alexander Haig put it in 1982: "The catastrophic consequences of another world war—with or without nuclear weapons—make deterrence our highest objective and our only rational military strategy."[7]

None of this is meant to deny that nuclear war is appalling to contemplate and mind-concentratingly dramatic, particularly in the speed with which it could bring about massive destruction. Nor is it meant to deny that decision makers, both in times of crisis and otherwise, are fully conscious of how horribly destructive a nuclear war could be. It is simply to stress that the sheer horror of repeating World War II is not all that much *less* impressive or dramatic, and that people with that experience behind them will strive to avoid anything that they feel could lead to *either* calamity.[8]

Moreover, if the experience of World War II deterred anyone, it probably did so to an extreme degree for the Soviets. Officially and unofficially they seemed obsessed by the memory of the destruction they suffered. In 1953, Ambassador Averell Harriman, certainly no admirer of Stalin, observed that the Soviet dictator "was determined, if he could avoid it, never again to go through the horrors of another protracted world war." As historian David Holloway put it 40 years later after an extensive analysis of newly available documents from the era, "There is no evidence to show that Stalin intended to invade Western Europe, except in the event of a major war, and his overall policy suggests that he was anxious to avoid such a war, and not merely because the United States possessed the atomic bomb." And the Soviets presumably picked up a few messages from their experience in World War I as well; as political scientist William Taubman notes, they learned the "crucial lesson" that world war "can destroy the Russian regime."[9]

Georgy Kornienko, a member of the Soviet foreign ministry from 1947, forcefully asserted that he was "absolutely sure" the Soviets would never have initiated a major war even in a nonnuclear world. The weapons, he thought, were an "additional factor" or "supplementary," and "not a major reason." In his memoirs, Nikita Khrushchev is quite straightforward about the issue: "We've always considered war to be against our own interests"; he says he "never once heard Stalin say anything about preparing to commit aggression against another [presumably major] country." And the memories lingered: President Gerald Ford recalls how Soviet leader Leonid Brezhnev at a meeting in 1974 "reached over and grabbed my left hand with his right hand. He began by telling me how much his people had suffered during World War II. 'I do not want to inflict that upon my people again,' he said."[10]

Postwar Contentment

For many of the combatants World War I was as destructive as World War II, but its memory did not prevent another world war. Of course, most nations *did* conclude from the horrors of World War I that such an event must never be repeated: if the only nations capable of starting World War II had been Britain, France, the USSR, and the United States, the war would probably never have occurred. Unfortunately other major nations sought direct territorial expansion, and conflicts over these desires finally led to war.[11]

Unlike the situation in the 1930s, however, the only countries capable of creating another world war after 1945 were the big victors, the United States and the Soviet Union, each of which emerged comfortably dominant in its respective sphere: as Waltz has observed, they had "more reason to be satisfied with the status quo than most earlier great powers had."[12] (Indeed, except for the dismemberment of Germany, even Hitler might have been content with the empire his archenemy Joseph Stalin controlled at the end of the war.) While there have been many disputes after the war, neither country had a grievance so essential as to make a world war—whether nuclear or not—an attractive means for removing it.

Soviet Ideology

The Soviet Union and international communism did have visions of changing the world in their preferred direction. However, their ideology, both before and after the invention of the atomic bomb, stressed revolutionary procedures over major war. The Soviet Union may have harbored some sort of hegemonic desire (or dream), as many argued, but, with a few possible exceptions (especially the Korean War) to be discussed below, its tactics stressed subversion, revolution, diplomatic and economic pressure, seduction, guerrilla warfare, local uprising, and civil war—activities for which nuclear weapons have little relevance. The Communist powers never— before or after the invention of nuclear weapons—subscribed to a Hitler-style theory of direct, Armageddon-risking conquest, and they have been extremely wary of provoking Western powers into large-scale war.

Founder Vladimir Lenin did suggest in 1919 that a series of "frightful collisions" between the Soviet Republic and the capitalist states was "inevitable" before international capitalism collapsed. But the Soviets have expected those collisions to arise only from attacks on them by the enemy, citing continually the example of Western intervention in their civil war in the aftermath of World War I. And by 1935 at the latest, official proclamations had abandoned the notion that such wars were inevitable, concluding that the solidarity of the international working class and the burgeoning strength of the Soviet armed forces had made them avoidable.[13]

Moreover, Lenin's methodology contains a strong sense of cautious pragmatism: A good revolutionary moves carefully in a hostile world, striking when the prospects for success are bright and avoiding risky undertakings. Indeed, three central rules for Soviet leaders were "avoid adventures," "do not yield to provocation," and "know when to stop." The approach was, in Gaddis' apt construction, "a combination of appetite with aversion to risk."[14]

Khrushchev puts the policy this way: "we Communists must hasten" the "struggle" against capitalism "by any means at our disposal, *excluding war*." Similarly, Russian specialist and cold war hawk Richard Pipes concludes that Soviet interests were "to avoid general war with the 'imperialist camp' while inciting and exacerbating every possible conflict within it," and he also stresses the Soviet tactical emphasis on "utmost caution," patience, and prudence. Major war, whether nuclear or not, simply does not fit into this worldview. As one of the Soviet Union's top reformers recalls, although the regime felt an ideological commitment to help revolutions in places like Cuba and Angola, there was not a single person among the Communist Party elders "who believed that one day we were going to take over the United States or that we could defeat the United States, or that we were seriously preparing for a nuclear war with the United States. No one, as far as I know, had this absurd notion."[15]

The Fear of Escalation

Given the postwar contentment with the territorial status quo and given the focus embedded in Soviet ideology on revolution rather than on direct warfare, it is not clear that *any* form of military deterrence has been necessary to prevent world war. However, even assuming military deterrence was necessary, or at least desirable, cataclysm has been prevented not so much by visions of nuclear horror as by the generally accepted belief that a direct conflict between the major countries could easily escalate to a level, nuclear or not, that those essentially satisfied states would find intolerably costly.[16]

To deal with this important issue, it is useful to assess two phenomena of the early postwar years: the potential for a Soviet postwar invasion of Europe and the Korean War.

A POTENTIAL SOVIET INVASION OF EUROPE? Some have argued that the Soviets would have been tempted to take advantage of their conventional strength after World War II to snap up a prize like Western Europe if its chief defender, the United States, had not possessed nuclear weapons. Winston Churchill, as usual, put the proposition most eloquently when he advanced the "melancholy thought" in 1950 that "nothing preserves Europe from an overwhelming military attack except the devastating resources of the United States in this awful weapon." A decade later the prominent American military strategist Albert Wohlstetter asserted that the Soviets had been "deterred from taking over Europe" solely by fear of an American nuclear response. So widely embraced had this highly consequential proposition become by then that Wohlstetter did not even bother to justify it.[17]

This argument requires at least three questionable assumptions. The first is that the Soviets really thought of Western Europe as a prize worth taking risks for. This assumption was certainly not obvious to defense analyst Bernard Brodie at the time: "It is difficult to discover what meaningful incentives the Russians might have for attempting to conquer Western Europe." Nor to diplomat George Kennan: "I have never believed that they have seen it as in their interests to overrun Western Europe militarily, or that they would have launched an attack on that region generally even if the so-called nuclear deterrent had not existed." Historian Hugh Thomas has aptly characterized Stalin's postwar policy as "conflict which should not be carried into real war.... Thus, though expansion should be everywhere attempted, it should not come too close to fighting in zones where the United States, and probably Britain, would resort to arms." After the cold war was over, a great amount of documentary evidence became available, but as Robert Jervis notes, "the Soviet archives have yet to reveal any serious plans for unprovoked aggression against Western Europe." Or, in the words of historian Stephen Ambrose, "*At no time* did the Red Army *contemplate*, much less plan for,*" an offensive against West Europe.[18] It is possible, of course, that the sole reason the Soviets neglected even to contemplate an attack on the West derived from concern about American nuclear weapons. Far more likely, however, is that, as Kennan suggests, such a venture, given their global game plan stressing revolutionary upheaval and given their experience with two disastrous world wars, scarcely made any sense whatever.

The second assumption is that, even without the atomic bomb to rely on, the United States would have disarmed its conventional forces after 1945 as substantially as it did. And the third is that the Soviets actually ever had the strength to be quickly and overwhelmingly successful in a conventional attack in Western Europe, an assumption that was strongly questioned by some analysts during the cold war and has been increasingly challenged since.[19]

However, even if one accepts these three very questionable assumptions, the Soviet Union would in all probability still have been deterred from attacking Western Europe by the enormous potential of the American war machine. The problem for the USSR was that, even if it had the ability and the desire to blitz Western Europe and even if there were no nuclear weapons to worry about, it could not have stopped the United States from repeating what it did after 1941: mobilizing with deliberate speed, putting its economy onto a wartime footing, and wearing the enemy down in a protracted conventional major war of attrition massively supplied from its unapproachable rear base.

The economic achievement of the United States during the war was astounding. While holding off one major enemy, it concentrated with its allies in defeating another, then turned back to the first. Meanwhile, it supplied everybody. With 8 million of its ablest men out of the labor market, it increased industrial production 15 percent per year and agricultural production 30 percent overall. Before the end of *1943* it was producing so much that some munitions plants were closed down, and even so it ended the war with a substantial surplus of wheat and over $90 billion in surplus war goods (national governmental expenditures in the first peacetime year, 1946, were only about $60 billion).[20]

And if anyone was in a position to appreciate this, it was the Soviets. By various circuitous routes the United States supplied the Soviet Union with, among other things, 409,526 trucks, 12,161 combat vehicles (more than the Germans had in 1939), 32,200 motorcycles, 1,966 locomotives, 16,000,000 pairs of boots (in two sizes), and over one-half pound of food for every Soviet soldier for every day of the war (much of it Spam).[21] It is the kind of feat that concentrates the mind, and it is extremely difficult to imagine the Soviets willingly taking on this somewhat lethargic, but ultimately hugely effective, juggernaut.

That Stalin was fully aware of the American achievement—and deeply impressed by it—is clear. Adam Ulam has observed that Stalin had "great respect for the United States' vast economic and hence military potential, quite apart from the bomb," and that his "whole career as dictator had been a testimony to his belief that production figures were a direct indicator of a given country's power." As a member of the Joint Chiefs of Staff put it in 1949, "If there is any single factor today that would deter a nation seeking world domination, it would be the great industrial capacity of this country rather than its armed strength." Or as Thomas has concluded, "If the atomic bomb had not existed, Stalin would still have feared the success of the U.S. wartime economy."[22]

After a successful conventional attack on Western Europe, the Soviets would have been in an unenviable position similar to that occupied by Japan after Pearl Harbor: they might have gains aplenty, but they would have no way to stop the United States (which along with its major allies, Canada and Japan, would be out of the reach of Soviet arms) from eventually gearing up for, and then launching, a costly and enervating war of attrition.[23] All they could hope for, like the Japanese in 1941, would be that their victories would cause the Americans to lose their fighting spirit. But if Japan's Asian and Pacific gains in 1941 propelled the United States into war, it is to be expected that the United States would find a Soviet military takeover of an area of far greater importance to it—Western Europe—to be alarming in the extreme. Not only would the United States be outraged at the American casualties in such an attack and at the loss of an important geographic area, but it would very likely conclude (as many Americans did conclude in the late 1940s even without a Soviet invasion of Europe) that an eventual attack on the United States itself was inevitable. Any Hitler-style protests by the Soviets that they had no desire for further territorial gains would not be very credible.

Thus, even assuming that nuclear weapons had never been invented and even assuming that the Soviets had the desire and the conventional capability easily to take over Western Europe, the undoubted American capacity to wage a huge, continent-hopping war of attrition from south, west, and east could be a highly effective deterrent.[24]

LESSONS FROM THE KOREAN WAR. Despite the vast American superiority in atomic weapons in 1950, Stalin was willing to approve or at least acquiesce in an outright attack by a Communist state on a non-Communist one in Korea, and it must be assumed that he would have done so at least as readily had nuclear weapons not existed. The American response was essentially the result of the lessons learned from the experiences of the 1930s: comparing this to similar incursions in Manchuria, Ethiopia, and Czechoslovakia, Western leaders resolved that such provocations must be firmly countered. If they were allowed to succeed, they would only encourage more aggression in more important locales later.[25]

For the Soviets the lessons of the Korean War must have enhanced those of World War II: once again the United States was caught surprised and inadequately armed, once again it rushed hastily into action, once again it soon applied itself in a forceful way to combat—and in this case for an area that it had previously declared to be of only peripheral concern. If the Korean War was a limited probe of Western resolve, the Soviets seem to have drawn the lessons the Truman administration intended. Unlike Germany, Japan, and Italy in the 1930s, they were tempted to try no more such probes: there were no Koreas after Korea.[26] It is likely that this valuable result would have come about regardless of the existence of nuclear weapons, and it suggests that the Korean War helped to delimit the methods the Soviet Union would be allowed to use to pursue its policy.[27]

CRISIS BEHAVIOR

Because of the harrowing image of nuclear war, it is sometimes argued, the United States and the Soviet Union were notably more restrained than they might otherwise have been, and thus crises that might have escalated in earlier eras to dangerous levels were resolved safely at low ones.[28]

There is, of course, no definitive way to refute this notion, since we are unable to run the events over again without nuclear weapons. And it is certainly true that decision makers were well aware of the horrors of nuclear war and clearly could not ignore the possibility that a crisis could lead to such devastation.

However, it should not be assumed that crises normally lead to war. Indeed, very often they don't.[29] Moreover, the notion that it is the fear of nuclear war that kept behavior restrained looks far less convincing when its underlying assumption is directly confronted: that the major countries would have allowed their various crises to escalate if all they had to fear at the end of the escalatory ladder was a catastrophic exercise like World War II. Whatever the rhetoric in these crises, it is difficult to see why the unaugmented horror of repeating World War II, combined with a considerable comfort with the status quo, wouldn't have been enough to inspire restraint.

Once again: what deters is the belief that escalation to something intolerable will occur, not so much the details of the ultimate unbearable punishment. Where the belief that the conflict will escalate is absent, nuclear countries *have* been militarily challenged with war—as in Korea, Vietnam, Afghanistan, Algeria, and the Falklands.[30]

Did the existence of nuclear weapons keep the Korean conflict restrained? As noted, the Communist venture there seems to have been a limited probe—though somewhat more adventurous than usual and one that got out of hand with the massive American and Chinese involvement. As such, there was no particular reason—or meaningful military opportunity—for the Soviets to escalate the war further. In justifying *their* restraint, the Americans continually stressed the danger of escalating to a war with the Soviet Union—something of major concern whether or not the Soviets possessed nuclear weapons.

Interestingly, it seems that, even in the great "nuclear" crisis over Cuba in 1962, the central figures would have been about equally anxious to keep the conflict under control even if they could have been guaranteed that any ensuing armed conflict would remain conventional.

From the start, Khrushchev was clearly moved by the wars he had already experienced and had no intention of working his way closer toward a repeat of those calamities—much less a worse one. "I have participated in two world wars," Khrushchev wrote Kennedy at the height of the crisis, "and know that war ends only when it has carved its way across cities and villages, bringing death and destruction in its wake."[31] In a speech to Soviet textile workers a year after the crisis Khrushchev recalled the loss of his son in World War II and the millions of other deaths suffered by the Russians, and then laid into his critics: "Some comrades abroad claim that Khrushchev is making a mess of things, and is afraid of war. Let me say once again that I should like to see the kind of bloody fool who is genuinely not afraid of war." The Soviet press reported that it was this statement that was cheered more loudly and wholeheartedly than any other by his audience. Or there was his earthy comment to some naval officers shortly after the crisis: "I'm not a czarist officer who has to kill himself if I fart at a masked ball. It's better to back down than to go to war."[32] The Soviets never even went on a demonstration alert.

For his part, American president John Kennedy was also intensely concerned about escalation, though he expressed it less colorfully. In particular, he was haunted by the experience with the conventional conflagration that began in 1914. He had been greatly impressed by Barbara Tuchman's *The Guns of August* and concluded that in 1914 the Europeans "somehow seemed to tumble into war...through stupidity, individual idiosyncrasies, misunderstandings, and personal complexes of inferiority and grandeur." He had no intention, he made clear, of becoming a central character in a "comparable book about this time, *The Missiles of October*."[33]

Of course the Cuban missile crisis would not have happened, at least in the same way, had there been no nuclear weapons for the Soviets to deploy to the island. The point here, however, is that even with the image of nuclear war staring at them, Kennedy and Khrushchev were referencing horrors remembered from prenuclear wars to warrant their intense concern about escalation.

STABILITY OVERDETERMINED

The postwar situation contained (and continues to contain) redundant sources of stability. The United States and the Soviet Union were essentially satisfied with their lot and, fearing escalation to another costly war, were deeply determined to keep their conflicts limited.

In 1961, strategist Thomas Schelling set up an elaborate, multiday simulation war game in which several high government officials participated. The Pentagon-sponsored exercise was taken very seriously by the players, and Schelling threw in various modifications to see what consequences might lead to war. However, no matter what he did, the response on both sides was to move to dampen the tensions, and Schelling simply could not get a war started no matter how desperate and outrageous the provocations he dreamed up. Similarly, in the 1980s, at a time of high war alarm, three Harvard analysts were struck at how difficult it was to come up with a plausible scenario for a major war even when it was assumed that deliberate choices would be confounded by accidents.[34]

Nuclear weapons were part of the thinking in these exercises, and they may well have enhanced or reinforced the stability found. And they are certainly dramatic reminders of how horrible a big war could be. But it seems highly unlikely that, in their absence, the leaders of the major powers would be so unimaginative as to need such reminding. In his exhaustive and extensive examination of wars over the centuries, historian Evan Luard notes that what he calls "a willingness for war" can "make war almost as inevitable, sooner or later, as a definite intention of war." However, if a willingness for war can make war nearly inevitable, continues Luard, "a general unwillingness for war" means that "precisely the opposite is the case."[35] That is, to reformulate a famous observation by impresario Sol Hurok, if people don't want to fight, nothing will stop them.

Even allowing considerably for stupidity, ineptness, miscalculation, viciousness, and self-deception in their considerations, it does not appear that a large war, nuclear or otherwise, has been remotely in the interest of the essentially contented, risk-averse, escalation-anticipating countries that have dominated world affairs since 1945. Nuclear weapons were not required to bring the cautious contestants to this elemental conclusion.

However, although nuclear weapons haven't been necessary either to prevent World War III or to keep leaders cautious about major war both during and between crises, there are imaginable circumstances under which it might be useful to have nuclear weapons around—such as the rise of another lucky, clever, risk-acceptant, hyperconfident, aggressive fanatic like Hitler.[36] Therefore, even if one concludes that nuclear weapons have not been necessary to preserve peace thus far, it might conceivably still make sense to have some for added insurance against severe anachronism. Insofar as a military deterrent was necessary, the fear of another World War II has been quite sufficient (indeed, far more than sufficient, I expect) for the *particular countries* that have actually existed since 1945. But it does not follow that that fear alone could necessarily prevent all imaginable wars.

In the world we've actually experienced, however, major war doesn't seem ever to have really been in the cards. Accordingly, any enhancement of stability engendered by nuclear weapons has been theoretical—extra insurance against unlikely calamity.

4

Modest Influence on History

In the previous chapter I argued that, had nuclear weapons never been invented, World War III would still not have occurred and decision makers of the major countries would still have had essentially the same strong incentive to keep their various crises under control. This chapter examines the influence of nuclear weapons on other historical developments and finds them to have had at most a rather limited substantive impact.

ENDING WORLD WAR II: WERE HIROSHIMA AND NAGASAKI NECESSARY?

The atomic bombings of the Japanese cities of Hiroshima and Nagasaki in August 1945 were followed in fairly short order by the surrender of the Japanese and then by the almost miraculous casualty-free occupation of their country by American forces. This agreeable cascade of events has led to the widespread acceptance of the notion that the bombs were the reason, even the sole reason, the Japanese surrendered so abruptly and completely, thus saving the lives of hundreds of thousands of Americans and countless Japanese who were expected to die in the planned invasion of the country.

That the weapons might be crucial was by no means obvious to all of those who knew about them at the time. The American

Chiefs of Staff treated the atomic bomb as just another weapon. Admiral William Leahy was doubtful that it would be effective, and General George Marshall anticipated that it would primarily be useful as protection and preparation for landings on Japan. Such thinking was probably inspired in part by the knowledge that the atomic bomb mostly differed from earlier weapons only in that a single explosion could cause vast damage. Using conventional bombing methods, tens of thousands had previously been killed in the German city of Dresden, and the raids of Tokyo in March 1945 had killed about 100,000. It was anticipated that the bombs dropped on Hiroshima and Nagasaki would kill 20,000 each. While the actual total death toll turned out to be greater, the atomic bombs could cause no more damage than the United States was already fully capable of inflicting with its command of the air, though now the Japanese had to scurry for cover when just a couple of bombers appeared.[1]

The Americans' chief hope was that the new weapon would somehow have a beneficial shock effect on the Japanese, and their surrender shortly after the bombings has widely been accepted to confirm the validity of this hope. However, the evidence that it had this impact is less than fully convincing. Some Japanese did indeed find the attack shocking—or were caught off guard.[2] However, no vote in the Japanese cabinet was changed by the two bombings, nor did the Japanese modify their key surrender terms—the crucial demand that the emperor and the imperial institution be retained. The most that can be said for the bombs is that they helped to undercut the Japanese army's romantic pretensions that victory could somehow be salvaged in a last glorious battle for its never previously conquered homeland, and that they helped the emperor, who had been on the side of surrender for months, to exert himself in the cabinet debates. That is, while they may have helped to tip a balance, they were effective only because a delicate balance happened to exist.[3]

Had the Americans refused to keep the emperor, or had the emperor decided, like the craven Adolf Hitler in Germany, to preside over a final drawn-out, suicidal conflagration, the war would have continued, bomb or no bomb. When the emperor went on the radio a week after the atomic bombings to announce surrender, the reaction of the Japanese people was almost universally one of astonishment and shock: it was generally expected that he would urge them on to greater efforts or to fight to the last. Many in the leadership wanted to do exactly that. The Communists in Vietnam fought one enemy or another (including two different nuclear powers) almost continuously between 1940 and 1990; the Japanese certainly might have been capable of similar fanaticism.[4]

Hatreds were intense in the Japanese-American war, and many Japanese fully believed they would be tortured and killed by the American occupiers. Fed in part by that anticipation, Japanese soldiers had fought to the death or committed suicide rather than give up: usually less than 5 percent surrendered. Moreover, the last year of the war had seen thousands of attacks by suicidal kamikaze bombers and *shinyo* boats, as well as mass suicide among civilians. On Saipan, hundreds of Japanese civilians, forced to a cliff by advancing American forces, killed themselves and their children by exploding hand grenades or by leaping onto jagged rocks or into the sea. On Okinawa, civilians were pressed into military service while hundreds of others, particularly children and the elderly, turned over their food to the Japanese army and then killed each other with razors, hatchets, and sickles. "We will fight," the Japanese had vowed, "until we eat stones." Or, as the war minister exhorted the army *after* Hiroshima and Nagasaki: "All that remains to be done is to carry through to its end the holy war for the protection of the Land of the Gods. We are determined to fight resolutely although that may involve our nibbling grass, eating earth, and sleeping in the fields. It is our belief that there is little in death." Had the emperor actively supported the idea, the popular Japanese slogan "One hundred million die together!" might well have eventually been translated into vivid reality. Even without his blessing, a few Japanese soldiers, refusing to believe surrender had ever occurred, held out for decades in isolated caves.[5]

Conceivably, the bombs were sufficient to end the war by themselves, though this proposition has been considerably disputed.[6] More to the point for present purposes, however, is this issue: were the bombs *necessary* to bring about the Japanese surrender at that time, to tip the delicate balance? A strong case can be made—and has been made—for the proposition that a simultaneous event—the declaration of war upon Japan by the Soviet Union, that took place between the atomic bombings—would have done so by itself.

In 1958, Paul Kecskemeti argued that it was the simultaneous Soviet declaration of war that was crucial in the timing of Japan's eventual surrender offer. Because the Soviet Union could now no longer act as a neutral mediator, the Japanese were forced to meet and to make some new decisions about approaching the United States. More recent research allies itself with that proposition; as Ward Wilson puts it, for Japanese leaders "it is clear Soviet intervention touched off a crisis, while the Hiroshima bombing did not."[7]

Wilson emphasizes as well that the military challenge posed by the Soviets was also very important. Although the Japanese leaders had been aware that the Soviets might enter the war, their whole strategy for defending the homeland, argues historian Tsuyoshi Hasegawa, was "predicated on Soviet neutrality." The Soviet entry into the war came, then, as a "complete surprise" and "undermined the confidence of the army, punching a fatal hole in its strategic plan." In consequence, "the military's insistence on the continuation of war lost its rationale." Moreover, and even more important to Hasegawa, if the war continued, the Soviets were likely to take control not only of areas occupied by Japan on the Asian mainland but also considerable portions of Japan as well, potentially including all or most of Hokkaido, the more northern of the two main Japanese islands, splitting the country. Wilson concludes that "although hard-liners might have been able to convince themselves that an all-out effort against one invasion was possible, no one would have believed that a decisive battle could be fought against two opponents at the same time." Therefore, the Soviet invasion "was the event that dramatically changed the strategic landscape and left Japan with no option but to surrender unconditionally." By contrast, "The Hiroshima bombing was simply an extension of an already fierce bombing campaign."[8]

THE LIMITS OF ATOMIC DIPLOMACY IN THE EARLY COLD WAR YEARS

The notion that nuclear weapons would greatly influence historical events was widely accepted even before the first one was exploded. As the atom bomb was reaching its final stages of development, American decision makers were anticipating that the weapon might have a very substantial, and potentially beneficial, impact not only in speeding up the Japanese surrender but on the postwar political atmosphere as well.

"Members of the administration," notes historian David Holloway, came to believe "that the bomb could be a powerful diplomatic instrument in relations with the Soviet Union," although they didn't display much awareness of how exactly that would come about. Some historians have contended that, since Japan was already all but defeated, this was the main, or even sole, reason for dropping the bombs. The general consensus, however, is that no one really knew what it would take to induce Japan to surrender at that point and that any beneficial postwar effect on the Soviets would come about as a sort of "bonus."[9]

Holloway demonstrates that Hiroshima did succeed in bringing the atomic bomb squarely into Soviet strategic calculations, and it certainly impelled Soviet leader Joseph Stalin to put into place an expensive crash program to get an atom bomb of his own. However, Soviet diplomacy, far from softening out of fear, was focused on demonstrating that the country would not be forced into concessions. As Stalin put it in a 1946 interview, "atomic bombs are meant to frighten those with weak nerves," and he set out to make clear he would not be intimidated. American Secretary of State James Byrnes glumly concluded from the experience that the Soviets were "stubborn, obstinate, and they don't scare." More generally, concludes Holloway, Stalin's postwar policy was not affected by the atomic bomb: "there was no radical shift in the Soviet conception of war" or of international relations, and "there is little evidence to suggest that the United States was able to use the bomb to compel the Soviet Union to do things it did not want to do." As Soviet specialist Charles Bohlen said at the time, the American monopoly neither "influenced Soviet policy" nor "abated its aggressiveness."[10]

Any impact, concludes Holloway, was rather marginal and, even at that, could cut in either direction. The monopoly may have "made the Soviet Union more restrained in its use of force," but it also made it "less cooperative and less willing to compromise, for fear of seeming weak." Overall, observes historian John Gaddis, "the American monopoly over nuclear weapons, while it lasted, yielded unimpressive results."[11]

INFLUENCE ON SPECIFIC EVENTS

It is also far from clear that the existence of nuclear weapons vitally—or even significantly—influenced the outcomes of specific events. For example, President Harry Truman was of the opinion that his nuclear threat forced the Soviets out of Iran in 1946, and President Dwight Eisenhower believed that his threats drove the Chinese and the Soviets into productive discussions at the end of the Korean War in 1953. Actually, even if we assume the threats *were* important, it is not clear why they had to be peculiarly *nuclear*—a threat to commit destruction on the order of World War II would also have been arrestingly unpleasant. Moreover, McGeorge Bundy's reassessment of these events suggests that neither threat was very well communicated and that, in any event, other occurrences—the maneuverings of the Iranian government in the one case and the death of Stalin in the other—were more important in determining the outcome.[12]

Reviewing the evidence on Korea in the aftermath of the cold war with newly available documentary evidence, Gaddis argues that the atomic bombs "frightened both sides into thinking twice—indeed into thinking repeatedly—about the risks of escalation." However, this was a consideration, as suggested in the previous chapter, that would have been at the top of their minds even if all they had to worry about was a repetition of World War II. As to Eisenhower's supposed threats, Gaddis concludes that any nuclear warnings during the Korean War were decidedly imprecise and were not particularly nuclear. Moreover, they became explicit "only *after* the armistice, and in the context of how it would respond to a violation." In agreement with Bundy, he concludes that the decisive event was Stalin's death. Eager to relax tensions, his successors "saw Korea as the obvious place to start" and decisively shifted policy within two weeks of the dictator's demise.[13]

Much the same could be said about other instances in which there was a real or implied threat that nuclear weapons might be brought into play: the Taiwan Straits crises of 1954 and 1958, the Berlin Blockade of 1948–49, the Soviet-Chinese confrontation of 1969, the Six-Day War in 1967, the Yom Kippur War of 1973, and cold war disagreements over Lebanon in 1958 and over Berlin in 1958 and 1961. Morton Halperin finds that "the primary military factors in resolving the crisis" in the Taiwan Straits in 1954 were "American air and naval superiority in the area," not nuclear threats. Alexander George and Richard Smoke note that crises in Berlin in 1948–49 and in the Taiwan Straits in 1958 were broken by the ability of the Americans to find a technological solution to them. Richard Betts suggests that even if the American alert was influential with the Soviets in 1973 (which is quite questionable), it is "hard to argue against the proposition that the conventional force elements in it were sufficient, the nuclear component superfluous." He also finds "scant reason to assume...that the nuclear balance would be a prime consideration in a decision about whether to resort to nuclear coercion."[14]

THE IMPACT OF ATOMIC SPIES

The bomb's absence of historical impact is illustrated in a different manner by a consideration of the once intensely controversial case of atomic espionage. During World War II, atomic secrets were surreptitiously transmitted to the Soviet Union (an ally in that war) partly through the auspices of American Communists and Communist sympathizers. When the Soviets exploded their first atom bomb surprisingly quickly in 1949, it was widely contended that it was the purloined atomic secrets that made this possible. Then, when the Soviets' client state in North Korea launched an armed invasion of South Korea a year later to which the United States responded by engaging in a costly three-year war on the peninsula, it was commonly and alarmingly assumed the venture was engineered by a Soviet Union emboldened by its new bomb.

The most public expression of this concern came about in multiple trials of two American Communists, Julius and Ethel Rosenberg, who were executed for their crimes as atomic traitors in 1953. This spectacular case was in turn a key event in the country's preoccupation with the domestic Communist menace, often known after its most prominent spokesman as McCarthyism. The concern became internalized and led to decades of costly counterespionage efforts, even though it seems clear in retrospect that the scope of the internal threat was massively exaggerated and scarcely warranted such efforts.[15]

Extensive evidence that became available after the cold war puts a considerably different perspective on the historic importance of the atomic espionage. After Hiroshima, Stalin instituted a crash program to obtain an atomic bomb as soon as possible. To do so, the Soviets decided to make use of materials obtained from the United States that were for an "implosion" bomb built around plutonium. Some Soviet scientists strongly argued that there were better and far cheaper ways to obtain a bomb, ones that might even be quicker. However, apparently because this route to a bomb seemed to present a greater degree of uncertainty and perhaps because of a distrust of Soviet science, Stalin and other top leaders insisted on following the stolen designs. This procedure may have proved to be the fastest route, but it probably only speeded things up by a year or two. Moreover, by 1951, Soviet science had produced a uranium bomb, one that used designs that owed nothing to the purloined documents.[16] Conceivably, this latter achievement could have been speeded up some if it had been given the highest priority.

In some respects, then, the stolen documents were of only marginal significance, and they may even have actually been a disservice to the Soviet Union. Following designs for a complicated and expensive plutonium bomb required the Soviets to put forward an enormous investment in money and skilled personnel that the country, still reeling from the catastrophic destruction suffered in World War II, could ill afford.[17] Without the purloined documents, the country would have pursued the designs preferred by some Soviet scientists, resulting in a weapon of similar effectiveness at about the same time, but at a far lower cost.

It also seems clear that the idea of the Korean War was sold to Stalin by North Korean leaders as a surefire and inexpensive venture exploiting a weak spot in the encircling chain presented by the capitalist world. Stalin's somewhat reluctant approval of the plan was a miscalculation, notes Holloway, but, most important for present purposes, it was not an indication that Soviet policy had been emboldened by the country's atomic bomb.[18]

THE END OF COLD WAR

The essential irrelevance, or at most the merely ancillary relevance, of nuclear weapons to important historical events is neatly illustrated by the remarkable way the cold war ended in 1989. The key element in this monumental development derived from changes in ideas, not armaments. Indeed, just about the only thing that *didn't* change very much at the time was the balance of weaponry, particularly the supposedly crucial nuclear weaponry, arrayed on both sides.[19]

The important change in ideas came as the Soviet Union abandoned its threateningly expansionary ideology. Its love affair with revolution in the advanced capitalist world, frustrated for decades, ceased to have even theological relevance, and its venerable and once visceral attachment to revolution and to "wars of national liberation" in the Third World no longer even inspired much in the way of lip service. As Francis Fukuyama observed at the time, the role of ideology in defining Soviet foreign policy objectives and in providing political instruments for expansion steadily declined in the postwar period, and Soviet leader Mikhail Gorbachev further accelerated that process after he took office in 1985. Early in his tenure, Gorbachev said his country required "not only a reliable peace, but also a quiet, normal international situation." And in 1986, he began to forcefully undercut Communist ideology about the "class struggle" and about the Soviet Union's "internationalist duty" as the leader of world socialism. By 1988, the Soviets were admitting the "inadequacy of the thesis that peaceful coexistence is a form of class struggle," and their chief ideologist explicitly rejected the notion that a world struggle was going on between capitalism and Communism. Then, in a major speech in December 1988, Gorbachev specifically called for "de-ideologizing relations among states" and, while referring to the Communist revolution in Russia as "a most precious spiritual heritage," proclaimed that "today we face a different world, from which we must seek a different road to the future."[20] Most impressively, by February 1989, Gorbachev had matched deeds to words by carrying out his promise to remove Soviet troops from Afghanistan.

The United States was quick to react favorably. In December 1988, in his last presidential press conference, Ronald Reagan, stressing the ideological nature of the contest, said, "If it can be definitely established that they no longer are following the expansionary policy that was instituted in the Communist revolution, that their goal must be a one-world Communist state ... [then] they might want to join the family of nations and join them with the idea of bringing about or establishing peace." Six months later his successor, George Bush, was urging in a series of speeches that "it is now time to move beyond containment to a new policy" to "seek the integration of the Soviet Union into the community of nations." The New York Times editorially proclaimed the cold war to be over on April 2, 1989, and on May 24 the Wall Street Journal added, "We won!"[21]

Through all this, the Soviet Union's military and nuclear might still inspired awe. In its declaration of the cold war's end, the New York Times readily acknowledged that "two enormous military machines still face each other around the world." This view was widely shared. At the time, hardliner Frank Carlucci, stressed, "At present, and in spite of actual and announced reform initiatives, the Soviet Union is in sheer military terms more formidable than ever before," and even as he announced his "beyond containment" policy, George Bush pointed out that "We must not forget that the Soviet Union has acquired awesome military capabilities."[22] Yet the Times, and, it appears, Bush, concluded that the cold war was essentially over, even though the military and nuclear balance seemed to be as impressive and as potentially dangerous as ever.

ALLIANCES AND THE "STRUCTURE" OF INTERNATIONAL RELATIONS

As this suggests, nuclear weapons do not seem to have crucially affected the basic shape of the cold war. In contrast, some maintain that nuclear weapons have been the "defining feature" of the international relations in the postwar world. Thus, in constructing his influential "structural realist" model of international relations, Kenneth Waltz argues that the contest, the strategies, and the structure emerged from the way military, economic, and political capabilities were distributed at the end of World War II. At that point, two countries were far more "capable" than any others, and from this condition, concludes Waltz, stems the essential conflict: "the United States is the obsessing danger for the Soviet Union, and the Soviet Union for the United States, since each can damage the other to an extent no other state can match." The cold war between them, therefore, "is firmly rooted in the structure of postwar international politics, and will last as long as that structure endures."[23]

However, if the structure of international relations, and therefore of the cold war, was centrally about "capabilities" and particularly about nuclear weapons—since it is surely those which allow a country to inflict truly big-time damage—it should still be going on. Although the Soviet Union has fractured, Russia, however troubled economically or politically, remains a major player and, due to its atomic arsenal, continues to be able to inflict a kind of damage on the United States no other state can even *remotely* match.[24]

In contrast, the intense rivalry and the "bipolarity" nuclear weapons are supposed to be dominant forces in creating have ceased to exist. This suggests that the arms balance was more nearly an indicator of international cold war tensions than the cause of them, an issue to be discussed more fully in chapter 6.

Not only were nuclear weapons irrelevant to the "bipolarity" of the cold war world, they also seem to have been irrelevant to the construction of the two specific military alliances that formed its center: the North Atlantic Treaty Organization and the Warsaw Pact. In fact, the construction of the alliances better reflects political and ideological bipolarity than sound nuclear strategy.

As military economist (and later defense secretary) James Schlesinger once noted, the Western alliance "was based on some rather obsolescent notions regarding the strength and importance of the European nations and the direct contribution that they could make to the security of the United States. There was a striking failure to recognize the revolutionary impact that nuclear forces would make with respect to the earlier beliefs regarding European defense." Or, as another observer has put it, American policies in Europe were "essentially pre-nuclear in their rationale."[25]

Indeed, if nuclear weapons had been a major determinant of the alliance patterns, one might expect the United States and, to a lesser extent, the Soviet Union to have been only lukewarm members, because the alliances included nations that contributed little to nuclear defense but possessed the capability of unilaterally getting the core powers into trouble. Furthermore, one would expect the small countries in each alliance to tie themselves as tightly as possible to the core country in order to have maximum protection from its nuclear weapons.[26] However, any weakening of the alliances that occurred during the cold war did not come from the major partners, but rather from the minor ones like France and Romania.

The cold war, then, was an outgrowth not of "capabilities," nuclear or otherwise, but of various disagreements between the United States and the USSR over ideology and over the destinies of Eastern, Central, and Southern Europe. And the division of the world into two alliances centered on Washington and Moscow suggests that the participants were chiefly influenced by their prenuclear experience with Hitler and the Second World War. As with the other historical developments discussed in this chapter, the existence of nuclear weapons, however ominous, was substantially ancillary, atmospheric, or even irrelevant to the process.

5

Apocalyptic Visions, Worst-Case Preoccupations, Massive Expenditures

Although nuclear weapons seem to have had at most a quite limited substantive impact on actual historical events, as argued in the previous two chapters, they have had a tremendous influence on our agonies and obsessions. They have deeply affected international atmospherics, inspiring desperate rhetoric, extravagant theorizing, and frenetic diplomatic posturing. And they—or their attendant atmospherics—have had a severe and mostly wasteful effect on defense spending and planning, sometimes to a preposterous degree.

THE ANGUISHED RHETORIC OF ALARM

For many, World War II and the atomic bomb engendered a profound sense of despair: not only had the human race invented new and even more effective methods for devastating itself, but it also seemed utterly incapable of controlling its own destiny. The Great War of 1914–18, for all its horror, had often seemed to carry with it the potential for an equally great postwar healing. By destroying militarism and the warring nation-state system, thought many, it might be "the war that will end war," as H. G. Wells, the popular British writer and futurist, entitled a 1914 tract. By contrast, in the wake of World War II, Wells, ill and deeply embittered, abandoned his lifelong celebration of human progress and prophesied inevitable and inescapable doom. In his last writings he declared that "the end of everything we call life is close at hand and cannot be evaded," and that mankind was "the most foolish vermin that have ever overrun the earth." His epitaph, he told friends, should read: "God damn you all: I told you so."[1]

Curiously, however, the rhetoric of alarm over nuclear weapons and over the prospect of a nuclear World War III has waxed and waned over the decades. Moreover, it was often out of synch with the actual technical threat—with the numbers and destructive potential of the nuclear arsenals of the time and with the capacities of the means available to deliver them.

Nuclear Fear during the Classic Cold War

Nuclear fears, set into motion in the aftermath of World War II, flourished at first during what might be called the classic cold war period, which ended in 1963. In general, there seems to have been a popular, if glib, belief at this time that since some 20 years separated the first and second world wars, World War III would come to pass about 20 years hence. Thus, in 1950 historian Arnold Toynbee authoritatively proclaimed, "In our recent Western history war has been following war in an ascending order of intensity; and today it is already apparent that the War of 1939–45 was not the climax of this crescendo movement." Stalin himself said he anticipated that Germany would revive fairly rapidly, after which Germany and the USSR would fight again. In 1945, Ambassador Joseph Grew, one of America's most perceptive diplomats, concluded that "a future war with the Soviet Union is as certain as anything in this world." Public opinion polls conducted in the United States characteristically found very substantial percentages opining that the next world war would occur within 25 years.[2]

With some desperation, schemes were formulated at the war's end to try to invalidate such gloomy sentiments. Some Western scientists, apparently consumed with guilt over having participated in the development of a weapon that could kill with much-heightened effectiveness, helped found the *Bulletin of the Atomic Scientists* in 1945. It soon sported its "doomsday clock" on the cover, suggesting that there was hope of preventing Armageddon, but only if we were quick about it. The clock has remained poised at a few minutes before midnight ever since, from time to time nudged slightly one way or the other by various events. (Amazingly, in 2006 the *Bulletin* launched a subscription campaign boldly and unapologetically built around the slogan "Dispensing facts instead of fear for over sixty years.") Led by the legendary Albert Einstein, many atomic scientists quickly came to conclusions expressed with an evangelical certainty they would never have used in discussing the physical world. "As long as there are sovereign nations possessing great power," Einstein declaimed, "war is inevitable."[3]

Nuclear fears continued to be pronounced over the next decade and a half. And in the process, truly massive numbers of people—indeed, the entire population of the earth—several times lost their lives to nuclear explosions, but only in novels, on television, and in the movies. The world was depopulated at least twice on celluloid in 1959 alone, and one of those films, Stanley Kramer's *On the Beach,* stands as perhaps the genre's most prominent exemplar. Based on a 1957 novel by Nevil Shute, it depicts a forlorn group of survivors in Melbourne, Australia, as they make love and contemplate suicide while awaiting the inevitable arrival of a radioactive cloud from the north, the result of a nuclear war that had already eradicated the rest of the animate residents of the earth. In explaining his approach, Kramer insisted that "This is a serious picture, it's about the end of the world, and we have to give them romance and sex." The combination certainly suited the reviewer for the *Saturday Review of Literature,* who deemed it "a picture that aims at something big and emerges as something tremendous." Around the same time, strategist and futurist Herman Kahn was warning, "I have a firm belief that unless we have more serious and sober thought on various aspects of the strategic problem . . . we are not going to reach the year 2000—and maybe not even the year 1965—without a cataclysm," even as C. P. Snow was publishing his alarmist broadside proclaiming it to be a "certainty" that, if the nuclear arms race between the United States and the Soviet Union were to continue and accelerate, a nuclear bomb would go off "within, at the most, ten years."[4]

Nuclear Fear Subsides: The 1960s and 1970s

None did, as it happened. Indeed, within, at the most, four years after Snow's urgent pronouncement, anxiety about nuclear cataclysm began to subside. In the aftermath of the 1962 Cuban missile crisis, the United States and the Soviet Union signed some arms control agreements and, although these agreements did not reduce either side's nuclear capacity in the slightest, the generally improved diplomatic atmosphere engendered a considerable relaxation in fear that they would actually use their weapons against each other.

Accordingly, whereas over 400 articles per year on nuclear-related topics are listed in the *Readers' Guide to Periodical Literature* for 1961, 1962, and 1963, output dropped to less than 200 in 1964 and to about 120 in 1967. Polls reflect a similar change. Before 1963, the various polling agencies had regularly asked the public if it expected another world war within the foreseeable future. Reflecting declining interest in the issue, pollsters largely abandoned the question after 1963, and when they did manage to bring the issue up, they found the public far less concerned about war than earlier. One observer aptly called the phenomenon "forgetting about the unthinkable."[5]

Nuclear Fear Revives: The Early 1980s

In 1979, the prominent realist political scientist Hans J. Morgenthau proclaimed that "the world is moving ineluctably towards a third world war—a strategic nuclear war. I do not believe that anything can be done to prevent it." In the same year, John Hackett published a gloomily imaginative book, *The Third World War: August 1985*. A few years earlier, John McPhee had begun a best-selling book by ominously reporting that "to many people who have participated in the advancement of the nuclear age, it seems not just possible but more and more apparent that nuclear explosions will again take place in cities." As one of these put it, "I think we have to live with the expectation that once every four or five years a nuclear explosion will take place and kill a lot of people."[6]

Such hair-raising utterances were still comparatively unusual at that time. However, in short order the unthinkable exploded back into popular consciousness, and, as before, people didn't like what they found themselves thinking about. Accordingly, they launched protests, signed petitions, and organized marches. Between 1972 and 1978 the number of items on nuclear and disarmament issues in the *Readers' Guide* had averaged 71 per year; in 1981 it jumped to 318, and in 1983 it hit 665. The first ever World Congress of International Physicians for the Prevention of Nuclear War was held in 1981, and one address was cheerlessly entitled "Does Humankind Have a Future?," concluding gloomily that "The world is moving inexorably toward the use of nuclear weapons."[7]

Some of this consciousness raising, one might think, could be attributed to the vast increases in strategic nuclear arsenals that had taken place by that time. Both sides had built up their intercontinental ballistic missile forces until each had more than 1,000, and both had also vastly increased their stock of submarine missiles. More menacingly, major improvements in missile accuracy were being made, and it had become technologically feasible to put more than one warhead on a single missile; together, these developments raised the ominous, if theoretical, possibility that one side, or both, could achieve a "first-strike capability," at least against the other's land-based missiles.[8]

But these developments don't really explain the rise of nuclear consciousness of the early 1980s. The new, vastly expanded arsenals had been in place for a decade at least, and the peculiar dilemma posed by the existence of accurate multiple-warhead missiles was neither new nor well appreciated by the protesters. Instead, it was a relatively minor weapons development— the proposed implantation by NATO of a few hundred shorter-range missiles in Europe—that triggered much of the phenomenon. Political opportunism, both in the West and East, played its part, too.

As part of an expensive nuclear arms buildup that had begun after the Cuban missile crisis of 1962, Leonid Brezhnev's Soviet Union began adding sophisticated new intermediate-range (3,000 miles) triple-warhead missiles to its arsenal in Europe. NATO became alarmed because it had nothing comparable, and in 1979 it scheduled the deployment of similar countervailing weapons unless the Soviets could be prevailed upon to limit their missiles.[9]

Talks on this issue were ambling along unproductively when Ronald Reagan became president in the United States in 1981. Almost instantly he began to strike a lot of people as a fire-breathing warmonger. He announced that he would substantially build up U.S. military forces (expanding the policy of this predecessor, Jimmy Carter) and would seek to develop a strategy so that the United States might manage to come out ahead, or "prevail," in a nuclear war (basically continuing a policy developed by Kennedy, elaborated by Richard Nixon, and accepted by Carter). Reagan also speculated about the possibility of having an exchange of nuclear weapons in, for example, Europe, without either the United States or the USSR becoming a target—one of those small, self-evident truths, largely enshrined in NATO doctrine, that no previous president had so foolishly and so baldly expressed in public before, having preferred the politic suggestion that any sizable Soviet attack would necessarily escalate to strategic nuclear war. At about the same time, Reagan's secretary of state, Alexander Haig, came up with the well-seasoned observation that in response to a conventional attack by the Soviets in Europe the United States might lob a nuclear bomb or two in their direction "for demonstrative purposes."[10]

A lot of Europeans were appalled, and soon they had convinced themselves that Reagan was going to drag them into a war and then watch calmly from the sidelines as the war was fought out to the last radiated European: "Euroshima," one creative pamphleteer called it.[11] By the end of Reagan's first year in office, mass demonstrations aimed at preventing the installation of the new NATO missiles were regularly staged in several European countries.

The antinuclear movement also caught on in the United States, and a 1982 *New Yorker* essay and book by Jonathan Schell, both entitled "The Fate of the Earth," served as its focal point. Schell passionately, if repetitively, argued the not entirely novel proposition that nuclear war would be terrible, and concluded ominously, "One day—and it is hard to believe that it will not be soon—we will make our choice. Either we will sink into the final coma and end it all or, as I trust and believe, we will awaken to the truth of our peril . . . and rise up to cleanse the earth of nuclear weapons." Schell was far from alone. The *Cumulative Book Index* indicates that while fewer than 16 books on nuclear issues were published in the four-year period from 1977 to 1980, there were 25 in 1981, 54 in 1982, and 80 in 1983. In one of them, historian William McNeill asserted that unless there were global control over atomic weaponry, there would likely be "sudden and total annihilation of the human species." Nuclear bombs continued to go off on television, and *The Day After*, a 1983 show that grimly dramatized the aftermath of a nuclear explosion, attracted 100 million viewers, though it may not have been nearly as important as contemporary international events in alarming public opinion. As late as the mid-1980s, 20 to 37 percent of the American population told pollsters that they held the potential for nuclear war to be the most important problem facing the country.[12]

The Decline, Again, of Nuclear Fear

The protests neither changed the 1979 NATO decision nor Reagan's determination to implement it.[13] By the mid-1980s the Soviets were becoming distinctly aware that they were in deep trouble in many areas. The economic, military, and ideological excesses of the Brezhnev era were catching up with them, and soon Gorbachev led them out of the cold war.

In a book published in 1988, historian Spencer Weart characterized the decline of nuclear fear in the 1960s as an "astonishing event" and as "the only well-documented case in history when most of the world's citizens suddenly stopped paying attention to facts that continued to threaten their very survival."[14] Shortly after Weart's book was published, the "astonishing event" was to repeat itself as anxiety about nuclear weapons in the hands of the United States and the USSR almost completely vanished at the end of the cold war, even though the former cold war contestants continued (and continue) to maintain large numbers of the offending weapons in their arsenals and are far more capable of pulverizing each other with them than at most points during the cold war.

As this, and earlier, experience demonstrates, anxieties about thermonuclear destruction have not correlated at all well with objective factors such as the size or the destructive effectiveness of nuclear arsenals. Nuclear fears have been determined far more by the levels of political tension than by the levels of arms, including the dramatically threatening nuclear ones. And this process suggests the irrelevance of weaponry and the nuclear arms "race" to fundamental issues and perceptions of war and peace. During the 1970s, the United States and the USSR became more capable of pulverizing each other's society, and in that sense the world became increasingly dangerous. At the same time, however, it didn't *sound* less safe, and clearly it was tone, not content, that mattered. And now, in the aftermath of the cold war, huge numbers of nuclear weapons continue to exist in the arsenals of East and West, but fears they will be massively slung at each other have vanished. We have neither cleansed the earth of nuclear weapons nor descended into Schell's "final coma." The apocalypse never arrived—though Schell himself continues to be alarmed about the possibility.[15]

TABOO

In the aftermath of Hiroshima and Nagasaki, many people came to hold that atomic bombs, like chemical weapons earlier, had put warfare on a new and more terrible plane. And, also like gas, they were seen to be horrible not only for the damage they caused but also for the revolting way they inflicted it: lingering deaths and sickness from radiation poisoning, burns, and cancer, plus long-term genetic damage. That is, the notion has progressively been accepted that killing people in a nuclear explosion is, like killing them with gas, somehow worse—less moral perhaps—than killing them with bullets and shrapnel. It has become, as Thomas Schelling puts it, an established convention "that nuclear weapons are different." Indeed, it may even be true, as one commentator suggested on the 40th anniversary of Hiroshima, that the explosion had perhaps been, or was in the process of being, elevated to become "a profoundly mystical event, an event ultimately of the same religious force as biblical events."[16]

To the degree that this perception has been accepted, and to the degree that what Schelling calls the "nearly universal revulsion against nuclear weapons" has been embraced, the weapons have inspired something of a taboo or tradition or informal norm or convention holding that they should not be used. This condition hardly affects a nuclear state's physical capacity to set off a bomb, of course, but effectively it adds to the cost of doing so. A transgressor can anticipate incurring international disapproval and reputational pain far greater than if more conventional methods of destruction were used instead to accomplish the same military objective.[17]

It is not all that clear, however, that the taboo has had much practical consequence. Nuclear weapons have been "used," of course, to deter another major war but, as discussed in chapter 3, they do not seem to have been necessary to do so. In addition, although nuclear countries have been at war or at military loggerheads with other countries from time to time since 1945, their nuclear restraint in these contests, as will be put in broader context in chapter 8, seems to stem at least as much from perceptions of the weapons' military uselessness as from concerns about breaking any prohibitory tradition or taboo. That is, it has been less a tradition of nonuse than one of nonusefulness.

From time to time, particularly early in the nuclear era, their use has been contemplated, and sometimes preliminary plans for their application in battle have been formulated. And in many cases, reputational or moral reasons have been advanced, sometimes quite strenuously, by those who opposed using them.[18] It is just that there already were strong, and probably adequate—that is to say, sufficient—military arguments to conclude that they should not be employed. At no point, it may well be, were there reasons to use the weapons that were compelling from a strictly military point of view.

Most important has been an inability to identify suitable targets or ones that could not be attacked as effectively, or almost as effectively, by conventional munitions. For example, an American study during the Korean War pointed out that "the timely identification of large masses of enemy troops" was "extremely rare." One conducted during Vietnam noted that the weapons were of "little use against troops moving small groups under forest cover," while another was unable to come up with a battlefield use even for small tactical nuclear weapons. During the Gulf War of 1991, to satisfy the "curiosity" of defense secretary Dick Cheney on the issue, General Colin Powell conducted a study of nuclear options and concluded:

> The results unnerved me. To do serious damage to just one armored division dispersed in the desert would require a considerable number of small tactical nuclear weapons. I showed this analysis to Cheney and then had it destroyed. If I had had any doubts before about the practicality of nukes on the field of battle, this report clinched them.[19]

In addition, there have been other concerns—about saving the weapons for other potential conflicts deemed to be more important, for example, or about the escalatory danger that, once introduced even in a limited way, the situation could not be controlled and consequently ever more weapons would necessarily be unleashed. Moreover, as discussed at the end of chapter 1, there seems to be a considerable distaste within the military for the battlefield messiness involved—all that radiation to worry about in particular—something that also affected military thinking about the use of chemical weapons.[20]

As a result, insofar as their battlefield use has been contemplated, nuclear weapons have been held back as weapons of last resort—not so much as the "absolute" weapon but rather as the "ultimate" weapon, something one analyst labels their "all-or-nothing" character. It is commonly contended that Israel, in particular, envisions using them only when it is under a massive attack that credibly threatens its existence.[21] The nuclear taboo/convention/norm/tradition has probably helped nuclear countries come to that conclusion, but it does not seem to have been necessary for them to do so.

NUCLEAR METAPHYSICS: THE SEDUCTIVE LOGIC OF DETERRENCE

The mesmerizing existence of nuclear weapons spawned a truly massive theoretical literature—Robert Johnson has labeled it "nuclear metaphysics"—over their consequences and over how they might or might not be deployed. And, as Fred Kaplan has aptly observed,

> In the absence of any reality that was congenial to their abstract theorizing, the strategists in power treated the theory as if it *were* reality. For those mired in thinking about it all day, every day, in the corridors of officialdom, nuclear strategy had become the stuff of a living dreamworld.... The precise calculations and the cool, comfortable vocabulary were coming all too commonly to be grasped not merely as tools of desperation but as genuine reflections of the nature of nuclear war.[22]

The central concept explored and developed in that living dreamworld was deterrence. The thinking process is nicely summarized in the recent recollections of Brian Jenkins, who, as an analyst at the RAND Corporation, has been at the center of this intellectual development for decades. The italics are mine:

> Each [side in the cold war] possessed an arsenal capable of ending modern civilization. Avoiding nuclear war became the major preoccupation of leaders of both sides. This *required* military planners to persuade their opponents that neither side could gain sufficient advantage to make starting a nuclear war even thinkable—neither could escape annihilation by launching a preemptive attack. To achieve this balance each side *had to maintain* sufficient nuclear capability to retaliate with equal or greater force and to persuade the other side that it was willing to do so if attacked. It sounds simple, but it *required careful calculations,* convincing communications, and complex negotiations aimed at preventing either side from gaining a destabilizing advantage. Deterrence was maintained by mutual assured destruction (MAD), a tense standoff aimed at preventing nuclear war.[23]

The simple existence of the nuclear arsenals, therefore, somehow *required* all sorts of exquisite theorizing about their precise capacities and about how they should be deployed. The theory then ingeniously looped back on itself to further require that the arsenal be big and impressive enough to be persuasive to the presumed perspective of the theorists on the other side. With a careful calculated deployment on both sides, neither would have a "destabilizing advantage," and the nuclear contestants could take some sort of curious comfort in the fact that they had managed to calculate each other into a "tense standoff."

Central to that awesome and compelling formulation is its unexamined assumption that the only way to persuade the other side not to attack was through the careful development of weapons that could credibly threaten to inflict unacceptable punishment on the aggressor. Deterrence has, accordingly, almost always been looked at strictly as a military issue, and definitions routinely characterize it as "the threat to use force in response as a way of preventing the first use of force by someone else" or as "altering the behavior of a target by using, or threatening to use, force."[24] Starting with a perspective like that, there has been a tendency to concentrate on what military capabilities will effectively threaten the attacker with high costs and on what diplomatic and military actions can be taken to make the threat appear credible.[25]

By contrast, a broader and more fully pertinent concept would vigorously incorporate nonmilitary considerations as well as military ones into the mix, making direct and central application of the obvious fact that states do not approach the world solely in military terms.[26] When deterrence is recast this way, it becomes clear that the vast majority of wars that never happen are prevented—deterred—by factors that have little or nothing to do with military concerns. If outcomes are principally determined by military considerations in our chaotic state of international "anarchy," as so many have suggested, why is it that there are so many cases where a militarily superior country lives contentedly alongside a militarily inferior one?[27]

For example, the United States obviously enjoys a massive military advantage over its northern neighbor and could attack with little concern about punishing military retaliation or about the possibility of losing the war. Clearly something is deterring the United States from attacking Canada—a country with which the United States has been at war in the past and where, not too long ago many war-eager Americans felt their "manifest destiny" lay. But obviously this condition of deterrence has little to do with the Canada's military might.

Moreover, the absence of war—successful deterrence—does not necessarily prove that a policy of deterrence has been successful.[28] The United States had a clear and costly policy in which it tried to deter the Soviet Union by threatening nuclear punishment for any major Soviet aggression. But the fact that the Soviet Union did not launch a massive aggressive war cannot necessarily be credited to American policy; indeed, as argued in chapter 3, the USSR seems to have had no interest whatever in getting into any sort of major war, no matter how the United States happened to choose to array its nuclear (or nonnuclear) arsenal. Insofar as the Soviets wanted to "take over" other countries, they anticipated that this could come about through revolutionary or civil war processes within those countries, ones that, assisted and encouraged by the Communist states, would bring into control congenial, like-minded people and groups that would willingly join the Communist camp. Military measures designed to deter direct, Hitler-style military aggression simply have no relevance to such developments.

Discussions of deterrence, with their preoccupation on the military, and particularly on the nuclear, have been focused on establishing what might be called "crisis stability." This notion is concerned with the techno-logical and organizational problems of maintaining a secure "second strike" capability—that is, developing a retaliatory force so well entrenched that a country can afford to wait out a surprise attack fully confident it will be able to respond with a devastating counterattack. If each side is militarily con-fident in this way, then neither would see much advantage in launching a surprise attack, and neither would be tempted to start a war out of fear that the other could get a jump on it. Crises, therefore, would be "stable"—both sides would be able to assess events in a luxuriously slow manner and not feel compelled to act hastily and with incomplete information.

Many argued that such crisis stability was "delicate," easily upset by technological or economic shifts, This view was prominently advanced in the late 1950s by strategist Albert Wohlstetter, who alarmingly argued that the United States existed in a "world of persistent danger" and that deterring general war over the next decade would be "hard at best." (Later, at the end of the cold war, Wohlstetter insisted that he had never claimed World War III was "imminent"—only that the danger was "persistent"—and acknowl-edged that the likelihood such a cataclysm would transpire was "never very large"—he had just neglected to say it at the time, apparently.)[29]

At any rate, a great deal of agonizing thought went into assessing whether a given weapons system or military strategy was "stabilizing" or "destabilizing." These considerations were generally exceedingly technocen-tric and preoccupied with exquisite numerological questions such as calcu-lating just how many Multiple Independently Targetable Reentry Vehicles could, after all, balance on the head of an Intercontinental Ballistic Missile.

In one extended exercise, for example, very smart people in Robert McNamara's defense department in the 1960s set out to determine just what the United States would need to do in order to deter the Soviet Union from instituting a major war. Ignoring the fact that the likelihood of that event, as it happened, was vanishingly small, they sought to establish just how much of the Soviet Union it would be necessary to destroy in a retaliatory strike such that, after experiencing it, the USSR would no longer be able to function as a "viable nation." This, America's "assured-destruction capability," came in at about 20 percent of the enemy's population and 50 percent of its industrial capacity. These interesting numbers were determined not by bothering to assess Soviet cost tolerance or by considering whether they were likely to start any sort of war under any circumstance, but rather by observing that, after devastation of that magnitude had been wreaked, there were "strongly diminishing marginal returns" to further destruction because additional targets were so dispersed and so insufficiently populated that they would be a waste of otherwise perfectly good nuclear ordnance.[30]

In contrast, a broader conceptualization of deterrence would stress something that might be called "general stability." Concerned with broader needs, desires, and concerns, it holds when two countries, taking all the various costs, benefits, and risks into account, vastly prefer peace to war.[31] It's the sort of thing that has prevailed for a century between the United States and Canada. Even more strikingly, there is the comfortable neighbor relationship that has developed between Germany and France despite centuries of enmity and despite the fact that France could readily devastate Germany within minutes with its nuclear arsenal. And, insofar as direct warfare is concerned, it held for the relationship between the United States and the Soviet Union during the cold war.

When general stability is high, crisis instability is of little immediate concern or consequence. From a strictly technical point of view, crisis stability between Russia and the United States has declined since the end of the cold war because of Russia's increased military disarray.[32] But, because general stability has increased so much, no one seems to care—or even to notice.

In addition, this line of thinking suggests that many concerns about changes in arms balances, while valid in their own terms, miss the essential point. A change in military posture may increase or decrease crisis stability, but this may not alter the broader picture significantly. When general stability is high, the question of who could fight the most ingenious and effective war becomes irrelevant. Deterrence, and therefore peace, prevails.

DEFENSE EXPENDITURES

As it was developed, the deterrence logic, with its nuclear inspiration and with its overwhelmingly military focus, tended to induce and to justify calls for increased defense expenditures even as it encouraged exaggerations of the military threat posed by the other side. In 1966, Ivan Selin, Head of Strategic Forces Division in the Office of the Assistant Secretary of Defense, crisply made the connection: "Welcome to the world of strategic analysis, where we program weapons that don't work to meet threats that don't exist." Selin was presumably joking, at least in part, but the consequences of the connection proved essentially to be farcical. Or perhaps even worse: asked about the nuclear buildup he had done so much to foster, former defense secretary Robert McNamara, once one of the most important proponents of nuclear metaphysics, reflected later: "Each individual decision along the way seemed rational at the time. But the result was insane."[33]

Central to the process was the somber and focused examination of worst-case scenarios. Good analysis, of course, should include a consideration of extreme possibilities. However, particularly where nuclear weapons are concerned, these often become so mind-concentratingly appalling that they push aside other considerations and become essentially accepted, even embraced, as the norm. During the cold war, as Robert Johnson puts it, the process involved "making the most pessimistic assumptions possible about Soviet intentions and capabilities" and then assuming that the capabilities (which turned out almost always to have been substantially exaggerated) would be used "to the adversary's maximum possible advantage."[34]

Defense analyst Bernard Brodie was one of the few who were capable, at least at times, of stepping back from the doom-eager thinking processes. In 1966, he expressed support for "the capability of dreaming up 'far out' events," but he also demanded that it be accompanied by a "disciplined judgment" about their likelihood. To do otherwise, he pointed out, is to assume that "the worst conceivable outcome has as good a chance as any of coming to pass." And in 1978, he railed against the preoccupation with what he called "worst-case fantasies" and pointedly observed that the defense establishment was

> inhabited by peoples of a wide range of skills and sometimes of
> considerable imagination. All sorts of notions and propositions

are churned out, and often presented for consideration with the prefatory works: "It is conceivable that..." Such words establish their own truth, for the fact that someone has conceived of whatever proposition follows is enough to establish that it is conceivable. Whether it is worth a second thought, however, is another matter. It should undergo a good deal of thought before one begins to spend much money on it.[35]

But spend they did. The absurdity of the situation is poignantly captured in an exasperated comment by President Dwight Eisenhower at a 1956 National Security Council meeting: "We are piling up armaments because we do not know what else to do to provide for our security."[36]

Exasperated or not, to deal with an aggressive military threat that was essentially imaginary, the United States, as noted earlier, expended enough money on nuclear arms and related programs over the course of the cold war to have bought, according to one calculation, everything in the country except for the land. Things were even worse—or even more ludicrous— in the Soviet Union. Throughout, they flailed to keep up with the United States—"we had the psychology of an underdog," recalled one Soviet general in 1994—and the desperate scramble that went on for decades likely substantially speeded the country's demise.[37]

There were also enormous short- and long-term opportunity costs for both sides. If those defense monies had instead been invested in the economy, one estimate suggests, they would have generated an additional 20 or 25 percent of production each year *in perpetuity*. And there was also a substantial loss entailed in paying legions of talented nuclear scientists, engineers, and technicians to devote their careers to developing and servicing weapons that have proved, it certainly seems, to have been significantly unnecessary and essentially irrelevant.[38]

ATOMIC THEATER

The effect of nuclear weapons has been, as historian John Gaddis proposes, primarily theatrical. They created moods of "dark foreboding," and they "required statesmen to become actors: success or failure depended, or so it seemed, not on what one was really doing, but on what one *appeared* to be doing."[39] That is, nuclear weaponry has furnished its possessors with instruments with which they could sometimes express their concerns and displeasures, something they did with considerable frequency and alacrity during the cold war. It gave them rockets to rattle.

This theatrical process has been, as previous chapters have suggested, only minimally significant historically. However, it did inspire a tremendous forehead-furling literature on how the weapons ought to be deployed and on the various potential consequences, mostly dire, of miscalculation. The most likely path to World War III, as most analysts envisioned it, arose from a process in which the weapons designed to prevent and deter it were inadvertently deployed in a manner that caused it to happen.[40] Fortunately, as argued in chapter 3, stability has been greatly overdetermined, and therefore the mutual bluffmanship has ultimately had little consequence. Accordingly, the theatrical form the foreign policy posturing most nearly resembles has been farce.

Nuclear weapons did add a new element to international politics: new pieces for the players to move around the board, new terrors to contemplate and to anguish over, new ways to dole out the public treasury. But in counter to Albert Einstein's famous remark that "the atom has changed everything save our way of thinking," it seems rather that nuclear weapons changed little except our way of talking, posturing, and spending money.[41] That is, although the weapons altered history little, they have very substantially influenced, mostly in a detrimental manner, the way people have gesticulated, scurried about, and expended funds.

PART II

The Spread of Nuclear Weapons

6

Arms Races

Positive and Negative

The technological fixation on nuclear weapons and the concomitant assumption, or assertion, that weapons are a crucial cause of war have led to decades of focused anguish over nuclear arms control and disarmament issues.

There have been two streams of endeavor. One, the concern of this chapter, is the quest to control "vertical proliferation"—to reduce the number of, or at least to bring some degree of control over, nuclear weapons in the arsenals of countries that already have them. The other, focusing on what has been called "horizontal proliferation," seeks to prevent countries that do not have nuclear weapons from obtaining them, and is the subject of the following chapters.

FORMAL EFFORTS TO CONTROL THE ARMS RACE

Control of nuclear weapons in the arsenals of the major countries has been held to be vital out of fear that dire consequences are somehow inherent in a nuclear arms race, particularly the one that took place between the United States and the Soviet Union for several decades. In due alarm, strategist Herman Kahn in 1960 proclaimed it "most unlikely that the world can live with an uncontrolled arms race lasting for several decades."[1] In the ensuing half century, the world somehow managed to do exactly that. Although there have been strenuous, at times even desperate, efforts to fabricate formal agreements to control the arms race Kahn was so alarmed about, none proved to be of much consequence.

World Government

In the immediate aftermath of World War II, Albert Einstein, along with fellow scientists and many others, fancied with a confidence bordering on intellectual arrogance that he had managed to discover the single device that could solve the problem: "Only the creation of a world government can prevent the impending self-destruction of mankind." Or, as Edward Teller, a physicist who was later to be instrumental in the development of the hydrogen bomb, put it in 1946, world government "alone can give us freedom and peace." Philosopher Bertrand Russell was equally certain: "It is entirely clear," he declared, "that there is only one way in which great wars can be permanently prevented and that is the establishment of an international government with a monopoly of serious armed force." Proclaimed Robert Oppenheimer, with a similarly unclouded clarity of vision, "without world government, there could be no permanent peace, and without peace there would be atomic warfare."[2] They came up with a snappy slogan for the idea: "One World or None," and Rube Goldberg won a Pulitzer Prize in 1948 for an editorial cartoon showing a huge atomic bomb teetering on a precipice between "world control" and "world destruction."

Without concerning himself with the fact that states with well-armed governments have nonetheless often managed to devolve into catastrophic civil war, Einstein proclaimed world government to be both an "absolute" and an "immediate" necessity, and suggested that it might emerge naturally out of the United Nations. For the most part, however, the Soviet Union viewed the UN with contempt, and in 1947 a committee of Soviet scientists informed Einstein with as much politeness as it could muster that his idea of a world state was a "mirage" and a "political fad." For one thing, the world government plan as it applied to nuclear weapons would forever freeze an American advantage.[3]

Others in the West, while less visionary about world government, also hoped that somehow the victors of the war could band together one way or another to reduce military forces and to establish a lasting universal peace. Perhaps grand self-interest and a process of international domestication of the Soviets would eventually bring basic agreement and general, if not necessarily genial, cooperation. Proposals were made, meetings were held, and hands were wrung.

It was a worthy try, perhaps. But viscerally opposing policies and interests of the major members kept the United Nations from ever functioning as anything resembling a world government. Nevertheless, enthusiastic support for the UN continued for decades in the West: in 1961 President John F. Kennedy extravagantly called it "the only true alternative to war" and "our last best hope."[4] As it happens, peace between the major countries has been maintained—there have been, to use Russell's term, no "great wars." However, the United Nations deserves little credit for this remarkable development, and world government none at all.

The Partial Test Ban Treaty of 1963

Although grand schemes to fabricate an effective world government as a method for bringing nuclear weapons under control faded in the 1950s as the cold war flowered, less ambitious schemes for controlling and reducing the nuclear arms in the hands of the cold war contestants continued to be formulated with ever-increasing ingenuity and debated with ever-increasing sophistication.

In the West, there were frequent peace marches and noisy convocations urgently demanding disarmament. Philosopher Russell was a major spokesman for the movement, and at times of highest tension, such as during the Cuban missile crisis of 1962, he was given to putting out cheerless pamphlets with titles like "You Are to Die." In England he helped to organize the Campaign for Nuclear Disarmament (CND), which invented the peace symbol—a circle around a configuration that looks like a missile but is supposed to represent both a broken cross and an overlapping of the semaphore N and the semaphore D.[5]

A similar development occurred in the United States, where there was also an active ban-the-bomb movement. Much of its energy was focused on protesting Kennedy's arms buildup of 1961, particularly his ill-fated proposals for developing a fallout shelter program to protect some of the citizenry in the event of nuclear attack or accident.

When cold war tensions declined a bit after the Cuban missile crisis, the main contestants managed to come up, in 1963, with the Partial Test Ban Treaty, a measure that bans nuclear testing above ground, on the sea, and in outer space. However, since underground testing was still acceptable and since the nuclear countries were getting very good at using such tests to develop new and better bombs, the treaty scarcely cramped their style. Qualitative improvements therefore continued, even as the treaty obviously put no constrains at all on any quantitative embellishments. That is, the arms race continued apace.

In supporting the test ban treaty at a June 10, 1963, address at American University, Kennedy assured his audience that the treaty "would check the spiraling arms race in one of its most dangerous areas." It had no meaningful effect on that race at all. He further claimed that it "would place the nuclear powers in a position to deal more effectively with one of the greatest hazards which man faces in 1963, the further spread of nuclear arms." It didn't change much of anything, and China, Kennedy's central worry at the time, went ahead and exploded its first bomb the next year.[6] And Kennedy also insisted that it "would increase our security" and "decrease the prospects of war," but there was virtually no prospect of major war at the time in any event.

Indeed, insofar as it had any effect on vertical proliferation, the treaty may have speeded the arms race up a bit. A ban on underground tests, insisted the Americans, must include a system for on-site inspections in which monitors would travel to the locale of a suspicious, distantly detected seismic event to determine whether the cause of the disturbance was a natural earthquake or a forbidden nuclear test. Khrushchev could not agree to that proposal because he was afraid—like the Wizard of Oz, suggest historians Aleksandr Fursenko and Timothy Naftali—that intrusive inspectors would find out how weak the Soviet Union was.[7] Uncharmed, many in the West took his wary behavior to mean he must have something to hide, and they urgently proposed arms buildups to counter the Wizard's imaginary threat.

At the same time, the United States and the Soviet Union agreed to establish a "hot line" between their capitals, a direct communication link that could potentially be used in time of emergency to reduce tensions or to provide information about developments such as troop movements that might mistakenly be taken to be threatening by the other side. The hot line was used a few times in later years, but was of rather marginal significance, its value limited by the fact that the two major cold war contestants never really got themselves into a true nose-to-nose crisis after 1963. A tool of rather obvious, if probably limited, value to both sides, what is interesting about this measure is that it took so long to conclude. At any rate, it obviously did nothing to affect vertical proliferation.

SALT I of 1972

The test ban treaty was a limited measure, even a militarily irrelevant one, by just about anybody's standards, but it was hailed by its advocates as a potential "first step" toward more serious and effective nuclear arms control measures between the United States and the USSR. It took nearly a decade for the next step to be taken, and that one proved, essentially, to make things worse.

By the 1970s, both sides in the cold war, unhampered by the test ban treaty, built up their intercontinental ballistic missile forces until each had more than 1,000, and both also vastly increased their stock of submarine missiles.[8] In part, this buildup was caused by the effort to control it. Soviet leader Leonid Brezhnev was strongly interested in concluding arms agreements, but he considered it necessary to increase armaments in order to destroy the American sense of superiority so that productive discussions on limiting the arms he was building up could take place.[9] However, the United States found Brezhnev's buildup threatening, and so it responded in kind—or more than in kind.

As part of this process, there were major—and menacing—advancements in the arms race. By the 1970s missiles were becoming much more accurate even as it became technologically feasible to put more than one warhead on a single missile. Together, these developments raised the ominous, if theoretical, possibility that one side, or both, could achieve a "first-strike capability," at least against the other's land-based missiles. If two countries possess about the same number of single-warhead missiles, and if it takes, say, two bombs to destroy a missile, each is reasonably safe because an attacker could count on destroying only half of the other's retaliatory capability with a first strike. But if each missile on each side has, say, three warheads, an aggressor would need to use only two-thirds of its warheads to destroy the other side's entire force.

By 1972, the United States and the Soviet Union had labored and brought forth the first Strategic Arms Limitation Treaty as well as an agreement to restrict missile defenses both sides had come to realize wouldn't work anyway. The process of concluding these measures probably did help to reduce international tensions some, and it certainly generated a lot of self-congratulatory celebration all around. However, from a strictly military standpoint, SALT I was an absurdity because it systematically limited the *wrong* arms. Specifically, the treaty restricted the number of intercontinental ballistic missiles each side was allowed to have in its arsenal, but it placed constraints neither on the number of warheads each missile could carry nor on qualitative improvements in their accuracy. Accordingly, as each side continued its military developments under the treaty, each came closer to creating a missile force that could demolish the other side's missile force in a surprise attack but could not survive such an attack by the other. SALT I, then, very significantly increased the advantage of striking first, a profoundly foolish development if the idea is to reduce the danger of nuclear war.

SALT II of 1979

The second Strategic Arms Limitation Treaty, concluded in 1979, attempted to correct the bizarre dilemma enshrined in the first by limiting the number of warheads each side could implant on its land-based and submarine missiles. It also brought strategic bombers into the mix and established broad and sensibly flexible limits on the numbers of ICBMs, submarine missiles, and bombers each side could field.

However, the treaty kept these limits at extremely high levels and did nothing to restrict qualitative improvements. Therefore, although it began to get a handle on the SALT I problem, the fundamental dilemma remained substantially unhampered.

Moreover, SALT II quickly became an irrelevance anyway. Late in 1979, the Soviet Union invaded neighboring Afghanistan to rescue a threatened friendly regime there (a profoundly misguided effort that eventually proved to be disastrous for it), and President Jimmy Carter was electrified. He announced that his "opinion of what the Soviets' ultimate goals are" had undergone a "dramatic change." Embracing in the process what historian Raymond Garthoff has called "the *least* likely Soviet motivation—pursuit of a relentless expansionist design," Carter dramatically declared that the invasion "could pose the most serious threat to world peace since World War II" and insisted on seeing it as an aggressive ploy relevant to the entire Middle East and South Asia. Duly alarmed, Carter sternly threatened to use "any means necessary" to counter a further Soviet military move in the area, and began a defense buildup.[10]

As part of this frantic display of outrage, Carter withdrew the SALT treaty from the ratification process, even though it was supposedly intended to reduce the danger of strategic nuclear war and was obviously completely irrelevant to the Afghan issue. Then, in elections in 1980 the country replaced him with Ronald Reagan, who had always strenuously opposed the treaty, though once in office he continued to abide by its strictures, indicating how generous and substantially unlimiting they actually were.

The Freeze, SDI, INF

As discussed in the previous chapter, fear over thermonuclear war became all the rage for a few years in the early 1980s, as the unthinkable, all but banished from public discourse after 1963, exploded back into popular consciousness, first in Western Europe and then in the United States, for the reasons outlined there.

The American protesters coalesced around a proposal stipulating that the United States and the USSR should freeze their nuclear weapons programs at present levels. By early 1983, the idea had been approved in ten states, mostly by sizable majorities, and the House of Representatives had voted 278 to 149 in favor of a freeze resolution.[11] However, Reagan's defense buildup continued nonetheless, and nuclear weapons stocks remained decidedly unfrozen.

At about the same time, Reagan devised and promptly fell in love with an arms limiting gimmick of his own. At his suggestion, various defense researchers had been looking hard at the possibilities for building an effective defense against a nuclear attack. They came up with a proposal that relied on laser technology and space satellites to zap incoming intercontinental missiles—though they would do little against lesser missiles and nothing at all against strategic bombers. Rather than merely freezing nuclear weapons at present levels, as his noisy opponents were urging, Reagan delightedly proposed building a defense that would make at least those nuclear weapons (and perhaps his critics as well) "impotent and obsolete." He even offered to share the technology, which he called the Strategic Defense Initiative (and just about everyone else called "Star Wars"), with the Soviets under appropriate circumstances.[12]

The Soviets were deeply alarmed at this idea (which is one reason Congress went along with Reagan's proposal to work on it). In part they were concerned that the technology had offensive potential because it could be used either to destroy Soviet missiles on the ground or to neutralize a Soviet retaliatory strike. In addition, it also promised a new, extremely expensive arms race in an area in which they were well behind: highly sophisticated technology.

At the same time, however, they were becoming distinctly aware that they were in deep trouble in many other areas as well: their previous economic, military, and ideological excesses were catching up with them. A new leader, Mikhail Gorbachev, desperate to reduce defense spending,[13] worked with Reagan to establish the Intermediate-range Nuclear Forces agreement in 1987 that caused Europe to become missile-free. At the same time, he essentially abandoned international communism's class-struggle ideology that had appeared so threatening to the West, a process that two years later led to the end of the cold war, as discussed in chapter 4.

Richard Rhodes notes that before Gorbachev took office no arms control agreement had "significantly limited the arms race between the two nuclear superpowers."[14] However, although the Gorbachev-Reagan INF treaty was an impressive achievement, particularly from a political point of view, it scarcely made much difference in the arms balance. It eliminated a set of missiles in one area of the world, restoring Europe to the armed status quo of ten years earlier. But it diminished the cold war contestants' overall nuclear capacities very little.

ARMS CONTROL AND THE NEGATIVE ARMS RACE

Hans J. Morgenthau once proclaimed that "men do not fight because they have arms," but rather "they have arms because they deem it necessary to fight." If that is so, it follows that when countries no longer deem it necessary to fight, they will get rid of their arms. While it may not be entirely fair to characterize disarmament as an effort to cure a fever by destroying the thermometer, the analogy is instructive when it is reversed: when fever subsides, the instrument designed to measure it loses its usefulness and is often soon misplaced.[15]

After all, a country buys arms because its leaders espy a threat or opportunity which, it seems to them, requires them to arm, and during the cold war the United States and the Soviet Union did exactly that. Then, when tensions relaxed after the cold war, a fair amount of arms reduction began to take place between the former contestants. It was a negative arms race, and it required little in the way of formal agreement.

Formal arms agreements can actually hamper, or at least clutter, the process. They tend to take forever to consummate, and they often became irrelevant under conditions of arms competition because while one weapons system is being controlled by laborious negotiation, a better one is being invented. Overall, formal arms control measures have had little history of reducing defense spending when tensions were high—reductions in one defense area were characteristically compensated for by increases in another.[16]

Actually, the existence of arms control talks has often hampered arms reduction. In 1973, for example, a proposal for a unilateral reduction of U.S. troops in West Europe failed in the Senate because it was felt that this would undercut upcoming arms control negotiations—which then ran on unproductively for years. At least in part for moral reasons, Jimmy Carter never really liked the idea, prominently put forward during his administration, of a "neutron bomb"—an enhanced radiation weapon that would kill people while leaving property comparatively undamaged. However, he nonetheless kept open the possibility of proceeding with production so that he could use it as a bargaining chip with the Soviets in arms control negotiations, and his successor, Ronald Reagan, then went ahead with production. Similarly, opponents of the supermissile known as the MX and of Reagan's Strategic Defense Initiative failed in Congress in part because some of those who considered the weapons systems dangerous or valueless nevertheless supported them so that they could be used as bargaining chips in arms control talks. Whether those arms reductions were wise or not, they failed in considerable measure because arms control talks existed. A message of George H. W. Bush's 1988 campaign for the presidency seems to have been that a weapons system, no matter how costly, stupid, or redundant, should never be unilaterally abandoned if it could serve as a bargaining chip in arms control negotiations.[17]

This all falls rather naturally out of the notion that one must "arm to parley," to apply a felicitous (or facile) phrase generated by Winston Churchill that John Kennedy greatly fancied. The notion, stressed Kennedy repeatedly in 1960, was that the United States "cannot parley" with the Soviets unless it establishes "a military position of equality with them." Or, as strategist Albert Wohlstetter put it approvingly at the time, "the likelihood of concluding an arms agreement with the Russians is increased by a strengthening of our military posture."[18] In other words, the existence of talks designed to reduce and control arms impelled their manufacture.

The process was neatly summarized in the 1980s, complete with pertinent typographical blunder, by the Wooster (Ohio) *Daily Record* when it noted that many contend that "the United States cannot expect a fair agreement on arms limitation with Russia until it achieves military parody." In order to achieve "fair agreement" on limiting arms, that is, one has to build ever more weapons. Given the weapons' essential pointlessness, the result of the process was indeed more nearly parody than parity.

When arms are reduced by agreement under conditions of arms competition, both sides are going to strain to make sure that all dangers and contingencies are covered, and they will naturally try, if at all possible, to come out with the better deal. Reduction is possible under those circumstances, but it is likely to be slow, halting, and inflexible. Arms control is essentially a form of centralized regulation and carries with it the usual defects of that approach. Participants will volunteer for such regulation only with extreme caution, because once under its control they are often unable to adjust subtly to unanticipated changes. Moreover, they are often encouraged, perversely, to follow developments that are unwise. As noted earlier, the strategic arms agreement of 1972 limited the number of missiles each side could have, but it allowed them to embroider their missiles with multiple warheads and to improve missile accuracy, thereby encouraging them to develop a potentially dangerous first-strike capability.

The alternative to formal arms control is just to *do* it. The cold war arms buildup, after all, was not accomplished through written agreement; instead, there was a sort of free market in which each side, keeping a wary eye on the other, sought security by purchasing varying amounts of weapons and troops. As requirements and perspectives changed, so did the force structure of each side. The same process can work in reverse: as tensions decline, so can the arms that are their consequence.

A Precedent

There was an interesting and informative precedent for the phenomenon.[19]

Once there was enormous hostility between the United States and British Canada, registered in wars in 1775–83 and 1812–14. After the second of these wars, the contestants lapsed into a long period of wary coexistence—of cold war, in fact.

However, they nevertheless managed to agree to one formal arms control measure. Impelled as much by economic exhaustion as anything else, the United States reduced its fleet of warships on the Great Lakes and proposed that the British do likewise. The British eventually agreed, and the results were formalized in the Rush-Bagot Agreement of 1817, which placed exact limits on the number, size, and armament of warships. However, there was no provision actually to destroy warships, and both sides kept some in dockyards where they could always be put into action should the need arise. Furthermore, there was quite a bit of evasion and technical violation over the next half century, and both built ships that could easily be converted to military use if necessary. Moreover, an arms race continued in areas not specifically restricted by the treaty: each country continued to build forts along the border (at one point the overzealous Americans accidentally built one in Canadian territory and had to abandon it), and the British created an extensive and expensive canal system (there were cost overruns) at Ottawa as a military supply line.

The arms race was accompanied by a series of conflicts between the two neighbors. There were border skirmishes in 1837, a crisis in 1839 in disagreement over the boundary between Maine and New Brunswick, continual war apprehension concerning the Oregon boundary (settled in 1846), substantial tension during the American Civil War, and sporadic raids by Irish-Americans into British Canada. Meanwhile many Americans were caught up in the romantic notion that it was somehow in their "manifest destiny to overspread the continent allotted by Providence for the free development of our yearly multiplying millions," as one newspaper famously and exultantly put it.

By the early 1870s, however, most claims and controversies had been settled. Canada was granted independent status in part because British taxpayers were tired of paying to defend their large, distant colony and, with the Americans focusing on settling the West and on recovering from their calamitous civil war, it seemed safe to begin to withdraw the British army from Canada. Without formal agreement, disarmament gradually took place between the two countries. Their forts often became museums where obsolete cannon still point accusingly but impotently in the direction of the nearby former enemy. And Ottawa's canal has been designated by UNESCO as a World Heritage Site and enjoyed a listing in the *Guinness Book of Records* as the world's longest skating rink until 2008 when it was dislodged by an upstart effort in Winnipeg (since Ottawa's version is wider, however, it remains the world's *largest*, according to local boosters). In all this, "disarmament became a reality," observes a Canadian student of the era, "not by international agreement, but simply because there was no longer any serious international disagreement." Or as another puts it, when "points of dissension disappeared, or could be amicably reconciled, the armaments disappeared with them."[20]

In later decades there was actually a substantial *rearmament* on the Great Lakes because both sides found them a convenient place to conduct training exercises. Charmingly, to preserve niceties, this was accompanied by a genteel process in which the Americans and the Canadians formally amended their 1817 agreement, which by now had become a complete, and quite pleasant, historical artifact.[21]

The Post-Cold War Negative Arms Race

With the demise of the cold war, the reactive arms policy of earlier years continued between West and East, except that now it was focused on arms reduction.

It started at the end of 1988, when, under severe economic pressure to reduce arms expenditures, Gorbachev dramatically announced that he was going to begin to do so unilaterally. Months before Gorbachev's announcement, Lord Carrington, then retiring Secretary General and Chairman of NATO, warned about what he called "involuntary or structural disarmament" within the organization in which a relaxation of East-West tensions had "made support for defense harder to win." This was of concern, he held, because, although Gorbachev clearly "has a real interest in reducing military expenditures," he had apparently not done so yet. However, if the Soviet buildup did begin to swing into reverse, Carrington conceded, NATO's tendency toward what he called "structural" disarmament "would not matter." As if on cue, the press was observing within days of Gorbachev's announcement that there was a "new reluctance to spend for defense" within NATO. In a month, other reports observed that Gorbachev's pronouncements "make it harder for Western governments to justify large sums for military machines.... the Soviet bear seems less threatening to Western publics these days, so that they want to do less on the weapons front.... Western perceptions [are] that the Soviet threat is receding and that big armies are expensive and inconvenient—perhaps even irrelevant." A few months later, as more proposals and counterproposals were spun out by both sides, the

Wall Street Journal was calling the process a "race to demobilize."[22] Reports at the time suggested, in fact, that some officials, alarmed at the disarmament impetus, were hoping to use the formal arms control mechanism to slow the process.

At first both sides reduced cautiously, in sensible if perhaps overly sensitive concern that a severe arms imbalance could inspire the other to contemplate blackmail. Then, after the failure of the Soviet hard-line coup in August 1991, the negative arms race sped ahead. Nuclear testing came to a halt, and by 2002 the former contestants in the cold war had reduced the total number of deployed warheads in their arsenals by some 40,000—from 70,000 to around 30,000. "Real arms control," wistfully reflects a former assistant secretary of state for arms control, "became a possibility only when it was no longer necessary."[23]

In all this, both sides often found that arms reductions would be more difficult if they were accomplished through explicit mutual agreement, which would mean that an exquisitely nuanced agreement must be worked out for every abandoned nut and bolt. In 1991, for example, the Americans announced that they were unilaterally withdrawing all ground-launched and sea-based tactical nuclear weapons while reducing air-based ones by 90 percent, and the Soviet Union soon followed suit, a development hailed by a close observer as "the most radical move to date to reverse the arms race" and a "dramatic move away from 'warfighting' nuclear postures." This "radical" and "dramatic" feat was accomplished entirely without formal agreement. Indeed, if there was a contest, it was caused by the arms control process trying to catch up with reality. When the U.S. Senate in 1992 ratified a nuclear arms reduction treaty that had been signed in 1990, both sides had already moved to reduce arms even further than required by that treaty.[24]

The process also encouraged unilateral efforts to make remaining weapons safer from accident and unauthorized launch. At times of tension there is a tradeoff between security and accident prevention: anything that reduces the likelihood of accidental launch is likely at the same time to reduce the capacity to respond to an attack. However, when tensions sag, one can comfortably upgrade locking devices and procedures on retaliatory weapons and take them off alert, something that happened in the 1990s.[25]

During the cold war, the nuclear arms race had inspired endless breast-beating and brow-furling from protesters and participants alike. At one of its peaks, creative activists at Brown University demanded that their health service stockpile suicide pills for immediate dispensation in the event of a nuclear attack to those unfortunates who still remained unvaporized. Although the measure was approved by 1,044 to 687 in a student referendum, the school's administration uncooperatively insisted it would not stock the pills, sternly adding that, in fact, Brown "condemns the whole idea of suicide as an alternative."[26]

In the cold war's wake, by contrast, the most common emotion was benign neglect, despite the fact that tens of thousands of the diabolical weapons that so exercised the Brown students continued to be maintained, indeed nurtured, in the arsenals of the former scorpions now at long last released from their bottle. In January 2007, four august former defense and foreign policy officials promulgated a dramatic proposal to rid the world of nuclear weapons, and a year later they urgently issued it again. The public reaction was, not to put too fine a point on it, that perhaps the august former officials had too much time on their hands. Six months after the second foray, a concerned *New York Times* scold proclaimed it "a measure of how blasé Americans have grown about such things" that the initiative generated "so little public attention."[27]

In part perhaps because of such public neglect, total nuclear disarmament seems hardly to be in the offing—though the notion does seem to be increasing in trendiness. The possible reemergence of a dangerous hostility would have to be guarded against, and there were other foreign concerns that might require military preparedness. And, of course, inertial guidance remains: those who had previously generated so many justifications for nuclear weapons in such exquisite detail continue to have their skill sets in order. In a top secret 1997 Presidential Directive that soon leaked, Bill Clinton ordered the military to cease preparing for a long nuclear war, but then authorized them to put on their thinking caps and figure out how nuclear weapons might be used to respond to a chemical or biological attack. The Pentagon, in full creative flower, was quick to find a role for the weapons in nonproliferation, "rogue state," and terrorism scenarios, and "measured ambiguity" became the fancy new catchphrase. There also continues to be an enterprising quest to develop mininukes and bunker busters, driven, analyst Bruce Blair darkly suspects, by self-serving interests at the Los Alamos and Lawrence Livermore laboratories whose mission, otherwise, "is shrinking." Stephen Younger, formerly in charge of nuclear weapons research at Los Alamos Laboratory, agrees with the general sentiment: "The United States is spending billions of dollars every year to maintain and refurbish weapons whose practical use military planners are hard-pressed to justify."[28]

Other countries maintain nuclear arsenals as well, although, as with the Americans and the Russians, the quantity is in some degree of decline. France halved its nuclear stockpile after the cold war, and, faced by budgetary problems, announced in 2008 that it was going to further reduce it by another third, to 300 or so. However, why it needs even that many remains far from clear. Perhaps the French labor under the influence of the notion that the weapons might one day prove useful should Nice be savagely bombarded from the sea or should a truly unacceptable number of Africans in former French colonies take up English. The official reasons supplied for maintaining the diminished arsenal, while imaginative, are scarcely more credible. President Nicolas Sarkozy explained that "we care about our nuclear deterrent" because "the security of Europe...is at stake" in that "Iran is increasing the range of its missiles." France's nuclear arsenal, accordingly, is a "life insurance policy," but one that is, of course, "strictly defensive."[29]

COMPARING RACES

A negative arms race is likely to be as chaotic, halting, ambiguous, self-interested, and potentially reversible as a positive one, but arms can be significantly reduced.[30] However, history suggests that arms reduction will happen best if arms negotiators keep out of the way. There could be a role for agreements focused on tension-reducing measures like improved communications links, mechanisms to detect surprise attack preparations, or improved methods to verify the size of the other's military forces. But actual arms reduction will proceed most expeditiously if each side feels free to reverse any reduction it later comes to regret. Formal disarmament agreements are likely simply to slow and clutter the process.

And more generally, Winston Churchill seems to have had it right when he argued in a House of Commons speech on July 13, 1934, that "It is the greatest possible mistake to mix up disarmament with peace. When you have peace, you will have disarmament." In the aftermath of the cold war, we have both. With the demise of fears of another major war, vertical proliferation of the nuclear weapons that were designed to deal with that problem has been reversed, and many of the arms that struck such deep fear for so long are quietly being allowed—as the bumper sticker would have it—to rust in peace.

7

Proliferation

Slow and Substantially Inconsequential

Over the last several decades, forecasts about horizontal proliferation have shown a want of prescience that approaches the monumental—even the pathological. Since 1945, we've been regularly regaled with predictions about the impending and rampant diffusion of nuclear weapons to new states and about the dire consequences that would inevitably flow from such a development. This endlessly and urgently repeated wisdom continues to flourish despite the fact that it has thus far proven to be almost entirely wrong.

In fact, nuclear proliferation has proceeded at a remarkably slow pace and the nuclear club has remained a small one, confounding the somber prophesies of generations of alarmists: indeed, even the supposedly *optimistic* forecasts about nuclear dispersion have proven to be too pessimistic.[1] Moreover, despite decades of dire warnings, the proliferation that has actually taken place has been of only rather minor consequence.

CASCADOLOGY

For decades now, assorted visionaries have espied imminent proliferation cascades. In 1958, for example, the National Planning Association predicted "a rapid rise in the number of atomic powers...by the mid-1960s," and the official U.S. intelligence community anticipated that there might well be 16 states with nuclear weapons by 1968. C. P. Snow was very much on the same wavelength when he ominously predicted a couple of years later that "Within, at the most, six years, China and several other states [will] have a stock of nuclear bombs." Around the same time, British defense commentator F. W. Mulley contended that all the arguments that led Britain to decide to develop its independent nuclear arsenal were equally valid for France "and there is no reason why other members of NATO should not decide to follow suit." And Britain's sometime defense minister, Denis Healey, pointedly asserted that "no country has resisted the temptation to make its own atomic weapons once it has acquired the physical ability to do so."[2]

In debates during the 1960 election campaign, John Kennedy fancifully insisted that there might be "ten, fifteen, twenty" countries with a nuclear capacity by 1964. Then, after becoming president and after being presented in 1963 with a Defense Department list tidily enumerating 20 potential nuclear countries, Kennedy expressed his deep anxieties about the proliferation problem even while quietly abandoning—or dexterously advancing—his previous dire prognosis about the fateful year of 1964:

> Personally, I am haunted by the feeling that by 1970, unless we are successful, there may be ten nuclear powers instead of four, and by 1975, fifteen or twenty....I see the possibility in the 1970s of the President of the United States having to face a world in which fifteen or twenty or twenty-five nations may have these weapons. I regard that as the greatest possible danger.[3]

The Defense Department's list was stocked with countries like Canada, Belgium, the Netherlands, Norway, Switzerland, and Australia, as well as with a slew of countries then under the full control of the Soviet Union. Although it also included a few whose independent possession of nuclear weapons could be seen to be notably problematic from the perspective of the time—China and Egypt, perhaps—the notion that the acquisition of nuclear weapons by most of the itemized countries necessarily posed the "greatest *possible* danger" rather suggests a limitation of imagination on the president's part. In any event, over three decades after Kennedy's fateful year of 1975, only a few of the 20 listed countries have even sought a nuclear weapons capability, and only three of them—China, Israel, and India—have actually managed to attain one.

It was also anticipated that cascades of proliferation would be precipi-
tated—that "points of no return" would be passed—whenever a new country
joined the nuclear club. Thus, many held that a Chinese bomb would set off
a wave of proliferation in Asia and that an Israeli bomb would encourage
Arab states to follow suit. President Lyndon Johnson intoned at the time that
China's "expensive and demanding effort tempts other states to equal folly"
and "is dangerous to all mankind," while CIA Director John McCone was
reported to have divined that "an Israeli bomb would lead to escalation and
then you could just cross off oil from the Middle East for years." Without
missing a step, the Gilpatric Report of 1965, issued by a high-level committee
hastily formed in the wake of the Chinese bomb test of 1964, asserted that "the
world is fast approaching a point of no return in the prospects of preventing
the spread of nuclear weapons."[4] It is true that many in India (for example)
did find the Chinese bomb to be unsettling, but it took them 35 years to
respond with a bomb of their own—perhaps the most lethargic "cascade" in
history. And although Israel did more circumspectly acquire a nuclear weapons capacity in the late 1960s, no Arab state has yet followed suit.

There were occasional calmer voices during the period. For example, in
1964 Richard Rosecrance argued that nuclear dispersion would not necessarily fundamentally disturb the international system and that countries
looking into the process might well be dissuaded once they came to calculate the costs. And in 1967 I suggested that the issue of the spread of nuclear
weapons, trendily known as "the Nth country problem" at the time, "may
have already approached a finite solution." But such voices have been persistently and quite effectively drowned out, indeed overwhelmed, by generations of alarmists, in part perhaps because, as political scientist Richard
Betts suggests, "those interested in the question were those inclined to be
worried about it."[5]

The end of the cold war in 1989 prompted another flurry of dire forecasts, and proliferation, as defense analyst William Arkin has suggested,
seems to have become "methadone for Cold Warriors" who could "no longer get the real thing." To these people, the world somehow managed to
become more dangerous, demanding "prudence, vigilance, and, of course,
tax dollars." Or, as Betts puts it, without the Soviet Union to worry about,
hawks and defense experts shifted their focus to proliferation, because that's
"where the action is."[6]

Thus in 1993, Central Intelligence Agency Director James Woolsey, pro-
fessed to believe darkly, and not, perhaps, without a degree of institutional

self-interest, that "we have slain a large dragon, but we live now in a jungle filled with a bewildering variety of poisonous snakes." Woolsey then conveniently enumerated these "snakes"; the first was "the proliferation of weapons of mass destruction and the ballistic missiles to carry them," followed by "ethnic and national hatreds that can metastasize across large portions of the globe; the international narcotics trade; terrorism; the dangers inherent in the West's dependence on mideast oil; new economic and environmental challenges."[7] None of these snakes, of course, was new on the scene at the time, but, as discussed in chapter 1, there was something comparatively original in the alarm-enhancing expansion of the term "weapons of mass destruction" to include not only nuclear arms but also chemical, biological, and radiological ones—devices that are far less effective at killing.

At any rate, specific predictions about nuclear proliferation at the time include the confident assertion that "Germany will feel insecure without nuclear weapons" and that Japan by natural impulse must soon come to yearn for nuclear weapons—updating futurist Herman Kahn's prediction of 1970 that Japan would "unequivocally start on the process of acquiring nuclear weapons" by 1980. Despite such urgings, the uncooperative Japanese and Germans themselves appear to have remained viscerally uninterested.[8] Indeed, it appears that Japan has not even sought to achieve a nuclear "hedging" position in which it would be poised to become a nuclear weapons state in fairly short order should the need arise, and the same may be true for Germany.[9]

With this unenviable prediction record behind them, one might think proliferation pessimists would now be beginning to sober up a bit. But instead "the sky-is-still-falling profession," as Arkin once labeled it on the pages of the *Bulletin of the Atomic Scientists,* has been if anything reinvigorated. Unimpressed by Arkin's characterization in its own pages and unembarrassed by the fact that its cover clock had been perpetually hailing imminent catastrophe without result for over half a century, the *Bulletin* nudged the hands on its imaginary timepiece a bit closer to the doomsday mark and breathlessly assured anyone who would listen (and hopefully buy the magazine) that "we stand at the brink of second nuclear age."[10]

Joining the chorus in early 2003, shortly before the United States invaded Iraq in a determined quest after the many weapons of mass destruction that he was sure existed there, CIA Director George Tenet confidently proclaimed that

The desire for nuclear weapons is on the upsurge. Additional countries may decide to seek nuclear weapons as it becomes clear their neighbors and regional rivals are already doing so. The "domino theory" of the twenty-first century may well be nuclear.

Or, as Harvard's Graham Allison assures us without even a breath of qualification, if Iran and North Korea become nuclear-armed, "each will trigger a cascade of proliferation in its neighborhood." Former Secretary of State Brent Scowcroft was on very much the same alarmist wavelength when he assured us in 2008 that if Iran were allowed to enrich uranium, potentially on the way to a bomb, "that starts a wave of proliferation, both in the region—Egypt, Saudi Arabia, Turkey—and elsewhere in the world where you could have 20 or 30 countries close to nuclear weapons."[11]

In similar vein, William Langewiesche has concluded that we have passed "the point of no return" on weapons proliferation to established states. That is, the nuclear genie is out of the bottle, and any state, even quite poor ones (North Korea is a pertinent case in point), can eventually obtain nuclear weapons if they really want to make the effort. The driver in this process, he somewhat mysteriously concludes, will be "the desire for self-sufficiency."[12]

Perhaps the ultimate in cascadological hysteria in all this came in a pronouncement by Mohammed ElBaradei, Director General of the International Atomic Energy Agency, one that, incidentally, could perhaps be taken to suggest that his job of inspecting nuclear development in states without the bomb had become monumentally important:

> We are reaching a point today where I think Kennedy's prediction is very much alive. Either we are going to…move to nuclear disarmament or we are going to have 20 or 30 countries with nuclear weapons, and if we do have that, to me, this is the beginning of the end of our civilization.[13]

The preface to a compilation of policy papers published in 2004 by the Washington think tank the Brookings Institution eschewed points of no return to herald instead the prospects for a "nuclear tipping point." Its opening chapter ominously proclaims the existence of "something approaching consensus," not only among the book's authors but also among "our colleagues both in and out of government," that "we now stand on the verge of a new nuclear age" with more nuclear weapons states and "a much greater chance that these weapons will be used." Accordingly, a "proliferation epidemic" could be triggered, with the result that John Kennedy's urgent, if perennially discredited, "nightmare vision," after lingering puzzlingly in historical disrepute for half a century, "may yet occur."[14]

Rather charmingly, however, after musing over studies of eight potential nuclear entrants (Egypt, Germany, Japan, Saudi Arabia, South Korea, Syria, Taiwan, and Turkey), the culminating chapter of the same book suggests that, just possibly, the sainted "consensus" proclaimed so triumphantly in the book's introduction has the occasional chink. It cheerily concludes that "we are almost certainly" not at a tipping point yet—"in fact, we do not appear to be close." Moreover, it continues, "the global nonproliferation regime may be more durable and less fragile than has sometimes [almost always?] been suspected or feared."[15]

Perhaps because this reassuring, if unconventionally laid-back, conclusion is tucked away at the end of the book, it is ignored in a review in *Foreign Affairs* portentously entitled "The Next Nuclear Wave." Similarly, a set of former top government officials proclaimed in 2008 that we are indeed at a "nuclear tipping point," a sentiment urgently echoed by two congressional commissions at the end of the year.[16]

Reflecting on the state of the, well, art in 2008, William Potter and Gaukhar Mukhatzhanova observe:

> Today it is hard to find an analyst or commentator on nuclear proliferation who is not pessimistic about the future. It is nearly as difficult to find one who predicts the future without reference to metaphors such as proliferation chains, cascades, dominoes, waves, avalanches, and tipping points.

Although Potter is, as he admits, a lapsed (or recovering) cascadologist himself, he and his coauthor conclude that the metaphors (they fail to include "epidemics" as well as those dreaded "points of no return" in their catalog, but that is probably simply an oversight) are "inappropriate and misleading," since they imply "a process of nuclear decisionmaking and a pace of nuclear weapons spread that are unlikely to transpire." Nonetheless, cascadology, as political scientist Jacques Hymans notes, "somehow convinces itself that its past predictive failures only serve to underscore the danger that with just one more setback we may well reach a 'tipping point' at which not just 'rogue states' but the whole world defects from our side."[17] It is doubtful that this process, now with more than 60 years of momentum behind it, will shift very much, despite Potter's welcome, if recent, conversion.

THE LIMITED CONSEQUENCES OF PROLIFERATION

Not only has proliferation progressed at a far more leisurely pace than generations of alarmists have routinely and urgently anticipated, but the diffusion that has actually transpired has proven to have had remarkably limited, perhaps even imperceptible, consequences.

China: The Ultimate Rogue

Alarms about proliferation today tend to focus on the dangers inherent if seemingly threatening and irresponsible regimes—"rogue states" in contemporary terminology—obtain the bomb. As a deputy assistant secretary of defense in the George W. Bush administration ominously warned, today's potential enemies differ from the Soviet Union in that they may base their decisions on superstition or fanaticism and may not value the welfare of their own people or their own survival.[18]

Although the word had not yet become fashionable, the world has already had experience with a rogue *par excellence* in the proliferation sweepstakes: Communist China. It was moving toward a nuclear capacity in the early 1960s, and, as historian Francis Gavin has pointed out, at the time

> the threat posed by a nuclear-armed China under Mao Zedong was far more terrifying than anything Iraq's Saddam Hussein or current "rogue" rulers could muster. China, with a population of more than 700 million in 1964, had already fought the United States in Korea; attacked India; and threatened Indochina, Indonesia, and Taiwan. It supported violent revolutionary groups around the world whose goals clashed with U.S. interests. Mao's internal policies had led to the deaths of millions of Chinese citizens, and he had already declared that nuclear war with the United States was not to be feared. In Mao's words, "If the worse came to the worst and half of mankind died, the other half would remain while imperialism would be razed to the ground and the whole world

would become socialist." To the United States, such actions and statements made the PRC appear not only irrational but perhaps undeterrable.

Needless to say, this impending development inspired great alarm. John Kennedy reportedly considered a Chinese nuclear test "likely to be historically the most significant and worst event of the 1960s," and an American analyst pointed out at the time that, since the Chinese appeared "determined to eject the United States from Asia," they were sure to "exploit their nuclear weapons to that end." Actually, it turned out that "historically the most significant and worst event of the 1960s" evolved, arguably, from Kennedy's decision to send American troops in substantial numbers to Vietnam largely to confront the Chinese "threat" that was seen to lurk there.[19]

However that may be, Kennedy was convinced that the impact of Chinese possession of nuclear weapons would be instantaneous: "from that moment on they will dominate South East Asia," and some of his analysts suggested that if the United States adopted a hands-off policy with respect to the spread of nuclear weapons, not only would there be a proliferation cascade, but this would lead to "a U.S. departure from Southeast Asia," which would then "fall under the Chicom [Chinese Communist] domination." Others suggested that a Chinese bomb "could create a bandwagon effect, with greater political pressures on states in the region to accommodate Beijing and loosen ties with Washington." Gavin summarizes the alarm the impending Chinese bomb inspired in high policy circles this way: "China's ascension to the nuclear ranks threatened to weaken the United States' position in Asia, unleash worldwide proliferation, and undermine geopolitical stability in the heart of Europe." That's right: Europe. All this was capped at the time by presidential adviser and CIA Director John McCone, who sternly warned that unless the Chinese "threat" were met by a much strengthened Western alliance, nuclear war was "almost inevitable."[20]

Accompanying this dire prognostication and considerably inspired by it, there seems to have been rather serious consideration in Washington about bombing nuclear facilities in China, perhaps in coordination with the Soviet Union, then decidedly on the outs with their erstwhile Chinese allies. There were all sorts of practical reasons to think this was a really terrible idea, not the least being that the USSR remained notably unenthusiastic.[21]

However, also relevant was an uncharacteristically calm assessment of the situation in several State Department internal reports authored primarily by a staffer, Robert Johnson, who tried, as he recalled more than three decades later, to expose the bureaucracy to nonalarmist thinking about a nuclear-armed China. Avoiding language about a "menacing situation," he concluded that a Chinese capability "will not, for the indefinite future, alter the real relations of power among the major states or the balance of military power in Asia." It was, he continued, "exceedingly unlikely" that the Chinese would use nuclear weapons first, unless under "serious attack." They wanted a nuclear force to deter an attack on their territory, were unlikely to change their essentially prudent, risk-averse military policy, and would "eschew rash military actions" or even "nuclear blackmail." Instead they would use their new capability as a "political weapon . . . to earn respect, to promote neutralism, to encourage revolutionaries." To neutralize any political benefits that China might derive from a small nuclear capability, he concluded, the United States need not do much more than it was already doing.[22]

It was clearly an uphill battle, but not only did his point of view come to prevail at the time, Johnson's predictions, ones that prescribed complacency in the face of imaginable (or fancied) threat, came to pass. China continued to act rather roguish for another decade or so and then began to mellow.[23] But at all times, just as Johnson predicted, it did "eschew rash military actions" as well as "nuclear blackmail." Overall, it is not at all obvious that its nuclear weapons had much relevance either to its roguishness or to its later mellowing, that they benefited it in any way whatever, or that they significantly played any threatening purpose. As a key foreign policy figure of the time, McGeorge Bundy, reflected in 1988, despite their shrill propaganda it turned out that the Chinese sought the bomb for the reasons they gave at the time—as a counter to what they took to be American bullying. Moreover, "no Chinese nuclear threat has ever been made except in terms of a readiness to reply to a nuclear attack and Chinese deployments have been restrained." The United States did manage to undergo a foreign policy debacle in Vietnam, but, as it turned out, this came about because of its hysteria about China and its bomb, not as a result of anything the Chinese did with their bomb.[24]

Domination?

Proliferation alarmists (a category which seems to embrace almost the totality of the foreign policy establishment) may occasionally grant that countries principally obtain a nuclear arsenal to counter real or perceived threats, but many go on to argue that the newly nuclear country will then use its nuclear weapons to dominate the area. It was in this spirit that John Kennedy grandly prophesied in the early 1960s that from the moment the Chinese obtained a bomb, they "would dominate South East Asia" and "so upset the world political scene" that it would become "intolerable."[25]

Such warnings have persisted, focused variously on other posited demons. The domination argument was repeatedly used with dramatic urgency by many for the dangers supposedly posed by Saddam Hussein in Iraq, and it is now being dusted off and applied to Iran. Thus, in the run-up to his 2003 war against Saddam Hussein's Iraq, President George W. Bush insisted that a nuclear Iraq "would be in a position to dominate the Middle East," even as Senator John McCain contended that a nuclear Saddam "would hold his neighbors and us hostage." Later, Bush maintained that a nuclear Iran would become "the predominant state in the Middle East," lording it over its neighbors.[26]

Exactly how this domination business is to be carried out is never made very clear. The United States possesses a tidy array of thousands of nuclear weapons and for years had difficulty dominating downtown Baghdad—or even keeping the lights on there. But the notion apparently is that should an atomic China or Iraq (in earlier fantasies) or North Korea or Iran (in present ones) rattle the occasional rocket, all other countries in the area, suitably intimidated, would supinely bow to its demands. Far more likely is that any threatened states would make common cause with each other against the threatening neighbor, perhaps enlisting the convenient aid eagerly proffered by other countries, probably including the United States, and conceivably even, in the case of Iran, Israel.

One of the few to examine the glib domination assumption (or fantasy) in some detail is political scientist Stephen Walt. Pointing out that the United States alone has twice the population of your standard collection of rogue states combined, has 60 times the GNP, and spends over 23 times as much on defense, he suggests the country would be in a rather good position to form the bedrock of an alliance in opposition to efforts of a rogue to impose its ardent desires on unwilling neighbors—rather as George H. W. Bush showed when that Iraq rogue rashly invaded Kuwait in 1990. Moreover, continues Walt, construction of an alliance, even one that includes countries normally at odds with one another, should be facilitated because, as the rogue threatens, the dangers it poses would come to outweigh other possible interests, disagreements about how to respond would decline, and each alliance member would be inclined to maximize its contribution. In the end, it hardly seems credible that, in Walt's words, a "rogue state's leaders will be utterly unfazed by the vast nuclear and conventional capabilities of the United States."[27]

Stability and Complexity?

Then there is that dreadful, if vaporous, ogre "instability" and its even more vaporous cousin, "complexity." As noted, it was commonly believed in the early 1960s that China's "ascension to the nuclear ranks" not only "threatened to weaken the United States' position in Asia" and "unleash worldwide proliferation," but that the process would also "undermine geopolitical stability in the heart of *Europe*."[28] Similarly, the Gilpatric Committee Report of 1965 determined that:

> The spread of nuclear weapons poses an increasingly grave threat to the security of the United States. New nuclear capabilities, however primitive and regardless of whether they are held by nations currently friendly to the United States, will add complexity and instability to the deterrent balance between the United States and the Soviet Union, aggravate suspicions and hostility among states neighboring new nuclear powers, place a wasteful economic burden on the aspirations of developing nations, impede the vital task of controlling and reducing weapons around the world, and eventually constitute direct military threats to the United States.

Considered 40 years later, Europe seems to have survived rather well, and, although the report proved not surprisingly to be quite on target about the "economic burden" nuclear weapons have presented to their possessors, its prophecy that proliferation would somehow present a threat, whether "grave" or "direct military," to American security scarcely seems to have come true. As Thomas Powers observes, experience clearly demonstrates "that nuclear powers do not use them, and they seriously threaten to use them only to deter attack," while "none has behaved recklessly with its new power." Nonetheless, Jon Wolfsthal, writing in a prominent foreign policy journal in 2005, concludes, despite this experience, that the report's assessment, despite its 40-year wandering in the wilderness, somehow "still holds."[29]

Accidents?

It is a plausible argument that, all other things equal, if the number of nuclear weapons in existence increases, the likelihood one will go off by accident will also increase.

But, in fact, all things haven't been equal. As nuclear weapons have increased in numbers and sophistication, so have safety devices and procedures. Precisely because the weapons are so dangerous, extraordinary efforts to keep them from going off by accident or by an unauthorized deliberate act have been instituted, and these measures have, so far, been effective: no one has been killed in a nuclear explosion since Nagasaki.

Extrapolating further from disasters that have not occurred, many have been led to a concern that, triggered by a nuclear weapons accident, a war could somehow be started through an act of desperate irrationality or of consummate sloppiness. Before the invention of nuclear weapons, such possibilities were not perhaps of great concern, because no weapon or small set of weapons could do enough damage to be truly significant. Each nuclear weapon, however, is capable of destroying in an instant more people than have been killed in an average war, and the weapons continue to exist in the tens of thousands.

However, even if a bomb, or a few bombs, were to go off, it does not necessarily follow that war would result. For that to happen, it is usually assumed, the accident would have to take place at a time of high war-readiness, as during a crisis, when both sides are poised for action and when one side could perhaps be triggered—or panicked—into major action by an explosion mistakenly taken to be part of, or the prelude to, a full attack.[30] This means that the unlikely happening—a nuclear accident—would have to coincide precisely with an event, a militarized international crisis, something that is rare to begin with, became more so as the cold war progressed, and has become even less likely since its demise.

Furthermore, even if the accident takes place during a crisis, it does not follow that escalation or hasty response is inevitable, or even very likely. As Bernard Brodie points out, escalation scenarios essentially impute to both sides "a well-nigh limitless concern with saving face" and/or "a great deal of ground-in automaticity of response and counterresponse." None of this was in evidence during the Cuban missile crisis when there were accidents galore. An American spy plane was shot down over Cuba, probably without authorization, and another accidentally went off course and flew threateningly over the Soviet Union. As if that weren't enough, a Soviet military officer spying for the West sent a message, apparently on a whim, warning that the Soviets were about to attack.[31] None of these remarkable events triggered anything in the way of precipitous response. They were duly evaluated and then ignored.

Robert Jervis points out that "when critics talk of the impact of irrationality, they imply that all such deviations will be in the direction of emotional impulsiveness, of launching an attack, or of taking actions that are terribly risky. But irrationality could also lead a state to passive acquiescence." In moments of high stress and threat, people can be said to have three psychological alternatives: (1) to remain calm and rational, (2) to refuse to believe that the threat is imminent or significant, or (3) to panic, lashing out frantically and incoherently at the threat. Generally, people react in one of the first two ways. In her classic study of disaster behavior, Martha Wolfenstein concludes, "The usual reaction is one of being unworried."[32]

In addition, the historical record suggests that wars simply do not begin by accident. In his extensive survey of wars that have occurred since 1400, diplomat-historian Evan Luard concludes, "It is impossible to identify a single case in which it can be said that a war started accidentally; in which it was not, at the time the war broke out, the deliberate intention of at least one party that war should take place." Geoffrey Blainey, after similar study, very much agrees: although many have discussed "accidental" or "unintentional" wars, "it is difficult," he concludes, "to find a war which on investigation fits this description." Or, as Henry Kissinger has put it dryly, "Despite popular myths, large military units do not fight by accident."[33]

It may also be useful in this regard to make a comparison.

The cold war was characterized by a contest in advanced nuclear arms and delivery systems between two intense rivals. In this case, as noted in the previous chapter, any efforts to reduce the likelihood of accidents had to be balanced against the fact that any accident-reducing measure might well also reduce the country's capacity to respond effectively and expeditiously to a first strike by the other—a potential problem that has, of course, been substantially relaxed with the end of the cold war.[34]

This dilemma is not present to nearly the same degree in the case of the acquisition of nuclear weapons by states that are less militarily pretentious. In particular, the exquisite hair-trigger niceties of the first strike/second strike consideration—maintaining "crisis stability," as discussed in chapter 5—scarcely holds where a country, or pair of rival countries, builds a relatively small arsenal of nuclear weapons and keeps them in reserve as a sort of final equalizer, something sometimes known as the "bomb in the basement" approach. Countries in that situation are scarcely concerned about being able instantly to retaliate to a nuclear attack, and their rivals are unlikely to have the sophisticated delivery system required to destroy their atomic capacity in a surprise attack in any case. Accordingly, unlike the cold war contestants, such countries have the luxury of making their bombs exceedingly safe from accidental detonation. For example, when it had a small nuclear arsenal, South Africa disassembled its weapons and stored the parts in separate secure locations, an approach currently being adopted by Pakistan and perhaps others.[35]

Judicious efforts to further reduce the danger of an accidental nuclear detonation, like those devoted to dissuading new states from acquiring nuclear weapons, are certainly justified. But the myopic hype and hysteria that have so routinely accompanied such efforts are not.

8

The Limited Appeal and Value of Nuclear Weapons

With decades of cascadological prophecy and, effectively, apocalyptic cheerleading for would-be proliferators behind us, one might be set to wondering why more countries haven't taken the nuclear plunge. As analyst Moeed Yusuf observes, not only "has the pace of proliferation been much slower than anticipated," but the very considerable majority of the states arrayed on the alarmists' lists "never came close to crossing the threshold"—indeed, "most did not even initiate a weapons program."[1]

It rather appears that, insofar as most leaders of most countries (even rogue ones) have considered acquiring the weapons, they have come to appreciate several defects. Among them: the weapons are dangerous, distasteful, costly, and likely to rile the neighbors. If one values economic growth and prosperity above all, the sensible thing seems to be to avoid the weapons unless they seem vital for security or are required to stoke a leader's extravagant ego.

That is, as one observer puts it, "there have always been quite powerful disadvantages to acquiring nuclear weapons, costs that countries would not wish to bear unless they felt extremely vulnerable or extremely cocky." And the result, notes weapons inspector David Kay tersely, is that a considerable number of states "have largely on their own decided that nuclear arms do not offer them any real benefits."[2] This chapter assesses the quite considerable and often significantly consequential disincentives to go nuclear.

THE LACK OF A TECHNOLOGICAL IMPERATIVE

The literature and policy debate on proliferation has overwhelmingly been "techno-centric." Thus, the National Planning Association concluded in 1958 that the rate of nuclear diffusion was dependent upon such essentially mechanical factors as a "nation's present technology, its present industrial capacity, its level of education, and the rate at which these factors are changing." Then, two years later, the association boldly rated the countries of the world as potential nuclear powers and came up with no less than 26 to worry about. Twelve countries were declared to be "able to embark on a successful nuclear weapons program in the near future," eight were "economically capable, fairly competent technically, although perhaps somewhat more limited in scientific manpower," and six more were "probably economically capable, although more limited in industrial resources and scientific manpower" and thus unlikely successfully to achieve a nuclear weapons capacity within five years. Since that time, education levels and technological and industrial capacities have substantially increased, and by the end of the century nearly 50 could be deemed to have become nuclear-capable. But the only countries on NPA's list to develop nuclear weapons over the subsequent half century have been France and China (both of which had active and well-known programs in place at the time), India, and, temporarily, South Africa. The other entrants, Israel, Pakistan, and North Korea, did not, as it happens, enter the list-makers' minds in 1960.[3]

Clearly, as history has shown and as Stephen Meyer pointed out a quarter century ago after extensive analysis, there is no "technological imperative" for countries to obtain nuclear weapons once they have achieved the technical capacity to do so.[4]

It seems clear, then, that proliferation pessimists have rather consistently been extrapolating from the wrong cases. Although Denis Healey didn't happen to notice in 1960 when he claimed that no technologically capable country had "resisted the temptation" to make its own atomic bomb, there was even then one country with that ability that had been entirely able—and has since continued to be able—to restrain any incipient desire to become a nuclear weapons state: Canada. As more careful analysts pointed out at the time, "Alone among the nations up to the present, she has had the undoubted capacity to produce atomic bombs and has chosen not to do so."[5] And it has transpired that, as other countries have attained a nuclear capacity, the overwhelming majority have followed the Canadian example, not the British or French one.

Indeed, over the decades a huge number of countries capable of developing nuclear weapons have neglected even to consider the opportunity seriously—for example, Belgium, Norway, and Italy. And others—Brazil, Argentina, South Korea, Sweden, Libya, and Taiwan—have backed away from or reversed nuclear weapons programs or perspectives, while South Africa, Ukraine, Belarus, and Kazakhstan have actually surrendered or dismantled an existing nuclear arsenal.[6] Some of this, as will be discussed in the next chapter, is no doubt due to the hostility—and bribery—of the nuclear nations, but even without that, the Canadian case seems to have had wide and general relevance.

William Langewiesche may be right that quite a few states—even quite a few poor ones now—do possess the technical and economic capacity to obtain nuclear weapons, but experience certainly doesn't suggest that that capacity alone is remotely enough to encourage them to take the plunge.[7] For potential nuclear aspirants, there are quite a few other considerations.

LIMITED VALUE AS A STATUS SYMBOL

In addition to the "technology imperative" argument, it has been assumed that nuclear weapons would be seen as important status—or virility—symbols, and therefore that all advanced countries would lust after them to secure position and to decorate the national ego. Thus, political scientist Robert Gilpin once declared that "the possession of nuclear weapons largely determines a nation's rank in the hierarchy of international prestige."[8] It is in this tradition that some analysts who describe themselves as "realists" have insisted for decades that Germany and Japan must soon surely come to their senses and quest after nuclear weapons.

At least in some cases, there is surely something to this. When his country exploded its first bomb in 1960, President Charles de Gaulle of France was jubilant: "Hoorah for France!" he bellowed, "since this morning she is stronger and prouder," and in 1965 he opined, "No country without an atom bomb could properly consider itself independent." But de Gaulle had a number of particular hang-ups about status, and most countries—then and now—can obtain it in other ways. The costs and travails of nuclear ownership only hamper that process. Indeed, plenty of leaders and members of foreign policy elites, facing comparable external conditions, have concluded that any potential status benefit in acquiring the bomb have been secondary or even illusory.[9] In fact, when de Gaulle's successors carried out a modest set of underground nuclear tests in the Pacific in 1995 and 1996, they found that their actions mainly attracted international disgust, condemnation, and outrage (as well as economic boycotts), not admiration or awe.

The Canadian example is instructive in this consideration. During World War II, Canada cooperated with Britain and the United States in atomic research, and at the war's end it found itself in possession of a small, low-power atomic energy pile. The Canadian and British situations in world affairs at that point were in many respects similar: neither then had nuclear allies, neither was under a de facto nuclear umbrella, neither had any perceived enemy against which it was necessary to arm, both were essentially invulnerable to any potential enemy, and both had the necessary resources and skills to launch a nuclear weapons program.

Unlike Great Britain, however, the Canadians never considered the idea seriously, and it is likely that an important difference arises from the two countries' self-images.[10] At the time, Britain considered itself to be a "great" power, while Canada saw itself in substantially more modest terms. A great power might have among its attributes the possession of atomic weapons, while a middle power operates by careful application of informal, moral, and nonmilitary persuasion. Moreover, Canadians do not seem to place a high value on military grandeur and certainly have no zeal for expansion. Indeed, one book on the Canadian military is subtitled "The Military History of an Unmilitary People." As a result of this, the military in Canada, which presumably would be most amenable to a nuclear weapons program, seems weaker as a political influence than its counterpart in many other countries. Canada's self-image as an influential, but not militarily powerful, actor on the world scene has great appeal and is widely accepted, and a nuclear capability does not fit into this image at all.

Like Canada, most technologically capable potential entrants into the nuclear club do not happen to see military capacity as particularly valuable, and their number is probably growing. Indeed, it may now well include the vast majority of countries so portentously, and preposterously, placed on those lists of potential entrants to the nuclear club in the 1950s and 1960s.

The Canadian example probably even applies to much larger countries like Germany and Japan. As a recent analysis observes,

Undoubtedly some countries have pursued nuclear weapons more for status than for security. However, Germany, like its erstwhile Axis ally Japan, has become powerful because of its economic might rather than its military might, and its renunciation of nuclear weapons may even have reinforced its prestige. It has even managed to achieve its principal international objective— reunification—without becoming a nuclear state.[11]

In the end, of course, status, like beauty, tends to lie in the eye of the beholder. As political scientist Jacques Hymans points out, even leaders "who are clearly international prestige seekers do not necessarily view the bomb as the right ticket to punch." For example, many Indian nationalists "not only believed that the potential security costs of building the bomb outweighed the status benefits, but also that India could actually gain more international status by *abstaining* from the bomb."[12]

Although China began to construct its nuclear arsenal in 1964, it was in the 1990s that it began to be hailed as "a great power," and this was because its economy had pushed, by some measures, into the top tier in the world. In 1988, McGeorge Bundy observed that "the Chinese do not appear to believe the possession of the atomic bomb is in itself a badge of status," a judgment confirmed by a more recent analysis in which it is pointed out that China has persistently sought to establish a reputation as a good global citizen and regional neighbor, and has downplayed its nuclear arsenal, uncondition-ally promising not to use or threaten to use its nuclear weapons against others.[13]

Indeed, status is increasingly being expressed in the dreary but bloodless medium of economic statistics. Consider in this regard il sorpasso, the exu-berant boast of Italy in 1987 that its gross domestic product was now greater than Britain's. From this the Italians jubilantly concluded that they deserved admission into the rich nations club, the Group of Five, supplanting the British (members of this club got to stay for dinner at meetings of the Big People, while lesser entities were required to retire quietly after coffee). The fact that they now could brandish a larger economic number than the Brit-ish gave the Italian people a lot of pride, and they celebrated as if they had just won a great battle. Equally interesting is the way the distinctly unamused British chose to reply to this Latin impudence. The Italians were miscalcu-lating the economic statistics, they countered, and besides, the British had far more television sets and telephones per capita. What the British *didn't* do was to point to, or even slyly to imply the relevance of, their military superiority—particularly their possession of nuclear weapons.[14]

And there are other possible standards. China's decades-long quest to host the Olympics stemmed in part from the belief that it would be a "mark of entry into the big league of world powers." And some Koreans have apparently come to believe that status is achieved when a country has many entries in the *Guinness Book of World Records:* exults one, "The more records we have leads to world power."[15]

Overall, it appears, the weapons have *not* proved to be crucial status symbols. As Robert Jervis has observed, "India, China, and Israel may have decreased the chance of direct attack by developing nuclear weapons, but they have not increased their general political prestige or influence."[16] How much more status would Japan have if it possessed nuclear weapons? Would anybody pay a great deal more attention to Britain or France if their arsenals held 5,000 nuclear weapons, or would anybody pay much less if they had none? Did China need nuclear weapons to impress the world with its economic growth? Indeed, how many people anymore even remember whether China *has* nuclear weapons?

Perhaps the only status benefit the weapons have conferred is upon contemporary Russia: with an economy the size of Spain, the country might have been less likely to be invited to associate with the top economic club (now up to eight) if it had no atomic arsenal. Beyond this, nuclear weapons may sometimes have a kind of "naughty child" effect: nuclear behavior can attract notice. As Russia's nuclear arsenal perhaps causes people to be more concerned about its destiny than if it had no bombs, and as apprehensions about chaos in Pakistan are doubtless heightened by the fact that it has gone atomic, North Korea can get people to pay more attention to it if it seeks to develop a bomb than if it doesn't—as William Arkin puts it, its various atomic forays in the area mainly demonstrate "how desperate the country is for international attention."[17] However, this phenomenon hardly generates real status, and it is nothing compared to the kind of respect a country would attract if it were to become an important economic player on the world scene.

LIMITED MILITARY VALUE

It is not clear that the bomb has been of much value militarily, either. It is routinely argued that nuclear weapons are what kept the cold war from becoming a hot one. However, as discussed in chapter 3, the people who have been in charge of world affairs since World War II seem hardly to have required visions of mushroom clouds to conclude that another catastrophic world war, nuclear or nonnuclear, win or lose, could be distinctly unpleasant and that they should keep their crises under control.

Beyond this, it is also difficult to see how nuclear weapons benefited their possessors in specific military ventures. Kenneth Waltz argues that "contemplating war when the use of nuclear weapons is possible focuses one's attention not on the probability of victory but on the possibility of annihilation.... The problem of the credibility of deterrence, a big worry in a conventional world, disappears in a nuclear one."[18] Now, it may be true that if a would-be aggressor thinks a move might very well escalate to something terrible like a world war (with or without nuclear weapons), caution is likely to ensue. However, where that fear is lacking—as with the Argentines when they launched military action against the interests of the (nuclear-armed) United Kingdom in 1982—war can come about. British nuclear retaliation was certainly possible, yet the Argentines apparently did not find it credible or relevant.

Similarly, its nuclear weapons were scarcely of help, or relevance, to France in its war in Algeria, to Britain in its venture in Suez in 1956, or to the Soviet Union in its disaster in Afghanistan. Nor did Israel's probable nuclear capacity restrain the Arabs from attacking in 1973 or help it during its lengthy intervention in the civil war in Lebanon or its armed conflicts with neighboring substate groups in 2006 and 2009. Nor did the Chinese find the bomb helpful in their brief and rather humiliating war against their erstwhile ally, Vietnam, in 1979. And tens of thousands of nuclear weapons in the arsenals of the enveloping allied forces did not cause Saddam Hussein to order his occupying forces out of Kuwait in 1990. Nor, as noted in chapter 5, did possession of the bomb benefit America in its efforts in Iraq, Korea, or Vietnam. Keith Payne makes a plausible, if less than airtight, case that the implied American threat to use nuclear weapons if Iraq used chemical ones in the Gulf War of 1991 (a pure bluff, as he points out) may have been "at least part of the reason Saddam Hussein did not use WMD." In an effort to uncover concrete instances where the nuclear threat made a difference, this rather tenuous one is about all he can come up with.[19]

Not only have nuclear weapons failed to be of much value in military conflicts, they also do not seem to have helped the nuclear country to swing weight or "dominate" an area, as discussed in chapter 7. All this is quite contrary to the visions, and to the endlessly repeated predictions, of dedicated antiproliferators.

One might also look at this whole issue from the opposite perspective. Even as a few countries have managed to obtain nuclear weapons in the last quarter century, a larger number have given them up: South Africa, Belarus, Kazakhstan, and Ukraine. What conceivable military (or status) loss has been suffered by these countries for their decision to revert to nuclear virginity (or at least chastity)?

It is also of interest in this regard that the atomic arsenals of new nuclear states have generally been rather small—including even those of China.[20] If the weapons were so useful militarily, one would expect them to build many more.

Some in Israel apparently espy some military value in its nuclear arsenal because it furnishes the country with what some have labeled the "Samson Option"—if its surrounding enemies successfully invade and envelop it in military defeat, it will have the capacity to bring the entire structure down upon them.[21] A key difference with the biblical analogy, however, is that the temple Samson pulled down to crush himself and his enemies was not filled as well with Jews.

Even as they furnish little military value, the weapons may make things militarily worse by riling the neighbors in some cases. Few countries are engaged in military rivalries, but those that do see a rivalry out there may be disinclined to stir the pot by arming in a manner that may cause concern to the rival. Thus, although Argentine leaders for decades believed that nuclear technology would give them international status, they eventually came to realize that such benefits were heavily outweighed by the possibility of ensnaring the country in a dangerous, costly arms race with Brazil.[22]

ECONOMIC AND ORGANIZATIONAL COST

As Hymans stresses, a state's decision to go nuclear is a monumental, indeed a "revolutionary," one. It is a "leap in the dark" with "potentially massive consequences on every level of politics and policy, including profound effects in the areas of military strategy, diplomacy, economics, domestic institutions, and ethical or normative self-image." For the many politicians and administrators for whom "courage" is a four-letter word, that can be an insuperable barrier. Or, as two analysts put it a bit more mildly, "it is not so easy to reverse longstanding decisions to forswear nuclear weapons."[23]

The economic costs of fabricating a nuclear arsenal can be monumental, and in many cases might require, as a former president of Pakistan once colorfully put it, having to "eat grass"—or at least consciously to downgrade or even abandon other goals. As part of this, notes Langewiesche, there is "a premium for working fast and in the shadows," and during its lengthy quest to explode an atomic bomb, for example, Pakistan apparently had to pay two or three times the going rate for equipment and material it needed.[24]

Assessing the nuclear weapons programs of India, Pakistan, and Iraq, physicists Richard Garwin and Georges Charpak conclude that "making nuclear weapons is not trivial, even for a country with substantial wealth and scientific resources." Israel's nuclear program has taken up more than 10 percent of its military budget—money that could have been spent on social services or on conventional forces. As with other countries, the project has also been costly in that it drained away a great portion of the country's best scientific and technical talent from other pursuits. Nuclear advocates in Israel in the 1960s insisted, however, that only nuclear weapons could furnish an absolute and final deterrent to the Arab threat.[25] When the Arabs, undeterred, did invade in 1973, Israel's nuclear force was of no direct military value whatever—though the country certainly could have used larger and better-supplied conventional forces.

Significantly adding to the cost is the fact that a nuclear weapon is not simply an impressive explosive but an entire system. This includes advanced hardware and software, as well as human organization that must be strong and management that must be skillful—areas in which many countries, including some of the ones antiproliferators are most concerned about, are often severely lacking. As Hymans notes, "the historical record of nuclear weapons programs clearly shows many delays, detours, and wasted expenditures that had nothing to do with the quantity of fissile material."[26]

A failure to appreciate this has led to overestimations of a country's ability to fabricate nuclear weapons that have sometimes been massive. A key finding of the Silberman-Robb Commission on intelligence is that it is "a fundamental analytic error" to equate "procurement activity with weapons system capability." That is, "simply because a state can buy the parts does not mean it can put them together and make them work." It is extremely important, then, to understand "the scientific, academic, industrial, and economic base a country needs in order to develop and actually produce weapons."[27]

MORALITY AND CONCERNS ABOUT PRECEDENTS

For many countries and peoples, there is a degree of moral repugnance to the possession of nuclear weapons: they take the nuclear taboo, discussed in chapter 2, seriously.

For example, some Canadians, after careful, objective analysis, have concluded that their country is morally superior to their gigantic neighbor to the south, a view that was once caricatured by a Canadian political scientist: "Having studied thousands of Canadian editorials, and listened to as many speeches and conversations, I have come to the conclusion that the fault with North America is an improper division of resources: the Americans got the power; the Canadians the virtue and common sense." Additionally, some attach a moral value to being a nonnuclear power: nuclear weapons are seen as contaminating, and the possessor as committed to a policy of mass devastation. A Canadian journalist once dubbed Canada's defense position one of "nuclear virginity."[28] But in this case virginity is more than a state of being; it is almost a psychological complex.

Nina Tannenwald suggests another possible effect. To the degree that nuclear weapons have picked up taboo status, "nuclear deterrence has not been viewed as a legitimate practice" for most states, and this can "legitimize a hierarchical world order" of nuclear haves and have-nots by "helping to define the identities of 'civilized' states."[29]

The degree to which this perspective is general would need to be assessed on a case-by-case basis. Quite a few countries, including Japan, may well embrace a moral perspective similar to Canada's. However, at one point the same might have been said about India, and that country did somehow manage to rise above any moral inhibitions it might have once embraced about the bomb.

An additional reason often given by those opposed to Canada's acquisition of nuclear warheads was that such an action would encourage the spread of nuclear weapons and adversely affect progress on disarmament. As a prominent magazine editorialized in 1962, "refusal is the only way to limit membership in the 'nuclear club' effectively, and the only effective protest against the acceptance of nuclear war as a tolerable consequence of national policy." The idea that Canada has a special and significant mission to perform in limiting nuclear diffusion and in promoting disarmament is an accepted component of the political lore of the nation, and it has been proposed there that the country initiate a "self-denying ordinance" in the United Nations to help limit nuclear diffusion.[30] A nation with this attitude does not make a likely prospect for the nuclear club. At least some potential nuclear countries may labor under similar perspectives.

LEADERSHIP PERSONALITY AND DOMESTIC PRESSURES

Especially in the last four or five decades, the decision to go nuclear or to abandon nuclear programs has been a rather idiosyncratic one. Mostly, it has not been the product of grander forces but rather of internal politics stemming from the dedicated machinations, and the peculiar perspectives and personalities, of specific leaders or governing coalitions.

Thus Hymans finds that leaders who have pursued weapons in recent decades are "driven by fear and pride," must "develop a desire for nuclear weapons that goes beyond calculation, to self-expression," and are quite rare. Cascadology, he stresses, "paints an exceedingly dark picture by lumping the truly dangerous leaders together with the merely self-assertive ones."[31]

In like manner, political scientist Etel Solingen expresses understandable dismay at the "lack of rigorous examination of domestic sources of nuclear postures," and comes to a similar conclusion. She puts more emphasis on the leaders' peculiar needs for political survival, which, she observes, are not "merely loosely associated" with nuclear policies, but "joined at the hip." In particular, nuclearization has been more costly, and consequently less attractive, for leaders and coalitions who, mainly to satisfy domestic proponents of internationalization, wish to integrate into the global economy. At the same time, those relying on or promoting what she calls "inward-looking bases of support"—people who favor nationalism, religious radicalism, or autarky—have greater tolerance for, and incentives for, nuclear weapons programs. And another study, focusing mainly on countries that abandoned nuclear programs, finds that the single most important factor in influencing their behavior was the quality of the political leadership.[32]

INTERNATIONAL PRESSURE

In a number of instances, international pressure has played a role in encouraging states to reverse nuclear programs or even abandon actual weapons.

This process is assessed more extensively in the next chapter, but one summary observation particularly relevant to the current discussion may be useful here.

Except where the "pressure" has involved outright invasion (that would be the costly war in Iraq that began in 2003), it is not at all clear, in almost all cases, that the pressure was a necessary cause of the result. In part, this is because the pressures have sought essentially to enhance the disincentives to go nuclear, which, as discussed above, are already quite substantial. In some cases, this marginal enhancement may have been consequential, but at the same time it also expanded the capacity of some countries to exact payments—that is, to engage in a form of extortion—to obtain funds and support to do something they would likely have done anyway.

Or, to put it another way, if nuclear weapons are such valuable possessions, one might think that states pursuing a nuclear program or ones that find themselves in the possession of nuclear arms would not be so susceptible to various forms of international pressure and bribery.

In 2003 Kenneth Waltz pointed out that "in the past half-century no country has been able to prevent other countries from going nuclear if they were determined to do so"—although the war against Saddam Hussein's Iraq that began in the same year might be seen now to be something of a special exception.[33] But the key issue is that the countries—or, in particular, their leaders—need to be *determined,* not merely have a desire, to go nuclear. And, contrary to the insistent warnings of decades of cascadologists, few have been of that mind. The decision to go nuclear is a dramatic and costly one, and the vast majority of leaders over the decades have been able to contain their enthusiasm for engaging in the endeavor.

In consequence, although the atomic genie in a technical sense may be out of the bottle—and indeed for decades has been so for a large number of states—only a few have been seduced by its charms. This is likely to continue to be the case, particularly if eating grass is a prerequisite for obtaining a nuclear arsenal. Most potential nuclear countries are, like Canada, militarily unpretentious states with middle power complexes, moral objections to nuclear weapons, a nonnuclear inertia, genuine fears about encouraging nuclear diffusion, and far, far better ideas of what to do with their money.

9

Controlling Proliferation

Modest Success

Over the last few decades, there have been extensive persuasive and dissuasive efforts to prevent horizontal proliferation—the dispersion of nuclear weapons and, to a lesser degree, other "weapons of mass destruction" to states that do not already have them. The idea has been to halt or at least to slow the spread of nuclear weapons by establishing a worldwide nonproliferation "regime."

This chapter evaluates the (rather limited) successes of these antiproliferation efforts. It begins, however, by briefly exploring the almost completely neglected possibility that there may be some benefit to horizontal proliferation.

VALUE IN PROLIFERATION?

The proliferation fixation has so permeated the foreign policy establishment that it has been almost impossible even to consider the possibility that nuclear proliferation could have some positive aspects.[1] A full evaluation of the issue should, however, take at least a few potential benefits into account.

Reducing Effective Threat by Encouraging Wasteful and Pointless Expenditure

Defense analyst Thomas McNaugher has arrestingly observed that, since missiles are expensive and vastly inferior to aircraft for delivering ordnance, it may be sensible to encourage countries to waste their money on missiles rather than spending it on cheaper and more effective airplanes. A good example of the process in action comes from Nazi Germany's elaborate and very expensive efforts to develop and use missiles in World War II. As Michael Neufeld reports, even the best of the missiles were so inaccurate they could barely hit a large city, and the total explosive load of all the missiles launched was not much greater than that of a single large raid by the British air force. Moreover, for the yearly cost and effort of producing its V-missiles alone, the Germans could have turned out 24,000 fighters at a time when production totaled only 36,000 per year. Concludes Neufeld, "German missile development shortened the war, just as its advocates said it would, but in favor of the Allies."[2]

Given their cost and essential uselessness, it seems conceivable that a similar argument could be made about nuclear weapons. After all, if a potentially dangerous country foolishly expends scarce resources on trying to develop expensive nuclear weapons, it won't have nearly as much money to spend on far more usable conventional ones. It might eventually attain a satisfying capacity to scare the readily traumatized major countries (whose fondest desire, of course, is to expend their resources on these weapons oligopolistically), but it would be less able to cause actual trouble.

As it happens, the regimes most likely to want to develop nuclear weapons—"rogues" and such—also tend to be almost mindlessly incompetent, particularly from a bureaucratic point of view. However brutally capable they may be at preserving the privileges of the elite and of the top leader, they are headed by people who are selfish, prideful, mercurial, impatient, distrustful (if not fully paranoid), and often brutal, and they routinely promote political hacks, churn personnel, alienate the best scientists and technicians, find it difficult to make coherent long-term plans, make poor technical choices, and exhaust resources with repeated crash programs that have unreasonable deadlines and distracting side projects.[3] If the development of rocketry proved to be a very substantial waste to the comparatively well-oiled German regime in World War II, any attempt by contemporary dysfunctional rogue states to carry out an expensive high-tech venture like the development of nuclear weapons and their attendant delivery systems is likely to become a major, even overwhelming, economic and organizational strain. And, in particular, the effort might well divert them from producing or purchasing military equipment that they might actually know how, and be able, to use.

Deterring War

There is also the argument forcefully brought forward by a few analysts, including the prominent international relations scholar Kenneth Waltz, that, in Waltz's words, "more may be better." Although there are clearly potential problems in the proliferation of nuclear weapons to states, Waltz suggests that, on balance, proliferation may do more good than harm by deterring war and armed conflict. "Those who dread a world with more nuclear states do little more than assert that more is worse and claim without substantiation that new nuclear states will be less responsible and less capable of self-control than the old ones have been," he argues. In his view, by contrast, "The likelihood of war decreases as deterrent and defensive capabilities increase." Since this holds for small as well as for big countries, "the gradual spread of nuclear weapons is more to be welcomed than feared."[4]

I do not find this argument particularly compelling: I'm inclined instead to suggest that, although proliferation probably doesn't make very much difference one way or the other in most cases, on balance it is probably not all that great an idea.[5] However, it is impressive how casually the Waltz perspective—a plausible line of argument, whatever my reservations—is commonly dismissed without even much analysis or effort at refutation. As Richard Betts notes, the argument cannot simply be "brushed off," yet that is exactly what has happened; "surprisingly few academic strategists" have tried to refute it in detail.[6]

Thus the otherwise careful and thoughtful Mitchell Reiss worries (or did in 2004) that we are nearing a nuclear "tipping point" that could trigger a "proliferation epidemic." Should this occur, he assures us, "few would take comfort in the assurances of some academic theorists [a double putdown if there ever was one] that 'more may be better,'" directly quoting Waltz, but not even affording him a footnote.[7]

If academics have substantially ignored the argument, policymakers have been at least as oblivious. For example, James Kurth simply dismisses the Waltz argument out of hand: "There probably has not been a single foreign policy professional in the U.S. government," he noted in 1998, "that has found this notion to be helpful."[8] But not, one strongly suspects, because any has spent any time thinking about it.

Solving Specific Security Problems

If the Waltz perspective has simply gone unconsidered, this is an indicator of faulty decision making, because there are clearly specific instances in which nuclear proliferation could potentially be beneficial.

In the late 1970s, for example, the United States, in full zero-tolerance mode, put enormous pressure on Taiwan to cease any program that could lead it to develop nuclear weapons. For decades that island nation has faced the threatening prospect of a very hostile takeover by (nuclear-armed) mainland China, and by the late 1970s the United States was in the process of deciding to reduce its security guarantees, which would presumably make Taiwan more vulnerable. At the time, the mainland was still staggering under the impact of decades of Maoist misrule and was struggling massively to reform its internal economic system. Accordingly, it was in a poor military position to do much of anything about whatever arms Taiwan chose to develop.[9]

With this confluence of circumstances, it would have been a good time at least to *consider* whether the long-term stability of the area would be best served by letting Taiwan develop a deterrent nuclear capacity. There are certainly good reasons to conclude that this policy would be, on balance, unwise. But the problem is that, laboring under the sway of the proliferation fixation, policy toward Taiwan was fabricated in a knee-jerk fashion that precluded even the consideration of an obvious, and potentially productive, policy alternative.

THE LIMITED ACHIEVEMENTS OF ANTIPROLIFERATION EFFORTS

As discussed earlier, nuclear proliferation has been remarkably slow—and certainly far slower than alarmists have so persistently and so eagerly predicted over the decades. However, it is not clear that the exertions of dedicated antiproliferators deserve very much credit for this result.

The Nuclear Nonproliferation Treaty

To explain the remarkably slow pace at which nuclear weapons have spread to new states, many put a great deal of weight on the supposedly beneficial effects of the 1968 Non-Proliferation Treaty (NPT). For example, Joseph Cirincione, the director for nuclear policy at a prominent Washington think tank, suggests that, without that document, a "nuclear wave" would have taken place. As a result, he suggests, the 1958 National Intelligence Estimate prediction that a large number of countries might soon develop a nuclear weapons capacity would have proved correct rather than so completely and embarrassingly wrong.[10] (At the time, the same spooks were also predicting that the Soviet Union would have 500 intercontinental nuclear missiles by the early 1960s, an estimate that also proved to be spectacularly, and equally embarrassingly, off the mark.)

By contrast, as argued in the previous chapter, most countries seem to fail to pursue nuclear programs not because the weapons violate international agreements, but because of the dawning realization that the weapons are a waste of time, effort, and money. To be able to proclaim the effectiveness of the NPT and of related international conventions such as the Comprehensive Test Ban Treaty of 1996, one would, at a minimum, have to rise to the test proposed by Betts: if these treaties have prevented proliferation, "one should be able to name at least one specific country that would have sought nuclear weapons or tested them, but refrained from doing so, or was stopped, because of either treaty." But, Betts notes pointedly, "none comes to mind."[11]

In distinct contrast, Ambassador George Bunn's mind fairly bubbles with instances. Quoted with considerable approval by Cirincione, Bunn in 2002 expressed his belief that without the NPT, 30 to 40 countries would have nuclear weapons. These, he suggested, would include not only the nine nuclear states at the time, but also Argentina, Australia, Belarus, Brazil, Canada, Egypt, Germany, Indonesia, Italy, Japan, Kazakhstan, the Netherlands, Norway, Romania, South Africa, South Korea, Spain, Sweden, Switzerland, Taiwan, Ukraine, and the former Yugoslavia, as well as "some of their neighbors and rivals."[12]

In extensive recent studies, Jacques Hymans and Etel Solingen have provided especially careful and informed debunkings of the notion that the slow pace of nuclear proliferation has been the result of international conventions like the NPT. As Hymans points out, most state leaders (undoubtedly including many of those running the countries arrayed in Bunn's impressive list) simply "find going nuclear to be less than tempting," and therefore "a strong international regime is not necessary to deliver them from temptation." Although he can point to quite a few leaders who were both against building a bomb and in favor of the NPT, it was the former, he finds, that caused the latter, not the reverse. Actually, in many quarters the nonproliferation treaty, which determinedly separates the world into nuclear haves and have-nots—"nuclear apartheid," some call it derisively—is "downright offensive," and unlikely to change the minds of those who really want the bomb even as it angers many of those who do not.[13]

Solingen uncovers similar patterns. For example, in the case of Japan, "the decision to remain non-nuclear was logically prior to, not a consequence of, the decision to ratify the NPT," even as the treaty hardly prevented the development of nuclear weapons programs in signatory states like Iran, Libya, and Iraq. Indeed, the latter two states apparently sought access to civilian technology under the NPT "in order to bolster secret programs with military potential." The pattern is also suggested by the fact that after the demise of the cold war, there was something of what Nina Tannenwald calls a "small stampede" to join the NPT. It was not that the treaty suddenly somehow became objectively more attractive, but rather that reasons to stay out of it diminished. Joining, accordingly, became something of a no-brainer.[14]

Only somewhat more impressed by the NPT, another extensive analysis finds that the NPT and the nonproliferation regime more broadly played at best an indirect, though possibly useful, role in the decisions of nine states that have stopped, reversed, or slowed down nuclear programs. And another concludes that it has had a "modest, constraining effect."[15]

Since any signatory can legally withdraw from the NPT after giving suitable notice, it is not clear why one should put so much emphasis on a piece of paper. Interestingly, those who, like Cirincione, lavish praise on the NPT for containing proliferation are also among those most alarmed about the spread of nuclear weapons in the future: for example, he worries that a collection of signatory states in the Middle East will go nuclear if Iran gains a capability.[16] This could be taken to suggest, however, that, although the treaty may increase a signatory's cost of going nuclear, it would little hinder further proliferation under sufficiently provocative conditions. One can't credibly maintain at the same time that the NPT is key to nonproliferation and that it will fall apart at the first impressive challenge.

Efforts at Focused Dissuasion

In addition to the creation of international treaties and conventions, there have been strenuous efforts by the United States and others to persuade specific countries at specific times to refrain from attempting to obtain a nuclear capability. Some of these efforts have involved military threats, extensive (even draconian) economic sanctions, military strikes, or outright invasion, ventures discussed in the next two chapters. Most, however, have adopted more subtle methods of dissuasion and are discussed here. While these have sometimes been influential, any impact has generally been rather modest, more nearly permissive or facilitating than determining.

SOUTH AFRICA. In the late 1970s, South Africa began a nuclear bomb program, and by 1982 it had produced its first bomber-deliverable weapon. Although it never actually tested its bombs, it did eventually assemble an arsenal of six gun-type bombs using highly enriched uranium.[17]

The military value of this venture, which was fairly expensive, but bearable, was less than overwhelmingly obvious. There were concerns at the time about increased Soviet interest in, and involvement with, countries to the north, but any danger of invasion or nuclear blackmail was remote. Moreover, any actual use of the bombs against Soviet forces was unthinkable because it would invite overwhelming retaliation, while any use against other forces was unnecessary because of the country's superior conventional capacity. Accordingly, there was no great pressure from the military to divert its budget in this manner, and it was not even involved in the decision. A major driving force appears to have been the personal preferences of Defense Minister, and later President, P. W. Botha, who was reportedly singularly fixated on obtaining nuclear weapons. It became something of a pet project for him.[18]

His successor, F. W. de Klerk, set about dismantling the project shortly after taking office in September 1989. By that time, Soviet connections to South Africa's northern neighbors had been much scaled back, and the cold war was in the process of evaporating. However, de Klerk had never had enthusiasm for what he called a "massive spending programme," and the changing security environment, concludes analyst Peter Liberman, "was at best a permissive condition for dismantling."[19]

In addition to his hostility to a costly and seemingly pointless weapons program, de Klerk was substantially motivated by a desire to lead his country, shunned and sanctioned by most countries for its racial apartheid policy, back into the world. Although these outside pressures were not primarily or specifically focused on nuclear weapons, they did create an environment in which dismantlement had distinct benefits for those with the appropriate mindset. Initially, international ostracism actually intensified the government's bunker mentality and played a large role in its decision to develop the weapons. But this perspective changed under de Klerk. Although international pressures to dismantle did not intensify at the time, South Africa's sensitivity to the program's diplomatic liabilities did. As such, the process is consistent with Solingen's conclusion that liberalizing regimes tend to be hostile toward nuclear weapons programs—or at least are more sensitive to their costs.[20]

Although the general international atmosphere may have further encouraged de Klerk to carry out a policy he already strongly favored, two important participants in the decision-making process firmly deny that specific pressure from the United States had an effect. Asked what impact American pressure had on the decision to reverse South Africa's nuclear policy, one bluntly proclaimed, "None!" and another went even further: "We found pressure from the U.S. counterproductive. It kept us out of the NPT longer."[21]

UKRAINE, BELARUS, KAZAKHSTAN. When the Soviet Union peacefully fractured into a set of independent countries at the end of 1991, three of the new states in addition to Russia had Soviet nuclear weapons on their soil. In fairly short order, all of the weapons outside Russia were either dismantled or moved to Russia. Accordingly the three states, after becoming members, at least technically, of the exclusive nuclear club for a while, willingly abandoned that status.[22]

From the beginning, the leaders of the new countries seemed to grasp that the weapons would be of little value to them. In considerable part, their patterns of thinking traced those of the many other technically capable states that have been content to follow a nonnuclear path, as discussed in the previous chapter. In Ukraine, and particularly Belarus, the experience with enhanced radiation levels that followed the meltdown of the

Chernobyl nuclear reactor in 1986 generated a special hostility toward—or wariness about—the weapons, something like a "nuclear allergy."[23] And in both countries, as well as in the third entity of concern, Kazakhstan, the economic costs of maintaining the weapons and of generating the expertise to do so were quite significant, particularly given the economic degradation and chaos that followed the splintering of the Soviet Union.

These attitudes and perspectives, possibly encouraged by the NPT atmosphere, might by themselves have led to an abandonment of the nuclear weapons by the three countries, perhaps more or less following the path taken a bit earlier by South Africa. That is, the countries would tend to model themselves more nearly on Canada than on France.[24] At the very least, that perspective would have led the three countries to make very sure the weapons were locked down and secure, perhaps through protective disassembly. Accordingly, the international consequences of retaining the weapons would likely have been minimal, though worst-case scenarists could doubtless nightmarishly envision potential future conflicts between, say, Russia and Ukraine that might conceivably go nuclear.

Concerned outsiders, particularly in Russia and the United States, had at their disposal techniques to enhance the reluctance of the three countries to hang onto their nuclear arsenals. To begin with, the Russians quickly removed the most potentially usable armaments—the smaller, more portable, tactical nuclear weapons—and they were able to do so without having to coordinate, or even to consult, with local authorities. Fifteen hundred were spirited away from Belarus, a couple of hundred from Kazakhstan, and four thousand from Ukraine. The governments of the three countries were left, then, with a smaller set of bulky, locked strategic weapons over which they did not have operational control and which they had not built and did not know how to maintain, unlock, or operate.[25]

Given that condition, the three governments, after mulling it over at bit, mostly sought to exact the best possible price from Russia and the United States for handing over their remaining, substantially useless, weapons. For example, for its troubles Ukraine received hundreds of tons of nuclear fuel for its nuclear reactors, forgiveness of a multibillion-dollar oil and gas debt to Russia, $900 million in aid from the United States, and security assurances from Russia, Britain, and the United States. Belarus also received aid, as well as a guaranteed trading partnership with Russia without which it might not have been able to survive. Kazakhstan, with a weak economy, was mostly interested in obtaining Western recognition and in establishing a secure international environment—sprawled as it is between nuclear-armed Russia and nuclear-armed China—within which to develop.[26]

SOUTH KOREA, TAIWAN. Both South Korea and Taiwan, to varying degrees, have to worry about an external threat in their neighborhood: South Korea about the strange and erratic cousin country to its north, Taiwan about mainland China, which routinely threatens to swallow it whole as a natural right and as part of its equally natural destiny. In both cases, one can easily understand the argument that either or both might find an independent nuclear force to be attractive to deter the external threat. Yet neither country has ever significantly moved to develop such a program.

Notable in their calculations has been the intense hostility of the United States to such a development. Should either seek to develop a nuclear weapons capacity, their large friend and important trading partner across the Pacific regularly promises to do terrible things—reduce security and weapons commitments, cease cooperation on reactor technology, fracture bilateral economic relations.[27]

But the deeper question is posed by Solingen: given their security concerns, why were these countries receptive to American threats? In both cases, she concludes, it was because they had harnessed themselves to—had put their highest priority on—a politically popular economic growth strategy that vitally depended on international trade and access.[28] This made them not only susceptible to American blandishments but also wary of doing anything that might alienate international institutions or cause concern among commercial partners.

At the same time, however, they were quite happy to extract the highest price for their nuclear cooperation. In the case of South Korea, this included stronger U.S. security commitments, more advanced weapons, nuclear energy support, and improved access to international financing.[29]

LIBYA. Colonel Muammar Qaddafi, Libya's resident dictator, achieved devil du jour status by the 1980s. A committed, if self-styled and somewhat flaky, revolutionary, he was good at spouting hostile rhetoric aimed at other Arab and African states, at the United States, and at Israel. He was also unapologetic about supporting terrorism as a method for, as he saw it at that time, improving the world.[30]

Libya was never the most notable state sponsor of terrorism during the cold war, but it had in Qaddafi terrorism's noisiest and most colorful spokesman. Moreover, because it was isolated within the Arab world, the country could be attacked with little risk of wider political ramifications. At any rate, the Reagan administration increasingly focused its attention on that particular rogue, and by 1986 had determined the distant, militarily feeble Libya somehow to have become a threat to America's national security. Qaddafi was fully up to the rhetorical challenge: he bellowed that "a state of war" existed between his little country and the United States, that all American and NATO bases within reach were to be legitimate targets, and, shades of Osama, that "all Arab people" should attack anything American, "be it an interest, goods, ship, plane or a person." In that spirit he called for Arabs to go nuclear, suggesting rather curiously that "We should be like Chinese—poor and riding donkeys, but respected and possessing an atomic bomb."[31]

Eager to "do something" about terrorism, Reagan in 1986 bombed Libya after terrorists linked to Libya had set off an explosion in a Berlin discotheque, killing three people, two of them American. However, the bombing raid, in which one plane crashed and scores of people were killed (none of them Qaddafi), enhanced Qaddafi domestically and caused him to be lionized in the developing world. He also continued and furthered a program to acquire or develop nuclear weapons, driven mostly, argues Solingen, not by strategic threats but by his drive for domestic control and by his "international, grandiose, and ultimately personal ambitions." Moreover, as Reagan's Secretary of State, George Shultz, wistfully noted later of the 1986 attack, "it didn't stop him" on the terrorism front either. In rather short order Libyan agents launched several attacks, and then Libya participated in the bombing of a Pan Am airliner over Lockerbie, Scotland, that killed 270 people, 187 of them American. Three years after the attack, investigators were lucky enough to find evidence that led to the indictment of two Libyan agents who eventually were found guilty of the bombing. With the indictments, the Americans were able to convince many in the international community to slap economic sanctions on Libya.[32]

In time, devil du jour Qaddafi mellowed. As the cold war ended, he became isolated and his ideas came to be seen as anachronistic. By the end of the 1990s, he was amiably blowing with (or in) a new wind: "We cannot stand in the way of progress....he fashion now is free markets and investments....the world has changed radically and drastically...and being a revolutionary and a progressive man, I have to follow this movement." His tent was no longer host to guerrilla leaders and terrorists, but to investment consultants and Internet executives. Economic travail encouraged this development. The sanctions were a component in this, as was the depressed price of Libya's main export, oil, at the time. But it is not at all clear they were essential to his ideological transformation. Concerns about domestic opposition may also have helped move him in this direction.[33]

In 2003, Qaddafi agreed to abandon his limited programs for "weapons of mass destruction" (mainly chemical ones), a development caused, claimed the George W. Bush administration, by its invasion of Iraq in that year. However, Qaddafi's decision had been in the cards for years and, others argue, would have come about anyway. In fact, Qaddafi had agreed to do the same thing in 1999, but had been turned down at the time until other issues were resolved, particularly ones concerning compensation to the families of people killed on the downed Pan Am airliner.[34]

Moreover, despite extensive help from the network set up by Pakistan's A. Q. Khan, and after three decades of labor, Libya had been unable to make any progress whatever toward an atomic bomb. Libya paid $100 million for Khan's favors, but when its nuclear materials were surrendered, much of it, relates chief inspector Mohamed ElBaradei, "was still in boxes." One might be tempted to wonder whether what Qaddafi had could credibly be called a nuclear weapons program at all. But ElBaradei, without any apparent sense of irony, decided that Libya was (1) "in the preparatory stage" (2) "of developing a capability" (3) "that would move it to acquire a nuclear weapon."[35] Preparing to develop a capability to move: how does that differ from being sound asleep?

At any rate, by the new century, Qaddafi had lost all sentimental attachment to Chinese on donkeys and was proclaiming the nuclear arms race to be "crazy." Instead, "we would like to have a better economy and an improved life." This sentiment was echoed by his premier, who declared, "Weapons of mass destruction are very costly. It is better that we concentrate on our economic development," and, noting that its WMD program was not making Libya safer but simply poorer, concluded that it was better to spend its money "on butter rather than guns."[36]

MODEST SUCCESS

Efforts by the antiproliferation community at focused persuasion, including measures designed to increase the costs of going nuclear or to create a nonproliferation atmosphere, have undoubtedly had some effect, as some of the discussion in this chapter suggests. Moreover, because any new atomic states are apt to find, like their unamused predecessors, that the weapons bring them little advantage at a distinctly burdensome cost, antiproliferation exertions, to the degree they are successful, have done them a favor.

However, for the most part the successes have been limited and might well have happened anyway. In addition, given the low value of the weapons and their high costs under the best of circumstances, it is not clear that the antiproliferation community has had to do all that much. As Waltz argues, the fact that so many fewer countries have developed nuclear weapons programs than have the capacity to do so "says more about the hesitation of countries to enter the nuclear military business" than it does about the effectiveness of the nonproliferation regime.[37]

Against any modest proliferation gains must be balanced the costs, which can become excessive when efforts are pushed too far. These costs and other negative consequences of the proliferation fixation are assessed in the next two chapters.

10

Costs of the Proliferation Fixation

Foreign policy analysts and advocates urgently and routinely argue that nonproliferation—"no new nuclear weapons states"—must be a prime foreign policy principle or a "supreme" or "number one" national security priority, and that, if lesser measures fail, the United States has somehow acquired a "duty" to use military force unilaterally to stop unpleasant regimes from developing nuclear, or even lesser, "weapons of mass destruction."[1] Although seeking to dissuade additional countries from becoming nuclear weapons states may be at base quite a good idea, the antiproliferation quest, following such policy logic, has sometimes been pushed to an extreme, especially after the end of the cold war and even more so after the terrorist attacks of September 11, 2001, and the results have been disastrous.

Any persuasive or dissuasive gains of the nonproliferation regime, as argued in the previous chapter, have been rather modest. Against these must be balanced the costs exacted, whether intended or unintended, by the antiproliferation fixation. When persuasive techniques have been hardened into severe sanctions and military action, these costs have been anything but modest—and, most tragically, they have come in the form of human lives as well as excessive government expenditures.

My plea, then, is not to abandon antiproliferation policies, but to warn about the dangers inherent in the "supreme priority" approach. This chapter seeks to lay out the human, foreign policy, and economic costs and drawbacks of the zero-tolerance proliferation policy.[2] The next chapter assesses its counterproductive aspects and proposes reconsideration.

HUMAN COSTS

The most important costs of the proliferation fixation are the human ones, and they have been extensive.

Iraq

The greatest destruction has occurred in Iraq.

The antiproliferation war there that began with military invasion in 2003 has inflicted deaths that may well run into the hundreds of thousands. This costly venture sprang primarily from the atomic obsession. Its sellers almost entirely billed it as a venture required to keep Saddam Hussein's pathetic and fully containable rogue state from developing nuclear and other presumably threatening weapons and to prevent him from palming off some of these to eager and congenial terrorists—the common collective nightmare of antiproliferation fantasists.[3]

Thus, in his influential 2002 book, *The Threatening Storm: The Case for Invading Iraq*, Kenneth Pollack continually cited the dangers of what would transpire if Saddam were to acquire nuclear weapons. He acknowledged the war he advocated might be costly—it might cause, he reckoned, thousands of deaths and run into the tens of billions of dollars. But war would be worth this price, concluded Pollack under heavy influence of the domination fantasy, because with nuclear weapons, Saddam would become the "hegemon" in the area, allowing him to control global oil supplies. Indeed "the whole point" of a war would be to prevent him from acquiring nuclear weapons, which Western intelligence agencies, he reported, were predicting would occur by 2004 (pessimistic) or 2008 (optimistic).[4]

The nuclear theme was repeatedly applied in the run-up to the war. In 2002, President George W. Bush pointedly and prominently warned that "The United States of America will not permit the world's most dangerous regimes to threaten us with the world's most destructive weapons." And Senator John McCain insisted that a nuclear Iraq would use its weapons to "hold his neighbors hostage." Most famous, perhaps, is National Security Adviser Condoleezza Rice's dire warning in September 2002. Two years earlier she had contended that there should be "no sense of panic" about an Iraqi bomb and that weapons like that in the hands of Iraq would be "unusable because any attempt to use them will bring national obliteration." But now, she ominously warned, we may not be able to wait for firm evidence before launching a war: "We don't want the smoking gun to be a mushroom cloud"—a snappy construction Bush applied in a major speech the next month. As the Defense Department's Paul Wolfowitz has pointed out, nuclear weapons, or at any rate weapons of mass destruction, became the "core reason" for the war, and Karl Rove, one of Bush's top political advisers, acknowledged in 2008 that, absent the belief that Saddam Hussein possessed WMD, "I suspect that the administration's course of action would have been to work to find more creative ways to constrain him like in the 90s."[5]

When no weapons of mass destruction or programs to create them were found in Iraq, the war's instigators quickly moved—"shifted rapidly," in the words of neoconservative Richard Perle—to promote the advancement of democracy as the reason for the war. Indeed, as Francis Fukuyama has crisply put it, a prewar request to spend "several hundred billion dollars and several thousand American lives in order to bring democracy to…Iraq" would "have been laughed out of court."[6] As it happens, the word "democracy" nowhere appears in Bush's address to the nation of March 19, 2003, announcing the war, and at a press briefing on April 10, shortly after the fall of Baghdad, White House press secretary Ari Fleischer insisted, "we have high confidence that they have weapons of mass destruction. That is what this war was about and it is about."

For their part, Democrats and liberals have derided the war as "unnecessary," but the bulk of them only came to that conclusion after the United States was unable to find either weapons or weapons programs in Iraq. Many of them have made it clear they would have supported putatively preemptive (actually, preventive) military action and its attendant bloodshed if the intelligence about Saddam's programs had been accurate. Thus, five years into the bloody war, the disillusioned war-supporting liberal columnist Jacob Weisberg glumly confessed, "I thought he had WMD, and I thought there was a strong chance he'd use them against the United States or one of our allies.…Had I known Iraq had no active nuclear program, I wouldn't have supported an invasion."[7]

Operative in the run-up to the Iraq War, then, was what Jacques Hymans calls a "Washington threat consensus," and it seems to have been based on three propositions.[8] First, Iraq would eventually rearm and would likely fabricate WMD, including a small supply of atomic arms. Second, once so armed, Saddam Hussein would be incapable of preventing himself from engaging in extremely provocative acts such as ordering a military invasion against a neighbor or lobbing weaponry against nuclear-armed Israel, despite the fact that such acts were extremely likely to trigger a concerted multilateral military attack upon him and his regime. And third, if Saddam were to issue such a patently suicidal order, his military would dutifully carry it out, presumably with vastly more efficiency, effectiveness, and élan than it demonstrated in the Gulf War of 1991.

The first proposition remained a matter of some dispute. At worst there was a window of several years before the regime would have been able to acquire significant arms, particularly nuclear ones. Some experts, however, seemed to think it could be much longer, while others questioned whether Saddam's regime would ever be able to gather or make the required fissile material.[9] Obviously, if effective weapons inspections had been instituted in Iraq, they would have reduced this concern greatly.

The second proposition rested on an enormous respect for what could be called Saddam's "daffiness" in decision making. Saddam did sometimes act on caprice, and he often appeared to be out of touch—messengers bringing him bad news rarely, it seems, got the opportunity to do so twice.[10] He does seem to have been an egomaniac, although egomania is rather standard equipment for your average Third World tyrant. At the same time, Saddam had shown himself capable of pragmatism. When his 1980 invasion of Iran went awry, he called for retreat to the prewar status quo; it was the Iranian regime that kept the war going. After he invaded Kuwait in 1990, he quickly moved to settle residual issues left over from the Iran-Iraq War so that he had only one enemy to deal with.

Above all, he seems to have been entirely nonsuicidal and was primarily devoted to preserving his regime and his own personal existence. Much of his obstruction of arms inspectors seems to have arisen from his fear that intelligence agents among them could fatally triangulate his whereabouts—a suspicion that press reports suggest was not exaggerated.[11] Even if Saddam did acquire nuclear arms, it seems most likely that he would have used them as all others have since 1945: to deter an invasion rather than to trigger one (and, also, of course, to stoke his ego). He was likely to realize that any aggressive military act in the region was almost certain to provoke a concerted, truly multilateral counterstrike that would topple his regime and remove him from existence.

The third proposition was rarely considered in discussions of the war, but it is important. One can't simultaneously maintain that Iraq's military forces can easily be walked over—something of a premise for the war makers of 2003, and one that proved to be accurate—and also that this same demoralized and incompetent military presented a coherent international threat. Even if Saddam did order some sort of patently suicidal adventure such as lobbing an atomic weapon at some target or other, his military might very well disobey—or simply neglect to carry out—the command. His initial orders in the 1991 Gulf War, after all, were to stand and fight the Americans to the last man. When push came to shove, his forces treated that absurd order with the contempt it so richly deserved. Moreover, the regime appeared to enjoy very little support, and Saddam Hussein so feared a coup by his own army that he supplied his troops with little or no ammunition and would not allow the army to bring heavy weapons anywhere near Baghdad. In addition, the regime really controlled only a shard of the country. The Kurds had established a semi-independent entity in the north, and the antipathy toward Saddam's rule was so great in the Shiite south that government and party officials often considered it hostile territory.[12]

However, the devastation of Iraq in the service of limiting proliferation did not begin with the war in 2003. For the previous 13 years, that country had suffered under economic sanctions, visited upon it by both Democratic and Republican administrations, that were designed to force the evil, if pathetic, Saddam Hussein from office (and, effectively, from life, since he had no viable sanctuary elsewhere) and to keep the country from developing weapons, particularly nuclear ones. The goals certainly had their admirable side, but, as multiple studies have shown, the sanctions proved to be a necessary cause (another is the administrative practices of Saddam's regime) of hundreds of thousands of deaths in the country, most of them children under the age of five—the most innocent of civilians.[13]

The additional deaths are attributed to inadequate food and medical supplies (between 1990 and 1996, pharmaceuticals were allowed in at only 10 percent of 1989 levels) as well as breakdowns in sewage and sanitation systems and in the electrical power systems needed to run them—systems destroyed by bombing in the 1991 Gulf War that had often gone unrepaired due to sanctions-enhanced shortages of money, equipment, and spare parts.

It was not until 1998—nearly eight years after sanctions began—that Iraq was allowed to buy material for rebuilding its agricultural sector, water supply facilities, oil fields, and once impressive medical system. Furthermore, imports of some desperately needed materials were delayed or denied because of concerns that they might contribute to Iraq's WMD programs. Supplies of syringes were held up for half a year because of fears they might be used in creating anthrax spores. Chlorine, an important water disinfectant, was not allowed into the country because it might be diverted into making chlorine gas, the first chemical weapon used in World War I but later abandoned when more effective ones were developed. Cancer soared because requested radiotherapy equipment, chemotherapy drugs, and analgesics were often blocked. Medical diagnostic techniques that make use of radioactive particles, once common in Iraq, were banned under the sanctions, and plastic bags needed for blood transfusions restricted. The sanctioners were wary throughout about allowing the importation of fertilizers and insecticides, fearing their use for WMD production, and as a result, disease-carrying pests that might have been controlled proliferated. Similarly restricted at times were cotton, ambulances, and pencils.[14]

Policy makers were clearly aware of the effect the sanctions were having. As Robert Gates, George H. W. Bush's deputy national security adviser put it in 1991, while Saddam remains in power, "Iraqis will pay the price." One might have imagined that the people carrying out this policy with its horrific and well-known consequences would from time to time have been queried about whether the results were worth the costs. To my knowledge, this happened only once, on television's *60 Minutes* on May 12, 1996. Madeleine Albright, then the American ambassador to the United Nations, was asked, "We have heard that a half a million children have died. I mean, that's more children than died in Hiroshima....Is the price worth it?" Albright did not dispute the number and acknowledged it to be "a very hard choice." But, she concluded, "we think the price is worth it," pointing out that because of sanctions Saddam had come "cleaner on some of these weapons programs" and had recognized Kuwait.[15]

In her memoirs, Albright, who later had been promoted to Secretary of State, frankly recalls of the incident, "As soon as I had spoken, I wished for the power to freeze time and take back those words. My reply had been a terrible mistake, hasty, clumsy and wrong. Nothing matters more than the lives of innocent people. I had fallen into the trap and said something that I did not mean."[16] Presumably, what was mistaken and wrong about the reply was not its content, but the fact she said it, because she continued to support the sanctions even while knowing (and publicly acknowledging) they were a necessary cause of the deaths of large numbers of "innocent people." Obviously, something did matter more to her than the lives of such people.

A Lexis-Nexis search suggests that Albright's remarkable dismissal on a prominent television show of the devastation sanctions had inflicted on innocent Iraqi civilians went completely unremarked upon by the country's media. In the Middle East, by contrast, it was widely and repeatedly covered and noted. Among the outraged was Osama bin Laden, who repeatedly used the punishment that sanctions were inflicting on Iraqi civilians as a centerpiece in his many diatribes against what he considered to be heartless and diabolical American policy in the area.[17]

Earlier, Saddam Hussein's nuclear weapons potential had been used to gain support for another war against Iraq—the one conducted by the George H. W. Bush administration in 1991. After it was discovered that the nuclear argument polled well, the administration started to stress the argument that, contrary to earlier reports indicating that the Iraqis were five to ten years from making a bomb, they might be able to do so within one year. It is likely, however, that Iraq was still very far from having a workable bomb at the time. The ensuing 1991 war inflicted deaths in the low thousands among Iraqis, and then tens of thousands more perished in its immediate aftermath in which massive, U.S.-encouraged uprisings against Saddam were brutally put down.[18]

North Korea

A similar process has taken place with North Korea.

Already the most closed and secretive society in the world, North Korea became even more isolated after the cold war when its former patrons, Russia and China, notably decreased their support. Its economy descended into a shambles, and it was having trouble even feeding its population, conditions that were exacerbated by the fact that it continued to be led by an anachronistic Communist dictatorship whose leaders celebrated theory and persistent self-deception over reality. In incessant fear of attack from the outside, the regime continued to spend 25 percent of its wealth to maintain a huge, if fuel-short, military force of over a million underfed troops.[19]

According to some American analysts, North Korea was also trying to develop nuclear weapons as part of this process. By 1994, one of those inevitable U.S. National Intelligence Estimates somberly concluded that there was "a better than even" chance that North Korea already had the makings of a small nuclear bomb. This conclusion, hotly contested at the time by some analysts, was later "reassessed" and found possibly to have been overstated. In addition, even if North Korea had the "makings" in 1994, skeptics pointed out, it still had several key hurdles to overcome in order to develop a deliverable weapon.[20]

Nonetheless, the Clinton administration, in full antiproliferation mode, was apparently prepared to go to war with the miserable North Korean regime to prevent or to halt its nuclear development, fearing the North Koreans might produce an arsenal of atomic bombs that could be sold abroad or used to threaten a country that possessed thousands of its own. Accordingly, the United States moved to impose deep economic sanctions to make the isolated country even poorer (insofar as that was possible) and, effectively, to cause its long-suffering population (aka "innocent people") to become even more miserable—a potential venture that garnered no support even from neighboring Russia, China, and Japan. The United States also moved to engage in a major military buildup in the area. So apocalyptic (or simply paranoid) was the North Korean regime about these two developments that some important figures think (perhaps fancifully) it might have gone to war on a preemptive basis if the measures had been carried out. A full-scale war on the peninsula, estimated the Pentagon, not perhaps without its own sense of apocalypse, could kill 1,000,000 people, including 80,000 to 100,000 Americans; cost over $100 billion; and do economic destruction on the order of a trillion dollars.[21] A considerable price, one might think, to prevent a pathetic regime from developing weapons with the potential for killing a few tens of thousands—if the weapons were (a) ever actually developed, and then (b) exploded, an act that would surely be suicidal for the regime.

In effect and perhaps by design, however, the North Korean leaders seem mainly to have been practicing extortion. No one ever paid much attention to their regime except when it seemed to be developing nuclear weapons, and they appear to have been exceedingly pleased when the 1994 crisis inspired a pilgrimage to their capital by ex-president Jimmy Carter, the most prominent American ever to set foot in the country. Carter quickly worked out a deal whereby North Korea would accept international inspections to guarantee that it wasn't building nuclear weapons, for which it would graciously accept a bribe from the West: aid, including some high-tech reactors that were capable of producing plenty of energy, but no weapons-grade plutonium, as well as various promises about normalizing relations. These promises went substantially unfulfilled in the hope and expectation that the North Korean regime would soon collapse.[22]

In the next years, that hope sometimes seemed justified as floods and bad weather exacerbated the economic disaster that had been inflicted upon the country by its rulers. Famines ensued, and the number of people who perished reached hundreds of thousands or more, with some careful estimates putting the number at over two million. Food aid was eventually sent from the West, though particularly in the early days of the famine, there seem to have been systematic efforts to deny the famine's existence in fear that a politics-free response to the humanitarian disaster would undercut its efforts to use food aid as a diplomatic weapon.[23]

That is, in a futile attempt to wring concessions on the nuclear issue from North Korea, efforts were knowingly made to increase the suffering of the North Korean people by exacerbating famine conditions.

FOREIGN POLICY AND ECONOMIC COSTS

In addition to being a necessary cause of hundreds of thousands of deaths, the proliferation fixation has had costs and negative consequences, albeit less dramatic ones, in other areas.

The fixation has served to inform and enforce a tolerant attitude toward Vladimir Putin's Russia, where democratic, and to a lesser extent capitalistic, reforms are being gradually dismantled. Clearly, if halting the spread of nuclear weapons, especially to terrorists, is some sort of absolute foreign policy priority, then it becomes "realistic" to accept just about anything else Putin's regime happens to want to do. As some prominent foreign policy analysts put it, "it is hard to take seriously the argument that the United States can realistically expect to try to undermine Putin's role in Russia and Russia's influence on its periphery on the one hand and receive whole-hearted Russian cooperation on matters nuclear."[24] However, regardless of what the Americans do, the Russians already have a very substantial interest in preventing the proliferation of weapons to terrorists (particularly, of course, Chechen ones) and to bordering states like Iran and North Korea.

In addition, major countries infected by the proliferation fixation have often allowed themselves to become victims of extortion, turning to bribery in response to threats to obtain or use nuclear weapons. North Korea has undoubtedly been the greatest winner in this somewhat tricky process—they accepted a $4 billion energy package for their cooperation in 1994.[25] But Taiwan and South Korea have also essentially extorted funds from the hand-wringers by accepting funds and favors and then giving in to what is likely to be their own best interests. Even though the nuclear weapons they inherited after the collapse of the Soviet Union were costly and essentially useless to them, Ukraine, Belarus, and Kazahkstan graciously accepted generous inducements from the United States and Russia to give up their valueless treasures. Israel played the game in a different way during its 1973 war. After being attacked by Egypt and Syria, Israel made it known that it might use its nuclear weapons (it may have had 20 at the time) in the conflict, a move that reportedly forced the United States desperately to initiate an immediate and massive resupply of the Israel military, aiding in Israel's subsequent victory against the invading Arab armies.[26] The American reputation generated by this episode for being a willing victim of extortion also had the perverse result of fueling, or supplying a rationale for, South Africa's nuclear ambitions. As one South African official put it,

> We argued that if we cannot use a nuclear weapon on the battlefield (as this would have been suicidal), then the only possible way to use it would be to leverage intervention from the Western Powers by threatening to use it. We thought that this might work and the alleged Israel-USA case gave some support to our view.[27]

The nonproliferation fixation has also imposed or inspired considerable economic costs in addition to those exacted by extortion. To begin with, antiproliferation efforts hamper worldwide economic development by increasing the effective costs of developing nuclear energy, sometimes even making them prohibitive for some countries. As countries grow, they require ever increasing amounts of power. Any measure that limits their ability to acquire this vital commodity—or increases its price—effectively slows economic growth and reduces the gains in life expectancy inevitably afforded by economic development. In the various proclamations about controlling the proliferation of nuclear weapons, this basic—and potentially massive—cost goes almost entirely unconsidered. For example, one of the common proposals by antiproliferators is that no country anywhere (except those already doing it) should be able to construct any facilities that could produce enriched uranium or plutonium—substances that can be used either in advanced reactors or in bombs. The NPT does specifically guarantee to signing nonnuclear countries "the fullest possible exchange of technology" for the development of peaceful nuclear power. However, as Richard Betts points out, this guarantee has been undermined by the development of a "nuclear suppliers cartel" that has worked to "cut off trade in technology for reprocessing plutonium or enriching uranium," thereby reducing the NPT to "a simple demand to the nuclear weapons have-nots to remain so." Under some proposals, the cartel would be extended to fuel as well.[28]

Moreover, the proliferation fixation has resulted in the summary dismissal of potentially promising ideas for producing energy. Thomas Schelling points out that there was a proposal in the 1970s (a decade that experienced two major oil-price shocks) to safely explode tiny thermonuclear bombs in underground caverns to generate steam to produce energy in an ecologically clean manner. According to Schelling, the proposal was universally rejected by both arms control and energy policy analysts at the time "without argument, as if the objections were too obvious to require articulation." On closer exploration, of course, this scheme might have proved unfeasible for technical or economic reasons. But to dismiss it without any sort of analysis was to blithely sacrifice energy needs—and therefore human welfare—to the nuclear knee-jerk. Something similar may now be in the cards. Currently in the research phase, it may become possible in the future to reduce radically the cost of producing nuclear energy by using lasers for isotope separation to produce the fuel required by reactors.[29] This, of course, might also make it easier, or at any rate less costly, for terrorists and rogue states to develop nuclear weapons. Accordingly, a balanced assessment of costs and benefits would have to be made if the technique ever proves to be feasible. But there is an excellent chance no one will ever make it: like the technology Schelling discusses, it will be dismissed out of hand.

There is also something of a security aspect to this process. Ever since the oil shocks of the 1970s, it has become common in American politics to espy a danger to the country's security in allowing it to be so dependent on a product that is so disproportionately supplied to the world by regimes in the Middle East that are sometimes contemptible, hostile, and/or unstable. Little or no progress has been made on this constantly repeated goal, but one obvious solution would be to rely much more on nuclear energy. There are a number of reasons why this has failed to happen, but the association of nuclear power with nuclear weapons and with worries about nuclear proliferation have had the result of making it much more difficult and expensive—often prohibitively so—to build nuclear reactors.[30]

In addition, because nuclear power does not emit greenhouse gases, it is an obvious potential candidate for helping with the problem of global warming, an issue many people hold to be of the highest concern for the future of the planet.[31] Since many of the policies arising from the nonproliferation fixation increase the costs of nuclear power, they, to that degree, exacerbate the problem.

The nonproliferation focus has also exacerbated the costly nuclear waste problem in the United States. In the late 1970s, the Carter administration banned the reprocessing (or recycling) of nuclear fuel in the United States—something that radically reduces the amount of nuclear waste—under the highly questionable, even rather fanciful, assumption that this policy would somehow reduce the danger of nuclear proliferation.[32]

Moreover, concern about proliferation—in this case primarily about atomic and WMD terrorism—has informed a huge amount of homeland security attention and spending. Indeed, if a proposal for spending can be spun so that it can be made to appear to deal with the atomic threat, it is a long way on the path to funding as thoughtful analysis gives way to anxiety.

The process could be seen in action in an article published in 2008 by Michael Chertoff when he was the secretary of homeland security. He felt called upon to respond to those who observe that the number of people who die each year from international terrorism, while tragic, is actually rather small, and that in consequence, the lifetime probability of someone living outside a war zone of being killed in an attack is something like one in 80,000. "This fails to consider," the secretary pointed out, "the much greater loss of life that a weapon of mass destruction could wreak on the American people."[33] That is, he was justifying his entire budget—only a limited portion of which is concerned with WMD—by the WMD threat.

Among other ventures, this concern has led to a rather bizarre, and highly expensive, preoccupation with port security, driven by the assumptions, apparently, 1) that after manufacturing their device at great expense and effort overseas, an atomic terrorist or desperately diabolical rogue state would supply a return address and then entrust his or her precious product to the tender mercies of the commercial delivery system, and 2) that analyst Randall Larsen is incorrect to conclude that "anyone smart enough to obtain a nuclear device will be smart enough to put half an inch of lead around it." As a result, a great deal of money has been hurled in that direction to inspect and to install radiation detectors, generating 500 false alarms daily at the Los Angeles/Long Beach port alone, triggered by such substances as kitty litter and bananas. This obsession is impressive as well because there seems to be no evidence that any terrorist has indicated any interest in, or even much knowledge about, using transnational containers to transport much of anything.[34]

In a like manner, concern about the bomb has productively been used to fuel support for costly wars. This process was seen, of course, in the run-up to George Bush's war in Iraq in 2002 and 2003, and it was applied again in 2009 to justify Barack Obama's continuing military venture in Afghanistan. If we don't defeat al-Qaeda through our efforts there, explained Bruce Riedel, a former CIA analyst who led Obama's interagency review on the issue early in the new president's term, there is a "serious possibility" al-Qaeda would be able to go nuclear.[35]

COMPARING COSTS

When the United States and other countries, mesmerized by the proliferation fixation, imposed drastic sanctions on Iraq in large part to keep it from becoming a nuclear power, and when that country was invaded in 2003 with the same goal principally in mind, few seemed to want to assess and compare the costs inflicted by sanctions and war with those likely to be inflicted by Saddam Hussein's potential atomic arsenal. But that consideration should be central to any reasonable policy consideration.

As discussed, the sanctions were a necessary cause of the demise of tens of thousands, then hundreds of thousands of people, and the war eventually resulted in deaths of a similar magnitude. Together, or perhaps even separately, the sanctions and the war resulted in more human destruction than was inflicted by Hiroshima and Nagasaki (103,000) combined with the human costs of that other extensive use of a "weapon of mass destruction"—gas in World War I—which caused some 78,000 deaths.

Against this tally would be balanced the potential human costs of letting Saddam Hussein seek to obtain nuclear weapons. It is possible, of course, that that impoverished, unpopular, conflictual, organizationally incompetent, and ultimately pathetic regime might *never* have been able to pull off such a technically difficult task, particularly if restrictions remained on some of the most useful technology. It is also possible that the regime would have been toppled or that Saddam (and his sons) would have died or been killed before the Iraqi bomb became a reality.

But setting those possibilities aside, what would Saddam have done with his bomb? The most likely outcome, surely, is that he would never have exploded it, using it perhaps for deterrence, for stoking his ego, and maybe for trying to intimidate his neighbors, an effort unlikely to be successful because those threatened would probably quickly combine themselves into an opposing coalition (as they had when he invaded Kuwait in 1990), one that would include in its membership countries with tens of thousands of nuclear weapons and with military budgets that surpassed his by several orders of magnitude.

Despite all this, worst-case scenarists of the proliferation fixation persuasion imagine that he might eventually have been daffy enough to order the lobbing of an atomic weapon or two from his tiny arsenal at some target or other. Even assuming his highly unreliable army would carry out such a self-destructive order, and even assuming his delivery system (unlike the Scud missiles he showered at Israel and Saudi Arabia in 1991, almost entirely unproductively) was good enough to carry the bomb to a target, and even assuming that his bomb would explode once it got there, the casualties inflicted would likely be nowhere near as large as those that resulted from the efforts to keep this wildly improbable scenario from coming to pass.

As this line of thinking suggests, perhaps it is time to reconsider proliferation policy. That is a task of the next chapter.

11

Reconsidering Proliferation Policy

Not only has the proliferation fixation cost lives and imposed a number of other foreign policy and economic costs, as argued in the previous chapter, it has also sometimes been counterproductive by effectively encouraging countries to consider going nuclear. This chapter assesses this issue, and it also evaluates current proliferation policy toward Iran and North Korea and proposes substantial changes.

ENHANCING THE APPEAL OF NUCLEAR WEAPONS

As discussed in chapter 8, the handful of countries to have acquired nuclear weapons programs seem to have done so sometimes as an ego trip for their leaders, and more urgently (or perhaps merely in addition) as an effort to deter a potential attack on themselves: China to deter the United States and the Soviet Union, Israel to deter various enemy nations in the neighborhood, India to deter China, Pakistan to deter India, and now North Korea to deter the United States and maybe others.

Insofar as nuclear proliferation is a response to perceived threat, efforts to threaten, sanction, or attack potential new nuclear states can have the opposite effect, encouraging them to seek their own bomb in response to the pressure. That is, strenuous efforts to prevent nuclear proliferation can act as a spur to the process, enhancing the appeal of—or desperate desire for—nuclear weapons for at least a few regimes, an effect that is often ignored.[1] Antiproliferation efforts have sometimes enhanced the appeal of nuclear weapons in other ways as well.

Threats

Political scientist Jacques Hymans argues that "the causal link between nuclear threats and actual decisions to go nuclear is at best unclear." As he points out, some leaders presented with exactly the same threat have reacted by seeking nuclear weapons, while others have not. However, as he also notes, perceptions of the surrounding threat matrix often do play into the nuclear decision.[2]

Although concerns about external threat are not sufficient to explain a decision to develop nuclear weapons and in some cases may not even be necessary, they can importantly contribute to the process. Thus, it seems quite possible, though difficult to prove conclusively, that the quintessential superrogue, Communist China, might not have developed nuclear weapons in the absence of persistent, and ultimately empty, nuclear threats from the United States. In an extensive analysis of the evidence, John Wilson Lewis and Xue Litai conclude that, faced with "increased American threats to use nuclear weapons against them," the Chinese in 1955 "resolved to acquire nuclear weapons of their own." McGeorge Bundy sees it similarly, observing pointedly that "the weapon was first sought when Mao felt bullied by Washington."[3]

From that perspective, George W. Bush's 2002 declaration dramatically and imaginatively grouping Iraq, Iran, and North Korea into an "axis of evil" was one of the most ill-advised presidential pronouncements ever made. These states did have regimes that could be considered evil—though those less inclined to the theological might rather prefer the word "contemptible." But, as defense analyst William Arkin puts it, "From the perspective of an Iran or North Korea, the 1990's erosion of absolute sovereignty and the post-9/11 presumption of preemption, together with the abandonment of meaningful disarmament by the permanent five, makes WMD seem both necessary and justified."[4]

Thus, commentator Kaveh Afrasiabi notes that Iran's nuclear program originated decades ago and was kept alive out of fears over Iraq, during and after its costly war with that country in the 1980s. Although Iran was generally happy to see the United States take down the Saddam Hussein regime in Iraq in 2003, "putting Iran in the same bracket as Iraq with the 'axis of evil' terminology, simply introduced new national security fears just as the old ones were disappearing."[5]

It follows from this experience, then, that one way to reduce the likelihood that new nuclear states will emerge is a simple one: *stop threatening them*. That is, the intense hostility toward particular regimes, due in considerable part to worst-case fantasies over what might conceivably happen should they obtain an atomic bomb, has had the perverse effect of enhancing the appeal of such weapons to the threatened regimes for the sake of deterrence if nothing else.

Threats can also have somewhat more subtle undesirable effects. In case of a political and societal breakdown in Pakistan, a persistent nightmare for many, it would be exceedingly valuable for the United States to know exactly where Pakistan's nuclear arsenal is located. Out of understandable fear of (or deep respect for) the threats the United States is constantly issuing in their area of the world, however, the Pakistanis, despite persistent entreaties from the Americans who supply them with considerable aid, have refused to supply that information. Moreover, they have rejected the idea of cooperating directly with the United States and the British on measures to secure their nuclear arsenal. They have accepted an offer to help design systems of controls, barriers, locks, and sensors to protect the weapons, but instead of allowing U.S. officials access to their facilities, they have insisted that Pakistani technicians travel to the United States for training on the systems. Out of fear of what could happen during a Pakistan political or civil meltdown, American intelligence officials say they have long had contingency plans for intervening to remove any Pakistani weapons at risk of falling into unfriendly hands.[6] It is a bit difficult to imagine how they would manage to accomplish that feat if they don't know where the relevant weapons are.

Sanctions

If threats can be counterproductive in seeking to reduce nuclear proliferation, specific punishing actions such as economic sanctions can be so as well.

At times, various apparent nuclear aspirants, particularly Iraq, North Korea, Libya, and most recently Iran, have been subjected to economic sanctions by the world community, or at least by substantial elements of it. Although these sanctions have often inflicted substantial pain, their record at preventing or halting the development of nuclear weapons is less than stellar. In some cases they may have cramped an aspirant's style, but organizational incompetence and divisiveness has often furnished a far more effective obstacle, while the country's determination to go nuclear has sometimes been heightened by outside pressures.[7]

The experience with sanctions on Iran suggests some of the difficulties. In that case, the internal group likely to benefit most from sanctions is the Pasdaran, or Revolutionary Guards, which, coincidentally, may also prove to be the group most in favor of developing a nuclear weapons capacity. At the same time, sanctions strongly enhance the desire—or even the need—to insulate the economy from unreliable foreigners. In the process, this undercuts the influence of those who want to internationalize—the very group that is most likely to oppose nuclear weapons development.[8]

In some cases sanctions may have a more exquisite counterproductive consequence. By effectively isolating the sanctioned country, as Hymans notes, scientists are less able to connect to peers in the international community. By contrast, in an open situation, top scientists often join research institutes abroad and become less able, and perhaps less willing, to work on secret parochial projects at home. This sort of actual or effective brain drain can hamper a country's ability to fabricate a nuclear arsenal and, as physicist Richard Muller puts it, "a nuclear weapon designed by anything less than a top-level team is likely to fizzle."[9]

The sanctions on Iran have also had another negative effect. Those desperately imploring Iran to eschew nuclear weaponry have, as a sweetener, sometimes offered to supply the Iranians with the nuclear fuel they need for their nuclear energy program. But because of the sanctions and the threat environment they are embedded in, the Iranians have been notably wary of such a deal because it would require them to be dependent on foreign suppliers who have proven themselves to be strongly hostile and could cut off the vital material at whim at any time, no matter what guarantees initially accompany the deal. To avoid the possibility of an externally induced energy crisis within the country, they have insisted on creating the fissile material required for their reactors themselves, a process that, however, would also allow them to produce a bomb more readily should they decide to do so at some point.

In addition, while causing substantial suffering for ordinary people, as discussed in the previous chapter, sanctions have often strengthened, rather than, as usually intended, reduced, a regime's ability to maintain control. By creating artificial shortages and driving up prices for scarce commodities, sanctions make smuggling an extremely lucrative enterprise. As shown in Iraq in the 1990s, the regime can readily award this business to the chosen, assuring that they remain ardent supporters of its rule. The system of food rationing, made necessary by the sanctions, was also used by the government to its advantage: as one Iraqi put it, "I have to pledge loyalty to the party. Any sign of disobedience and my monthly card would be taken away."[10]

Military Attacks

A military invasion followed by an occupation like the one perpetrated upon Iraq by the United States and a few allies in 2003 can obviously arrest weapons development—at enormous cost to the attacker. However, as Mitchell Reiss observes, "one of the unintended 'demonstration' effects" of the American antiproliferation war against Iraq "was that chemical and biological weapons proved insufficient to deter America: only nuclear weapons, it appeared, could do this job."[11]

In addition, less expensive attacks, such as air strikes, can be decidedly counterproductive. This is a key lesson from Israel's highly touted air strike against Iraq's nuclear program in the Osirak attack of 1981. The best analyses suggest the attack actually caused Saddam Hussein to speed up his nuclear program, increasing its budget 25-fold while decreasing its vulnerability by dispersing its elements and putting them underground—a lesson Iran has also learned.[12]

Status Effects

Most countries, as argued in chapter 8, do not seem to have seen the possession of nuclear weapons to be particularly helpful for attaining international status—particularly that of the long-lasting variety. Those determinedly embarked upon the nonproliferation quest ought, accordingly, to routinely seek to enhance this effect. Sensibly, for example, they ought to devote considerable energy to obtaining permanent seats on the UN Security Council for Germany and Japan. As often noted, the five permanent members now are also the five first to obtain nuclear weapons, and the expansion measure might critically signal to other aspirants that international status today very substantially derives from other state attributes.

Instead, the signal coming from dedicated antiproliferators is often that the weapons do carry status utility. As noted in chapter 8, nuclear weapons often cause major countries to pay more attention to the possessing country than they might otherwise. This is hardly a new phenomenon. Assessing the period when China's bomb was inspiring a great deal of official hysteria in the United States, historian Francis Gavin notes:

> The more effort the United States made to halt proliferation, the more political capital it spent, the more attractive these weapons must have seemed to smaller powers. If a single atomic detonation by China, a country with no conceivable means of delivery and decades away from a secure second-strike force, could provoke grave concern and prompt a shift in policy from the world's most powerful country, the U.S. government would have great difficulty convincing others that these weapons had no political utility.[13]

That observation continues to be pertinent.

Antiproliferators are playing counterproductively with the status issue in another way by seeking to dumb down the definition of a nuclear weapon state. Commonly, this designation has been conferred upon a state when it first tests a nuclear weapon or device. Although this approach makes a good deal of sense, there are problems with it because it is possible to create an arsenal of (presumably workable) nuclear weapons without actually testing them (or before testing them), as both Israel and South Africa have demonstrated. To deal with this and other perceived problems, there has been a tendency in recent years to consider countries possessing, or capable of producing, plutonium or highly enriched uranium to be nuclear weapons states—or, as Mohammed ElBaradei, head of the International Atomic Energy Agency puts it, to be "virtual nuclear weapons states"—even though they may have no intention whatever of using the material to make nuclear weapons. Accordingly, as Hymans aptly points out, whereas 20 years ago the idea of launching a military attack on a country with a growing competence to enrich uranium would have been viewed as "completely preposterous," today it has become "common coin in the Washington security debate."[14]

This redefinition process not only massively underestimates the technical difficulties in fabricating a bomb—particularly for the countries antiproliferators are most worried about—but it could have the entirely perverse result of encouraging proliferation. If countries become labeled

nuclear weapons states merely because they have, entirely for peaceful purposes, acquired the capacity to produce fissile material, the process effectively lowers the barriers for them to develop nuclear weapons, though
perhaps only marginally so.[15]

NORTH KOREA AND IRAN

It may be useful at this point to bring the discussion in this and in earlier
chapters to bear on the main current proliferation issues: policies designed
to deal with the North Korean and Iranian nuclear programs.

After the dustup over the prospective North Korean bomb in 1994, an
extreme perspective on the issue continues to be strenuously advocated by
many. Typical is Graham Allison, who insists that keeping North Korea from
obtaining nuclear weapons is no less than a "supreme priority." In 2004, he
anticipated—conservatively, he says—that North Korea would soon have
the capacity to produce 50 to 70 nuclear weapons by 2009. To deal with this
alarming prospect, he proposed several steps of diplomacy, including the
screening of a horror video for North Korea's Kim Jong Il ("known to be
a great fan of movies") that would graphically depict the kind of destruction American munitions could visit upon Kim's errant country. Should
diplomacy fail and this vivid bluff be called, however, Allison essentially
advocated launching a military attack on North Korea, even though he
acknowledged that potential targets had been dispersed and disguised and
that a resulting war might kill tens of thousands in the South. (To cut down
on the civilian body count there, however, he suggested preemptively evac-
uating Seoul, one of the world's largest cities and one that already boasts
some of the most impressive traffic jams on the planet.) Curiously and
rather elliptically, Allison considers such an attack not to be an act of war—
it would be the North Korean response to the attack, not the attack itself,
which would end up "initiating a second Korean War."[16] By that imaginative
standard, it was the United States that started the Pacific War by responding
to the Japanese attack on Pearl Harbor.

Members of the Bush administration, perhaps because they had
become immersed in their own antiproliferation war in Iraq, failed to
accept Allison's urgent advice. And then in 2006, North Korea apparently
became something of a nuclear weapons state by testing a nuclear device
underground.[17]

In 2004 Allison had sternly insisted that to allow such an outcome would be "gross negligence" and would foster "a transformation in the international security order no great power would wittingly accept." So, with all that behind us, we are now in a position to see if Allison's cascadological predictions come true. If North Korean became accepted as a nuclear weapons state, he assured us in 2004, this "would unleash a proliferation chain reaction, with South Korea and Japan building their own weapons by the end of the decade" (by 2009, that would be), with Taiwan "seriously considering following suit despite the fact that this would risk war with China," and with North Korea potentially "becoming the Nukes R' Us for terrorists." A similar perspective has been advanced by Philip Bobbitt who assures us that once North Korea deploys nuclear weapons, "only tragedy and terror will follow."[18]

This sort of alarmism about the North Korean bomb continues to be common coin in the foreign policy establishment, and it has now been focused even more emphatically on the potential for an Iranian nuclear weapon. And many people, including many of those who gave us the Iraq War to wipe out its imagined weapons of mass destruction programs, seem to be contemplating air strikes or even an invasion of Iran to keep that country from getting an atomic bomb. The only thing worse than military action against Iran, says Senator John McCain repeatedly, would be a nuclear-armed Iran, while Secretary of State Hillary Clinton has insisted that Iran must be kept from getting the bomb "at all costs"—without, of course, tallying up what those might be. Nor do the potential costs (or the unlikelihood of success) burden the mind of Graham Allison when, assuming other pressures don't work to stop Iran's enrichment program, he advocates destroying that country's nuclear facilities with American precision-guided missiles. And during his successful 2008 campaign for the presidency, Barack Obama repeatedly announced that a nuclear weapon in the hands of the Iranians was "unacceptable" and pledged that, as president, he would "do everything in my power to prevent Iran from obtaining a nuclear weapon—everything." Indeed, notes former weapons inspector David Kay, "there seem to be few in the mainstream of American politics ready to go on the record with a plan for 'the day after' that does not involve military action."[19]

Particularly in recent years, Israeli anxieties about their country's security have been amalgamated into extreme apprehensions about atomic annihilation at the hands of Iran, apprehensions stoked by some of the

fulminations of Iran's president, Mahmoud Ahmadinejad, a populist wind-
bag whose tenuous hold on office has been enhanced by foreign overreaction to his bloviating. Together with the other concerns, those about Iran
have sometimes inspired a sense of despair and desperation, and in many
quarters, apparently, a loss of hope.[20] Not only do Israelis constantly and
extravagantly compare the Iranian problem to the Holocaust, but the process has required them to insist without qualification that Iran is inevitably
going to develop an atomic weapon despite that country's repeated denial of
such intentions, that its acquisition of those weapons is a near-term prospect, and that its leadership is so deranged and suicidal that it will actually
use the weapon on Israel despite Israel's ability to retaliate massively—not
to mention the capacity of its ardent backer, the United States, to react in a
similar manner.[21]

TOWARD A CALMER ASSESSMENT

If Iran and North Korea really do want to develop a nuclear weapons capacity, there is no way this can be prevented, at least in the long term, except by
invading the countries directly—enterprises that in both cases would likely
make America's costly war in Iraq look like child's play in comparison. If the
experience with the Osirak bombings of Iraq holds, a comparable air strike
would at best merely slow down the countries' atomic progress somewhat,
and the Iranians' most likely response would be to launch a truly dedicated
effort to obtain a bomb, something now required, as they would see it, for
defensive purposes.[22]

Moreover, the casualties inflicted by direct invasion, or by "collateral
damage" in the case of air attacks, could rival those suffered by Iraq under
sanctions or during the current war there, particularly because air defense
installations would need to be attacked before going after nuclear targets.
Moreover, any released nuclear radiation from a military attack could not
only be harmful to life, but also, if the response to Chernobyl is an indication, would create alarm, some of it desperate, over a very wide area, including Iraq and Turkey for an attack on Iran and China and South Korea for
one on North Korea. In the case of an attack on Iran, there would likely also
be radicalization throughout the Muslim world, including Pakistan. The
outrage could make it unsafe for an American to be anywhere in the Middle
East except Israel (and perhaps not even there), while Iran would probably

exercise its considerable capacity for helping to make the U.S. position both in Iraq and in Afghanistan markedly more difficult.

Short of outright invasion or a military attack, diplomacy and various forms of bribery to dissuade North Korea and particularly Iran from pursuing a nuclear weapons program may have some prospects for success. However, these seem always to be tied to various forms of economic sanctions, which can be, as discussed earlier, not only quite destructive but also effectively counterproductive, especially in the way they play into the hands of the hard-liners in the targeted countries.

A calm—that is to say, nonhysterical—policy discussion of the North Korean and Iran issues should take several additional considerations into account.

For its part, North Korea remains essentially the most pathetic country in the world. If there were a contest for the country on whose side history is most fully not, it would win handily. Its leaders have apparently wanted to become nuclear for decades, and that extravagant goal has been delayed more by the country's monumental administrative incompetence than anything else, although increased threats from abroad may have had an enhancing effect on its efforts. In 2006, the country did manage to stage something of an atomic bomb test, though it may well have been simply a fizzle, and they tried once again in 2009.[23]

In the meantime, the country simply can't feed itself. Not only was there a massive famine in the 1990s, discussed in the previous chapter, but the general condition of undernourishment—the "eating problem," it is called within the country—continues to the point where both the bodies and the minds of millions of its citizens are being stunted. In the meantime, it remains beholden to foreign food aid and uses its nuclear program, such as it is, as a lever of extortion. It has become, as one observer put it, "the world's first nuclear-armed, missile-wielding beggar."[24]

Its leadership does seem at times to have what appears to be a poor grasp of reality, and it does seem to be desperate for attention. But, while the situation there is distinctly unpleasant, its leaders seem far from suicidal.

And some consideration should be given to what North Korea could possibly do with a nuclear capacity, assuming this ill-led and monumentally incompetent regime were ever able to attain one. Beyond using its weapons to stoke its nationalist ego and to deter an attack on itself—which, given the threatening fulminations of its many glowering opponents, it has good reason to be concerned about—the country is likely, even more than earlier entrants into the nuclear club, to find the weapons to be useless.

Delivery outside the country by airplane would be hugely problematic due to the air defenses of its neighbors. And North Korea's missile capacity remains pathetic: its missiles are small and exceedingly inaccurate—though they have managed to hit the Pacific Ocean several times, in each instance stirring worldwide angst. To even begin to make use of this missile potential (if any), the common expectation is that the country would have to develop only very small nuclear weapons with concomitantly small yields. Assuming such weapons could be delivered to their intended target and would actually go off when they got there, they would likely destroy an area no larger than a city block. North Korea is already capable of doing far greater damage (without, however, any radioactive fallout effects) with artillery on nearby targets such as South Korea's capital city.

There remains a fantasy about how the North Koreans might give or sell weapons to others, particularly to terrorists. North Korea has apparently assisted some countries in their nuclear programs in the past (to very little effect), but it can of course continue to do that now if it wants to—it doesn't need actual weapons on hand. Parting with a laboriously developed member of a tiny nuclear arsenal supposedly needed to deter an attack on itself is another thing. As will be discussed more fully in the next chapter, there would be a huge danger that any weapon given away or sold would be misused and that its origins would be discovered either before or after detonation.

A viable policy toward this pathetic regime, then, might be to calm down while continuing to be extorted for the sake of the miserable North Korean people. Conceivably (but only conceivably), a reduction in the threat environment might nudge the North Korean regime into reducing its armed forces some, while spending more on its people. For the rest, one would simply wait for the leadership to come around. It might be a long wait, but getting hysterical over this regime and launching a war against it seems a far inferior option.[25]

Similarly, a calmer policy discussion of the Iranian bomb issue should take the following considerations into account.

1) Iran claims it has no intention of developing nuclear weapons; there is some chance this is true and that it never will actually do so. The country's supreme leader, Ali Khamenei, has forcefully proclaimed that "We do not need these weapons." Using nuclear bombs would be against "Islamic rules" of warfare, he insists, and, moreover, they would be extremely

expensive to make while there are no policy purposes for which they would be useful.[26] I do not wish in this book even to begin to adjudicate the first of these three propositions, but it certainly seems that Khamenei has gotten the other two right.

2) If Iran does develop nuclear weapons under present conditions, the process, contrary to intelligence exaggerations persistently spun out, will likely take years[27]—or even decades, if the Pakistan experience is any guide.

3) Iran scarcely has a viable delivery system for nuclear weapons and nothing in the way of an adequate missile capacity.[28]

4) Although the ravings of people like Iran's president Ahmadinejad can be distinctly unsettling, he does not have final control of the military, is in considerable disrepute within Iran because of economic difficulties, and, while distinctly hostile to the state of Israel, apparently meant his remark, routinely translated as calling for Israel to be "wiped off the map," to mean that the state of Israel should eventually disappear from history, not that its Jewish population should be exterminated. The United States and West Europe lived for decades under a similar sort of threat from the Soviet Union, which was explicitly dedicated to overthrowing their form of government and economy. And from time to time Soviet leader Nikita Khrushchev would casually point out how few of his nuclear bombs would be required to annihilate France or Britain.[29]

5) Comparing people like Ahmadinejad with Hitler, as has commonly been done, verges on the absurd. Far more valid would be comparisons with such devils du jour as Egypt's Nasser, Indonesia's Sukarno, Iraq's Saddam, and Libya's Qaddafi, all of whom were variously envisioned to be new incarnations of the Nazi leader and all of whom eventually subsided into history's dustbin—or are doing so now.[30] Moreover, each of those venom-spouting and seemingly threatening dictators had far greater control over their countries than does anyone in Iran.

6) While hostile and unpleasant in many ways, the leadership of Iran does not consist of a self-perpetuating gaggle of suicidal lunatics.

7) If Khamenei is lying or undergoes a conversion and Iran does develop nuclear weapons, it will most likely "use" them in the same way all other nuclear states have: for prestige and deterrence.[31] Indeed, suggests Thomas Schelling, deterrence is about the *only* value the weapons might have for Iran:

What else can Iran accomplish, except possibly the destruction of its own system, with a few nuclear warheads? Nuclear weapons would be too precious to give away or to sell, too precious to waste killing people when they could, held in reserve, make the United States, or Russia, or any other nation hesitant to consider military action.[32]

8) If Iran does develop nuclear weapons, it is exceedingly unlikely that it will ever detonate them or give them to a substate group like Hezbollah to detonate, particularly on a country like Israel—not least because the nonlunatics in charge would fear that the source of the weapon would be detected by nuclear forensics (discussed in the next chapter), inviting devastating retaliation.[33]

9) It seems overwhelmingly likely that, if Iran does develop nuclear weapons and brandishes them to intimidate others or to get its way, it will find that those threatened, rather than capitulating to its blandishments, will ally with others (including conceivably Israel) to stand up to the intimidation. As discussed in chapter 7, the popular notion that nuclear weapons furnish a country with the capacity to "dominate" its area has little or no historical support—a fact, however, that hardly cramps the style of obsessive antiproliferators. Actually, in the wake of the Iraq disaster, an invasion by the ever-threatening Americans can probably now be creditably deterred simply by maintaining a trained and well-armed cadre of a few thousand troops dedicated to, and capable of, inflicting endless irregular warfare on the hapless and increasingly desperate invaders, although the Iranians may not yet have grasped this new reality.

10) In the end, if Iran actually does develop something of an atomic arsenal, it will likely find, following the experience of all other states so armed in the "nuclear age," that the bombs are essentially useless and a very considerable waste of money and effort.

REEVALUATING THE "SUPREME PRIORITY" APPROACH

In assessing policy concerning the prospect that Iran might eventually build nuclear weapons, David Kay is understandably bewildered that so many "invite either the humiliation of having to back down from their previous unequivocal declarations of the necessity of an attack in response to an Iranian nuclear weapon, or the obvious economic and political disasters that would follow from such an action."[34]

A case in point is supplied in a thoughtful article by specialists Colin Dueck and Ray Takeyh. Assessing the situation, they argue that an invasion of Iran "is simply not going to happen" and that air strikes would probably fail to destroy the program, while causing such serial unpleasantnesses as a nationalist backlash in Iran, international condemnation, the strengthening of Iran's hard-liners, the potential disruption of oil supplies, and Iranian-sponsored attacks against both American troops and American interests throughout the area. Further, they conclude that, if Iran gets nuclear weapons, it is "extremely unlikely" that its leaders would use them against the United States or its allies "either directly or through transfer to terrorist groups," because either act "would bring about their own utter destruction." Rather, the Iranians would use them for deterrence and for "amplifying Iran's diplomatic leverage within the region" (whatever that means). However, despite their effective conclusion that any impact of Iran's nuclear weapons would be essentially atmospheric, Dueck and Takeyh somehow think it important to "terminate Iran's nuclear program." This, they suggest, should be done primarily through diplomacy—backed, however, by the threat of "new, intensified economic sanctions" (even though they acknowledge that these tend to help the hard-liners) and of military action, despite their recognition of the "immense" political fallout that would follow from such action. Like most analysts, they appear to be untroubled by the fact that a considerable number of people might be killed by the action, even though they are convinced that Iran's nuclear weapons would never actually be used to kill *anybody*.[35]

Devoted antiproliferator Joseph Cirincione paints a different dark picture, but comes to a similar conclusion. He thinks a nuclear Iran or North Korea could readily be deterred from using a nuclear weapon against their neighbors or the United States, and he discounts the likelihood that either might "intentionally give a weapon to a terrorist group they could not control." What sets Cirincione off instead is an extravagant fear cascade that envisions "a nuclear reaction chain where states feel they must match each other's nuclear capability," something "underway already in the Middle East," where "a dozen Muslim nations suddenly declared interest in starting nuclear-power programs," which, he asserts, are a "nuclear hedge against Iran" (or, one might add, against the United States). This, continues Cirincione, "could lead to a Middle East with not one nuclear-weapons state, Israel, but four or five," and that, he dramatically concludes, "is a recipe for nuclear war." Effectively, Cirincione is in line with President George W. Bush's view: "if you're interested in avoiding World War III, it seems like you ought to be interested in preventing [Iran] from having the knowledge necessary to make a nuclear weapon."[36]

Following such imaginative, if vague and underspecified, chains of thinking, it becomes clear that if countries like North Korea and Iran cannot be stopped by lesser means from getting a bomb (or, in Bush's terms, even from acquiring the *knowledge* of how to do so), the world has no choice but to apply military force to stop them, killing in the process thousands, or even tens or hundreds of thousands, of people. After all, however regrettable, that would be better than World War III or a nuclear war. All this to avoid finding out if the extreme imaginings have any substance. This was essentially the approach applied to Iraq in 2003, and tens or hundreds of thousands have since paid the price.

That's the kind of policy that logically (and actually) follows when nuclear proliferation is determined to be an international "duty," a "supreme priority" or "our number one national-security priority."

Kay is further amazed that, in contrast to such curious reasoning, there is so little discussion of constructing arrangements with other states in the region to prevent states from gaining any decisive advantage from acquiring nuclear weapons. It is the sort of discussion that, as suggested in the previous chapter, should have taken place for Iraq during the reign of Saddam Hussein.[37]

With these considerations in mind, it seems time to reconsider the "supreme priority" approach to nuclear proliferation.

It would certainly be preferable that a number of variously designated regimes (including Iran and North Korea) never obtain a nuclear arsenal. But if they do so they are by far most likely to put them to use—if that is the term—the same way other nuclear countries have: to stoke their collective egos and to deter real or perceived threats.

If leaders of a state are determined to obtain a nuclear capacity, dedicated antiproliferators have a choice of two policy options: 1) let them have it, or, in distinct contrast, 2) let them have it.

Under the first option, antiproliferators might seek to make things difficult and costly for the nuclear aspirant, but in the end they would stand back and let the undesirable development come about, trusting (or hoping) that the new nuclear country could be kept in line by deterrence and containment. In this, they would remain mindful of historical experience, which strongly suggests that new nuclear countries—even ones that once seemed to be hugely threatening, like China in 1964—have been content to use their weapons for purposes of prestige and deterrence even while discovering them to be a very considerable waste of time, money, effort, and scientific talent.

Under the second option, antiproliferators would give in to the spell they have fashioned for themselves. Under extravagant imaginings about their international "duty" and about dire developments that could conceivably transpire should the nuclear aspirant succeed, they would desperately apply military action or sanctions against the determined nuclear aspirant, policies that will inevitably result in the deaths of a very considerable number of people.

This book warns against the second of these and recommends the first. "It is dangerous," muses Hymans aptly, "to fight smoke with fire."[38] Nuclear proliferation, while not necessarily desirable, is unlikely to accelerate or prove to be a major danger. And extreme policies based, however logically, on dire proliferation fancies need careful reconsideration. They can impose costs far higher than those likely to be generated by the imagined problems they seek to address, and they can be counterproductive.

I have nothing against making nonproliferation a high priority. I would simply like to top it with a somewhat higher one: avoiding policies that can lead to the deaths of tens or hundreds of thousands of people under the obsessive sway of worst-case scenario fantasies.

PART III

The Atomic Terrorist?

12

Task

The 9/11 Commission attributed the fact that the United States was surprised on 9/11 to a "failure of imagination." That defect was substantially reversed in the aftermath. Notes one commentator, "no one" in the American national security community considered (or imagined) that disaster to be an "isolated occurrence," and it was apparently inconceivable that the country would go over eight years (and counting) without some sort of repetition. Or even three: it was in 2004 that another characterized the post-9/11 period as one in which, "contrary to every expectation and prediction," the second shoe never dropped. As Rudy Giuliani, New York's mayor on 9/11, reflected in 2005, "Anybody—any one of these security experts, including myself—would have told you on September 11, 2001, we're looking at dozens and dozens and multiyears of attacks like this. It hasn't been quite that bad." No, not nearly. Precisely what Giuliani's "security experts" were basing their expert opinion on is not entirely clear, but there certainly was no failure—or at any rate, lack—of imagination.[1]

As this suggests, it is clearly possible to have a surfeit of imagination as well. In the aftermath of World War II, for example, popular and expert opinion mostly imagined that another war like that was just around the corner, as noted in chapter 5, and, as documented in chapter 7, for decades imagined estimates about the future pace of nuclear proliferation have been persistently on the high side, often extravagantly so.

In this spirit, alarm about the possibility that small groups could fabricate and then set off nuclear weapons have been repeatedly raised at least since 1946, when, as noted in chapter 2, atomic bomb maker J. Robert Oppenheimer contended that if three or four men could smuggle in units for an atomic bomb, they could "destroy New York." Assertions like that proliferated after the 1950s, when the "suitcase bomb" appeared to become a something of a practical possibility. And it has now been well over three decades since a prominent terrorism specialist, Brian Jenkins, published his (not unreasonable) warnings about how "the world's increasing dependence on nuclear power may provide terrorists with weapons of mass destruction," and since a group empowered by the Atomic Energy Commission darkly noted that "terrorist groups have increased their professional skills, intelligence networks, finances, and levels of armaments throughout the world." And because of "the widespread dissemination of instructions for processing special nuclear materials and for making simple nuclear weapons," the group warned, "acquisition of special nuclear material remains the only substantial problem facing groups which desire to have such weapons."[2]

At around the same time, journalist John McPhee decided that, although only a small proportion of nuclear professionals expressed a "sense of urgency" about the issue, he would devote an entire book to a physicist he was able to find who did (nothing, of course, is as boring as a book about how urgent something isn't). That was Theodore Taylor, who proclaimed the problem to be "immediate" and who explained to McPhee at length "how comparatively easy it would be to steal nuclear material and step by step make it into a bomb." To fabricate a crude atomic bomb, Taylor patiently, if urgently, pointed out, was "simple": all one needed was some plutonium oxide powder, some high explosives, and "a few things that anyone could buy in a hardware store." "Everything is a matter of probabilities," Taylor assured his rapt auditor, and at the time he thought either that it was already too late to "prevent the making of a few bombs, here and there, now and then," or that "in another ten or fifteen years, it will be too late."[3] Thirty-five years later, we continue to wait for terrorists to carry out their "simple" task.

In the wake of 9/11, concerns about the atomic terrorist surged, even though the terrorist attacks of that day used no special weapons. "Nothing is really new about these perils," notes the *New York Times*' Bill Keller, but 9/11 turned "a theoretical possibility into a felt danger," giving "our nightmares legs." Jenkins has run an Internet search to discover how often variants of the term *al-Qaeda* appeared within ten words of *nuclear*. There were only seven hits in 1999 and eleven in 2000, but this soared to 1,742 in 2001 and to 2,931 in 2002.[4]

In this spirit, Keller relays the response of then Secretary of Homeland Security Tom Ridge when asked what he worried about most: Ridge "cupped his hands prayerfully and pressed his fingertips to his lips. 'Nuclear,' he said simply." On cue, when the presidential candidates were specifically asked by Jim Lehrer in their first debate in September 2004 to designate the "single most serious threat to the national security of the United States," the candidates had no difficulty agreeing on one. It was, in George W. Bush's words, a nuclear weapon "in the hands of a terrorist enemy." Concluded Lehrer, "So it's correct to say the single most serious threat you believe, both of you believe, is nuclear proliferation?" George W. Bush: "In the hands of a terrorist enemy." John Kerry: "Weapons of mass destruction, nuclear proliferation.... There's some 600-plus tons of unsecured material still in the former Soviet Union and Russia.... there are terrorists trying to get their hands on that stuff today." And Defense Secretary Robert Gates contends that *every* senior leader in the government is kept awake at night by "the thought of a terrorist ending up with a weapon of mass destruction, especially nuclear."[5]

If there has been a "failure of imagination" over all these decades, however, perhaps it has been in the inability or unwillingness to consider the difficulties confronting the atomic terrorist. Thus far, terrorist groups seem to have exhibited only limited desire and even less progress in going atomic. This may be because, after brief exploration of the possible routes to go atomic, they, unlike generations of alarmed pundits, have discovered that the tremendous effort required is scarcely likely to be successful.

OBTAINING A FINISHED BOMB: ASSISTANCE BY A STATE

One route a would-be atomic terrorist might take would be to be given or sold a bomb by a generous like-minded nuclear state for delivery abroad. This is highly improbable, however, because there would be too much risk, even for a country led by extremists, that the ultimate source of the weapon would be discovered. As one prominent analyst, Matthew Bunn, puts it, "A dictator or oligarch bent on maintaining power is highly unlikely to take

the immense risk of transferring such a devastating capability to terrorists they cannot control, given the ever-present possibility that the material
would be traced back to its origin." Important in this last consideration are
deterrent safeguards afforded by "nuclear forensics," the rapidly developing
science (and art) of connecting nuclear materials to their sources even after
a bomb has been exploded.[6]

An indication of the natural sensitivity of governments on this issue
can be found in the experience of the Pakistani journalist Hamid Mir. In
an interview conducted as al-Qaeda's position in Afghanistan was about to
be overrun, Osama bin Laden contended to Mir that al-Qaeda possessed
chemical and nuclear weapons (this episode is assessed more fully in chapter 14). According to Mir, the Pakistani government told him "not to mention the nuclear weapon under any circumstance because the Americans
might think Pakistan had sold it" to bin Laden.[7] Although the Pakistanis
appear to have gotten the point on their own, it was presumably hammered
home a bit later in that year when CIA Director George Tenet flew to the
country in part to inform Pakistan's president, with a notable absence of
diplomatic subtlety, "You cannot imagine the outrage there would be in my
country if it were learned that Pakistan is coddling scientists who are helping Bin Ladin acquire a nuclear weapon. Should such a device ever be used,
the full fury of the American people would be focused on whoever helped
al-Qa'ida in its cause."[8]

Moreover, there is a very considerable danger to the donor that the
bomb (and its source) would be discovered even before delivery or that
it would be exploded in a manner and on a target the donor would not
approve—including on the donor itself. Another concern would be that the
terrorist group might be infiltrated by foreign intelligence.[9]

It is also worth noting that, although nuclear weapons have been
around now for well over half a century, no state, thus far at least, has ever
given another state—even friendly allies—a nuclear weapon (or a chemical, biological, or radiological one either, for that matter) that the recipi-
ent could use independently, though there have been cases of state-to-state
assistance with nuclear programs. For example, during the cold war, North
Korea tried to acquire nuclear weapons from its close ally, China, and was
firmly refused.[10]

There could be some danger that terrorists would be aided by private (or semiprivate) profiteers, like the network established by Pakistani
scientist A. Q. Khan. However, Khan's activities were easily penetrated by

intelligence agencies (the CIA, it is very likely, had agents within the network), and the operation was abruptly closed down when it seemed to be the right time. And although the Khan case is understandably unsettling, it did not, as analyst Michael Levi notes, "involve nuclear weapons or explosive materials, the most sensitive part of the Pakistani nuclear program." Moreover, the aid he tendered was entirely to states with return addresses whose chief aim in possessing nuclear weapons would be to deter (or to gain prestige). As with previous examples of state-to-state assistance, Khan did not aid stateless terrorist groups whose goal presumably would be actually to set the weapons off.[11]

In addition, al-Qaeda—the chief demon group and the only one that has claimed to see value in striking the United States—is unlikely to be trusted by just about anyone. As one observer has pointed out, the terrorist group's explicit enemies list includes not only Christians and Jews, but all Middle Eastern regimes; Muslims who don't share its views; most Western countries; the governments of India, Pakistan, Afghanistan, and Russia; most news organizations; the United Nations; and international NGOs. Most of the time it didn't get along all that well even with its host in Afghanistan, the Taliban government. And, although there is concern that a re-Talibanized Afghanistan would facilitate an al-Qaeda bomb program, the main Taliban elements are strongly opposed to foreign fighters like al-Qaeda and have reportedly sought to distance themselves from the terrorist group, in part to ingratiate themselves with bin Laden's number-one enemy, Saudi Arabia, whose support they would need if they ever tried again to run Afghanistan.[12]

STEALING OR ILLICITLY PURCHASING A BOMB: LOOSE NUKES

There has also been great worry about "loose nukes," especially in post-Communist Russia—weapons, "suitcase bombs" in particular, that could be stolen or bought illicitly. In 1997, Russian politician and general Alexander Lebed announced on CBS' *60 Minutes* that dozens of suitcase bombs were missing from his country's arsenal. However, he later recanted this testimony, and both Russian nuclear officials and experts on the Russian nuclear programs have adamantly denied that al-Qaeda or any other terrorist group could have bought such weapons. They further point out that the bombs, all built before 1991, are difficult to maintain and have a lifespan of one to three years, after which they become "radioactive scrap metal." Similarly, a careful assessment conducted by the Center for Non-proliferation Studies has concluded that it is unlikely that any of these devices have actually been lost and that, regardless, their effectiveness would be very low or nonexistent, because they (like all nuclear weapons) require continual maintenance. After an extended assessment, Jenkins dismisses the story as a "persistent urban legend," and even some of those most alarmed by the prospect of atomic terrorism have concluded, "It is probably true that there are no 'loose nukes,' transportable nuclear weapons missing from their proper storage locations and available for purchase in some way."[13]

It might be added that Russia has an intense interest in controlling any weapons on its territory, since it is likely to be a prime target of any illicit use by terrorist groups, particularly Chechen ones, of course, with whom it has been waging a vicious on-and-off war for well over a decade. The government of Pakistan, which has been repeatedly threatened by al-Qaeda, has a similar very strong interest in controlling its nuclear weapons and material—and scientists. Notes Stephen Younger, former head of nuclear weapons research and development at Los Alamos National Laboratory, "regardless of what is reported in the news, all nuclear nations take the security of their weapons very seriously."[14]

Even if a finished bomb were somehow lifted somewhere, the loss would soon be noted and a worldwide pursuit launched. And most bombs that could conceivably be stolen use plutonium, which emits more radiation than highly enriched uranium and can therefore be detected somewhat more readily by sensors in the hands of pursuers.[15]

Moreover, as technology has developed, finished bombs have been out-fitted with devices that will trigger a nonnuclear explosion that will destroy the bomb if it is tampered with. Experts polled by a *Washington Post* reporter point out that "it would be very difficult for terrorists to figure out on their own how to work a Russian or Pakistan bomb," because even the simplest of these "has some security features that would have to be defeated before it could be used." One of them, Charles Ferguson, stresses:

> You'd have to run it through a specific sequence of events, includ-ing changes in temperature, pressure and environmental condi-tions before the weapon would allow itself to be armed, for the

fuses to fall into place and then for it to allow itself to be fired. You
don't get it off the shelf, enter a code and have it go off.

And there are other security techniques: bombs can be kept disassembled
with the component parts stored in separate high-security vaults, and things
can be organized so that two people and multiple codes are required not
only to use the bomb but also to store, maintain, and deploy it. If the terrorists seek to enlist (or force) the services of someone who already knows
how to set off the bomb, they would find, as Younger stresses, that "only few
people in the world have the knowledge to cause an unauthorized detonation of a nuclear weapon." Weapons designers know *how* a weapon works,
he explains, but not the multiple types of signals necessary to set it off, and
maintenance personnel are trained only in a limited set of functions.[16]

Despite this array of inconvenient facts, five suitcase bombs did show up
one day in 2007 on Fox Television's *24*. One of these, sadly, did go off in Valen-
cia, California, at 9:58:07 a.m., destroying several square blocks and instantly
killing the 12,000 people who had been concentrated there for dramatic pur-
posed by the scriptwriters. Fortunately, all the others were disarmed or recovered unexploded with the successful and increasingly ingenious application
of torture as featured prominently in episodes 1, 2, 5, 6, 7, 8, 12, and 17.

Returning closer to reality, there could be dangers in the chaos that
would emerge if a nuclear state were utterly to fail, collapsing in full
disarray—Pakistan's troubles with the Taliban are frequently brought up in
this context. The notion that a few thousand Taliban combatants based in a
small, distant, and backward area of Pakistan could terminally disrupt—or
even manage to take over and control—the rest of a country with a population of over 150 million that is hostile to them and possessed of a large
army does seem to be a considerable stretch. However, even under chaotic conditions, nuclear weapons would likely remain under heavy guard
by people who know that a purloined bomb would most likely end up
going off in their own territory, would still have locks (and, in the case of
Pakistan would be disassembled), and could probably be followed, located,
and hunted down by an alarmed international community. The worst-case
scenario in this instance requires not only a failed state but a considerable
series of additional conditions, including consistent (and perfect) insider
complicity and a sequence of hasty, opportunistic decisions or developments that click flawlessly in a manner far more familiar in Hollywood
scripts than in real life.[17]

It is conceivable that stolen bombs, even if no longer viable as weapons, would be useful for the fissile material that could be harvested from them. However, Christoph Wirz and Emmanuel Egger, two senior physicists in charge of nuclear issues at Switzerland's Spiez Laboratory, point out that even if a weapon is not completely destroyed when it is opened, its fissile material yield would not be adequate for a primitive design, and therefore several weapons would have to be stolen and then opened successfully.[18] Moreover, potentially purloinable weapons generally use plutonium, a substance that is not only problematic to transport but far more difficult and dangerous to work with than highly enriched uranium.

BUILDING A BOMB OF ONE'S OWN

Since they are unlikely to be able to buy or steal a useable bomb, and since they are further unlikely to have one handed off to them by an established nuclear state, the most plausible route for terrorists would be to manufacture the device themselves from purloined materials. This is the course identified by a majority of leading experts as the one most likely to lead to nuclear terrorism.[19]

Because of the dangers and difficulties of transporting and working with plutonium, it is generally further agreed that a dedicated terrorist group would choose to try to use highly enriched uranium.[20] The idea would be to obtain as much of this stuff as necessary and then fashion it into an explosive. To cut corners, the group would presumably be, to the degree possible, comparatively cavalier about safety issues such as radiation exposure.

The likely product of this effort would not be a bomb that can be dropped or hurled, since this would massively complicate the delivery problem. Rather, the terrorists would seek to come up with an "improvised nuclear device" (IND) of simple design, one that could be set off at the target by a suicidal detonation crew. The simplest design is for a "gun" type of device in which masses of highly enriched uranium are hurled at each other within a tube. At best, such a device would be, as the deeply concerned Graham Allison acknowledges, "large, cumbersome, unsafe, unreliable, unpredictable, and inefficient."[21]

The process is a daunting one even in this minimal case. The terrorists would confront, as the set of counterterrorism and nuclear experts interviewed by the *Post* point out, enormous technical and logistical obstacles.[22] In particular, the task requires that a considerable series of difficult hurdles be conquered in sequence. The following discussion attempts to lay these out in a systematic manner.

Procuring Fissile Material

To begin with, at the present time and likely for the foreseeable future, stateless groups are simply incapable of manufacturing the required fissile material for a bomb, because the process requires an effort on an industrial scale. Moreover, they are unlikely to be supplied with the material by a state for the same reasons a state is unlikely to give them a workable bomb.[23] Thus, they would need to steal or illicitly purchase this crucial material.

Although there is legitimate concern that some fissile material, particularly in Russia, may be inadequately secured, things have improved considerably on this score, and Pakistan keeps exceedingly careful watch over its bomb-grade uranium. Moreover, even sleepy, drunken guards will react with hostility (and noise) to a raiding party.[24]

Thieves also need to know exactly what they want and where it is, and this presumably means trusting bribed, but not necessarily dependable, insiders. And to even begin to pull off such a heist, they need to develop a highly nuanced street sense in foreign areas often filled with people who are congenitally suspicious of strangers.[25]

But outright armed theft is exceedingly unlikely, not only because of the resistance of guards but because chase would be immediate. A more plausible route would be to corrupt insiders to smuggle out the required fissile material. However, this approach requires the purchasers to pay off a host of greedy confederates, including brokers and money transmitters, any one of whom could turn on them or, either out of guile or incompetence, furnish them with stuff that is useless.[26] Even under the best of circumstances, the conspirators would still have to anticipate that the missing HEU would soon be noticed.

Not only could the exchange prove to be a scam, it could also be part of a sting—or become one. Although there may be disgruntled and underpaid scientists in places like Russia, they would have to consider the costs of detection. A. Q. Khan, the Pakistani nuclear scientist, was once a national hero for his lead work on his country's atomic bomb, but he was brought down in 2004 for selling atomic secrets to other governments and was placed under severe house arrest for years.[27] Renegade Russian scientists who happen not to be national heroes could expect a punishment that would be considerably more unpleasant.

Moreover, because of improving safeguards and accounting practices, it is decreasingly likely that the theft would remain undetected.[28] This is an important development, because once it is noticed that some uranium is missing, the authorities would investigate the few people who might have been able to assist the thieves, and one who seems suddenly to have become prosperous is likely to arrest their attention right from the start. There is something decidedly worse than being a disgruntled Russian scientist, and that is being a dead disgruntled Russian scientist. Thus even one initially tempted by, seduced by, or sympathetic to the blandishments of smooth-talking foreign terrorists might well soon develop sobering second thoughts and go to the authorities.

Insiders might also come to ruminate over the fact that, once the heist was accomplished, the terrorists would, as Jenkins puts it none too delicately, "have every incentive to cover their trail, beginning with eliminating their confederates." He also points out that no case of a rogue Russian scientist working for terrorists or foreign states has ever been documented.[29]

It is also relevant to note that over the years, known thefts of highly enriched uranium have totaled less than 16 pounds or so. This is far less than required for an atomic explosion; for a crude bomb, over 100 pounds are required to produce a likely yield of one kiloton.[30] Despite huge concerns about the chaos that engulfed Russia in the 1990s, only minute amounts of weapons-grade material has been stolen as far as we know—1994 proved to be the peak, with declines thereafter.[31]

None of these thieves was connected to al-Qaeda, and, most strikingly, none had buyers lined up—nearly all were caught while trying to peddle their wares. Indeed, concludes analyst Robin Frost, "there appears to be no true demand, except where the buyers were government agents running a sting." Since there seems to be no real commercial market for fissile material, each sale would be a one-time affair, not a continuing source of profit like drugs, and there is no evidence of established underworld commercial trade in this illicit commodity.[32] Consequently, sellers need to make all their money on the single transaction.

Of course, there may also have been additional thefts that went undiscovered.[33] However, the difficulty of peddling such a special substance suggests that any theft would have to be done on consignment—the thief is unlikely to come across likely purchasers while wandering provocatively down the street like a purveyor of drugs or French postcards. It is tricky to peddle stolen goods under the best of circumstances—and even then, the purchaser of purloined materials, the fence, generally takes the lion's share of the profit. The atomic thief's task would be like trying to find a buyer for a stolen Rembrandt painting. The thief is far more likely in the process to be noticed and reported or to become the victim of a sting than to reap sumptuous reward.

Even a "theft on spec" requires that the sellers advertise or that they know where and how to contact their terrorist buyer—presumably through middlemen trusted by both sides, all of whom have to be paid off. Moreover, it is likely that no single seller would have a sufficient amount of purloined material, requiring multiple clandestine buys.[34]

In the end, concludes Levi in agreement with Frost, "there may be no such thing as a true nuclear black market." This conclusion would presumably come as some relief to the specialists surveyed on the issue by Senator Richard Lugar, who overwhelmingly picked "black market purchase" as the "most likely method through which terrorists would acquire nuclear weapons or weapons grade nuclear material."[35] Or it could perhaps be taken to suggest that many of those experts haven't really thought the problem through.

Nor, it would seem, had the people at charge at CBS's 60 Minutes when they did a story on a 2007 break-in at a South African nuclear facility. It is not clear what the thieves were looking for—they apparently tried to make off with a laptop, and there had been another break-in attempt a couple of years earlier. But the television show very pregnantly notes that "certainly the most valuable single thing at that site" was a store of some 1,000 pounds of highly enriched uranium worth, they suggest, "millions of dollars on the black market." The thieves did break through some perimeter defenses, but, as the program makes clear, they still had fences, cameras, and locks between them and the HEU. The likelihood they could have successfully breached all these and successfully made off with the HEU seems exceedingly small. However, even more questionable is the program's casual assumption that they could have successfully peddled the purloined material at the high price the program invents in a market that essentially does not seem to exist and is filled with sting and scam operators.[36]

If terrorists were somehow successful at obtaining a sufficient mass of relevant material, they would then have to transport it hundreds of miles out of the country over unfamiliar terrain and probably while being pursued by security forces.[37]

Crossing international borders would be facilitated by following established smuggling routes, and, for a considerable fee, opium traders (for example) might provide expert, and possibly even reliable, assistance. But the routes are not as chaotic as they appear and are often under the watch of suspicious and careful criminal regulators.[38] If they became suspicious of the commodity being smuggled, some of these might find it in their interest to disrupt passage, perhaps to collect the bounteous reward money likely to be offered by alarmed governments if the uranium theft had been discovered. It is not at all clear, moreover, that people engaged in the routine, if illegal, business of smuggling would necessarily be so debased that, even for considerable remuneration, they would willingly join a plot that might end up killing tens of thousands of innocent people.

To reduce dangers, the atomic terrorists might decide to split up their booty and smuggle it out in multiple small amounts. In this, however, they would have to rely on the hope that every single container would escape notice and suspicion.

Constructing an Atomic Device

Once outside the country with their precious booty, terrorists would need to set up a large and well-equipped machine shop to manufacture a bomb, and then populate it with a very select team of highly skilled scientists, technicians, and machinists. Moreover, stresses one physicist, the process would also require good managers and organizers. Physicist Richard Muller, who has been shown bomb designs in detail, concludes, as noted earlier, that "a nuclear weapon designed by anything less than a top-level team is likely to fizzle"—rather like the one tested by the North Koreans in 2006 after the country had invested enormous resources and effort over decades on the project.[39]

The group would have to be assembled and retained for the monumental task while no consequential suspicions were generated among friends, family, and police about their curious and sudden absence from normal pursuits back home. Pakistan, for example, maintains a strict watch on many of its nuclear scientists even after retirement.[40] The Japanese terrorist group Aum Shinrikyo did establish and maintain a fairly extensive research facility, which suggests that this tricky task is not impossible, though that enterprise was not carried out in an environment in which police were scouring the world for recently purloined fissile material.

Members of the bomb-building team would also have to be utterly devoted to the cause, of course. And, in addition, they would have to be willing to put their lives, and certainly their careers, at high risk, because after their bomb was discovered or exploded, they would likely become the targets in an intense worldwide dragnet operation, facilitated by the fact that their skills would not be common ones. Applying jargon that emerged in the aftermath of an earlier brutal conspiracy, their names would become Mudd.

Some observers have insisted that it would be "easy" for terrorists to assemble a crude bomb if they could get enough fissile material, and one popular article even declared the task to be "child's play." But there are those who beg to differ. Atomic scientists, perhaps laboring under the concern, in the words of investigative journalist William Langewiesche, that "a declaration of safety can at any time be proved spectacularly wrong," have been comparatively restrained in cataloguing the difficulties terrorists would face in constructing a bomb. However, physicists Wirz and Egger have published a paper that does so, and it bluntly concludes that the task "could hardly be accomplished by a subnational group." They point out that precise blueprints are required, not just sketches and general ideas, and that even with a good blueprint the terrorist group "would most certainly be forced to redesign." They also stress that the work, far from being "easy," is difficult, dangerous, and extremely exacting, and that the technical requirements "in several fields verge on the unfeasible." They conclude that "it takes much more than knowledge of the workings of nuclear weapons and access to fissile material to successfully manufacture a usable weapon."[41]

These problems are also emphasized in an earlier report by five Los Alamos scientists: although schematic drawings showing the principles of bomb design in a qualitative way are widely available, the essential detailed design drawings and specifications are not. Moreover, to prepare these drawings requires a large amount of labor and the direct participation of individuals thoroughly informed in such distinct areas as the physical, chemical, and metallurgical properties of the materials used; the characteristics affecting their fabrication; nuclear and biological radiation effects;

and technology concerning high explosives and/or chemical propellants, hydrodynamics, and electrical circuitry. They also point out that designing and building a bomb requires experimenting over many months, assessing the results, and making corrections or improvements for follow-on experiments. Although they think the problems can be dealt with "provided adequate provisions have been made," they also stress that "there are a number of obvious potential hazards in any such operation, among them those arising in the handling of a high explosive; the possibility of inadvertently inducing a critical configuration of the fissile material at some stage in the procedure; and the chemical toxicity or radiological hazards inherent in the materials used. Failure to foresee *all* the needs on these points," they conclude laconically, "could bring the operation to a close." Or, as weapons expert Gary Milhollin puts it, "a single mistake in design could wreck the whole project."[42]

Los Alamos research director Younger has more recently made a similar argument. It is simply "wrong to assume that nuclear weapons are now easy to make," he says, expressing his amazement at "self-declared 'nuclear weapons experts,' many of whom have never seen a real nuclear weapon," who "hold forth on how easy it is to make a functioning nuclear explosive." Information is readily available for getting the general idea behind a rudimentary nuclear explosive, but none of this is detailed enough to "enable the confident assembly of a real nuclear explosive." Although he remains concerned that a terrorist group could buy or steal a nuclear device or be given one by an established nuclear country, Younger is quick to enumerate the difficulties the group would confront when attempting to fabricate one on their own. He stresses that uranium is "exceptionally difficult to machine," while "plutonium is one of the most complex metals ever discovered, a material whose basic properties are sensitive to exactly how it is processed," and both require special machining technology.[43]

Others contend the crudest type of bomb would be "simple and robust" and "very simple" to detonate. Younger disagrees:

> Another challenge…is how to choose the right tolerances. "Just put a slug of uranium into a gun barrel and shoot it into another slug of uranium" is one description of how easy it is to make a nuclear explosive. However, if the gap between the barrel and the slug is too tight, then the slug may stick as it is accelerated down the barrel. If the gap is too big, then other, more complex, issues may arise.

All of these problems can be solved by experimentation, but this experimentation requires a level of technical resources that, until recently, few countries had. How do you measure the progress of an explosive detonation without destroying the equipment doing the measurement? How do you perform precision measurements on something that only lasts a fraction of a millionth of a second?

Stressing the "daunting problems associated with material purity, machining, and a host of other issues," Younger concludes, "to think that a terrorist group, working in isolation with an unreliable supply of electricity and little access to tools and supplies" could fabricate a bomb or IND "is far-fetched at best."[44]

In addition, the bomb makers would not be able to test the product to be sure they were on the right track. Although it is true, as Allison points out, that the bomb dropped on Hiroshima had not been tested, Levi parses the issue more fully, noting that, during the project, scientists and engineers spent years testing not only the gun device itself, but the trigger for the chain reaction, the casting and machining of the uranium metal in order to detect impurities in the product and to avoid fires and criticality accidents during production, and different configurations of material to determine how it would behave—a project that led to the death of one of the physicists.[45]

The work would also be dangerous, particularly if, as seems likely, standard safety procedures were relaxed in an effort to save money and to speed the manufacturing process. Levi quotes the Iraq Study Group Report, "working with molten highly enriched uranium requires special consideration for criticality during the melting and solidification process," and then adds: "Criticality accidents, which occur when so much nuclear material is collected together that a chain reaction takes place, may kill or disable scientists," people who would, he further notes, "be difficult to replace in a group with few technical experts."[46]

Under the best of circumstances, the process could take months or even a year or more, and it would all, of course, have to be carried out in utter secrecy even while local and international security police are likely to be on the intense prowl. As Milhollin presents the terrorists' problem, "the theft of the uranium would probably be discovered soon enough, and it might be only a short matter of time before the whole world showed up on their doorstep." Moreover, "in addition to all the usual intelligence methods," note the

Los Alamos scientists, "the most sensitive technical detection equipment available would be at their disposal," and effective airborne detectors used to prospect for uranium have been around for decades and "great improvement in such equipment have been realized since."[47] In this case, however, the "prospectors" would be hunting for comparatively small quantities of uranium.

Another problem is that people in the area may observe with increasing curiosity and puzzlement the constant coming and going of technicians unlikely to be locals. Unless they live constantly in the shop (itself a noticeable situation), the conspirators would eat, sleep, drink, and recreate elsewhere, constantly bumping into curious, and potentially inquiring, people. It would obviously be vital to keep from inadvertently giving away any information about their project that might incite suspicion—a wariness that could itself inspire suspicion—and to maintain perfectly a plausible and consistent cover story. Their activities must fail to incite curiosity not only by the police but also by local criminal gangs. Through all this they would have to remain completely loyal to the cause, avoiding disillusionment as well as consequential homesickness and interpersonal frictions.[48] This task is clearly not impossible: for nearly a decade now, al-Qaeda central has successfully been able to hole up in a remote corner of the world. However, as discussed more fully in chapter 15, it hasn't really done much of anything either, except for issuing propaganda messages, an enterprise quite a bit simpler than fabricating an atomic explosive.

The process of fabricating an IND requires, then, the effective recruitment of people who have great technical skills and will remain completely devoted to the cause. This is not impossible—some of the terrorists who tried (and failed) to commit mayhem in Britain in 2007 had medical and engineering degrees—but it certainly vastly complicates the problem. In addition, corrupted coconspirators, many of them foreign, must remain utterly reliable, international and local security services must be kept perpetually in the dark, and no curious outsider must get consequential wind of the project over the months or even years it takes to pull off.[49]

Transporting and Detonating the Device

The finished product could weigh a ton or more.[50] Encased in lead shielding to mask radioactive emissions, it would then have to be transported to, and smuggled into, the relevant target country.

The conspirators could take one of two approaches. Under one of these, they would trust their precious and laboriously fabricated product to the tender mercies of the commercial transportation system, supplying something of a return address in the process, and hoping that transportation and policing agencies, alerted to the dangers by news of the purloined uranium, would remain oblivious.

Perhaps more plausibly, the atomic terrorists would hire an aircraft or try to use established smuggling routes, an approach that, again, would require the completely reliable complicity of a considerable number of criminals, none of whom develops cold feet or becomes attracted by bounteous reward money. And even if a sufficient number of reliable coconspirators can be assembled and corrupted, there is still no guarantee their efforts will be successful. A common crack is "just put the bomb inside a bale of marijuana," and the suggestion that international borders, including those of the United States, are anything but impervious is well taken, of course. But there is a key difference between smuggling drugs and smuggling an atomic weapon. Those in the drug trade assume that, although a fair portion of their material will be intercepted by authorities, the amount that does get through will be enough to supply them with a tidy profit. For example, the portion of cocaine sent from South America that fails to reach its destination has been estimated at something like 35 to 70 percent. Odds like that may be tolerable for drug smugglers, but a risk of interception in that range, or even one quite a bit lower, might be distinctly unsettling for terrorists seeking to smuggle in a single large, and very expensively obtained, weapon.[51]

However transported, the dense and remarkably heavy package would then have to be received within the target country by a group of collaborators who are at once totally dedicated and technically proficient at handling, maintaining, detonating, and perhaps assembling the weapon after it arrives. For this purpose, it would be necessary earlier to have infiltrated such people into the country or else to have organized locals.

The IND would then have to be moved over local roads by this crew to the target site in a manner that did not arouse suspicion. And, finally, at the target site, the crew, presumably suicidal, would have to set off its improvised and untested nuclear device, one that, to repeat Allison's description, would be "large, cumbersome, unsafe, unreliable, unpredictable, and inefficient." While doing this, they would have to hope, and fervently pray, that the machine shop work has been perfect, that there were no significant shakeups in the treacherous process of transportation, and that the thing, after all this effort, doesn't prove to be a dud.

The Financial Costs

The discussion so far has neglected to consider the financial costs of the extended operation in all its cumulating, or cascading, entirety, but these could easily become monumental. There would be expensive equipment to buy, smuggle, and set up, and people to pay—or pay off. Some operatives might work for free out of utter dedication to The Cause, but the vast conspiracy would require in addition the subversion of a considerable array of criminals and opportunists, each of whom would have every incentive to push the price for cooperation as high as possible. Any criminals competent and capable enough to be an effective ally in the project are likely as well to be at once smart enough to see boundless opportunities for extortion and psychologically equipped by their profession to be willing to exploit them.

In an analysis, Peter Zimmerman and Jeffrey Lewis suggest the entire caper could be pulled off for $10 million. This seems to understate the costs wildly; the conspirators would be lucky to buy off three people with such a paltry sum. Moreover, the terrorists would be required to expose their ultimate goals to at least some of the corrupted, and at that point (if not earlier) they would become potential extortion victims. They could not afford to abandon unreliable people who know their goals (though they could attempt to kill them), and such people would enjoy essentially monopoly powers to escalate their price. The cost of the operation in bribes alone could easily become ten times the sum suggested by Zimmerman and Lewis.[52]

And even at that, there would be, of course, a considerable risk that those so purchased would, at an exquisitely opportune moment of their own choosing, decide to take the money and run—perhaps to the authorities representing desperate governments with essentially bottomless bankrolls and an overwhelming incentive to expend resources to arrest the atomic plot and to capture or kill the scheming perpetrators.

ASSESSING THE TASK

In his article on the prospects for atomic terrorism, Bill Keller of the *New York Times* suggests that "the best reason for thinking it won't happen is that it hasn't happened yet," and that, he worries, "is terrible logic."[53] However, "logic" aside, there is another quite good reason for thinking it won't happen: the task is bloody *difficult*. The next chapter attempts to estimate just *how* difficult that task is.

13

Likelihood

In his thoughtful, influential, and well-argued 2004 book, *Nuclear Terrorism: The Ultimate Preventable Catastrophe*—a work Nicholas Kristof of the *New York Times* finds "terrifying"—Graham Allison relayed his "considered judgment" that "on the current path, a nuclear terrorist attack on America in the decade ahead is more likely than not." He repeated that judgment in an article published two years later—albeit without reducing the terminal interval to compensate—and he had presumably relied on the same inspirational mechanism in 1995 to predict: "In the absence of a determined program of action, we have every reason to anticipate acts of nuclear terrorism against American targets before this decade is out."[1]

He has quite a bit of company in his perpetually alarming conclusions. In 2003, UN Ambassador John Negroponte judged there to be a "a high probability" that within two years al-Qaeda would attempt an attack using a nuclear or other weapon of mass destruction. When some 85 foreign policy experts were polled by Senator Richard Lugar in 2004 and 2005, they concluded on average that there was a 29 percent likelihood a nuclear explosion would occur somewhere in the world within the next ten years, and they overwhelmingly anticipated that this would likely be carried out by terrorists, not by a government. And in 2007, physicist Richard Garwin put the likelihood of a nuclear explosion on an American or European city by terrorist or other means at 20 percent per year, which would work out to 87 percent over a ten-year period.[2]

In late 2008, after working for six months and interviewing more than 250 people, a congressionally mandated task force, the Commission on the Prevention of Weapons of Mass Destruction Proliferation and Terrorism (possibly known as COPWOMDPAT to its friends) issued its report, portentously entitled *World at Risk*. It led by expressing the belief that "unless the world community acts decisively and with great urgency, it is more likely than not that a weapon of mass destruction will be used in a terrorist attack somewhere in the world by the end of 2013." Although the report is careful to reassure its readers that it does not intend to frighten them about the current state of terrorism and weapons of mass destruction, it failed miserably in that admirable goal almost immediately. Representative Ellen Tauscher (D-Calif.), chairwoman of the Strategic Forces Subcommittee of the House Armed Services Committee, proclaimed shortly after the report was issued, that it "scared the pants off of most of us."[3]

In its dire forecast, the report's phraseology echoes, of course, Allison's formulation of 2004, and this may owe something to the fact that he was one of the commission's nine members. There are a couple of differences, however. In Allison's earlier rendering, bad things happen only if we stay on "the current path." Thus, should bad things fail to occur, this happy result could be taken as proof that we somehow managed somewhere along the line to alter our path, and who, pray, will be able exactly to designate what a "current path" actually is (or was)? The commission, in stark contrast, claims bad things are likely to happen "unless the world community acts decisively and with great urgency," something, experience suggests, that is next to impossible.

On the other hand, the commission artfully broadens its definition of bad things from Allison's "acts of nuclear terrorism against American targets" to the use of a "weapon of mass destruction" by terrorists "somewhere in the world." As one critic points out, there is certainly a good chance that someone somewhere will release some germs, killing few, if any, or, as insurgents have done in Iraq, ineffectually lace the occasional bomb with chlorine. Although no normal person would consider either act to constitute "mass destruction," the report can, strictly speaking, claim vindication. Actually, the report is on even safer ground. A man in Rockford, Illinois, who purchased some bogus hand grenades from an FBI informant with the intent to detonate them at a local shopping mall, has been convicted of attempting to use weapons of mass destruction under laws that creatively define hand grenades to be weapons of mass destruction.[4]

Even those who decidedly disagree with such scary-sounding, if somewhat elusive, prognostications about nuclear terrorism often come out *seeming* like they more or less agree. In his *Atomic Bazaar,* William Langewiesche spends a great deal of time and effort assessing the process by means of which a terrorist group could come up with a bomb. Unlike Allison—and, for that matter, the considerable bulk of accepted opinion—he concludes that it "remains *very, very* unlikely. It's a possibility, but unlikely." Also:

> The best information is that no one has gotten anywhere near this. I mean, if you look carefully and practically at this process, you see that it is an enormous undertaking full of risks for the would-be terrorists. And so far there is no public case, at least known, of any appreciable amount of weapons-grade HEU [highly enriched uranium] disappearing. And that's the first step. If you don't have that, you don't have anything.

The first of these bold and unconventional declarations comes from a book discussion telecast in June 2007 on C-SPAN and the second from an interview on National Public Radio. Judgments in the book itself, however, while consistent with such conclusions, are expressed more ambiguously, even coyly: "at the extreme is the possibility, entirely real, that one or two nuclear weapons will pass into the hands of the new stateless guerrillas, the jihadists, who offer none of the retaliatory targets that have so far underlain the nuclear peace" or "if a would-be nuclear terrorist calculated the odds, he would have to admit that they are stacked against him," but they are "not impossible."[5]

The previous chapter arrayed a lengthy set of obstacles confronting the would-be atomic terrorist—often making use in the process of Langewiesche's excellent reporting. Those who warn about the likelihood of a terrorist bomb contend that a terrorist group could, if often with great difficulty, surmount each obstacle—that doing so in each case is, in Langewiesche's phrase, "not impossible."[6] But it is vital to point out that, while it may be "not impossible" to surmount each individual step, the likelihood that a group could surmount a series of them could quickly approach impossibility.

If the odds are "stacked against" the terrorists, what are they? Lange-wiesche's discussion, as well as other material, helps us evaluate the many ways such a quest—in his words, "an enormous undertaking full of risks"—could fail. The odds, indeed, are stacked against the terrorists, perhaps massively so. In fact, the likelihood a terrorist group will come up with an atomic bomb seems to be vanishingly small.

ARRAYING THE BARRIERS

Assuming terrorists have some desire for the bomb (an assumption questioned in the next chapter), fulfillment of that desire is obviously another matter. Even the very alarmed Matthew Bunn and Anthony Wier contend that the atomic terrorists' task "would clearly be among the most difficult types of attack to carry out" or "one of the most difficult missions a terrorist group could hope to try." But, stresses the CIA's George Tenet, a terrorist atomic bomb is "possible" or "not beyond the realm of possibility." In his excellent discussion of the issue, Michael Levi ably catalogues a wide array of difficulties confronting the would-be atomic terrorist, adroitly points out that "terrorists must succeed at every stage, but the defense needs to succeed only once," sensibly warns against preoccupation with worst-case scenarios, and pointedly formulates "Murphy's Law of Nuclear Terrorism: What can go wrong might go wrong." Nevertheless, he holds nuclear terrorism to be a "genuine possibility," and concludes that a good defensive strategy can merely "tilt the odds in our favor."[7]

Accordingly, it might be useful to take a stab at estimating just how "difficult" or "not impossible" the atomic terrorists' task, in aggregate, is—that is, how far from the fringe of the "realm of possibility" it might be, how "genuine" the possibilities are, how tilted the odds actually are. After all, lots of things are "not impossible." It is "not impossible" that those legendary monkeys with typewriters could eventually output Shakespeare.[8] Or it is "not impossible"—that is, there is a "genuine possibility"—that a colliding meteor or comet could destroy the earth, that Vladimir Putin or the British could decide one morning to launch a few nuclear weapons at Ohio, that an underwater volcano could erupt to cause a civilization-ending tidal wave, or that Osama bin Laden could convert to Judaism, declare himself to be the Messiah, and fly in a gaggle of mafioso hit men from Rome to have himself publicly crucified.[9]

As suggested, most discussions of atomic terrorism deal in a rather piecemeal fashion with the subject—focusing separately on individual tasks such as procuring HEU or assembling a device or transporting it. However, as the Gilmore Commission, a special advisory panel to the president and Congress, stresses, setting off a nuclear device capable of producing mass destruction presents "Herculean challenges," requiring that a whole series of steps be accomplished: obtaining enough fissile material, designing a weapon "that will bring that mass together in a tiny fraction of a second," and figuring out some way to deliver the thing. And it emphasizes that these merely constitute "the *minimum* requirements." If each is not fully met, the result is not simply a less powerful weapon, but one that can't produce any significant nuclear yield at all or can't be delivered.[10]

Following this perspective, an approach that seems appropriate is to catalogue the barriers that must be overcome by a terrorist group in order to carry out the task of producing, transporting, and then successfully detonating an improvised nuclear device, an explosive that, as Allison acknowledges, would be "large, cumbersome, unsafe, unreliable, unpredictable, and inefficient." Table 13.1 attempts to do this, and it arrays some 20 of these— *all* of which must be surmounted by the atomic aspirant. Actually, it would be quite possible to come up with a longer list: in the interests of keeping the catalogue of hurdles down to a reasonable number, some of the entries are actually collections of tasks and could be divided into two or three or more. For example, number 5 on the list requires that heisted highly enriched uranium be neither a scam nor part of a sting nor of inadequate quality due to insider incompetence, but this hurdle could as readily be rendered as three separate ones.

In contemplating the task before them, would-be atomic terrorists effectively *must* go through an exercise that looks much like this. If and when they do so, they are likely to find the prospects daunting and accordingly uninspiring or even terminally dispiriting.

ASSESSING THE LIKELIHOOD

To gain some additional feel for how daunting the task is, one could assign probabilities to each barrier and then see how easy or difficult it would be, given those estimates, for a terrorist to fabricate and then explode an

TABLE 13.1 The atomic terrorist's task in the most likely scenario

1   An inadequately secured source of adequate quantities of highly enriched uranium (HEU) must be found.

2   The area must be entered while avoiding detection by local police and locals wary of strangers.

3   Several insiders who seem to know what they are doing must be corrupted.

4   All the insiders must remain loyal throughout the long process of planning and executing the heist, and there must be no consequential leaks.

5   The insiders must successfully seize and transfer the HEU, the transferred HEU must not be a scam or part of a sting, and it must not be of inadequate quality due to insider incompetence.

6   The HEU must be transported across the country over unfamiliar turf while its possessors are being pursued.

7   To get the HEU across one or more international borders, smugglers must be employed, and they must remain loyal despite, potentially, the temptations of massive reward money even as no consequential suspicion is generated in other smugglers using the same routes who may be interested in the same money.

8   A machine shop must be set up in an obscure area with imported, sophisticated equipment without anyone becoming suspicious.

9   A team of highly skilled scientists and technicians must be assembled, and during production all members of the team must remain absolutely loyal to the cause and develop no misgivings or severe interpersonal or financial conflicts.

10 The complete team must be transported to the machine shop, probably from several countries, without suspicion and without consequential leaks from relatives, friends, and colleagues about the missing.

11 The team must have precise technical blueprints to work from (not general sketches) and must be able to modify these appropriately for the precise purpose at hand over months (or even years) of labor, and without being able to test.

12 Nothing significant must go wrong during the long process of manufacture and assembly of the improvised nuclear device (IND).

13 There must be no inadvertent leaks from the team.

14 Local and international police, on high (even desperate) alert, must not be able to detect the project using traditional policing methods as well as the most advanced technical detection equipment.

15 No criminal gangs or other locals must sense that something out of the ordinary is going on in the machine shop with the constant coming and going of nonlocal people.

16 The IND, weighing in a ton or more, must be smuggled without detection out of the machine shop to an international border.

17 The IND must be transported to the target country either by trusting the commercial process, filled with people on the alert for cargo of this sort, or by clandestine means, which requires trusting corrupt coconspirators who may also know about any reward money.

18 A team of completely loyal and technically accomplished coconspirators must be assembled within, or infiltrated into, the target country.

19 The IND must successfully enter the target country and be received by the in-country coconspirators.

20 A detonation team must transport the IND to the target place and set it off without anybody noticing and interfering, and the untested and much-traveled IND must not prove to be a dud.

atomic device. Levi considers such an approach, but rejects it in favor of a qualitative one. "Because nuclear terrorism is so complex and so poorly understood," he suggests, a more quantitative approach "normally becomes intractable or meaningless." Although he then approvingly cites a study that takes exactly that approach, and does it himself in a different place, his wariness is certainly justified.[11]

The discussion in the previous chapter has followed the kind of qualitative approach Levi favors: synthesizing a considerable amount of material to lay out the route a terrorist group must take to acquire and detonate an atomic bomb in the scenario generally taken to be the most likely. It seems to me that this exercise by itself suggests the almost breathtaking enormity of the difficulties facing the would-be atomic terrorist. This conclusion can be reinforced by a quantitative assessment, but readers who, like Levi, are wary of that sort of approach may wish to skip past it.

Assigning and Calculating Probabilities

Assigning a probability that terrorists will be able to overcome each barrier is, of course, a tricky business, and any such exercise should be regarded as rather tentative and exploratory, or perhaps simply as illustrative—though it is done all the time in cost-benefit analysis. One might begin a quantitative approach by adopting probability estimates that purposely, and heavily, bias the case in the terrorists' favor. In my view, this would take place if it is assumed that the terrorists have a fighting chance of 50 percent of overcoming each of the 20 obstacles displayed in Table 13.1, though for many barriers, probably almost all, the odds against them are surely much worse than that. Even with that generous bias, the chances that a concerted effort would be successful comes out to be less than one in a million, specifically 1,048,576. Indeed, the odds of surmounting even seven of the 20 hurdles at that unrealistically, even absurdly, high presumptive success rate is considerably less than one in a hundred. If one assumes, somewhat more realistically, that their chances at each barrier are one in three, the cumulative odds they will be able to pull off the deed drop to one in well over three billion—specifically 3,486,784,401. What they would be at the (still entirely realistic) level of one in ten boggles the mind.

One could also make specific estimates for each of the hurdles, but the cumulative probability statistics are likely to come out pretty much the same—or even smaller. There may be a few barriers, such as numbers 13 or

16, where one might perhaps plausibly conclude that the terrorists' chances are better than 50/50. If the device were set off on a container ship in port, numbers 17 to 20 would be partially collapsed—though an ill-timed detonation would destroy only the ship itself. And perhaps the 20th barrier, the actual detonation of the device, could be assessed in a somewhat broader context: even if the bomb failed to go off, the horror induced by the fact that the terrorists got that far would still be very significant, though, obviously, it would be less than would be provoked by an actual explosion.[12] However, any such considerations are likely to be more than counterbalanced by those many barriers for which the likelihood of success is almost certainly going to be exceedingly small—for example, numbers 4, 5, 9, and 12, and, increasingly, the (obviously) crucial number 1. Moreover, in this formulation, the actual process of creating the device—a highly challenging technological task by almost all accounts—is rendered as only one (or maybe two) barriers (number 12 plus, perhaps, number 11). As alarmist Garwin notes in a book he coauthored before 9/11, "the task of actually fabricating a nuclear explosive, once the design is fixed, is not trivial. It could be done, but not on a tight schedule and not with high confidence."[13] By assigning a likelihood of success in this task of one chance in two or one chance in three, I suspect I very much err on the generous side.

In assembling the list, I sought to make the various barriers independent, or effectively independent, from each other, although they are, of course, related in the sense that they are substantially sequential. However, while the terrorists must locate an inadequately secured supply of HEU to even begin the project, this discovery will have little bearing on whether they will be successful at securing an adequate quantity of the material, even though, obviously, they can't do the second task before accomplishing the first. Similarly, assembling and supplying an adequately equipped machine shop is effectively an independent task from the job of recruiting a team of scientists and technicians to work within it. Moreover, members of this group must display two qualities that, although combined in hurdle 9, are essentially independent of each other: they must be *both* technically skilled *and* absolutely loyal to the project.

Nonetheless the cumulative probability estimate might be attenuated by the fact that there are at least a few synergies between the barriers— although it could be argued that they are intellectually independent, they may not, strictly speaking, be statistically so. For example, in assembling its bomb-making team, a terrorist group might be inclined to let the quality of absolute loyalty trump the one of technical competence. This would increase the chances that the bomb-making enterprise would go undetected, while at the same time decreasing the likelihood that it would be successful. However, given the monumentality of the odds confronting the would-be atomic terrorist, adjustments for such issues are scarcely likely to alter the basic conclusion. That is, if one drastically slashed the one in 3.5 billion estimate a thousandfold, the odds of success would still be one in 3.5 million.

Moreover, all this focuses on the effort to deliver a single bomb. If the requirement were to deliver several, the odds become, of course, even more prohibitive.

Getting away from astronomical numbers for a minute, Levi points out that even if there are only ten barriers and even if there were a wildly favorable 80 percent chance of overcoming each hurdle, the chance of final success, following the approach used here, would only be 10 percent. Faced even with such highly favorable odds at each step, notes Levi, the would-be atomic terrorist might well decide "that a nuclear plot is too much of a stretch to seriously try." Similarly, Jenkins calculates that even if there are only *three* barriers and each carried a 50/50 chance of success, the likelihood of accomplishing the full mission would only be 12.5 percent.[14] Odds like that are not necessarily prohibitive, of course, but they are likely to be mind-arrestingly small if one is betting just about everything on a successful outcome.

Multiple Attempts

The odds considered so far are for a single attempt by a single group, and there could be multiple attempts by multiple groups, of course. Although Allison considers al-Qaeda to be "the most probable perpetrator" on the nuclear front, he is also concerned about the potential atomic exploits of other organizations such as Indonesia's Jemaah Islamiyah, Chechen gangsters, Lebanon's Hezbollah, and various doomsday cults.[15]

However, few, if any, groups appear to have any interest whatever in striking the United States except for al-Qaeda, an issue to be discussed more fully in the next chapter. But even setting that consideration aside, the odds would remain long even with multiple concerted attempts.[16] If there were a hundred such efforts over a period of time, the chance at least one of these would be successful comes in at less than one in over 10,000 at the one chance in two level. At the far more realistic level of one chance in three, it would be about one in nearly 35 million. If there were 1,000 dedicated attempts, presumably over several decades, the chance of success would be worse than one in a thousand at the 50/50 level and one in nearly 3.5 million at the one in three level.[17] Of course, attempts in the hundreds are scarcely realistic, though one might be able to envision a dozen or so.

Additionally, if there were a large number of concerted efforts, policing and protecting would presumably become easier because the aspirants would be exposing themselves repeatedly and would likely be stepping all over each other in their quest to access the right stuff. Furthermore, each foiled attempt would likely expose flaws in the defense system, holes the defenders would then plug, making subsequent efforts that much more difficult. For example, when the would-be peddler of a tiny amount of purloined highly enriched uranium was apprehended in 2006, efforts were made to trace its place of origin using nuclear forensics.[18]

Also, the difficulties for the atomic terrorists are likely to *increase* over time because of much enhanced protective and policing efforts by self-interested governments. Already, for example, by all accounts Russian nuclear materials are much more adequately secured than they were 10 or 15 years ago.[19]

Other Acquisition Scenarios

These odds are for the most plausible scenario by means of which a terrorist group might gain a bomb: constructing one from HEU obtained through illicit means. As noted in the previous chapter, there are other routes to a bomb: stealing a fully constructed one or being given one as a gift by a nuclear state. However, as also noted there, those routes are generally conceded, even by most of the most alarmed, to be considerably *less* likely to result in a terrorist success than the one outlined in Table 13.1.

Assistance by a state would shorten the terrorist group's list of hurdles considerably, of course, but they would be replaced by the big one: the exceedingly low likelihood that a nuclear state would trust it with one of its precious bombs. Moreover, the gift bomb would probably emit more radioactivity and therefore be far easier to detect than the modest, comparatively simple uranium IND. In addition, the science of nuclear forensics will inevitably advance, continually increasing the likelihood that the source of a terrorist bomb can be detected and therefore decreasing the likelihood of any sort of voluntary state complicity.

The theft of a finished bomb would also shorten the list of hurdles. However, it would generate new ones as well, such as the necessity to defeat locks and the difficulty of even beginning to be able to find a purloinable nuclear weapon in an age in which these weapons are increasingly under lock and key and in which insiders who could productively help with the theft are small in number and ever more likely to be found out after the deed was accomplished.

COMPARISONS

Improbable events, even highly improbable ones, do sometimes take place in the world, of course. But although any event that is improbable is, at the same time and by definition, possible, it is obviously a fundamental fallacy to conclude that, because improbable events do occasionally occur, an improbable event should somehow be taken to be likely. Peter Zimmerman and Jeffrey Lewis pointedly conclude an article on atomic terrorism by declaring, "just because a nuclear terrorist attack hasn't happened shouldn't give us the false comfort of thinking it won't."[20] However, just because something terrible is possible shouldn't send us into hysterics thinking it will surely come about, either. For every one in a million chance that does actually come off, there are going to be 999,999 equally improbable (or probable) events that don't. But people tend to focus on the long shot that happens to pay off, not on the overwhelming majority that don't.

Huge numbers of people buy public lottery tickets despite the fact that the odds can easily be worse than a million to one against them, and a (very) few of these gamblers do, of course, cash in. However, that a few people do eventually win the lottery should not be allowed to overshadow the fact that the vast majority do not—though of course the triumphs of the rare, improbable winner make for much more arresting newspaper copy than do the travails of the many (and therefore uninteresting) losers.

It is also instructive to contrast the costs of failure in entering a lottery with those involved in a terrorist's effort to acquire and set off an atomic bomb. A lottery loser forfeits only a limited amount of money in each million-to-one fling, while losers in the atomic terrorism enterprise could easily end up sacrificing not only all their financial resources in a single concerted attempt, but their lives as well. If the price of a lottery ticket at those odds were not only one's life savings but one's life as well, there would be a notable absence of buyers.

Another comparison might be made with the 9/11 events. The difficulties confronting the hijackers were considerable, and the conspirators certainly were extremely lucky. But there has never been a terrorist attack that has been remotely as destructive and, despite innumerable predictions that 9/11 was a harbinger, it has thus far remained an aberration.[21]

Moreover, whatever the hijackers' difficulties, they were nothing like those confronting the would-be atomic terrorist. Because of the extraordinary results of the 9/11 attack, notes counterterrorism analyst Bernard Finel, "we implicitly assume the plot must have had a high level of technical sophistication." However, he continues, "it simply didn't." Required were "nineteen thugs with stabbing implements," four of whom possessed "the sort of rudimentary flight training that could be acquired by playing a computer game." The conspiracy also required "simple strategic planning" and "a small amount of money." The 9/11 conspirators did maintain extensive secrecy and group loyalty on their daring and risky endeavor, and their planning does seem to have been meticulous. But the size of the conspiracy was very small, they never had to trust strangers or criminals, technical requirements were minimal, obtaining flight training only took the money to pay for it, the weapons they used could legally be brought on planes, and, most importantly, they were exploiting an environment in which the policy was to cooperate with hijackers rather than fight and risk the entire plane. Indeed, only a few months earlier, three Muslim terrorists, in this case Chechens, had commandeered a Russian airliner, demanding that it be flown to Saudi Arabia at which point they were overcome by local security forces with almost no loss of life. To physicist Richard Muller, in fact, "the genius of the operation was its low risk."[22] Even in that enormously advantageous policy environment, the 9/11 hijackers failed to accomplish their mission with the last of the four planes.

In addition, the personnel requirements are far higher in the atomic case. The 9/11 plot necessitated the recruitment and the training (minimal, except for the pilots) of a single group of men who were absolutely loyal to the cause. However, aside from a general physical ability and a capacity to carry out orders, they needed little in the way of additional qualities. In the case of the terrorist bomb, the conspiracy—or, actually, the sequential sets of conspiracies—mandate the enlistment of a much larger number of people, and most of these must not only be absolutely loyal, but also extremely skilled at an elaborate series of technical, organizational, and conspiratorial tasks: the 9/11 conspirators could put loyalty ahead of competence, while an atomic terrorism conspiracy would likely need to reverse those priorities. Moreover, the 9/11 plotters did not have to rely on criminals, while the steadfast cooperation of such people would be central to an atomic conspiracy. And carrying out the 9/11 operation itself required a few hours of concentrated work and dedication, not the months or even years that would be required of atomic terrorists.

The Japanese, too, were extremely lucky in their carefully planned attack on Pearl Harbor, and, like the 9/11 hijackers, they (obviously) had the technical ability to pull it off. However, their luck rested not on the lengthy sequence of technical and conspiratorial efforts that loom for the would-be atomic terrorist, but rather on a single convenient circumstance: the Americans were, for fairly good reasons, expecting any attack to take place elsewhere, a rather familiar, even predictable, situation in warfare.[23]

Interestingly (and perhaps instructively), as in the case of 9/11 (at least so far), Japanese skill and luck at Pearl Harbor proved to be anything but a harbinger. At the subsequent battle of Midway, notes historian H. P. Willmott, the Japanese commander who had been so successful at Pearl Harbor "insisted upon a tactical deployment that incorporated every possible risk and weakness and left his forces inferior to the enemy at the point of contact, despite their having what should have been an irresistible numerical and qualitative superiority." As for the Japanese army, Willmott observes, "One cannot ignore the simple fact that not a single operation planned after the start of the war met with success."[24]

POLICY: REDUCING THE LIKELIHOOD

The purpose of this discussion has not been to argue that policies designed to inconvenience the atomic terrorist are necessarily unneeded or unwise. Rather, in contrast with the many who insist that atomic terrorism under current conditions is rather—indeed, *exceedingly*—likely to come about, I have contended that it is hugely unlikely. That is, in part because of the current policy environment but also because of a wealth of other technical and organizational difficulties inherent in the deed, the atomic terrorists' task under present conditions is already monumental, and their success is most improbable.

Efforts to further enhance this monumentality, if cost-effective and accompanied with tolerable side effects, are generally desirable—although to me they scarcely seem as urgent as their proponents repeatedly proclaim. Moreover, sometimes the efforts can impose excessive economic costs by instituting unnecessary or overwrought growth-dampening security measures and policies.

Some policy projects do seem to be worth the effort. For example, since a terrorist group cannot manufacture fissile material itself, it makes sense to try to secure existing stocks around the world. Most of those stocks, as it happens, are in Russia, and for over a decade a considerable number of people, including Allison and his colleagues, have been advocating for strenuous efforts to get the stuff controlled and locked up. As part of this process, the Nunn-Lugar legislation has provided funds and impetus for this generally desirable and rather inexpensive project.[25] And indeed, as noted earlier and in the previous chapter, there is substantial consensus that Russian nuclear materials are much more adequately secured than they were 10 or 15 years ago. The process, thus, seems to be proceeding well, albeit at a pace too slow for some.

In my view, establishing a reliable inventory of fissile material may be almost as important as securing it. If authorities are able to detect immediately when some goes missing, international policing efforts would be triggered. These are likely to considerably hamper the terrorists' prospects for success in their necessarily complex and wide-ranging conspiracy, not only by setting investigators into action but also by alerting the public worldwide (including the criminal element) to what has happened and by establishing and publicizing generous rewards for productive tips.

It would also be sensible to devote funds for further development of the science of nuclear forensics to identify the source of the fissile material in a bomb or device. Indeed, this seems to be a no-brainer. An inexpensive project, it may also have desirable scientific spin-offs.

I suspect nuclear sting operations are rather inexpensive, and it probably makes sense to continue these to deter sellers and to keep a viable black market from emerging. However, sting efforts have thus far come up with little: even if all of the sellers rolled up by the police had been successful in peddling their illicit product to a single dedicated terrorist group, the group would not have been able to accumulate even enough for a single bomb. Therefore it is not completely clear that sting operations are all that necessary or useful.

Some of those who consider a terrorist atomic explosion to be a likely prospect have logically come to stress the need to plan for such an eventuality. Since I find that likelihood to be far lower, I certainly do not see this as an urgent necessity. Inexpensive exercises to game a response to a terrorist bomb may generate some useful information and may be worthwhile, and protection measures that might in addition increase a certain area's ability to survive more probable disasters like earthquake or hurricane might become cost-effective.[26]

The issue is complicated, however, by the fact that it is very difficult to predict where a bomb might be set off. During the cold war, one could at least begin to come up with a list of targets—particularly military ones—that might be expected to appeal to a Soviet war planner (as the United States had a list of choice targets in the Soviet Union). However, if the terrorists' goal is simply to kill substantial numbers of people, there is virtually an infinite number of places where this can be effectively accomplished. And if the terrorists' goal is primarily to terrorize rather than to kill, an atomic explosion in a cornfield in the remotest part of Kansas is likely to do the trick. Moreover, any process that reduces the chance that a terrorist IND could be successfully set off in, say, Times Square necessarily (if microscopically) increases the chance that the Upper East Side or downtown Boston or suburban Chicago will be struck.[27]

An area that needs much more attention concerns education about the effects of radiation. This concern is relevant not only to an atomic explosion, particularly a groundburst one, but also to the effects of a somewhat more likely "dirty bomb" explosion and of accidental radiation releases like ones that occurred in Brazil in 1987 from an abandoned medical instrument and in the Soviet Union in 1986 from a nuclear reactor meltdown. There are no immediate dangers from even fairly substantial increases in radiation, but people are simply not aware of that, and radiation fears may induce overly evasive behavior in the immediate and short term, and this should very much be a primary concern. In fact, if radiation levels are raised only somewhat above normal backgrounds levels in a small area by a dirty bomb, accident, or nuclear fallout, a common recommendation from nuclear scientists and engineers is that those exposed should calmly walk away. Those in charge have failed to advance this information much—or even, perhaps, at all. Effectively, therefore, they encourage panic, and the danger is, as one nuclear engineer puts it, "if you keep telling them you expect them to panic, they will oblige you. And that's what we're doing." Risk analyst Baruch Fischoff, noting how rare real panic actually is, puts the issue bluntly: "while people are amazing under pressure, it cannot help to have predictions of panic drummed into them by supposed experts." Other specialists urge that the public should be "psychologically immunized" against radiation fears through an extensive public education campaign stressing that radiation usually does not pose immediate threats to life.[28]

Fear and anxiety about radiation can also have negative health consequences in the long term, and if the anxieties are unjustified, that should be of concern. Extensive studies that have been conducted of the Soviet nuclear disaster of 1986 found that the largest health effect came not from the accident itself but from the negative and often life-expectancy-reducing impact on the mental health of people traumatized by relocation and by lingering, and greatly exaggerated, fears that they would soon die of cancer. In the end, lifestyle afflictions like alcoholism, drug abuse, chronic anxiety, and fatalism have posed a much greater threat to health, and essentially have killed far more people, than exposure to radiation.[29] The fact that public officials and the media have done so little to explain the problem and to publicize what one should do under conditions of enhanced radiation is, in my view, something of a scandal.

A systematic—if politically dicey—reexamination of the almost absurdly conservative standards for acceptable radiation levels is also long overdue. The ALARA principle is currently applied: it demands that the radiation levels be As Low As Reasonably Achievable. Working chiefly from concerns about radiation leakage from reactors, which are characteristically situated in remote areas, regulators demand that people evacuate the area until radiation levels are cleaned down to acceptable levels even though, as noted in chapter 1, the heightened levels may be lower than one would experience by moving from Biloxi to many places in Colorado. The procedure could also have the damaging effect of unnecessarily increasing fears about radiation. In the context of enhanced radiation levels in a city from a dirty bomb attack or fallout, adhering to severely conservative cleanup standards could become spectacularly expensive—unnecessarily costing billions of dollars—and potentially result in the forcible evacuation of millions of people, with no real gain to public safety or health.[30]

There are some indications that the Department of Homeland Security is beginning to reevaluate cleanup standards, which currently require radiation to be reduced to 15 percent of the amount that is emitted by building materials in the United States Capitol and therefore routinely absorbed by people working there.[31] However, there seems to have been rather little progress.

At any rate, if trusted governmental officials can truthfully say after a limited radiation release has been detected that the "contamination" does not reach levels considered unsafe, undesirable negative psychological and economic reactions might be beneficially reduced and might far outweigh any risks involved. The risk communication literature, however, suggests that this would be a difficult sell—perhaps even a counterproductive one.[32] And given the tendency of bureaucrats to cover their bases against any potential calamity, it is unlikely to be seriously undertaken.

One final policy suggestion. It would be exceedingly desirable if opportunistic politicians, bureaucrats, and security entrepreneurs would cease evoking the atomic terrorist bogeyman to justify expenditures that have nothing to do with the nuclear issue. But a change like that is, surely, much too much to hope for.

ACCEPTABLE RISK

As Allison appropriately points out, it is important to consider not only the likelihood that an event will take place but also its consequences. Therefore, one must be concerned about catastrophic events even if their likelihood is small.[33]

At some point, however, probabilities, become so low that, even for catastrophic events, it begins to make sense to ignore, or at least to back-burner, them: the risk becomes "acceptable." Consider the odds that a wheel on a speeding automobile will suddenly shear off. That horror is surely "not impossible," yet legions of motorists effectively find it so improbable that they are routinely willing to risk their lives that it will not happen—it is, in short, an acceptable risk.

The British could at any time attack the United States with their submarine-launched missiles and kill millions of Americans—far more than even the most monumentally gifted and lucky terrorist group. Yet the risk that this potential (and fully possible) calamity might take place evokes little concern; essentially, it is "accepted." Meanwhile, Russia, with whom the United States enjoys a rather strained relationship, could at any time do vastly more damage with its nuclear weapons, a fully imaginable calamity that goes substantially ignored.

In constructing what he calls "a case for fear," Cass Sunstein notes that if there is a yearly probability of one in 100,000 that terrorists could launch a nuclear or massive biological attack, the risk would cumulate to one in 10,000 over 10 years and to one in 5,000 over 20 years. These odds, he suggests, are "not the most comforting."[34] Comfort, of course, lies in the viscera of those to be comforted, and, as he suggests, many would probably have difficulty settling down with odds like that. But there must be *some* point at which the concerns even of these people would ease. Just perhaps it is at some of the levels suggested here: one in a million or one in three billion per attempt.

The same consideration holds for Vice President Dick Cheney's "one percent doctrine." A top CIA analyst late in 2001 told him that al-Qaeda probably did not have a nuclear weapon, but that he couldn't "assure you that they don't." To this, Cheney replied, "If there's a one percent chance that they do, you have to pursue it as if it were true."[35] Cheney's observation is a somewhat confused, but effective, way of saying that one should take low probability events that could have an exceedingly high impact very seriously indeed. And a one percent chance of a terrorist atomic attack would clearly fit into that category. It's just that the chances, while perhaps not zero, do not seem to be anywhere remotely near one percent. It's not that they are necessarily one in 3.5 billion, but they aren't anything like one in ten, one in a hundred, or one in a thousand. Perhaps, in fact, they are comparable to, or even lower than, those for a thermonuclear attack from Russia.

14

Progress and Interest

The degree to which al-Qaeda has pursued, or even has much interest in, a nuclear weapons program may have been exaggerated—often by the same people who so alarmingly warned us about Saddam Hussein's nonexistent WMD development.

Al-Qaeda and its potential atomic capacity are the central concerns here because it "is the only Islamic terrorist organization that targets the U.S. homeland," as stressed by Glenn Carle, 23-year veteran of the Central Intelligence Agency, where he was deputy national intelligence officer for transnational threats.[1] Somewhat more broadly, Middle East specialist Fawaz Gerges points out that, over time, mainstream Islamists—the vast majority within the Islamist political movement—have given up on the use of force. That is, the jihadis who are still willing to apply violence constitute a tiny minority. But he also notes that the vast majority even of this small group primarily focuses on various "infidel" Muslim regimes (as well as on Israel) and consider those among them who carry out violence against the "far enemy"—mainly Europe and the United States—to be irresponsible and reckless adventurers who endanger the survival of the whole movement.[2] Al-Qaeda, then, is a fringe group of a fringe group.

Some other terrorist organization or a millennial one, either within the country or without, could in the future generate designs to harm the United States directly. But for now, certainly, al-Qaeda stands essentially alone.

There is some occasional evidence to indicate that the group might have some interest in atomic weapons, but this is limited and often ambiguous. The same can said about evidence that it has actively sought to achieve an atomic capacity. This chapter evaluates that evidence.

BIN LADEN'S REPORTED "HIROSHIMA" REMARK AND THE URANIUM SCAM

The 9/11 Commission cites two specific indications that al-Qaeda is seeking nuclear weapons: reports from 1998 "that Bin Ladin's associates thought their leader was intent on carrying out a 'Hiroshima'" and evidence that "al Qaeda has tried to acquire or make nuclear weapons for at least ten years."[3]

Information about the "Hiroshima" remark obviously comes from thirdhand reports speculating about Osama bin Laden's mind-set. Moreover, the Commission elsewhere notes that the reports suggest he was hoping to inflict "at least 10,000 casualties."[4] Many times that many casualties were suffered at Hiroshima, and this could suggest that if bin Laden did utter the word, he was using it as many others have, as a synonym for a "major disaster," not necessarily an atomic one. In many respects, of course, the devastation of 9/11 could be envisioned as a sort of "Hiroshima."

The only evidence the Commission supplies to support its conclusion that al-Qaeda had been working on nuclear weapons for at least ten years comes from an episode that is supposed to have taken place around 1993 in Sudan, when bin Laden's

> business aides received word that a Sudanese military officer who had been a member of the previous government cabinet was offering to sell weapons-grade uranium. After a number of contacts were made through intermediaries, the officer set the price at $1.5 million, which did not deter Bin Ladin. Al Qaeda representatives asked to inspect the uranium and were shown a cylinder about 3 feet long, and one thought he could pronounce it genuine. Al Qaeda apparently purchased the cylinder, then discovered it to be bogus. But while the effort failed, it shows what Bin Ladin and his associates hoped to do. One of the al Qaeda representatives explained his mission: "it's easy to kill more people with uranium."[5]

Information about this supposed venture apparently comes entirely from Jamal al-Fadl, who defected from al-Qaeda in 1996 after he had been caught stealing $110,000 from the organization. As Lawrence Wright relates in his prize-winning *The Looming Tower*, Fadl "tried to sell his story to various intelligence agencies in the Middle East, including the Israelis," but only found a buyer "when he walked into the American Embassy in Eritrea." Although Fadl clearly lied repeatedly in early interviews, some CIA investigators came to trust him, and he spun out his tale about the bogus uranium. He became a government witness, and by 2001 the government had spent nearly $1 million on him. One of his FBI debriefers says, "He's a lovable rogue. He's fixated on money…He likes to please. Most people do."[6]

In the text of his book Wright narrates the uranium story in much the same way as the 9/11 Commission.[7] However, Wright's discussion of bin Laden's finances suggests that it might well have been difficult for him to lay his hands on anything like $1.5 million at the time—he was living on a limited monthly stipend from a business in Saudi Arabia even while investing and disbursing his money foolishly, and by the end of 1994 claimed he had "lost all my money."[8]

In addition, Wright relays the testimony of the man who allegedly actually purchased the substance for bin Laden, as well as that of a Sudanese intelligence agent. Both assert that, although there were various other scams going around at the time that may have served as grist for Fadl, the uranium episode never happened. Perhaps because an alarming tale in the hand is worth considerably more that two debunkings in the bush, Wright buries the conflicting testimony in an endnote.[9]

Fadl's reliability is also called into question by another of his revelations: he was a key (perhaps the only) inspiration for the CIA's notion that bin Laden was developing chemical weapons in Sudan. This supposition, or extrapolation, eventually led in 1998 to the American bombing of a Sudanese pharmaceutical plant erroneously suspected of producing such a product. After the fall of al-Qaeda in Afghanistan in 2001, investigators found evidence that the terrorist group had been experimenting with chemical weapons and may have produced small quantities of World War I–era agents. This hardly suggests, however, that it had been churning out quantities of chemical weapons for the better part of a decade in a facility in distant Sudan. Indeed, concludes weapons expert Milton Leitenberg, the evidence in Afghanistan provides "little confidence in the competence of the al-Qaida group to carry out either chemical or biological agent production." In the meantime, the loss of the vital medications the plant was actually making in that impoverished country—fully half of Sudan's pharmaceuticals were produced at the destroyed plant—may have led to a very considerable number of Sudanese deaths over time.[10]

It also seems possible that it was Fadl who started the CIA thinking that al-Qaeda was out to get nuclear weapons. According to Michael Scheuer, who created the agency's bin Laden unit in 1996—which was the year of Fadl's defection—"We had found that he [bin Laden] and al-Qaeda were involved in an extraordinarily sophisticated, professional effort to acquire weapons of mass destruction. In this case, nuclear material. So by the end of 1996 it was clear that this was an organization unlike any other one we had ever seen."[11]

It's possible, of course, that Fadl, a "lovable rogue" who "likes to please," is telling the truth, or at least what he thinks (or by now has come to think) is the truth. But his allegations, now endlessly repeated, have gone from a colorful and reasonably credible story relayed by an admitted embezzler on the lam to an unquestioned and fully accepted fact. "We know," it is repeatedly declared, that bin Laden tried to purchase weapons-grade uranium in Sudan in the early 1990s. Qualifications, even modest ones, concerning the veracity of the evidence behind that declaration have vanished in the retelling.

THE CHECHEN CONNECTION

By the late 1990s, there was a sort of competition for leadership within the violent radical Islamist movement between bin Laden's Afghanistan-based al-Qaeda and a similar group in Chechnya run by another Saudi, Ibn al-Khattab. Information about this episode comes from two sources: diaries written by a leading al-Qaeda ideologue published in Arabic in 2005, and letters exchanged by courier between bin Laden and Khattab over several months in 1999 that were found on an al-Qaeda computer captured in Afghanistan in 2001.

There was no consequential meeting of minds. Khattab deemed the Russians to be the chief enemy of Muslims worldwide and wanted al-Qaeda to join his armed conflict against them, and his military venture into the neighboring Russian republic of Dagestan was substantially responsible for triggering the second Chechen war in late 1999, resulting eventually in his death in 2002. For his part, bin Laden wanted Khattab to accept his leadership and to focus a joint effort on the United States, the country he considered to be the real enemy.

As part of this, there were incidental discussions of nuclear weapons, more likely dirty bombs than atomic explosives. Khattab had the idea that he should try to obtain some by stealth from Russia to use as a deterrent. Bin Laden seems to have encouraged that idea and suggested that Khattab bring the weapons with him when he came to join the (correct) fray in Afghanistan.

That seems to have been the extent of it. However, the diaries suggest that there were radical elements in bin Laden's entourage who were interested in pursuing atomic weapons or other weapons of mass destruction. The diaries report the disappointment of the author that bin Laden did not have much interest in this, and that he essentially sabotaged the idea by refusing to fund a WMD project, or even to initiate planning for it. After the fall of Chechnya's capital city, the diaries report, a delegation of Chechen fighters visited Afghanistan seeking assistance and inquiring whether there were any WMD available there that they could then smuggle back to use against the Russians.[12]

CONVERSATIONS WITH PAKISTANI SCIENTISTS

As a key indication of al-Qaeda's desire to obtain atomic weapons, Graham Allison and many others have focused on a set of conversations in Afghanistan in August 2001 that two Pakistani nuclear scientists, Sultan Bashiruddin Mahmood and Abdul Majid, who had been working on relief and reconstruction programs in the country, reportedly had with Osama bin Laden, Ayman Zawahiri, and two other al-Qaeda officials. A key source for information about these meetings is a front-page *Washington Post* article written by Kamran Khan and Molly Moore and published in late 2001.[13] It is based on information supplied by Pakistani intelligence officers, and the reporters were able neither to interview the scientists, who had been interrogated for two months by that time, nor to determine (as the article puts it delicately) "the nature of the investigatory techniques being used."

The article says the conversations took place over two or three days and concerned chemical, biological, and nuclear weapons. Graham Allison contends that the talks were "especially about" nuclear weapons and that bin Laden was "particularly interested in nuclear weapons," but that emphasis does not appear in the *Post* article, the source he specifies. To further darken the issue, Allison says, quoting from another newspaper article, "Pakistani military authorities found it 'inconceivable that a nuclear scientist would travel to Afghanistan without getting clearance from Pakistani officials,' because Pakistan 'maintains a strict watch on many of its nuclear scientists, using a special arm of the Army's general headquarters to monitor them even after retirement.'" He also discloses that "American operatives have sought to intercept further 'vacations' in Afghanistan by Pakistani nuclear physicists and engineers."[14] But the Khan-Moore article makes it completely clear that Mahmood and Majid *did* have permission from the Pakistani government to travel to Afghanistan (they were allowed three trips in 2001), and it nowhere indicates that the trip was in any sense considered a "vacation."

At any rate, the Pakistani intelligence officers interviewed for the article characterize the discussions as "academic," and they also maintain that to be the descriptor the scientists "insisted" on using. The officers do report, however, that the scientists "described bin Laden as intensely interested in nuclear, chemical and biological weapons."[15]

Also important: the scientists reportedly said that "bin Laden indicated he had obtained, or had access to, some type of radiological material that he said had been acquired for him by the radical Islamic Movement of Uzbekistan" and that he "asked them how the material could be made into a weapon or something usable." At the time, there were many rumors and reports in the area about radioactive materials being purveyed by entrepreneurs hailing from the former Soviet Union. Many, and perhaps all, of these were scams or leftover material from X-ray machines of highly questionable value, and it is possible bin Laden's supply, if any, came from that source. At any rate, the scientists reportedly told him "it would not be possible to manufacture a weapon with the material he might have." Although Mahmood is not allowed to speak to reporters, his son is. According to him, "My father never went along." Bin Laden "asked him about how to make a bomb and things like that. But my father wouldn't help him. He told him, 'It's not so easy, you can't just build a bomb, you can't just do it with a few thousand rupees. You need a big institution. You should forget it.'"[16]

Mahmood had been vocally sympathetic to militant Islamic groups and had advocated sending weapons-grade plutonium and uranium to other

Muslim states (not terrorist groups), positions that resulted in his being pressured to resign from office in 1999, two years before the conversations with al-Qaeda took place. He is also something of a mystic; he has recommended that spirits be tapped as a free source of energy and is convinced that sunspots influence major human events, predicting in 1998 that 2002 would be a year of upheaval and that "millions, by 2002, may die through mass destruction weapons, hunger, disease, street violence, terrorist attacks, and suicide." Mahmood's talents as an economist are equally fanciful: it is his opinion that Afghanistan would have become a strong industrial country within 10 years had the United States not invaded in 2001. According to CIA Director George Tenet, "Mahmood was thought of as something of a madman by many of his former colleagues in the Pakistan nuclear establishment."[17]

It is possible to believe that the two scientists "provided detailed responses to bin Laden's technical questions about the manufacture of nuclear, biological and chemical weapons," as another *Washington Post* report puts it.[18] But the questions do not seem to be very sophisticated, and as the scientists themselves have reportedly insisted, it seems that the discussion was wide-ranging and academic (even rather basic) and that they provided no material or specific plans.

Moreover, as the Pakistani officials stressed to Khan and Moore, Mahmood had been involved with uranium enrichment and plutonium production but not bomb building. Therefore he "had neither the knowledge nor the experience to assist in the construction of any type of nuclear weapon," nor, it seems, were the scientists experts in chemical or biological weapons. Therefore, they likely were incapable of providing truly helpful information, because their expertise was not in bomb design, which might be useful to terrorists, but rather in the processing of fissile material, which is almost certainly beyond the capacities of a nonstate group, as discussed in chapter 12. As a Pakistani nuclear scientist working at Princeton put it, Mahmood "may not actually have much more knowledge than you would get from an undergraduate degree in nuclear physics. My suspicion is if you gave him a bucket full of plutonium he wouldn't know what to do with it, because he never worked with nuclear weapons, as far as we know." Nonetheless, reports Allison, U.S. intelligence agencies have convinced themselves that the two errant Pakistani scientists provided al-Qaeda with a "blueprint" for constructing nuclear weapons.[19]

EVALUATING THE EVIDENCE IN AFGHANISTAN

Khalid Sheikh Mohammed, the apparent mastermind behind the 9/11 attacks, reportedly says that al-Qaeda's atom bomb efforts never went beyond searching the Internet. After the fall of the Taliban in 2001, technical experts from the CIA and the Department of Energy examined documents and other information uncovered by intelligence agencies and the media in Afghanistan and came up with conclusions generally supportive of that assertion. According to an official American report, the experts "judged that there remained no credible information that al-Qa'ida had obtained fissile material or acquired a nuclear weapon." Moreover, they found no evidence of "any radioactive material suitable for weapons." They did uncover, however, a "nuclear-related" document discussing "openly available concepts about the nuclear fuel cycle and some weapons-related issues."[20]

Physicist and weapons expert David Albright has also examined this evidence. He contends in one interview that "there is no indication that al Qaeda's nuclear work has gone beyond theory," but in a report he more provocatively concludes that "if al Qaeda had remained in Afghanistan, it would have likely acquired nuclear weapons eventually" and that "al Qaeda was intensifying its long-term goal to acquire nuclear weapons and would have likely succeeded if it had remained powerful in Afghanistan for several more years."[21]

Albright's findings in the report include the following:

1. Only a relatively small portion of the records found were about nuclear weapons or WMD, though perhaps some documents were destroyed or taken along on the flight.

2. A handwritten 25-page document entitled "Superbomb" was found. It has some relatively sophisticated sections, while others are remarkably inaccurate or naive. It is not a cookbook for making nuclear weapons, as many critical steps are missing, and it includes designs for atomic bombs that are not credible. It looks like the type used by lecturers at Arab universities.[22]

3. Student notebooks suggesting that people learning how to make conventional explosives were also given a brief primer at the end of the sessions about nuclear weapons.

4. There was no evidence al-Qaeda had acquired nuclear weapons or had collected a cadre of nuclear scientists or engineers.

Albright concludes that, although their efforts in making nuclear weapons were far less sophisticated than known state programs, their determination to get nuclear weapons is "astounding." However, if al-Qaeda had any visions at all about obtaining an atomic bomb or device, these seem to have been at most a distant glint based on some very limited and preliminary probes. That they may have had dreams at all is perhaps "astounding," given the rudimentary state of the group's science capacities, its limited resources, and its severe isolation.

Albright argues that the group "was putting together a serious program to make nuclear weapons," but it is difficult to see how one can come to that conclusion from the evidence he supplies. He seems to believe that they were creating something of a state within a state, and that the Taliban government could provide cover while they, unnoticed, put together over time (it took Pakistan 27 years) the infrastructure necessary to build a bomb (including the production of fissile material) while importing the scientists, technicians, and material necessary to carry out the task.

As CIA adviser and arms inspector Charles Duelfer has stressed, the development of nuclear weapons in such a manner requires thousands of knowledgeable scientists and large physical facilities. Pakistan would seem to have been the logical, and perhaps only possible, supplier, and Albright suggests that, although "al Qaeda's nuclear program seems to have been relatively primitive," Pakistani scientists like Mahmood "would probably have provided extensive and ongoing assistance" if the 9/11 attacks had not led to cutting off contacts between Pakistani scientists and al-Qaeda (that is, the subsequent invasion of Afghanistan was not required for this).[23]

However, as noted earlier, the Pakistanis were keeping careful watch on their materials and on their scientists (including retirees) even before 9/11. Specifically, Mahmood had been sacked merely for suggesting aiding the nuclear programs of other Muslim states (not terrorists), and they had allowed him only three visits to Afghanistan in all of 2001. This process was much intensified after Pakistan's A. Q. Khan network—which had informally supplied nuclear information to several states (but not to the Taliban or to any substate groups)—was exposed in 2004. Moreover, as Tom Fingar, assistant secretary of state for intelligence and research, rather bluntly acknowledged in 2005, "We have seen no persuasive evidence that al-Qaida has obtained fissile material or ever has had a serious and sustained program to do so." And analyst Anne Stenersen notes that evidence from a recovered al-Qaeda computer indicates that the group had earmarked some

$2000–$4000 for WMD research at the time, all of it apparently for (very crude) chemical work with some potentially for biological weapons. By contrast, she points out that the millennial terrorist group Aum Shinrikyo appears to have invested $30 million in its sarin gas manufacturing program alone.[24]

Be all that as it may, Albright concludes that any al-Qaeda atomic efforts were "seriously disrupted"—indeed, "nipped in the bud"—by the invasion of Afghanistan in 2001. Whatever his evaluation of the situation before the event, Albright concludes that after the invasion "the overall chance of al Qaeda detonating a nuclear explosive appears on reflection to be low."[25]

RUMORS OF THE PURCHASE OF LOOSE NUKES

Rumors and reports that al-Qaeda has managed to purchase an atomic bomb, or several, have been around now for over a decade, beginning around 1998. In assessing these, it would be useful to keep in mind Wright's conclusion that bin Laden's funds were very limited when he fled from Sudan to Afghanistan in 1996—he may only have had some $50,000 to his name.[26]

Louise Richardson catalogues a number of the loose-nuke stories. They include one based on a leaked Israeli intelligence report of 1998 stating that bin Laden had paid more than two million British pounds to a middleman in Kazakhstan for a "suitcase" bomb. Another arises from information supplied by Russian intelligence services in 1998 that bin Laden had given a group of Chechens $30 million in cash and two tons of opium in exchange for 20 nuclear warheads. A third tells of the arrest in Germany in September 1998 of an alleged aide of bin Laden, Mamdouh Mahmud Salim, for trying to obtain highly enriched uranium. There are also various reports of expensive failed efforts by bin Laden to acquire enriched uranium in Eastern Europe, and allegations in 2000 from Arab security sources that a shipment of about 20 nuclear warheads originating from Kazakhstan, Turkmenistan, Russia, and Ukraine had been intercepted en route to bin Laden. One 2001 report claimed that al-Qaeda had acquired a Russian-made suitcase nuclear bomb from Central Asian sources that had a serial number of 9999 and could be set off by mobile phone. And there was the 2004 report in an Egyptian newspaper that al-Qaeda had bought tactical nuclear weapons from Ukraine in 1998 and was holding them in storage.[27]

Brian Jenkins has also sifted through these reports, adding a few more: 2001 warnings from a Pakistani newspaper that al-Qaeda might already have spirited several bombs into the United States; assertions that the purchase of 20 warheads was only one of three nuclear deals al-Qaeda had consummated; claims that by 1990 bin Laden had hired hundreds of atomic scientists from "the former Soviet Union" (the Soviet Union actually did not collapse, and therefore did not become "former," until the end of 1991) and had them hard at work at a secret laboratory in Kandahar, Afghanistan; alarms in 2005 that al-Qaeda had several nuclear weapons forward deployed to the United States where it planned to set them off simultaneously in Boston, New York, Washington, Las Vegas, Miami, Chicago, and Los Angeles. He also documents a warning that a nuclear blast would rock New York on February 2, 2004; another predicting that atomic explosions would take place in New York, Washington, Baltimore, and Miami on August 5, 2004; and a third about a plan to set off such bombs sometime in 2006 between September 24 and October 23.[28]

Related warnings include the one issued by former CIA spook Michael Scheuer on *60 Minutes* on November 14, 2004, when he assured his rapt and uncritical CBS interviewer that the explosion of a nuclear weapon or dirty bomb in the United States was "probably a near thing." And author Paul Williams has written at least two books proclaiming the likelihood of a nuclear attack on the United States in the near future. In the most recent of these, he concludes, "It could occur within a month or a year or two. But most experts believe it will happen soon.... As this book goes to press, millions of Americans may be living on borrowed time."[29] The publication date of the book is September 6, 2005.

For his part, Allison relays many of these reports, including the extravagant one about the 1998 purchase of 20 nuclear warheads "from Chechen mobsters in exchange for $30 million in cash and two tons of opium." He does so without any effort at critical evaluation, much less skepticism, even though his source is a *Seattle Times* article which specifically notes that the original reports inspired "a spate of alarming, unconfirmed and exaggerated news reports" that played off those original reports and that the original reports themselves remain unconfirmed.[30]

Reviewing this remarkable litany, Richardson concludes, "there can be little doubt that most of these reports are as reliable as the reports that Saddam Hussein was developing and stockpiling weapons of mass destruction." In his assessment of these "vague rumors and reports," Jenkins points out that "although the facts of these reported contacts, deals, and deliveries were shrouded in mystery, the 'shocking revelations' were often shorn of uncertainty and offered as 'empirical proof,' presented as fact and accepted on faith."[31]

If any of the several reports suggesting al-Qaeda had acquired an atomic arsenal over a decade ago were true, one might think the terrorist group (or in the case of the most spectacular of the reports, the Chechen suppliers) would have tried to set one of those things off by now. Or one might be led to suspect that al-Qaeda would have left some trace of the weapons behind in Afghanistan after it made its very hasty exit in 2001. But as noted earlier, none was found.

However, absence of evidence, we need hardly be reminded, is not evidence of absence. Thus, Allison approvingly reports that when no abandoned nuclear weapons material was found in Afghanistan, some intelligence analysts responded, "We haven't found most of the Al Qaeda leadership either, and we know that they exist."[32] Since we know Mount Rushmore exists, maybe the tooth fairy does as well.

Interesting in this regard is a discussion in a book cowritten before the trauma of 9/11 by one of today's top alarmists, physicist Richard Garwin. The book reports what it calls "an authoritative update" by the head of the U.S. Strategic Command in 1998—a peak year for loose-nuke stories—after several visits to Russian military bases. The general was quite insistent: "I want to put to bed this concern that there are loose nukes in Russia. My observations are that the Russians are indeed very serious about security." And he then noted pointedly that, whereas he had actually gone to Russia to check out the situation, those in the intelligence community responsible for various alarming interpretations of the time had not done so. However, reports Garwin and his coauthor, this forceful firsthand testimony failed to persuade the intelligence community, "perhaps because it had access to varied sources of information."[33] A decade and more later, it rather looks like it was the general, not the spooks, who had it right.

HAMID MIR'S INTERVIEW

Pakistani journalist Hamid Mir was brought in to interview bin Laden just a day or two before al-Qaeda was to flee from Afghanistan in 2001. There are varying published texts of what was actually said, but in one

of them bin Laden supposedly asserted, "If the United States uses chemical or nuclear weapons against us, we might respond with chemical and
nuclear weapons. We possess these weapons as a deterrent."[34] Bin Laden
declined to discuss the weapons' origins, but, according to Mir, Zawahiri,
bin Laden's second in command, separately explained, "If you have thirty
million dollars, go to the black market in the central Asia, contact any disgruntled Soviet scientist and...dozens of smart briefcase bombs are available. They have contacted us, we sent our people to Moscow, to Tashkent,
to other central Asian states and they negotiated and we purchased some
suitcase bombs."[35]

Given the military pressure they were under at the time, and taking
into account the evidence of the primitive nature of al-Qaeda's nuclear program (if it could be said to have had one at all), the reported assertions by
the two al-Qaeda leaders, while unsettling, appear to be best interpreted as a
desperate bluff. Or, perhaps better, as flagrant lies: previously bin Laden had
massively inflated both the number of men he had sent to fight in Somalia
and their role there, and he had flagrantly and repeatedly betrayed the trust
of the Taliban in Afghanistan. Although the nuclear lies of 2001 have often
been uncritically accepted at face value, they seem comparable to some
of the colorful pronouncements issued around the same time by Mullah
Omar, leader of the Taliban in Afghanistan, who was also under siege. Contacted by the BBC, Omar railed about "the destruction of America" and
claimed that a plan to carry out that project "is being implemented. But it is
a huge task, which is beyond the will and comprehension of human beings.
If God's help is with us, this will happen within a short period of time; keep
in mind this prediction."[36]

OTHER BIN LADEN STATEMENTS

Bin Laden has pronounced on the nuclear weapons issue a few other
times.

A State Department "Fact Sheet," apparently issued in 1998, contained
this information:

> On or about May 29, 1998, bin Laden issued a statement entitled
> "The Nuclear Bomb of Islam," under the banner of the "Interna-
> tional Islamic Front for Fighting the Jews and Crusaders," in which

he stated that "it is the duty of Muslims to prepare as much force as possible to terrorize the enemies of God."[37]

This assertion, in those exact words, has been repeated a number of times without source reference.[38] However, a fuller version, with a somewhat different date, has been published by Peter Bergen. "On May 14, 1998," says Bergen, "bin Laden issued a statement following the Indian government's nuclear tests three days earlier." In context, it is clear that bin Laden is urging Muslims, and particularly Pakistan, to obtain nuclear weapons to deal with the Indian threat. In no sense does it suggest he is out to obtain this own bomb:

> The world was awakened last Tuesday by the sound of three underground Indian nuclear explosions, accompanied by explosive statements from the Hindu government in India. The leaders of the Islamic world were struck by political blindness and failed to see this danger. We call upon the Muslim nation in general, and Pakistan and its army in particular, to prepare for the Jihad imposed by Allah and terrorize the enemy by preparing the force necessary thereto. This should include a nuclear force to raise fears among all enemies led by the Zionist Christian Alliance to overthrow the Islamic world, and the Hindu enemy occupier of Muslim Kashmir.[39]

In an interview variously dated as 1998 or 1999, bin Laden was asked about accusations or charges that he was attempting to acquire nuclear, chemical, or biological weapons, and said, "We believe that this right to defend oneself is the right of all human beings. At a time when Israel stocks hundreds of nuclear warheads and when the western crusaders control a large percentage of this weapon, we do not consider this an accusation, but a right." He also dismissed the charges as "shabby" or "worn-out," and he "supported and congratulated the Pakistani people when God blessed them with possession of a nuclear weapon."[40]

Around the same time he was asked by *Time* about reports that he was trying to acquire nuclear and chemical weapons. His reply:

> This is a multi-dimensional question. It presupposes that I do possess such weapons, and goes on to ask about the way in which we will use them. In answer, I would say that acquiring weapons for the defense of Muslims is a religious duty. To seek to possess the

weapons that could counter those of the infidels is a religious duty. If I have indeed acquired these weapons, then this is an obligation I carried out and I thank God for enabling us to do that. And if I seek to acquire these weapons I am carrying out a duty. It would be a sin for Muslims not to try to possess the weapons that would prevent the infidels from inflicting harm on Muslims. But how we could use these weapons if we possess them is up to us.[41]

Some of these pronouncements can be seen to be threatening, but they are rather coy and indirect, indicating perhaps something of an interest, but not acknowledging a capability. And, as Richardson concludes, "statements claiming a right to possess nuclear weapons have been misinterpreted as expressing a determination to use them. This in turn has fed the exaggeration of the threat we face."[42]

OTHER POSSIBLE EXPRESSIONS OF INTEREST

Tenet reports that his agency in 1998 received "fragmentary information from an intelligence service" that Osama bin Laden may have tried to establish contact with A. Q. Khan's network. The same source, presumably equally fragmentarily, said that Khan had rebuffed the entreaties.[43]

Tenet also relates that in 2001 the CIA received a set of "unsubstantiated rumors" that "some sort of small nuclear device had been smuggled into the United States and was destined for New York City." They also received information supplied by an al-Qaeda "senior paramilitary trainer" who claimed—but then "later recanted"—that the terrorist group had collaborated with Russian organized crime to import "canisters containing nuclear material" into that very same city. Reports Tenet, the CIA dutifully incorporated these unsubstantiated rumors and recanted claims into its "threat matrix." It is to be hoped that said matrix was not terribly burdened by the intelligence about the small nuclear device in New York because that was generated by an informant dubbed "Dragonfire," and just about everything he had to say, observes Michael Levi, "turned out to be a lie."[44]

And, again according to Tenet, in 2002 and 2003, the agency received what he characterizes as "a stream of reliable reporting" that senior al-Qaeda leaders in Saudi Arabia were "negotiating for the purchase of three

Russian nuclear devices," and that "no price was too high to pay" for them. If so, they must have been using their own money, because, judging by Lawrence Wright's account, bin Laden's finances were severely strained when he went to Afghanistan in 1996, and they hardly improved after he was chased from the country in hasty disarray in 2001. At any rate, Tenet notes that after this information was impressed upon Saudi leaders (and in particular after some terrorist attacks in Saudi Arabia starting in early May 2003 that he neglects to mention), "the Saudis staged a remarkable series of preemptive actions that thwarted a number of terrorist attacks in the kingdom, and which gutted the al-Qa'ida leaders in Saudi Arabia in the process."[45]

Quite a few commentators, including Allison and Tenet, place considerable weight on an Internet posting in June 2002 by a former al-Qaeda spokesman, an obscure Kuwaiti cleric named Suleiman Abu Ghaith. Putting his mathematical skills to a grisly test, Abu Ghaith calculated that the terrorist group had the "right to kill four million Americans" to compensate for Muslim losses at the hands of the Americans in Iraq and the Israelis in Palestine. From this extravagant rant, reports Tenet ominously, his agency "had to consider the possibility that Abu Ghaith was attempting to justify the future use of weapons of mass destruction that might greatly exceed the death toll of 9/11. Such weapons could be nuclear."[46]

Tenet, Scheuer, and others also are impressed by a pronouncement by a Saudi cleric in 2003 that millions of civilian casualties would be acceptable "if they came as part of an attack aimed at defeating an enemy." After subsequently spending some six months under arrest, however, the cleric has rescinded his fatwa and expressed regret for errors in his religious analysis.[47]

THE RECORD

Although "it is likely that al-Qaeda central has considered the option of using non-conventional weapons," concludes Anne Stenersen of the Norwegian Defence Research Establishment after an exhaustive study of available materials, there "is little evidence that such ideas ever developed into actual plans, or that they were given any kind of priority at the expense of more traditional types of terrorist attacks."[48]

That is, when examined, the evidence of al-Qaeda's desire to go atomic and about its progress in accomplishing this exceedingly difficult task is remarkably skimpy, if not completely negligible. The scariest stuff— a decade's worth of loose-nuke rumor and chatter and hype—seems to have no substance whatever. For the rest, there is perhaps reason for concern, or at least for interest. But alarm, and certainly hysteria, are scarcely called for.

15

Capacity

The previous chapter concluded that the evidence that al-Qaeda—the only terrorist group that appears even to want to target the United States and perhaps the West in general—ever had much in the way of an atomic weapons program is quite limited. Moreover, the notion that it ever seriously (or even not so seriously) had a pressing desire to obtain such weapons is equally limited.

The concern in this chapter, however, is this: assuming the group, or one like it, actually would like to be able to make or steal an atomic bomb or two, how capable is it of accomplishing a task that, as chapter 12 contends, is enormously difficult?

Physicist David Albright, as noted in the previous chapter, is quite impressed—overimpressed, in my view—by the evidence that al-Qaeda once had a program to do so when it was ensconced in Afghanistan. But even he concludes that the program was nipped in the bud by the reaction to 9/11, which included the cutoff of aid from Pakistan and then the invasion of Afghanistan.

The current question, then, concerns the present and potential capacities of al-Qaeda. Could these somehow be marshaled effectively to attain some sort of atomic capability or to steal and then manage a purloined weapon? Albright judges the likelihood to be "low." This chapter evaluates al-Qaeda's capacities and its record since 2001 quite broadly, then focuses the discussion on the nuclear issue. It concludes that Albright's assessment of its future atomic prospects is sound.

EMPTY THREATS AND ALARMED RESPONSE

However hampered they may be in other ways, the leaders of al-Qaeda have retained their ability to posture and to issue threats. In the years since 9/11, its key spokespeople, principally Osama bin Laden and Ayman al-Zawahiri, have regaled the world with audio and video declarations—more than 20 in 2006 alone.[1] Some of these have boasted about various nefarious operations that are under way, and these threats have been taken very seriously—indeed, internalized—by many of their opponents in the West.

A few examples of the threats will give the flavor.

In December 2001, as he was fleeing the American onslaught in Afghanistan, bin Laden somehow managed to imagine that it was *America* that at the time was "in retreat by the grace of God Almighty and economic attrition is continuing up today." However, he continued, "it needs further blows. The young men need to seek out the nodes of the American economy and strike the enemy's nodes."[2] All American nodes (and non-nodes) thus far remain free of terrorist blows.

A year after 9/11, in October 2002, bin Laden called upon the American people to "understand the lesson of the New York and Washington raids, which came in response to some of your previous crimes." He went on to assure them: "God is my witness, the youth of Islam are preparing things that will fill your hearts with fear. They will target key sectors of your economy until you stop your injustice and aggression or until the more short-lived of us die." Although quite a few short-lived people have died in the intervening interval (which is how we know they were short-lived), Islamic youths have yet to hit those key sectors. A month later bin Laden renewed his threat: "Leave us alone, or else expect us in New York and Washington."[3]

It was in May 2003 that Zawahiri, al-Qaeda's second in command, promised attacks in Saudi Arabia, Kuwait, Qatar, Bahrain, Egypt, Yemen, and Jordan, and shortly thereafter Osama himself cited Italy, Japan, Australia, and the United States as targets.[4] In the same year, Zawahiri managed to imagine that "We are still chasing the Americans and their allies everywhere, even in their homeland."[5] Six years later, bombs had gone off in Saudi Arabia, Egypt, Yemen, and Jordan (as well as in some unlisted countries), but not in the other explicitly threatened countries, and no perceptible chasing of the kind that so worked up Zawahiri has been going on in the American homeland.

In October 2004, a misplaced Californian, Adam Gadahn, born Adam Pearlman, aka Azzam the American, issued his first propaganda video, in which he proclaimed in steamy, colorful English, "People of America, I remind you of the weighty words of our leaders, Osama bin Laden and Dr. Ayman Al Zawahiri, that what took place on September 11 was but the opening salvo of the global war on America...The magnitude and ferocity of what is coming your way will make you forget about September 11.... The streets of America shall run red with blood...casualties will be too many to count and the next wave of attacks may come at any moment."[6] That moment has yet to arrive, and Americans, as it happens, have not forgotten September 11.

Nor did they forget Vietnam and Afghanistan in response to Zawahiri's 2005 screed: "As for you, the Americans, what you have seen in New York and Washington, what losses that you see in Afghanistan and Iraq, despite the media blackout, is merely the losses of the initial clashes. If you go on with the same policy of aggression against Muslims, you will see, with God's will, what will make you forget the horrible things in Vietnam and Afghanistan."[7]

In 2006, bin Laden, perhaps concerned that his group's credibility was under some degree of strain because of its endless and endlessly unfulfilled threats, issued yet another one: "As for the delay in carrying out similar operations in America, this was not due to failure to breach your security measures. Operations are under preparation, and you will see them on your own ground once they are finished, God willing."[8] Thus far, we are presumably to suppose, God has been unwilling.

Although these threats have thus far proven to be almost completely empty, they have been embraced, inflated, and internalized by al-Qaeda's designated targets. Polls suggest that Americans remain concerned about becoming the victims of terrorism and that the degree of worry hasn't changed all that much in the years since the 2001 attacks. The public appears to have chosen, then, to wallow in a false sense of insecurity (to apply a phrase suggested by Leif Wenar), and it will therefore be likely to continue to demand that its leaders pay due deference to its insecurities and will uncritically approve as huge amounts of money are shelled out in a quixotic and mostly symbolic effort to assuage those insecurities. In response to this apparent demand, something that might be called a "terrorism industry" has sprung up. This entity, consisting of politicians, bureaucrats, journalists, and risk entrepreneurs, also takes the threat very seriously and, moreover, benefits in one way or another from exacerbating anxieties about terrorism. And the result, as Bart Kosko points out, is a synergistic situation in which "government plays safe by overestimating the terrorist threat, while the terrorists oblige by overestimating their power." Brian Jenkins puts it this way: "We stack the threats, extrapolate from there, estimate high probabilities of occurrence, and credit terrorists with greater capabilities." Thus, Homeland Security czar Michael Chertoff proclaimed in 2008 that the "struggle" against terrorism was a "significant existential" one—carefully differentiating it, apparently, from all those insignificant existential struggles we have waged in the past.[9]

This process has a long tradition. It strongly appears that, with the benefit of hindsight, there has been a tendency to inflate national security threats in the past and then, partly in consequence, to overreact to them. Not all concerns that could potentially have been seized upon have evoked anxiety and overreaction, but it does appear that every foreign policy threat in the last several decades that has come to be accepted as significant has then eventually been greatly exaggerated.[10]

ASSESSING AL-QAEDA'S RECORD AND CAPABILITIES

In contrast to the reception al-Qaeda's threats have been given, the record of the group's achievements suggests that its threatening proclamations have mostly been flagrant efforts at deception and desperate self-promotion and that the anxieties the proclamations have so routinely produced have been overwrought.

Size

In evaluating al-Qaeda's general capacity to carry out its violent threats, a good place to start is with analyses provided by Marc Sageman.[11] A former intelligence officer with experience in Afghanistan, Sageman has carefully and systematically combed through both open and classified data on jihadists and would-be jihadists around the world. In the process, he sorts the al-Qaeda enemy into three groups and assesses its size.

First, there is a cluster left over from the struggles in Afghanistan against the Soviets in the 1980s. Currently they are huddled around, and hiding out with, Osama bin Laden somewhere in Afghanistan and/or Pakistan. This band, concludes Sageman, probably consists of a few dozen individuals. Joining them in the area are perhaps a hundred fighters left over from al-Qaeda's golden days in Afghanistan in the 1990s.

These key portions of the enemy forces would total, then, less than 150 actual people. They may operate something resembling "training camps," but these appear to be quite minor affairs. They also assist with the Taliban's distinctly separate, far larger, and very troublesome insurgency in Afghanistan and Pakistan.

Beyond this tiny band, concludes Sageman, the third group consists of thousands of sympathizers and would-be jihadists spread around the globe who mainly connect in Internet chat rooms, engage in radicalizing conversations, and variously dare each other to actually do something.[12]

All of these rather hapless—perhaps even pathetic—people should of course be considered to be potentially dangerous. From time to time they may be able to coalesce enough to carry out acts of terrorist violence, and policing efforts to stop them before they can do so are certainly justified. But the notion that they present an existential threat to just about anybody seems at least as fanciful as some of their schemes.

Sageman's remarkable and decidedly unconventional evaluation of the threat resonates with other prominent experts who have spent years studying the issue. One of them is Fawaz Gerges, whose book *The Far Enemy,* based on hundreds of interviews in the Middle East, parses the jihadist enterprise. As an additional concern, he suggests that Sageman's third group may also include a small, but possibly growing, underclass of disaffected and hopeless young men in the Middle East, many of them scarcely literate, who, outraged at Israel and at America's war in Iraq, may provide cannon fodder for the jihad. However, these people would present problems mainly in the Middle East (including Iraq), not elsewhere.[13]

Other estimates of the size of al-Qaeda central generally come in with numbers in the same order of magnitude as those suggested by Sageman and Gerges. Egyptian intelligence, for example, puts the number at less than 200, while American intelligence estimates run from 300 to upwards of 500. One retired U.S. intelligence officer suggests it could be "as many as 2,000," but that number should obviously be taken essentially to define the upper range of contemporary estimates.[14]

Activity

Some analysts have cited al-Qaeda threats as evidence that "Osama bin Laden's deadly outfit is back in business," and have suggested the messages are particularly important because "when bin Laden speaks, his followers still listen—and act."[15] However, al-Qaeda's activities worldwide since 9/11 seem to have been, despite all the huffing and puffing, quite limited.

Whatever the threats may be taken to signify, not only has there been no al-Qaeda attack whatever in the United States since 2001, but, after years of well-funded sleuthing, the FBI and other investigative agencies have been unable to uncover a single true al-Qaeda sleeper cell within the country. (In interesting synergy, that would be exactly the number of weapons of mass destruction uncovered by the U.S. military in Iraq over the same period.) Indeed, they have been scarcely able to unearth anyone who might even be deemed to have a "connection" to the diabolical group. Over a billion and a half foreigners have been admitted to the United States legally since 9/11 and many others, of course, have entered illegally. Even if security were so good that 90 percent were turned away or deterred from trying to get it, some would have made it in. And of those, it seems reasonable to suggest, some would have been picked up by now. Accordingly, the inability of the FBI to find *any* in the country suggests the terrorists are either far less diabolically clever and capable than usually depicted or that they are not trying very hard.[16]

Some homegrown "plotters" have been apprehended and, while perhaps potentially somewhat dangerous at least in a few cases, most have been flaky or almost absurdly incompetent. There is, for example, that would-be bomber of shopping malls in Rockford, Illinois, who exchanged two used stereo speakers (he couldn't afford the opening price of $100) for a bogus handgun and four equally bogus hand grenades supplied by an FBI informant. Had the weapons been real, he might actually have managed to do some harm. How much is a matter of question, however. It was his idea to set off the grenades in garbage cans in order to "create shrapnel." Since grenades are essentially made of shrapnel, his approach would be comparable to trying to shoot somebody through a wooden board in hopes they would be impaled by flying splinters. At any rate, he clearly posed no threat that was existential (significant or otherwise) to the United States, to Illinois, to Rockford, or, indeed, to the shopping mall.[17]

The situation seems scarcely different in Europe. Political scientist Michael Kenney has interviewed dozens of officials and intelligence agents and analyzed court documents, and finds that Islamic militants there are operationally unsophisticated, short on know-how, prone to make mistakes, and poor at planning, and they have a limited capacity to learn. Another study documents the difficulties of network coordination that continually threaten operational unity, trust, cohesion, and the ability to act collectively.[18]

It is also useful to assess the actual amount of violence perpetrated around the world by Muslim extremists since 9/11 outside of war zones. Included in the count would be terrorism of the much-publicized and fear-inducing sort that occurred in Bali in 2002, in Saudi Arabia, Morocco, and Turkey in 2003, in the Philippines, Madrid, and Egypt in 2004, and in London and Jordan in 2005.

Three publications from think tanks have independently provided lists or tallies of violence committed by Muslim extremists outside of such war zones as Iraq, Israel, Chechnya, Sudan, Kashmir, Afghanistan, and Pakistan, whether that violence is perpetrated by domestic terrorists or by ones with substantial international connections.[19] The lists include not only attacks by al-Qaeda but also those by its imitators, enthusiasts, look-alikes, and wannabes, as well as ones by groups with no apparent connection to it whatever. Although these tallies make for grim reading, the total number of people killed in the years after 9/11 in such incidents comes to some 200 to 300 per year. That, of course, is 200 to 300 too many, but it hardly suggests that the destructive capacities of the terrorists are monumental. Moreover, the rate of terrorist mayhem outside of war zones seems, if anything, to be declining.[20]

Al-Qaeda central's seeming impact has been inflated by a tendency to conflate that organization with those fighting the American occupation in Iraq and with the destructive insurgency conducted by the Taliban in Afghanistan.

After the American invasion of Afghanistan in 2001, Abu Musab al-Zarqawi, an especially bitter and violent jihadist who sympathized with al-Qaeda's ideology and agenda, moved with 30 supporters from Afghanistan to Iraq. Pursued by Saddam Hussein's security services, this tiny band had difficulty linking up with antiregime elements. However, this problem, of course, was conveniently removed in 2003 by the Americans, whose war and subsequent disorder and chaos played perfectly into Zarqawi's hands. Soon he was the leader of a small army of dedicated and brutal terrorists numbering perhaps in the thousands, recruited or self-recruited from within and abroad. In late 2004, Zarqawi linked himself up with al-Qaeda (although bin Laden harbored considerable misgivings about Zarqawi's violently anti-Shiite sentiments), and this connection may have helped in attracting recruits and in generating financial and logistical support for Zarqawi's insurgents. They were further benefited by the tendency of the Americans to credit them with a far larger portion of the violence in Iraq than they probably committed, a process that also helped to burnish Zarqawi's image in much of the Muslim world as a resistance hero.[21]

For their part, the Taliban, which were distinctly uncomfortable as hosts to al-Qaeda in the past, are quick to point out that they are running their own war. It seems clear that al-Qaeda plays only a limited role in their efforts. "No foreign fighter can serve as a Taliban commander," insists one Taliban leader. An extensive study of the Taliban operation in Afghanistan includes al-Qaeda as part of the coalition, but mentions it only very occasionally when discussing the details of the insurgency. And, as noted in chapter 12, there are reports that the main Taliban leaders are very hostile to the foreign forces and have explicitly distanced themselves from al-Qaeda in discussions with Saudi Arabia, whose government has been repeatedly threatened by bin Laden and whose aid and goodwill the Taliban would desperately need were it ever to succeed in Afghanistan.[22]

Actually, one might wonder whether al-Qaeda has really done much of anything since 9/11 except issue threats. Although the terrorist organization designed, equipped, and executed several large attacks before 9/11, every al-Qaeda-"linked" terrorist attack since seems to have been perpetrated by unaffiliated or, at best, "franchised" groups.[23]

Opposition and Counterproductive Violence

One reason for the remarkably low activity is that 9/11 proved to be substantially counterproductive from al-Qaeda's standpoint. Notes Patrick Porter of Britain's Joint Services Command and Staff College, the group has a "talent at self-destruction," and one disillusioned former al-Qaeda associate says, "al-Qaeda committed suicide on 9/11 and lost its equilibrium, skilled leaders, and influence." Their activities, beginning with 9/11—or even with the African embassy bombings of 1998—have also turned many radical jihadists against them, including some of the most prominent and respected.[24]

To begin with, by this action, the group massively heightened concerns about, and outrage over, terrorism around the world. Recalls Gerges, "less than two weeks after September 11, I traveled to the Middle East and was pleasantly surprised by the almost universal rejection—from taxi drivers and bank tellers to fruit vendors and high school teachers—of Al Qaeda's terrorism." Indeed, the key result among jihadis and religious nationalists was a vehement rejection of al-Qaeda's strategy and methods.[25]

Moreover, no matter how much they might disagree on other issues (most notably on America's war on Iraq), there is a compelling incentive for states—including Arab and Muslim ones—to cooperate to deal with any international terrorist threat emanating from groups and individuals connected to, or sympathetic with, al-Qaeda.

Important in this process was the almost immediate move, after 9/11, of the Pakistan government from support of the Taliban regime in neighboring Afghanistan to dedicated opposition. More generally, there has been a worldwide, cooperative effort to deal with the terrorist problem. The FBI may not have been able to uncover much of anything within the United States since 9/11, but quite a few real or apparent terrorists overseas have been rounded, or rolled, up with the aid and encouragement of the Americans. Given what seems to be the limited capacities of al-Qaeda and similar entities, these cooperative international policing efforts may not have prevented a large number of attacks, but more than 3,000 "suspects" have been arrested around the world, and doubtless at least some of these were dangerous. Although these multilateral efforts, particularly by such Muslim states as Sudan, Syria, Libya, and even Iran, may not have received sufficient publicity, these countries have had a vital interest because they felt directly threatened by the militant network, and their diligent and aggressive efforts have led to important breakthroughs against al-Qaeda.[26]

This post-9/11 willingness of governments around the world to take on international terrorists has been much reinforced and amplified by subsequent, if sporadic, terrorist activity in such places as Pakistan, Saudi Arabia, Turkey, Indonesia, Egypt, Spain, Britain, Morocco, and Jordan. The phenomenon is hardly new: in 1997, for example, terrorists attacked a Luxor temple in Egypt, killing 68 foreigners and Egyptians, and it triggered a very substantial revulsion against the perpetrators that critically set back their cause.[27]

Thus, the terrorist bombing in Bali in 2002 galvanized the Indonesian government into action and into extensive arrests and convictions. When terrorists attacked Saudis in Saudi Arabia in 2003, that country seems, very much for self-interested reasons, to have become considerably more serious about dealing with internal terrorism, including a clampdown on radical clerics and preachers. Some inept terrorist bombings in Casablanca in 2003 inspired a similar determined crackdown by Moroccan authorities. The main result of al-Qaeda-linked suicide terrorism in Jordan in 2005 was to outrage Jordanians and other Arabs against the perpetrators. Massive protests were held, and in polls the percentage expressing a lot of confidence in Osama bin Laden to "do the right thing" plunged from 25 to less than one. In polls conducted in 35 predominantly Muslim countries, over 90 percent condemn bin Laden's terrorism on religious grounds.[28]

If this weren't enough, al-Qaeda has continually expanded its enemies list in its declarations to the point where, as noted in chapter 12, it has come to include all Middle Eastern regimes, Muslims who don't share its views, and the governments of India, Pakistan, Afghanistan, and Russia. The group's "literalist, narrow ideology," notes Porter, "warrants aggression against anyone who fails to meet its rigid standards," with the result that, while claiming to be "the knight of Islam," it mostly "persecutes and impoverishes Muslims."[29]

In sum, with 9/11 and subsequent activity, bin Laden and gang seem mainly to have succeeded in uniting the world, including its huge Muslim portion, against their violent global jihad. In 2008, CIA director Michael Hayden was willing to go on the record to note that there had been a "significant setback for al-Qaeda globally—and here I'm going to use the word 'ideologically'—as a lot of the Islamic world pushes back from their form of Islam."[30]

This has also been the experience in Iraq. Al-Qaeda's Zawahiri once described the war there as "the greatest battle of Islam in this era." However, the mindless brutalities of his protégés—staging beheadings at mosques, bombing playgrounds, taking over hospitals, executing ordinary citizens, performing forced marriages—eventually turned the Iraqis against them, including many of those who had previously been fighting the American occupation. In fact, they seem to have managed to alienate the *entire* population: data from polls conducted in Iraq in 2007 indicate that 97 percent of those surveyed opposed efforts to recruit foreigners to fight in Iraq, 98 percent opposed the militants' efforts to gain control of territory, and

100 percent considered attacks against Iraqi civilians "unacceptable." In Iraq as in other places, "al-Qaeda is its own worst enemy," notes Robert Grenier, a former top CIA counterterrorism official. "Where they have succeeded initially, they very quickly discredit themselves."[31]

In addition, continuing, and perhaps accelerating, a long-range trend, state sponsorship of terrorism (at least against countries other than Israel) seems to be distinctly on the wane after 9/11, a phenomenon noted even by the Department of Homeland Security in a 2005 report.[32]

AL-QAEDA'S CAPACITY FOR ATOMIC TERRORISM

Any "threat," at least outside the Middle East, appears, then, to derive princi-pally from Sageman's leaderless jihadists: self-selected people, often isolated from each other, who fantasize about performing dire deeds. From time to time some of these characters, or ones closer to al-Qaeda central, may actually manage to do some harm; since it can be carried out by individuals or by very small groups, terrorism, like crime, will always be with us. And occasionally, they may even be able to pull off something large, like 9/11. But in most cases their capacities and schemes—or alleged schemes—seem to be far less dangerous than initial press reports vividly, even hysterically, suggest. Indeed, as Porter suggests, "incompetence is the norm."[33]

Most importantly for present purposes, however, any notion that the actual al-Qaeda enemy has the capacity to come up with nuclear weapons, even if it wanted to, looks far-fetched in the extreme, as does the notion that they could effectively handle a pilfered one or one given them by a state. Although there have been plenty of terrorist attacks in the world since 2001, all (thus far, at least) have relied on conventional destructive methods. There hasn't even been the occasional gas bomb, not even in Iraq, where the technology is hardly much of a secret—Saddam Hussein's government had extensively used chemical weapons 20 years earlier. A few terrorist bombs used there have been laced with chlorine, but with little or no effect. In gen-eral, the experience with unconventional weapons cannot be too encourag-ing to the would-be atomic terrorist. One group that tried, in the early 1990s, to use them was the Japanese apocalyptic group, Aum Shinrikyo. Unlike al-Qaeda, it was not under siege, and it had money, expertise, a remote and secluded haven in which to set up shop, even a private uranium mine. After making dozens of mistakes in judgment, planning, and execution in its nuclear quest, it turned to biological weapons, which, as it happened, didn't work either, and finally to chemical ones, resulting eventually in a somewhat botched release of sarin gas in a Tokyo subway that managed to kill a total of 12 people.[34]

It was in 1996 that one of terrorism studies' top gurus, Walter Laqueur, assured the world that "proliferation of the weapons of mass destruction does not mean that most terrorist groups are likely to use them in the foreseeable future, but some almost certainly will." Presumably any future foreseeable in 1996 is now history, but in contrast to Laqueur's confident assertion, terrorists seem in effect to be heeding the advice found in a memo on an al-Qaeda laptop seized in Pakistan in 2004: "Make use of that which is available... rather than waste valuable time becoming despondent over that which is not within your reach." That is: Keep it simple, stupid. "Say what you want of terrorists," observes pilot Patrick Smith, "they cannot afford to waste time and resources on schemes with a high probability of failure."[35]

And, in fact, it seems to be a general historical regularity that terrorists tend to prefer weapons that they know and understand, not new, exotic ones. As Jenkins notes, any increase in terrorist violence was "not driven by new weapons or other technology." In fact, "none of the bloodiest attacks involved any weapons that had not already been in the terrorist arsenal for many years." Indeed, the truly notable innovation for terrorists over the last few decades has not been in qualitative improvements in ordnance at all, but rather in a more effective method for delivering it: the suicide bomber.[36]

FBI Director Robert Mueller has been highly alarmist about the terrorist potential in testimony over the years.[37] However, by the time he got around to testifying before the Senate Select Committee on Intelligence on January 11, 2007, Mueller had become notably reticent, and his chief rallying cry had been reduced to a comparatively bland "We believe al-Qaeda is still seeking to infiltrate operatives into the U.S. from overseas," even as he stressed that his chief concern within the United States had become homegrown groups. Moreover, while remaining concerned that things could change in the future, he testified that "few if any terrorist groups" were likely to possess the required expertise to produce nuclear weapons—or, for that matter, biological or chemical ones.

As Glenn Carle warns, "We must not take fright at the specter our leaders have exaggerated. In fact, we must see jihadists for the small, lethal, disjointed and miserable opponents that they are." Al-Qaeda "has only a handful of individuals capable of planning, organizing and leading a terrorist organization," and although they have threatened attacks with nuclear weapons, "its capabilities are far inferior to its desires." Terrorism specialist Bruce Hoffman remains quite worried about the loose terrorist networks, but he also points out that they are likely to be "less sophisticated" and "less technically competent" than earlier terrorists.[38]

Indeed, despite the rain of threats issued by its loquacious leaders and spokesmen over the years, one might be led to wonder whether al-Qaeda even "desires" to set off an atomic explosion—or to attack the United States at home at all. One former radical jihadist, Libya's Noman Benotman, remembers attending a high-level meeting with 200 top jihadists from around the world at bin Laden's headquarters in Afghanistan in 2000. At the meeting, Benotman says he cited various jihadist failures of the 1990s, particularly the spectacularly counterproductive insurgency in Algeria— precursor to the later failure in Iraq—and urged bin Laden to "stop his campaign against the United States because it was going to lead to nowhere." According to Benotman, bin Laden, apparently with 9/11 in mind, replied, "I have one more operation, and after that I will quit." He couldn't call back the one under way, he said, "because that would demoralize the whole organization."[39] The counterproductive results of the 9/11 aftermath are likely to embellish that perspective.

Moreover, as two analysts independently suggest, the terrorist use of unconventional weapons can be especially counterproductive by turning off financial supporters, dividing the movement, and eliciting major crackdowns.[40]

DETERRENCE, TERRORISM, "ROOT CAUSES," AND EXISTENTIAL BOMBAST

In Sageman's estimation, any threat presented by al-Qaeda is likely to simply fade away in time. Unless, of course, the United States overreacts and does something to enhance their numbers, prestige, and determination— something that is, needless to say, entirely possible.[41]

In sharp contrast, there have been fears for years now about a resurgent al-Qaeda. As early as 2002, CIA Director George Tenet was assuring a joint congressional committee without even a wisp of equivocation that al-Qaeda was "reconstituted," planning in "multiple theaters of operation," and "coming after us." And that perspective continues to attract official and unofficial adherents. For example, in 2007 American intelligence had reportedly convinced itself that al-Qaeda was "marshaling its reconstituted forces for a spectacular new attack on the United States."[42]

And the threat posed by this entity has been repeatedly rendered in the most extreme terms. In 2002, National Security Adviser Condoleezza Rice insisted that "after 9/11, there is no longer any doubt that today America faces an existential threat to our security—a threat as great as any we faced during the Civil War, the so-called 'Good War,' or the Cold War." A best-selling book of 2004 by Michael Scheuer, formerly of the CIA, repeatedly assures us that our "survival" is at stake and that, unless U.S. policy in the Mideast changes considerably, we are engaged in a "war to the death." Two years later, Scheuer remained comfortable in his alarm: "America faces an existential threat," he proclaimed, and, moreover, "time is short." Following this line of thinking, it has become fashionable in some alarmist circles to extravagantly denote the contest against Osama bin Laden and his sympa-thizers as (depending on how the cold war is classified) World War III or World War IV. Meanwhile, Democrats have routinely insisted that the ter-rorist menace has been energized and much heightened by the Republicans' misguided war in Iraq. Very much on this wavelength was the New York Times editorial board when it assured us on April 23, 2008, that "the fight against al-Qaeda is the central battle for this generation," and Senator John McCain more expansively, and repeatedly, points to what he calls "radical Muslim extremism," labels the struggle against it the "transcendental chal-lenge of the 21st century," and expresses the belief that, if it prevails, it can affect "our very existence."[43]

Many (though not all) of those proclaiming the struggle against, and the threat presented by, al-Qaeda to be an "existential" one hinge their alarm on the prospect that the group could obtain atomic weapons, or at least weapons of mass destruction.

As discussed in chapter 2, few alarmists even attempt to spell out how the atomic terrorist would actually go about causing a huge country like the United States to cease to exist—nor, disappointingly, are they ever closely queried on this truly spectacular alarmism by journalists or others. Mostly, to make their proclamations resonate, they rely on the overstatements of the destructive capacities of atomic weapons that have been so uncritically spewed out now for two-thirds of a century—the ones about Armaged-don and apocalypse and stuff like that. A groundburst atomic device of Hiroshima proportions could certainly devastate an area of a few blocks and, if the right set of blocks were selected, this could result in the deaths of tens of thousands and perhaps even more. If more than one were set off at the same time, this would of course be even more destructive and would multiply alarm severalfold. A massive calamity, to be sure, but how does this lead to the extinguishment of the rest of the country? Do farmers in Iowa cease plowing because an atomic bomb went off in an Eastern city? Do manufacturers close down their assembly lines? Do all churches, businesses, governmental structures, community groups simply evaporate?

As Jenkins points out, even if terrorists could obtain nuclear weapons, they will never have enough of sufficient destructive power to destroy an entire nation. Any losses from a terrorist bomb would be "tragic, but the republic will still survive," albeit "wounded, angry, determined, and very dangerous." In 1999, two years before 9/11, the Gilmore Commission pressed a point it considered "self-evident," but one that, it felt, nonetheless required "reiteration" because of the "rhetoric and hyperbole" surrounding the issue: although a terrorist attack with a weapon of mass destruction could be "serious and potentially catastrophic," it is "highly unlikely that it could ever completely undermine the national security, much less threaten the survival, of the United States." To hold otherwise "risks surrendering to the fear and intimidation that is precisely the terrorist's stock in trade."[44] The fact that terrorists subsequently managed to ram airplanes into three buildings on a sunny September morning does not render this point less sound.

"Fear warps our judgment," warns Jenkins. "If nuclear terrorism is assumed to be Armageddon, then we operate in an artificial environment of absolutes, not the real world of relative risks." And military analyst William Arkin stresses that a danger in all this is that, although terrorists cannot destroy America, "every time we pretend we are fighting for our survival we not only confer greater power and importance to terrorists than they deserve but we also at the same time act as their main recruiting agent by suggesting that they have the slightest potential for success."[45]

Moreover, existential bombast could even encourage further attacks. Contrary to accepted wisdom, notes Jenkins, terrorists *can* be deterred. It is probably true that they can't be deterred by threatening unacceptable punishment. But, as argued in chapter 5, there is much more to deterrence than that: it can be achieved as well by reducing the terrorists' likelihood of success.[46] That this approach can be productive is suggested by some of the earlier discussion. Many top jihadists, even before 9/11, were becoming disillusioned with the terror technique because it simply brought on harsh government clampdowns and alienated the public, including people who might otherwise be expected to be sympathetic to the cause.

Put another way, a key "root cause" of terrorism is the perception by a terrorist group—particularly by the leaders—that the technique will be productive. Therefore, as part of a deterrent strategy, threatened countries like the United States should seek to demonstrate that terrorist attacks will not bring about existential self-destruction, but rather that the country will be resilient and respond in a determined, yet self-controlled, manner.[47]

From this perspective, then, rhetorical declamations insisting that terrorism poses an existential threat are profoundly misguided. And so are self-destructive overreactions (like the war in Iraq) which are also encouraging to the terrorists. As Osama bin Laden crowed in 2004:

> It is easy for us to provoke and bait....All that we have to do is to send two mujahidin...to raise a piece of cloth on which is written al-Qaeda in order to make the generals race there to cause America to suffer human, economic, and political losses. Our policy is one of bleeding America to the point of bankruptcy. The terrorist attacks cost al-Qaeda $500,000 while the attack and its aftermath inflicted a cost of more than $500 billion on the United States.

Or perhaps, it is even worse. To the extent that we "portray the terrorist nuclear threat as the thing we fear most," notes Susan Martin, "we nurture the idea that this is what terrorists must do if they want to be taken seriously."[48]

Existential bombast can be useful for scoring political points, selling newspapers, or securing funding for pet projects or bureaucratic expansion. However, it does so by essentially suggesting that, if the terrorists really want to destroy us, all they have to do is hit us with a terrific punch, particularly a nuclear one. Although the attack may not in itself be remotely big enough to cause the nation to cease to exist, purveyors of bombast assure the terrorists that the target country will respond by obligingly destroying itself in anguished overreaction. The suggestion, then, is that it is not only the most feared terrorists who are suicidal. As Sageman points out, the United States hardly faces a threat to its existence, because even a nuclear strike by terrorists "will not destroy the nation." As things stand now, he adds, "only the United States could obliterate the United States."[49]

Atomic terrorism may indeed be the single most serious threat to the national security of the United States. Assessed in an appropriate context, however, the likelihood that such a calamity will come about seems breathtakingly small. Sensible, cost-effective policies designed to make that probability even lower may be justified, given the damage that can be inflicted by an atomic explosion. But unjustified, obsessive alarmism about the likelihood and imminence of atomic terrorism has had policy consequences that have been costly and unnecessary. Among them are the war in Iraq and the focus on WMD that seduced federal agencies away from due preparation for disasters that have actually happened, such as Hurricane Katrina.[50]

Arch-demon Zawahiri once noted that the group only became aware of biological weapons "when the enemy drew our attention to them by repeatedly expressing concerns that they can be produced simply with easily available materials."[51] By constantly suggesting that the United States will destroy itself in response to an atomic explosion, the existential bombast about a terrorist bomb that follows so naturally from decades of atomic obsession encourages the most diabolical and murderous terrorists to investigate the possibility of obtaining one. Fortunately, however, would-be atomic terrorists are exceedingly unlikely to be successful in such a quest, however intense the inspiration and encouragement they receive from the unintentional cheerleaders among their distant enemies.

Epilogue and an Inventory of Propositions

In *The Absolute Weapon,* a book published a year after Hiroshima, Bernard Brodie, who was to become one of the era's most important defense strategists, proclaimed there to be "twin facts" about the new bomb: "it exists" and "its destructive power is fantastically great."[1]

Working from that perspective, the central task Brodie set for himself in this seminal book was to consider how the new weapon could be applied to military strategy. At the time, he argued that the "chief purpose" of the weapons, indeed of the entire military establishment, should be to deter (or "avert") wars: indeed, he contended, there can be "almost no other useful purpose." Therefore, "the first and most vital step" in the atomic age would be "to guarantee to ourselves in case of attack the possibility of retaliation in kind."[2]

The quest to provide Brodie's "guarantee" led to decades of exquisite theorizing and massive expenditure, and Brodie was very much part of this development. Indeed, much of the atomic obsession and the fanciful exaggeration of external threats this book considers can be seen to stem semi-logically from Brodie's "twin facts" and from his book's somewhat overstated title—although Brodie nowhere calls the weapon "absolute" (whatever that means) in the text. Because the weapons exist and can inflict destruction that is "fantastically great," it might seem to follow that they are also fantastically important.

However, by the 1960s Brodie began to reexamine fundamental premises, and he came to conclude that it was wildly unlikely that the Soviet Union was poised, would ever likely be poised, or even wanted to be poised to launch any sort of direct military aggression against the United States or its prime interests in Europe.[3] That is, although he didn't put it this way, there was nothing to deter—or avert. He also became dismayed at the whole course of strategic analysis as it became ever more mathematized and mechanical, leading in the process to the endless production of what a few months before his death in 1978 he labeled "worst-case fantasies." It was all, he concluded dismally, "simply playing with words."[4] In the end, such highly unconventional, even iconoclastic, views caused him to be shunned in the intellectual community he had done so much to create.

Brodie was something of a guru for me. I don't know whether he would necessarily agree with everything in this book, but I'd like to think that much of it is essentially an extrapolation from some of his thinking as he sought to reevaluate both the intellectual and the practical implications of the premises he had so influentially set out in 1946. It is, in particular, an extension of his concern about policy perspectives spun out so prodigiously over the decades by what he called the "cult of the ominous."[5]

An inventory of some of the propositions put forward here in that spirit would include the following.

- Obsession with nuclear weapons, sometimes based on exaggerations of the weapons' destructive capacity, has often led to policies that have been unwise, wasteful, and damaging
- Nuclear weapons have been of little historic consequence and have not been necessary to prevent World War III or a major conflict in Europe
- Militarily, the weapons have proved to be useless and a very substantial waste of money and of scientific and technical talent: there never seem to have been militarily compelling reasons to use them, particularly because of an inability to identify suitable targets or ones that could not be attacked about as effectively by conventional munitions
- Although nuclear weapons seem to have at best a quite limited substantive impact on actual historical events, they have had a tremendous influence on our agonies and obsessions, inspiring

desperate rhetoric, extravagant theorizing, wasteful expenditure, and frenetic diplomatic posturing

- Wars are not caused by weapons or arms races, and the quest to control nuclear weapons has mostly been an exercise in irrelevance
- The atomic bombs were probably not necessary to induce the surrender of the Japanese in World War II
- Those who stole American atomic secrets and gave them to the Soviet Union did not significantly speed up the Soviet program; however, obsession about that espionage did detrimentally affect American foreign and domestic policy, something that led to a very substantial inflation in the estimation of the dangers that external and internal enemies presented
- Changes in anxieties about nuclear destruction have not correlated at all well with changes in the sizes or the destructive capacities of nuclear arsenals
- Arms reduction will proceed most expeditiously if each side feels free to reverse any reduction it later comes to regret; formal disarmament agreements are likely simply to slow and confuse the process
- The economic and organizational costs of fabricating a nuclear arsenal can be monumental, and a failure to appreciate this has led to considerable overestimations of a country's ability to do so
- The proliferation of nuclear weapons has been far slower than routinely predicted because, insofar as most leaders of most countries (even rogue ones) have considered acquiring the weapons, they have come to appreciate several defects: the weapons are dangerous, distasteful, costly, and likely to rile the neighbors
- The nuclear diffusion that has transpired has proved to have had remarkably limited, perhaps even imperceptible, consequences
- Nuclear proliferation is not particularly desirable, but it is also unlikely to accelerate or prove to be a major danger
- Strenuous efforts to keep "rogue states" from obtaining nuclear weapons have been substantially counterproductive and have been a cause of far more deaths than have been inflicted by all nuclear detonations in history
- The weapons have not proved to be crucial status symbols
- Not only have nuclear weapons failed to be of much value in military conflicts, they also do not seem to have helped a nuclear country to swing its weight or "dominate" an area

- Given the low value of the weapons and their high costs, any successes in the antiprolifertion effort have been modest and might well have happened anyway
- Strenuous efforts to prevent nuclear proliferation can act as a spur to the process, enhancing the appeal of—or desperate desire for—nuclear weapons for at least a few regimes, an effect that is often ignored
- The pathetic North Korean regime mostly seems to be engaged in a process of extracting aid and recognition from outside, and a viable policy toward it might be to reduce the threat level and to wait while continuing to be extorted rather than to enhance the already intense misery of the North Korean people
- If Iran actually does develop something of an atomic arsenal, it will likely find, following the experience of all other states so armed, that the bombs are essentially useless and a very considerable waste of money and effort
- Although there is nothing wrong with making nonproliferation a high priority, it should be topped with a somewhat higher one: avoiding policies that can lead to the deaths of tens or hundreds of thousands of people under the obsessive sway of worst-case scenario fantasies
- It is likely that no "loose nukes"—nuclear weapons missing from their proper storage locations and available for purchase in some way—exist
- It is likely there is no such thing as a true black market in nuclear materials
- The evidence of any desire on al-Qaeda's part to go atomic and of any progress in accomplishing this exceedingly difficult task is remarkably skimpy, if not completely negligible, while the scariest stuff—a decade's worth of loose-nuke rumor and chatter and hype—seems to have no substance whatever
- Because of a host of organizational and technical hurdles, the likelihood that terrorists will be able to build or acquire an atomic bomb or device is vanishingly small
- Despite the substantial array of threats regularly issued by al-Qaeda (the only terrorist group that may see attacks on the United States as desirable), and despite the even more substantial anguish these

threats have inspired in their enemies, the terrorist group's capacity seems to be quite limited

- One reason for al-Qaeda's remarkably low activity in the last years is that 9/11 proved to be substantially counterproductive from al-Qaeda's standpoint; indeed, with 9/11 and subsequent activity, the terrorist group seems mainly to have succeeded in uniting the world, including its huge Muslim portion, against its violent global jihad
- Any threat presented by al-Qaeda is likely to fade away in time, unless, of course, the United States overreacts and does something to enhance their numbers, prestige, and determination—something that is, needless to say, entirely possible
- The existential bombast suggesting that the United States will destroy itself in response to an atomic explosion encourages the most diabolical and murderous terrorists to investigate the possibility of obtaining one

In the end, it appears to me that, whatever their impact on activist rhetoric, strategic theorizing, defense budgets, and political posturing, nuclear weapons have had at best a quite limited effect on history, have been a substantial waste of money and effort, do not seem to have been terribly appealing to most states that do not have them, are out of reach for terrorists, and are unlikely to materially shape much of our future. Sleep well.

Notes

PREFACE

1. Pundit: Snow 1961, 259. Strategist: Kahn 1960, x. Scientist: McPhee 1964, 4. Political scientist (Hans J. Morgenthau) in Boyle 1985, 23.
2. For sources for these quotes, see pp. 90–99.
3. Speech in Prague, April 5, 2009.
4. Kean: interviewed for *Frontline*'s "The Enemy Within," PBS, on March 27, 2006 (www.pbs.org/wgbh/pages/frontline/enemywithin/interviews/kean. html). Keller 2002. Mueller: Kessler 2007, 221–22. Gates: Graham 2008, 43.
5. Mueller: Kessler 2007, 221–22. Mowatt-Larssen: Suskind 2008, 93 (existential), 92 (can't sleep), 4 (looking), 93 (grim).
6. Rhodes 2007, 306.

CHAPTER 1: EFFECTS

1. On this issue, see Jenkins 2008, 56.
2. Office of Technology Assessment (OTA) 1979, 22.
3. W. Allison 2006, 181.
4. OTA 1979, 19.
5. Garwin and Charpak 2001, 65–67. Smoke 1993, 259–61.
6. OTA 1979, 20–22. For an extended discussion of fire effects, see Eden 2004.
7. Destructive blast: OTA 1979, 16–19. Radius: Wilson 2007, 178 n. Brodie 1946, 60.
8. Two to ten years: OTA 1979, 22–25. GAO: Kolata 2001.
9. Ferguson et al. 2003, 21–22. Ferguson and Potter 2005, 267. See also Zimmerman and Loeb 2004, 8.
10. Acceptable levels: Zimmerman and Loeb 2004, 8; W. Allison 2006, 180. Moving: Understanding Radiation, National Safety Council: www.nsc.

org/issues/rad/exposure.htm (21 March 2005). China: Henriksen and Maillie 2003, 137. Denver: Zimmerman and Loeb 2004, 7. Studies around the world: Jones 2000.

11. Zimmerman and Loeb 2004, 8.

12. Factor of ten: Zimmerman and Loeb 2004, 10. W. Allison 2006, 316–17. Raised radiation good for health: on this "hormesis" hypothesis, see information at the Health Physics Society's website: http://www.hps.org/publicinformation/ate/q299.html (10 July 2006). For a useful discussion of the debate, see Kolata 2001.

13. Fishermen: Henriksen and Maillie 2003, 94. Chernobyl: Finn 2005; see also W. Allison 2006, 199–202; Henriksen and Maillie 2003, 109–12; Garwin and Charpak 2001, 189–95. Of the workers at Chernobyl, 20 out of 21 who received a dose of 6,000–16,000 mSv died, 7 of 21 who received a dose of 4,000–6,000 mSv died, 1 of 55 who received a dose of 2,000–4,000 mSv died, and none of the 140 who received a dose of less than 2,000 mSv died (W. Allison 2006, 200).

14. Garwin and Charpak 2001, 73–74. Smoke 1993, 256–61.

15. OTA 1979, 81–90.

16. OTA 1979, 94–100.

17. OTA 1979, 114–15.

18. Killed: Henriksen and Maillie 2003, 139. Other damage: De Seversky 1950, chs. 9, 10; USSBS 1946; U.S. Army 1946; Lapp 1949, ch. 7; Committee for Compilation 1981, 40, 106, 113; Brodie 1946, 25–26.

19. USSBS 1946, 33; on this issue, see also Brodie 1946, 24–25. One commentator, Major Alexander de Seversky, after inspecting the two bombed cities in 1945 at the request of the U.S. Secretary of War, reported to him and then to the public in lectures, books, articles, and congressional testimony that although destruction in the two cities was extensive, the damage was far less than popular accounts often indicated. De Seversky concluded that the bomb could not conceivably do damage on that scale to a modern city. Furthermore, he concluded that it would have taken at least 5,000 atomic bombs to accomplish the widespread damage that conventional bombers had inflicted on Germany and its occupied territories (1950, 127, 132, 155; 1946, 121). Physicist Ralph Lapp, noting that "A-bombs are too big for many military applications," and ignoring isolated targets, concluded it would take 75 atomic bombs to duplicate the bomb damage in Germany (1949, 61). In a 1946 article, de Seversky declared that an atomic bomb on New York or Chicago would do no more damage than a ten-ton blockbuster (1946, 121; for a contemporary refutation, see Littell 1946). See also Boyer 1985, 66–67, 72, 306.

20. Thus far, less than 1 percent excess cancers: Kolata 2001; see also Henriksen and Maillie 2003, 140. Kristof 1995. W. Allison 2006, 196–97.

21. Ferguson and Potter 2005, 51–52.

22. Ferguson and Potter 2005, 51–52.

23. Muller 2008, 35–36. See also Jenkins 2008, 56–57; Allison 2004, 10.

24. This can be seen to have been part of an effort to keep the "catastrophe quota" comfortably full: as big problems become resolved, there is a tendency to elevate smaller ones, sometimes by redefinition or by raising standards, to take their place. On this process, see J. Mueller 1995a, ch. 1.

25. On the history of "WMD" and for data on the use of the term, see Carus 2006; Hymans 2004, 37–39. For a good overview, see Easterbrook 2002. See also Pillar 2003, 21–26; McNaugher 1990; Rapoport 1999; Mueller and Mueller 1999, 2000; J. Mueller 2006, 18–24; Bergen 2008. Actually, the 1994 legal definition of the concept is so broad

that hand grenades, bombs bursting in air, and Revolutionary War muskets would be considered to be WMD. See Carus 2006, 10; Mueller and Mueller 2009.

26. Meselson 1991, 13. Evacuate: McNaugher 1990, 31. OTA 1993, 54. Gilmore 1999, 28. See also OTA 1993, 9, 46; Betts 1998, 30–31. For a discussion that begins by claiming that a single chemical weapon, like a nuclear one, could kill thousands of people, but then in its analysis of chemical weapons comes up with admittedly "simplified and worst-case" scenarios that might inflict deaths in the hundreds or less, see Falkenrath et al. 1998, 1, 147–51.

27. Tucker and Sands 1999, 51. See also Meselson 1995; Gilmore 1999, 25; Ruppe 2005, 1221; OTA 1993, 48–49, 62. After assessing, and stressing, the difficulties a nonstate entity would find in obtaining, handling, growing, storing, processing, and dispersing lethal pathogens effectively, biological weapons expert Milton Leitenberg compares his conclusions with glib pronouncements in the press about how biological attacks can be pulled off by anyone with "a little training and a few glass jars" or how it would be "about as difficult as producing beer." He sardonically concludes, "The less the commentator seems to know about biological warfare the easier he seems to think the task is." Leitenberg 2004, 35–39. See also Leitenberg 2005; Ropeik and Gray 2002, ch. 22.

28. Zimmerman and Loeb 2004, 11. Ferguson et al. 2003, 19. Allison 2004, 8. See also Rockwell 2003.

29. Levi and Kelly 2002.

30. They may also be peculiarly disgusting in the way they kill, but that characteristic has not stopped the military from finding battlefield uses for napalm.

31. Ineffective against troops: OTA 1993, 8, 58; Meselson 1991, 13. Uncomfortable: Edmonds and Maxwell-Hyslop 1947, 606. Distaste: Brown 1968, 33–38, 153–54.

CHAPTER 2: OVERSTATING THE EFFECTS

1. Weart, interviewed in *Bulletin of the Atomic Scientists,* May/June 2008, 12.

2. Blow up New York: Bird and Sherwin 2005, 349; see also G. Allison 2004, 104. Destroyer of worlds: Oppenheimer disclosed this recollection in a television broadcast in 1965, 20 years after the event, and he may have been creatively embellishing, or poeticizing, his actual reactions at the time; to one of his friends it sounded like one of Oppenheimer's "priestly exaggerations": Bird and Sherwin 2005, 309. Absolute weapon: Brodie 1946. On this issue, see also Muller 2008, 35–36.

3. Cirincione 2007b, 16. Gallucci 2008, 75. Sheets 2008.

4. Jenkins 2008, 277. Cirincione 2007b, 16. Physicist: McPhee 1974, 5; also 149.

5. Blow up airport: for example, Sanders 2005; Wright 2006, 262. Oklahoma bomb: Mlakar et al. 1998; Michel and Herbeck 2001, 164.

6. Lugar: *Fox News Sunday,* 23 June 2003; Lugar 2005, 3. Mowatt-Larssen: Suskind 2008, 92. Benjamin and Simon 2002, 399, 418. Myers: Kerr 2003.

7. G. Allison 2004, 191. Bunn and Wier 2006, 146. Ignatieff 2004b, 147. Bobbitt 2008, 9, 547.

8. Tenet and Harlow 2007, 279.

9. Goldstein 2004, 128. Ferguson and Potter 2005, 3; elsewhere they make a somewhat similar argument, but posit a nuclear explosion much larger than a "crude" one (2005, 46). Benjamin and Simon 2002, 398–99. Franks: Shanken 2003. For a contrast with such views, see Byman 2003, 160, 163; Seitz 2004; Sageman 2008, 148–49, 176.

10. Inexorably: Ignatieff 2004b, 146. Not forgive: Ignatieff 2004a, 46–48. At the time, Ignatieff predicted with equal assurance that there would be terrorist events in connection with the 2004 elections: Ignatieff 2004a, 48.

11. Bobbitt 2008, 425–26.

12. Japan: see also Wilson 2008. Confidence in government: Langer 2002. Socially responsible behavior: Furedi 2008, 178.

13. Katrina estimate: Dart 2005. 9/11 estimate: The estimate on September 24, for example, was that nearly 7,000 had died (*New York Times*, 24 September 2001, B2); on this issue, see Lipton 2001.

14. Snow 1961, 259. Doomsayers have been wryly advised to predict catastrophe no later than ten years into the future but no sooner than five, because that would be soon enough to terrify their rapt listeners, but far enough off for people to forget if the doom-saying proves to be wrong (Will 2004, working from the musings of Gregg Easterbrook). Snow seems to have gotten the point.

15. Destabilizing: Reiss 2004, 14. Welch 2000, vii.

16. Deaths: Gilchrist 1928, 7. Tonnage of gas used: Falkenrath et al. 1998, 75. Fatal: McNaugher 1990, 19 n. (For the United States, 2 percent of gas casualties died, while 24 percent of those incapacitated by other weapons died. The rates for Germany were 2.9 percent and 43 percent, and for the British 3.3 percent and 36.6 percent. Overall, the estimates are that there were 1,009,038 gas casualties in the war, of whom 78,390, or 7.7 percent, died. Gas fatalities were suffered very disproportionately by the Russians, who were ill protected against gas. However, even taking that into consideration, their ratio of gas deaths to total gas casualties, 11.7 percent, is so out of line with those found on the Western front that it seems likely that the number of gas fatalities is exaggerated. Gilchrist 1928, 7–8, 48.) Return to combat: McNaugher 1990, 20 n. Suffer less: Gilchrist 1928, 47. On the probable exaggeration of long-range effects, see Haber 1986, 258; he concludes, however, that although the cause-and-effect connections between being gassed and later maladies was "tenuous," it was "enough for people to believe that being gassed was the cause of illness years later, and thus the special anxiety created by chemical warfare continued into the peace and was kept alive in the public consciousness." See also Harris and Paxman 1982, ch. 4.

17. Harold Macmillan quoted in Bialer 1980, 158.

18. Brown 1968, 65, 164, 180–81. On Douhet and his exaggerations, see Brodie 1959, ch. 3. For a less alarmist contemporary view of gas bombing, see Dupuy and Eliot 1937, 208–09.

19. Churchill 1932, 246, 248. Freud 1930, 144. Baldwin: Kagan 1987, 26. See also Bialer 1980, 46–47. In a study of fictional accounts of future war, I. F. Clarke notes that World War I produced a pronounced change, which World War II and atomic weapons were later only to embellish: "Since 1914 the literature of imaginary warfare has seen a constant retreat from the old, heroic, and aggressive attitudes. The chief enemy is no longer some foreign power, it is the immense destructiveness of modern weapons.... All that has been written about future wars since Hiroshima merely repeats and amplifies what was said between the two world wars." Clarke 1966, 167–76. Typical was a 1931 novel, *The Gas War of 1940*, which envisioned a war begun by a German attack on Poland that escalated to worldwide ruin from poison gas and high explosives. Other British works of the era have such titles as *The Poison War, Empty Victory, War upon Women, People of the Ruins, The Last Man, The Collapse of Homo Sapiens, Invasion from the Air, Last of My Race, At the End of the World, Day of Wrath,* and *The World Ends.* Similar tales

were penned in Germany and France. The Germans even had a name for the genre: *Weltuntergangsroman*—world-downfall novel.

20. Kennedy 1961.

21. Gilchrist 1928, 47. Liddell Hart: Mearsheimer 1988, 90; see also Stockton 1932, 536–39. Helmet: interestingly, in Serge Eisenstein's classic 1938 film, *Alexander Nevsky*, invading Teutonic knights are made to appear menacing and inhuman precisely because of their masking helmets.

22. Boyer 1985, 65–66.

23. Boyer 1985, 70 (Morrison, Einstein, scientist, Rabinowitch), 70 (Oppenheimer), 66 (decisive fact), 74–75 (strategy).

24. Boyer 1985, 72, 336.

25. Rhodes 2007, 80.

26. Not a new phenomenon. For example, as part of their concerted program to entice the United States into the First World War on its side, the British launched intense propaganda efforts to stigmatize the Germans as inhuman monsters for having introduced chemicals into the art of war, and it is estimated that for dramatic effect they quintupled their gas casualty figures from the first German attack (Brown 1968, 14 n). Something similar may have happened during the costly war between Iran and Iraq in the 1980s. One episode during that war is often taken to indicate the extensive destructive potential of chemical weapons: the chemical attack in 1988, apparently by Iraqi forces, on the town of Halabja. It is commonly contended that 5,000 people died as a result of the gas attacks. However, attacks on the city took place over several days and involved explosive munitions as well, and there is a possible confusion over deaths caused by chemical weapons and those caused by other means. All the reports from journalists who were taken to the town shortly after the attack indicate that they saw at most "hundreds" of bodies. Although some of them report the 5,000 figure, this number is consistently identified as coming from Iranian authorities, an important qualification often neglected in later accounts. The Iranians apparently claimed that an additional 5,000 were wounded by the chemical weapons, even though experience suggests that an attack killing 5,000 would have injured far more—actually *vastly* more—than that. A Human Rights Watch report on the events has an appendix in which other Iraqi chemical attacks in the area are evaluated; in two of these attacks it is suggested that 300 or 400 might have been killed, while all the other estimates are under 100, most under 20. Human Rights Watch 1995, 262–64.

27. Wilson 2007, 175–76. See also Hasegawa 2005, 298–303.

CHAPTER 3: DETERRING WORLD WAR III

1. Shultz et al. 2007.

2. E. May 1999, 1–2.

3. Luttwak 1983, 82. Art and Waltz 1983, 28. Kenneth N. Waltz, Presidential Address, Annual Meeting, American Political Science Association, Washington, DC, September 1998. Rostow quoted in E. May 1999, 3. See also Gilpin 1981, 213–19; Knorr 1985, 79; Mearsheimer 1984/85, 25–26; Jervis 1988; Gaddis 1992, ch. 6; Gaddis 1999; van Creveld 1999, 337–44; van Creveld 2006; and the essays in Gaddis et al. 1999.

4. This formulation derives from Kaysen, McNamara, and Rathjens 1991, 99. See also J. Mueller 1985; Luard 1986, 396; J. Mueller 1988; Luard 1988, 25–31; Bundy 1988;

J. Mueller 1989, 110–16; Ray 1989, 428–31; Holmes 1989, 238–48; Vasquez 1991; J. Mueller 1995, ch. 5.

5. Pause: Gaddis 1997, 86. Drastically: Waltz 1990, 745. More robust: Mearsheimer 1990, 31. Unimaginably enormous: Jervis 1988, 31–36. Vision of future war: Gaddis 1992, 109. Amplified: Kaysen 1990, 61.

6. Gaddis 1992, 108.

7. *New York Times,* April 7, 1982. See also Michael Mandelbaum's comment in a book which in this respect has a curious title, *The Nuclear Revolution:* "The tanks and artillery of the Second World War, and especially the aircraft that reduced Dresden and Tokyo to rubble might have been terrifying enough by themselves to keep the peace between the United States and the Soviet Union" (1981, 21). And of course, given weapons advances, a full-scale *conventional* World War III could potentially be even more destructive than World War II.

8. To demonstrate that nuclear weapons have made an important difference, Carl Kaysen argues if that nuclear weapons had been invented in the 18th century, the war-loving absolute monarchs of that era "would certainly change their assessment of the relative virtues of war and peace" (1990, 61–62). But the leading countries after 1945 *already* vastly preferred peace to major war, and thus needed no conversion.

9. Harriman: *Newsweek,* 16 March 1953, 31. Holloway 1994, 271–72, also 368. Taubman 1982, 11.

10. Kornienko: comments at Conference of the Nuclear History Program, Washington, DC, September 1990. Khrushchev 1974, 511, 533. Ford: Leffler 2007, 247.

11. For the argument that the European half of World War II may not have been in the cards in any sense, but was mostly the product of the machinations of a single man—history's supreme atavism—Adolf Hitler, see J. Mueller 2004, ch. 4.

12. Waltz 1979, 190. See also Nye 1987, 377.

13. For an excellent analysis, see Burin 1963.

14. Rules: Leites 1953, 46–53. Gaddis 1997, 31.

15. Khrushchev 1974, 531, emphasis in the original. Pipes 1984, 65, 52–53. Reformer: Rhodes 2007, 129. Arkady Shevchenko, while stressing that "the Kremlin is committed to the ultimate vision of a world under its control," insists that the Soviets "are patient and take the long view," believing "that eventually [they] will be supreme—not necessarily in this century but certainly in the next" (1985, 285–86). Similarly, Michael Voslensky asserts that Soviet leaders desired "external expansion," but their "aim is to win the struggle between the two systems without fighting"; he notes that Soviet military ventures before and after World War II were consistently directed only against "weak countries" and only after the Soviets have been careful to cover themselves in advance—often withdrawing when "firm resistance" has been met (1984, 320–30). Taubman says that Stalin sought "to avert war by playing off one set of capitalist powers against another and to use the same tactic to expand Soviet power and influence without war" (1982, 12). MacGregor Knox argues that for Hitler and Mussolini "foreign conquest was the decisive prerequisite for a revolution at home," and in this respect those regimes differed importantly from those of Lenin, Stalin, and Mao (1984, 57). See also Jervis 1984, 156; MccGwire 1985, 122. For a study stressing the Soviet Union's "cautious opportunism" in the Third World, see Hosmer and Wolfe 1983.

16. For the argument that this belief was probably exaggerated, see J. Mueller 1989, 236–40. Jervis suggests that the fear of escalation is more vivid and dramatic in the nuclear case (1988, 35–36). This may be true, but to show that this quality is consequential, it is

necessary in addition to demonstrate that those running world affairs have needed such vivid reminders.

17. Churchill 1951, 356. Wohlstetter (from a 1961 article): Zarate and Sokolski 2009, 290.

18. Brodie 1966, 71–72; see also Kaplan 1983, 339. Kennan 1987, 888–89. Thomas 1986, 102. Jervis 2001, 59. Ambrose 1990, emphasis added. See also Johnson 1994, 75–78.

19. Evangelista 1982/83, 110–38. See also Ulam 1968, 414; Mearsheimer 1983, ch. 6; Posen 1984/85; Cockburn 1983; Johnson 1994, 75–78. Among Stalin's problems at the time was a major famine in the Ukraine in 1946 and 1947 (Khrushchev 1970, ch. 7).

20. Despite shortages, rationing, and tax surcharges, Americans increased consumer spending by 12 percent between 1939 and 1944. On these issues, see Lingeman 1970, 133, 357, and ch. 4; Milward 1977, 63–74, 271–75. As the British historian Denis Brogan observed at the time, "to the Americans war is a business, not an art" (quoted, Nevins 1946, 21).

21. Deane 1947, 92–95; Jones 1969, Appendix A. Additional information from Harvey DeWeerd.

22. Ulam 1971, 95, 5. Joint chief: Huntington 1961, 46. Thomas 1986, 548. Nor is it likely that this attitude changed later: "The men in the Kremlin are absorbed by questions of America's political, military, and economic power, and awed by its technological capacity" (Shevchenko 1985, 278). Or Khrushchev: "those 'rotten' capitalists keep coming up with things which make our jaws drop in surprise" (1974, 532).

23. Interestingly, one of Hitler's "terrible anxieties" before Pearl Harbor was that the Americans and Japanese might work out a rapprochement, uniting against Germany (Rich 1973, 228, 231, 246).

24. In fact, in some respects the memory of World War II was *more* horrible than the prospect of atomic war in the immediate postwar period. For a few years after World War II the United States enjoyed an atomic monopoly and there were proponents of an atomic preventive war against the USSR. These people were countered by General Omar Bradley and others who argued that this policy would be "folly" because the Soviets would still be able to respond with an offensive against Western Europe which would lead to something *really* bad: an "extended, bloody and horrible" struggle like World War II (Bradley 1949).

25. Stueck 2002, 71–77. Jervis 2001, 39–40.

26. The Soviet military intervention in Afghanistan in 1979 was an effort to prop up a faltering pro-Soviet regime. As such it was not like Korea but was more like American escalation in Vietnam in 1965 or the Soviet interventions in Hungary in 1956 and Czechoslovakia in 1968. For discussions of the importance of the Korean War in shaping Western perspectives on the cold war, see Gaddis 1974; Jervis 1980; May 1984.

27. The Korean experience may have posed a somewhat similar lesson for the United States. In 1950, amid talk of "rolling back" communism and sometimes even of liberating China, American-led forces invaded North Korea. This venture led to a costly and demoralizing, if limited, war with China and resulted in a considerable reduction in enthusiasm for such maneuvers. Had the United States been successful in taking over North Korea, there might well have been noisy calls for similar ventures elsewhere—though, of course, these calls might equally well have gone unheeded by the leadership.

28. Gilpin 1981, 218. Gaddis 1987, 229–32. Blacker 1987, 46. Holsti 1991, 305. Gaddis 1992, 110–12.

29. See Kennedy 1983, 170; Schroeder 2006, 36–37.

30. On military initiatives nonnuclear countries have taken against nuclear ones, see Paul 1994; Paul 2009.

31. Medvedev 1983, 190; G. Allison 1971, 221. Khrushchev's memoirs seem to support Shevchenko's conclusion that from the start the Soviets "were preoccupied almost exclusively with how to extricate themselves from the situation with minimum loss of face and prestige" (1985, 118).

32. Khrushchev: Werth 1964, xii, and Lebow and Stein 1994, 110; a report from a "reliable, well-placed" Soviet source says that the leadership issued a formalized secret directive that it had decided not to go to war even if the United States invaded Cuba: Garthoff 1987, 51. For an able refutation of the popular notion that it was American nuclear superiority that determined the Soviet backdown in the Cuban missile crisis, see Lambeth 1972, 230–34. Marc Trachtenberg has presented an interesting, if "somewhat speculative," case that Soviet behavior was influenced by their strategic inferiority. His argument is largely based on the observation that the Soviets never went on an official alert, and he suggests this arose from fear of provoking an American preemptive strike. But the essential hopelessness of the tactical situation and the general fear of escalation to what Lambeth (quoting Thomas Schelling) calls "just plain war" would also seem to explain this behavior (Trachtenberg 1985, 156–63).

33. Kennedy 1971, 40, 105. Although there were some dicey moments particularly in the first day or so, although there were hotheads on both sides, and although it was certainly possible to imagine an escalation sequence that could lead to war, the United States was extremely wary of the escalation process (and, anyway, had many lower rungs to climb first—tightening the blockade, bombing the sites, invading Cuba, fighting limited battles at sea—before getting there). Moreover, the president was apparently quite willing to consider formally removing missiles in Turkey if that is what it took to get the Cuban missiles out without further escalation. Defense Secretary Robert McNamara recalled Kennedy saying, "I am not going to war over worthless missiles in Turkey. I don't want to go to war anyhow, but I am certainly not going to war over worthless missiles in Turkey" (Trachtenberg 1985, 146). Transcripts of some of the climactic meetings at the White House tend to corroborate this view, as does the remarkable disclosure by Secretary of State Dean Rusk 25 years after the event that Kennedy had actually established mechanisms for arranging the missile trade should it come to that (Welch and Blight 1987/88, 27–28; Blight, Nye, and Welch 1987, 178–79; Lebow and Stein 1994, 127–28). As two analysts who have worked with the transcripts of the American meetings have observed, even if the Soviets had held out for a deal that was substantially embarrassing to the United States, the odds that the Americans would have gone to war "were next to zero" (Welch and Blight 1987/88, 27). See also Blight, Nye, and Welch 1987, 184; Brodie 1973, 426; Bundy 1988, 453–57, 461–62; Lebow and Stein 1994, ch. 6; Gaddis 1997, 269–72; Jervis 2001, 57.

34. Schelling: Kaplan 1983, 301–02. Harvard analysts: G. Allison et al. 1985, 208.

35. Luard 1986, 231.

36. On this issue, see Brodie 1973, 430.

CHAPTER 4: MODEST INFLUENCE ON HISTORY

1. Not obvious: Brown 1968, 286 n. 20,000: Freedman and Dockrill 1994, 201. No more damage: Compton 1956, 237; Dower 1986, 298, 301. Wilson points out that among

the bombing raids, Hiroshima ranked second in numbers of people killed, fourth in square miles destroyed, and seventeenth in percentage of the city destroyed (2008, 437n19).

2. Freedman and Dockrill 1994, 197–201 (shock); 193, 205–06, 208 (off guard).

3. See Butow 1954, 93, ch. 8; USSBS 1946; Kase 1950, 217; Freedman and Dockrill 1994, 201, 204–05; Bernstein 1995b, 136. On the "strategy" of the last glorious battle, see Ienaga 1978, 229–30.

4. Radio: Coffey 1970, 518–23; Kase 1950, 154–55; Craig 1967, 212–13. The Potsdam Declaration, issued several days before the atomic bombings, implied that the Japanese would be allowed to keep their emperor. The Japanese understood the message (Kase 1950, 210), so their public rejection of it, which set the plans for the atomic bombings in motion, proved to be a tragic mistake.

5. Kamikaze: Hoyt 1986, 396; Spector 1985, 410; see also Craig 1967, 13. Saipan: Ienaga 1978, 185, 197–98. Okinawa: Ienaga 1978, 185, 198. Stones: Brines 1944, 9. All that remains: Kase 1950, 249. Die together: Butow 1954, 49, 68, 93. The Japanese belief they would be killed was not entirely without foundation. Asked what should be done with the Japanese after the war, 10 to 15 percent of Americans in various polls conducted during the war volunteered the solution of extermination. After the war was over, 23 percent said they regretted that many more atomic bombs had not "quickly" been used on Japan before they "had a chance to surrender." For analysis, see J. Mueller 1973, 172–73. The U.S. Strategic Bombing Survey concludes that Japan would have surrendered by the end of 1945 even if the bombs hadn't been dropped and even if the Soviets had not entered the war (1946, 13). But this conclusion derives from postwar interviews with Japanese leaders detailing political progress toward surrender in the cabinet and indicating the emperor's position on the issue. It is not based on the notion that Japan would have been physically incapable of fighting by that time. On the willingness and ability of the military to continue to fight to the very end, see Bernstein 1995b, 119–20.

6. Hasegawa 2005, 296–98. Wilson 2007.

7. Kecskemeti 1958, ch. 6; see also Hoyt 1986, 420. Wilson 2007, 171.

8. Hasegawa 2005, 295–96. On Japanese awareness that the Soviets might enter the war, see in addition Freedman and Dockrill 1994, 205. Wilson 2007, 164, 167. Additionally, a Japanese study in 1945 found that imports from Korea and Manchuria—areas quickly taken over by the Soviet Union after its entry into the war—were vital in order to deal with a prospective gap in rice supplies (Bernstein 1995b, 122). For additional support for this general conclusion, see Bernstein 1995b, 136. For extended discussion of these issues, see the essays in Hasegawa 2007.

9. Holloway 1994, 122, 155. Some historians: in particular Alperovitz 1965. Bonus: Bernstein 1995a.

10. Holloway 1994, 122 (squarely); 129–30, 172 (impel Stalin); 156, 159, 253, 259–60, 368 (not be intimidated); 171, 253 (weak nerves); 156, 272 (Byrnes); 169 (not affected); 369 (no radical shift); 250 (international relations); 271 (little evidence). Bohlen: Gaddis 1997, 98. See also Wilson 2008, 434.

11. Holloway 1994, 272; see also Gaddis 1997, 98. Gaddis 1997, 111.

12. Bundy 1984, 44–47; Bundy 1988, 232–33, 238–43. For the argument that Truman never made a threat, see Thorpe 1978, 188–95. See also Gaddis 1987, 124–29; Betts 1987, 42–47; Holloway 1994, 271. On Soviet leader Nikita Khrushchev's fanciful conviction that his nuclear blandishments caused Britain and France to reverse their invasion at Suez in 1956, see Fursenko and Naftali 2006, 133–37.

13. Gaddis 1997, 107–10, emphasis in the original.

14. Halperin 1987, 30. George and Smoke 1974, 383. Betts 1987, 218–19. As for the Soviet-Chinese confrontations of the 1960s, Roy Medvedev notes Soviet fears of "war with a poorly armed but extremely populous and fanatical China" (1986, 50; see also Shevchenko 1985, 165–66; on many of these issues, see Bundy 1988). On the Berlin Blockade, see also Holloway 1994, 261. Israel's threat to use nuclear weapons in 1973, however, seems to have had an essentially extortionary impact on American policy at the time, a process discussed in chapter 10.

15. On this process, which may be repeating itself today with obsessions over the prospect of domestic terrorism, see J. Mueller 2008.

16. Holloway 1994, 138–44 (distrust); 222, 366 (fastest route); 222 (lower cost).

17. Holloway 1994, 283. However, the hydrogen bomb, which the Soviet scientists developed at about the same time as the United States entirely from their own designs (Holloway 1994, 366), required a plutonium implosion trigger. So to achieve that, they would have had eventually to devise that kind of bomb.

18. Holloway 1994, 283. However, almost all American policy makers simply assumed that the war was being directed from Moscow and was part of a Soviet strategic master plan. When State Department Counselor and Soviet specialist Charles Bohlen argued that Korea did not indicate a willingness to risk global war, he was ignored. Callahan 1990, 136–37. For a fuller discussion, see J. Mueller 2006, 72–75.

19. For a fuller discussion of these developments, see J. Mueller 2004–05; also J. Mueller 1995a, 31–34. See also Jervis 2001, 60.

20. Fukuyama 1987, 12. Reliable: Colton 1986, 191. Undercut: Oberdorfer 1992, 158–64. Inadequacy: Binder 1988. Ideologist: Keller 1988. 1988 speech: New York Times, 8 December 1988, A16; 9 December 1988, A18. For a 1986 analysis tracing the decline in fervor in the Soviet Union for its ideological commitment to the international Communist revolutionary movement and for the suggestions that this decline "could eventually result in the end of the cold war" and that "we may be coming to the end of the world as we know it," see J. Mueller 1986. On the Gorbachev transformation, see also Garthoff 1992; J. Mueller 1995a, ch. 2.

21. Reagan: New York Times, December 9, 1988, A18. Bush 1990, 541; see also 546, 553, 602, 606, 617, 667. Notably, Reagan tied this development to an end of the Soviet expansionary threat, not to the reform of its domestic system. That is, cooperation, even alliance, was not contingent on the progress of Soviet domestic reform. As long as the Soviet Union, like China in the 1970s or Yugoslavia after 1949, continued to neglect its expansionary and revolutionary ideology, it could be embraced by the West. Illiberal, nonexpansionist Portugal, after all, was a founding member of NATO. Much of this was anticipated in a comment made decades earlier by the quintessential cold warrior, John Foster Dulles: "The basic change we need to look forward to isn't necessarily a change from Communism to another form of government. The question is whether you can have Communism in one country or whether it has to be for the world. If the Soviets had national Communism we could do business with their government" (quoted, Gaddis 1982, 143). Economic and material factors may have helped to bring these changes about: the failure of the Soviet economic and administrative system clearly encouraged Gorbachev and others to reexamine their basic ideology. However, as Myron Rush observes, these problems by no means required a doctrinal change: had the Soviet Union done nothing about its problems, "its survival to the end of the century would have been likely," and "by cutting defense spending sharply... a prudent conservative leader in 1985 could have improved the Soviet economy markedly" (1993, 21).

22. Carlucci 1989. Bush 1990, 541. See also Vasquez 1998, 330.

23. Defining feature: Tannenwald 2007, 7. Waltz 1979, 98, 131, 170. Firmly rooted: Waltz 1988, 628.

24. That military capabilities are far more determining than economic ones in the Waltz perspective is suggested by his exclusion of the economically impressive, but militarily weak, United States from his list of major players on the international scene in the 19th century (1979, 162).

25. Schlesinger 1967, 6. Pre-nuclear: Schilling 1961, 26. See also J. Mueller 1995, ch. 2; Gaddis 1987, 230 n; Gaddis 1992, 112.

26. "The existence of nuclear weapons, especially of nuclear weapons that can survive attack, helps make empires and client states questionable sources of security" (M. May 1985, 150). "If France were truly fearful of a Soviet strike, it seems likely that she would seek a closer nuclear integration with the United States" (Richard Rosecrance in J. Mueller 1967, 881).

CHAPTER 5: APOCALYPTIC VISIONS, WORST-CASE PREOCCUPATIONS, MASSIVE EXPENDITURES

1. Wells 1914. Wells 1968, 67 (end). Wagar 1961, 13 n (vermin), 48 (epitaph).

2. Toynbee 1950, 4. Stalin: Djilas 1962, 114–15. Grew: Gaddis 1987, 218 n. For public opinion data and analysis, see J. Mueller 1979, 303–7.

3. Einstein 1960, 347.

4. Kramer: Billman 1997, 148. Reviewer: Green and Goldblatt 1973, 439. Kahn 1960, x. Snow 1961, 259.

5. Readers' Guide, observer: Paarlberg 1973, 133, 137; see also Brodie 1966, 21; Weart 1988, 262–69. Polls: J. Mueller 1977, 326–27; see also J. Mueller 1979.

6. Morgenthau: Boyle 1985, 73. Hackett 1979. McPhee 1974, 3–4.

7. Readers' Guide: McGlen 1986; see also Weart 1988, ch. 19. World Congress: Reiss 2004, 7.

8. Smoke 1993, ch. 10. On this first-strike dilemma, see also the discussion on pp. 66–67, 77 below.

9. Smoke 1993, 188–91.

10. Prevail: Smoke 1993, 111–12, 217–21. Reagan on war in Europe: Smoke 1993, 223; H. Mueller and Risse-Kappen 1987, 83. Haig: Gwertzman 1981. See also Kaplan 1983, 388–89.

11. H. Mueller and Risse-Kappen 1987, 83–84.

12. Schell 1982, 231. Book index: McGlen 1986. McNeill 1982, 383–84. Day After: Schuman et al. 1986, 528–29. Polls: J. Mueller 1994, 211.

13. Nor, apparently, did they significantly alter public opinion on the issue. For example, in November 1981, nuclear opponents in Amsterdam pulled off by far the biggest demonstration in Holland's history (Smoke 1993, 223). However, popular opposition to the new missiles changed hardly at all (DeBoer 1985, 128).

14. Weart 1988, 262.

15. Schell 2003.

16. Schelling 2005, 365. Commentator: Alvin M. Weinberg, quoted in Schelling 2005, 373.

17. Schelling 2005; on this process, see also Tannenwald 2007; Paul 2009; Bundy 1988, 586–88. Pain: Tannenwald 2007, 18.

18. See in particular Tannenwald 2007, Paul 2009.

19. Korea: Brodie 1959, 319; Paul 2009, 45–49; on nuclear restraint during that war, see also Brodie 1973, 64–65; Gaddis 1987, 115–23. Extremely rare: Paul 2009, 48. Vietnam: Paul 2009, 70; Zenko 2006, 93. Gulf: Powell 1995, 486. On this issue, see also Luard 1986, 396; Jervis 1989, 28; Gaddis 1992, 110; Paul 1994; Wilson 2008, 434; Paul 2009, ch. 7.

20. For consideration of the underexamined escalation assumption, see J. Mueller 1989, 236–40. Distaste: see also Tannenwald 2007, 133–35.

21. Paul 2009, 24 (all-or-nothing), 125–31 (examining the Israeli case).

22. Johnson 1994, 78. Kaplan 1983, 390, emphasis in the original.

23. Jenkins 2008, 193.

24. The threat: Morgan 1977, 9. Altering: Rothgeb 1993, 139. On these issues, see also Snyder 1961, ch. 1; Singer 1962, ch. 2; K. Mueller 1991.

25. See Huth and Russett 1990, 470.

26. As Huth and Russett point out, "Inclusion of positive inducements as a means to deter is not standard practice in academic writing or policy debates, but the lack of theoretical or practical attention cannot be justified on grounds of strict logic." And they label such considerations "a long-neglected and therefore underdeveloped component of deterrence theory" (1990, 471). For a fuller discussion, see J. Mueller 1995a, ch. 4; K. Mueller 1991; Rosecrance 1975.

27. For a critique of the concept of "anarchy" in international politics, see J. Mueller 1995, ch. 2.

28. Vasquez suggests the example of the boy in Brooklyn who runs out of his house once a day waving his arms in order to "keep the elephants away." When someone points out that there are no elephants in Brooklyn, the boy triumphantly observes, "See? It works!" (1991, 207). See also Wilson 2008.

29. Zarate and Sokolski 2009, 209; also 293 ("to deter a major power such as the Soviet Union is hard"); 637–38 (never large). See also Snyder 1961, 97–109.

30. Enthoven and Smith 1971, 207.

31. This is essentially what Kenneth Boulding (1978) calls "stable peace."

32. Lieber and Press 2006.

33. Selin: Cockburn 1983, vii. McNamara: Rhodes 2007, 99.

34. Johnson 1994, 29. On exaggerations of Soviet military capabilities, see Rhodes 2007, Cockburn 1983.

35. Brodie 1966, 59. Brodie 1978, 68, 83.

36. Gaddis 1997, 221.

37. Bought everything: Rhodes 2007, 306; a more conservative calculation, notes Rhodes, tags the expenditures at (merely) 55 percent of the country's nonland wealth. Underdog: Leffler 2007, 254.

38. Estimate (by Bruce Russett): Rhodes 2007, 307. Scientists: Reiss 1995, 3.

39. Gaddis 1997, 258. Emphasis in the original.

40. For a wide-ranging rumination on this issue, see Rosenberg 1994.

41. Einstein 1960, 426.

CHAPTER 6: ARMS RACES

1. Kahn 1960, 574.

2. Einstein 1960, 566. Teller and Russell: Grodzins and Rabinowitch 1963, 101, 124. Oppenheimer: Bird and Sherwin 2005, 341–42.

3. Einstein 1960, 382, 417, 482. Soviet scientists: Einstein 1960, 449.

4. Kennedy 1961.

5. On these developments, see also Joffe 1987, 39–40.

6. In Kennedy's view, China's nuclear program was the "whole reason for having a test ban." Trachtenberg 1999, 384.

7. Fursenko and Naftali 2006, 543–44. Possibly appropriate would be a comment made by the Wizard toward the end of the *Wizard of Oz* film: "I'm a very good man, but I'm a very bad Wizard."

8. Smoke 1993, ch. 10.

9. Leffler 2007, 254.

10. Ultimate goals: Hosmer and Wolfe 1983, 240. Garthoff 1994, 1070, emphasis in the original. See also Johnson 1994, 166–67, 169; Halperin 1987, 45.

11. Smoke 1993, 224–25. The resolution failed in the Senate. On public reaction to all this, see McGlen 1986; Schuman et al. 1986.

12. Smoke 1993, 236. Rhodes 2007, 252. One of Reagan's advisers said SDI was designed to "outflank the freeze" (Hymans 2004, 42).

13. Rhodes 2007, 191, 205, 271.

14. Rhodes 2007, 74.

15. Morgenthau 1948, 327. Thermometer: the image is proposed, but not adopted, in Rappard 1940, 490.

16. See Berkowitz 1987, especially ch. 2.

17. Unilateral reduction: Smoke 1987, 186. Carter: Paul 2009, 78–79; see also Smoke 1993, 187–88, 223. Bush: see, for example, his arguments in debate: *Congressional Quarterly,* 1 October 1988, 2750.

18. Kennedy campaign speech of October 23, 1960, at Milwaukee, Wisconson. Wohlstetter: Zarate and Sokolski 2009, 213.

19. For a valuable overview of this history, see Stacey 1953. See also Falk 1961.

20. Disarmament: Stacey 1953, 12. Points: Falk 1961, 73.

21. Stacey 1953, 15–16.

22. Carrington 1988, 3–5. Reluctance: Shlaes 1988. Harder to justify: Keatley 1989. Race to demobilize: *Wall Street Journal,* 31 May 1989, A1. An especially vivid acknowledgement of this tendency was put forward by John Tower in January 1989 in his ill-fated confirmation hearings for Secretary of Defense. While he foresaw no early reduction in the Soviet armed threat, Tower observed that if that threat *were* to diminish "we could obviously reduce our dedication of resources to defense.... We'd be maintaining the kind of army we had in 1938 [which was] about half the size of what the Marine Corps is now." Significantly, Tower did not insist that such a remarkable reduction would have to come about through formal agreement, but clearly implied it could happen naturally, even automatically, if the perceived threat diminished. (Confirmation Hearing for John Tower for Secretary of Defense, Senate Armed Services Committee, January 25, 1989.)

23. Coup: see, for example, Rhodes 2007, 293–94. Testing: Krepon 2009. Total number: Tannenwald 2007, 389. Former secretary: Bohlen 2009.

24. Nut and bolt: see also Kaysen, McNamara, and Rathjens 1991, 107. Unilaterally withdrawing: Tannenwald 2007, 329, 329 n. Radical move: Tannenwald 2007, 329. Senate: Cushman 1992.

25. Tannenwald 2007, 330.

26. "Atom War 'Suicide Pills' Backed," *New York Times,* 13 October 1984.

27. Defense officials: Shultz et al. 2007, 2008; for an extended spinoff, see Daalder and Lodal 2008. Little attention: Robbins 2008.

28. Pentagon: Tannenwald 2007, 331–32. Blair 2003. Younger 2009, 11.

29. Baum 2008.

30. To reduce cold war tensions, Charles E. Osgood once proposed something he called GRIT: Graduated Reciprocation In Tension-reduction (1962, especially ch. 5). He supposed high tension and then proposed a series of explicit unilateral initiatives to reduce arms and tensions. His initiatives had stringent requirements that made them very difficult to engineer in practice. For example, he required that they be diversified, publicly announced, explicitly capable of reciprocation, executed on precise schedule, unambiguous, and susceptible to verification. Although he referred to his approach as an "arms race in reverse," arms races are not so rigorous or formal. They are filled with deception, guesswork, ambiguity, abrupt lurches, whim, panic, and elaborate efforts to evade verification. The negative arms race, by contrast, supposes *low* tension. Since, as Morgenthau suggests, the progress of the arms race has been impelled by high tensions, low tensions, combined with economic pressures, should naturally encourage a negative arms race.

CHAPTER 7: PROLIFERATION

1. Hymans 2006, 5. See also Yusuf 2009, 4, 60–61.

2. National Planning Association 1958, 42. Intelligence community: Cirincione 2007a, 27. Snow 1961, 259. Mulley 1962, 79–80. Healey 1960, 3.

3. Ten, fifteen: Kraus 1962, 394. Personally: Rhodes 2007, 71.

4. China bomb: Kroenig 2008. Burr and Richelson 2000/01, 62; Gavin 2004/05, 104–05. Johnson and McCone: Hersh 1991, 149, 106. Gilpatric 1965, 3.

5. Rosecrance 1964, 312; J. Mueller 1967, 884; see also Brodie 1973, 383–86. Betts 2000, 54.

6. Arkin 1994. Betts 2000, 55. See also Hymans 2004, 38.

7. Woolsey 1993.

8. Germany: Mearsheimer 1990, 38. Japan: Layne 1993, 37. Kahn 1970, 165–66. On these cases, see Mackby and Slocombe 2004; Campbell and Sunohara 2004. On Japan, see also Berger 1993; Katzenstein and Okawara 1993, 115–16; Hughes 2007; Solingen 2007, ch. 3. For a listing of other unfulfilled predictions about Japan's likely nuclear future, see Solingen 2007, 314n68. For an excellent discussion of unfulfilled pessimistic prophesies about North East Asia more generally, see Choi 2006.

9. Japan: Hughes 2007, 81; Solingen 2007, 314n68. Germany: Mackby and Slocombe 2004, 206.

10. Arkin 1994. Bulletin: Solingen 2007, 6. See also Hymans 2006, 2.

11. Tenet: Reiss 2004, 4. G. Allison 2007; on concern in the Clinton administration a decade earlier about a North Korean cascade, see Kroenig 2008. Scowcroft: *The News-Hour with Jim Lehrer,* PBS, 11 November 2008.

12. Langewiesche 2007, 16, 177.

13. Solingen 2007, 7.

14. Reiss 2004, 12–13, 4. On the phenomenon of the "Washington threat consensus," see Hymans 2004.

15. Campbell and Einhorn 2004, 328.

16. Review: Wolfsthal 2005. Former officials: Schultz et al. 2008. First Commission: Graham 2008, 18. Second Commission: Pincus 2008.

17. Potter and Mukhatzhanova 2008, 159. Hymans 2006, 208–09.

18. Keith Payne in Ruppe 2003.

19. Gavin 2004/05, 101, see also 104. Worst event: Burr and Richelson 2000/01, 61. Sure to exploit: Gavin 2004/05, 104. For a contemporary comparison, see Zakaria 2007. For the importance of fear of an expansive China on U.S. decision making over Vietnam, see J. Mueller 1989, 168–73, 177–81.

20. Dominate: Trachtenberg 1999, 320. Chicom: Gavin 2004/05, 109–10. Bandwagon: Richelson 2006, 144. Gavin 2004/05, 107. McCone: Gavin 2004/05, 104.

21. Burr and Richelson 2000/01, 69–71.

22. Burr and Richelson 2000/01, 76–78. For Johnson's perspective more broadly, see his brilliant book, *Improbable Dangers,* published in 1994 and developed in part from earlier writings.

23. On this process, see J. Mueller 1989, 184–86.

24. Bundy 1988, 531. See also Walt 2000, 198.

25. Gavin 2004/05, 122.

26. Bush: Kroenig 2008. McCain: *Congressional Record,* 10 October 2002.

27. Walt 2000, 196 n (U.S.), 209 (alliance construction), 211 (unfazed).

28. Gavin 2004/05, 107, emphasis added.

29. Gilpatric 1965, 2. Powers 2008. Wolfsthal 2005.

30. For example, see Bracken 1983, 64–65.

31. Brodie 1966, 57. Plane shot down: Hilsman 1967, 220–21; without authorization: Bernstein 1987. Plane off course: Hilsman 1967, 221. Soviet officer: Garthoff 1987, 40–41. See also Bundy 1988, 455; Sagan 1993, ch. 2.

32. Jervis 1979, 299. Wolfenstein 1957, 17; see also Furedi 2008, 175–80.

33. Luard 1986, 232. Blainey 1973, 141. Kissinger 1979, 885. See also Brodie 1966, 53–57. A possible instance, however, is the "football war" between Honduras and El Salvador in 1969 in which unintended and undesired hostilities broke out, and peace was reestablished in a few days (Luard 1986, 227 n).

34. On this change, see also Sagan 1993, 9–10.

35. Basement: Sagan in Sagan and Waltz 2003, 169. South Africa: Reiss 1995, 11. Pakistan: Warrick 2007.

CHAPTER 8: THE LIMITED APPEAL AND VALUE OF NUCLEAR WEAPONS

1. Yusuf 2009, 61.

2. Observer: Betts 2000, 54–55. Kay 2008, 18–19. See also Cirincione 2007a, ch. 4; Hymans 2006, 225. Rosecrance 1964, 299–306.

3. Techno-centric: Hymans 2006, 11. National Planning Association 1958, 40. National Planning Association 1960, 27–28; the technical report is by William C. Davidon, Marvin Kalkstein, and Christoph Hohenemser. 50 deemed capable: Hymans 2006, 4. For a discussion of Israel's capabilities in the early 1960s, see Beaton and Maddox 1962, ch. 11.

4. Meyer 1984. See also Kaysen, McNamara, and Rathjens 1991, 98; Hymans 2006, 2–12; Yusuf 2009, 60.

5. Healey 1960, 3. Beaton and Maddox 1962, 98.

6. Reiss 1995. Paul 2000.

7. Langewiesche 2007.

8. Gilpin 1981, 215.

9. De Gaulle 1968, 103; see also Sagan 2000, 41–44. Illusory: Hymans 2006, 211.

10. Beaton and Maddox assert that Canada rejected a nuclear weapons policy "in 1946 by a deliberate and conscious decision" (1962, 98). But to call Canada's arrival at a nonnuclear policy a "decision," let alone a "deliberate and conscious" one, appears to be overly imaginative. It seems rather that a nuclear policy was never thought of. An analysis of the histories and periodicals of the time, of the atomic energy debates, and of the biographies of Mackenzie King, Canada's then prime minister, leads to the conclusion that there was no serious consideration of the pros and cons of developing an atomic weapons program. In all this literature the word "decision" is rarely used, and then only in a general way, referring to the policy arrived at, not the procedure for making it. As J. W. Pickesgill, an assistant to and biographer of Mackenzie King and a powerful backstage figure in Ottawa from 1937 to 1953, recalls, "there were never any serious proponents of the view that Canada should develop its own atomic force. Certainly Mr. King had no such view" (personal communication, 26 November 1962). No general announcement that the military policy of Canada was nonnuclear was ever made, but that this was indeed the policy was admitted in an offhand manner in the middle of a House of Commons debate on June 3, 1946, and this may be the date to which Beaton and Maddox refer. On this issue, see J. Mueller 1967, 866.

11. Mackby and Slocombe 2004, 210.

12. Hymans 2006, 211–12, emphasis in the original.

13. China as power: Greenhouse 1993; on this issue, see also Rosecrance 1986. Bundy 1988, 531. Unconditional: Cho 2009.

14. Revzin 1987.

15. China: WuDunn 1993; see also Bundy 1988, 531. Korea: Darlin 1990.

16. Jervis 1989, 4. See also J. Mueller 1967; Hymans 2006, 211–12.

17. Arkin 200.

18. Waltz 1990, 734; for an assessment of this perspective, see Sagan 2000, 20–27.

19. Payne 2009, 48–51.

20. Wilson 2007, 178–79. China: Cho 2009.

21. Hersh 1991, 137.

22. Hymans 2006, 212.

23. Hymans 2006, 9, 11. Not so easy: Campbell and Einhorn 2004, 328.

24. Eat grass: Langewiesche 2007, 88; Cirincione 2007a, 38. Expensive: Langewiesche 2007, 103.

25. Garwin and Charpak 2001, 352. Israel: Hersh 1991, 59, 65, 67–68, 136.

26. System: Hymans 2006, 11. Record: Hymans 2008, 273. See also Reed and Stillman 2009, 269, 281.

27. Silberman and Robb 2005, 260–61. See also Hymans 2008, 273.

28. J. Mueller 1967, 878 n (improper division), 879 (virginity).

29. Tannenwald 2007, 19.

30. J. Mueller 1967, 877.

31. Hymans 2006, 2, 208.

32. Solingen 2007, 275–77. Quality of political leadership: Reiss 1995, 329. See also Sagan 2000, 27–37. On the crucial importance of individual leaders in major decisions, see also Valentino 2004.

33. Waltz in Sagan and Waltz 2003, 38.

CHAPTER 9: CONTROLLING PROLIFERATION

1. On the rise of a "Washington threat consensus" on this issue, see Hymans 2004.

2. McNaugher 1990, 32–33. Neufeld 1995, 273–74.

3. On this process, see Hymans 2008, 273–74; Hymans 2007.

4. Waltz in Sagan and Waltz 2003, 44–45. See also Bueno de Mesquita and Riker 1982; Mearsheimer 1990, 1993.

5. Moreover, to espy benefit in proliferation Waltz focuses on international war, something that scarcely exists anymore, at least in its classic form. Indeed, over the last two decades, there has been only one substantial international war in which two countries directly have it out over some issue of mutual dispute, in this case territory: the almost unnoticed (but quite costly) conflict between Ethiopia and Eritrea that took place between 1998 and 2000. There have also been a considerable number of civil wars, a few border flare-ups, and several "policing wars"—militarized efforts by developed countries designed to bring order to civil conflicts or to deal with thuggish regimes. The relevance, if any, of nuclear weapons to these kinds of armed conflict is very limited. In addition, the policing war phenomenon, rather tentative at best, seems more likely to wane than to grow due to lack of interest, an extremely low tolerance for casualties in military missions that are essentially humanitarian, and an aversion to long-term policing, sentiments likely to be greatly enhanced by the experiences in Iraq and Afghanistan. See J. Mueller 2009a. Also J. Mueller 2004.

6. Betts 2000, 64.

7. Reiss 2004, 4. As noted on p. 94, however, the book actually ends up concluding that we are not anywhere near a tipping point.

8. Kurth 1998.

9. On this episode, see Solingen 2007, ch. 5; Jacob 2008.

10. Cirincione 2007b, 17.

11. Betts 2000, 69, emphasis removed.

12. Cirincione 2007a, 33–34.

13. Hymans 2006, 214–16. Hymans also notes that Argentina and Brazil engaged in cooperative nuclear developments in the 1980s in order to fend off pressure to join the NPT, developments that "led to fantastic assertions that the two might be planning to launch a 'bi-national' bomb program" (2006, 164).

14. Solingen 2007, 262 (Japan), 263 (Iran, Libya, Iraq), 194 (bolster). Tannenwald 2007, 330–31.

15. Useful: Reiss 1995, 391. Modest: Paul 2000, 151.

16. Cirincione 2007b, 16–17.

17. First weapon: Liberman 2001, 49–54. Arsenal: Reiss 1995, 29–31.

18. Costs: Liberman 2001, 55; Reiss 1995, 15, 30; Reiss notes, however, that the program "siphoned off many of the country's most talented scientists and engineers," and this must be factored in when assessing the costs of the program (43n117). Danger remote: Liberman 2001, 58. Unthinkable: Reiss 1995, 29. Military: Liberman 2001, 66–67. Fixated: from a "well-placed" source, Liberman 2001, 64. Pet project: according to F. W. de Klerk: Liberman 2001, 72–73.

19. Soviet connections: Liberman 2001, 74–75; Reiss 1995, 20–21. de Klerk: Liberman 2001, 74; see also Reiss 1995, 19. Permissive condition: Liberman 2001, 75.

20. Large role: Reiss 1995, 28. Sensitivity, consistent with Solingen: Liberman 2001, 83–84.

21. Reiss 1995, 32.

22. Asked at an open forum at the 1992 meetings of the Midwest Political Science Association, "What would happen if Ukraine were to give up nuclear weapons?" realist John Mearsheimer responded, "That would be a tremendous blow to realist theory." In 1993, he published an article making the case for a Ukrainian bomb.

23. Reiss 1995, 92, 129–30 (Belarus), 92 (allergy). See also Potter 1995.

24. For a thoughtful assessment of this possibility in the Ukraine case, see Sagan 2000, 44–49.

25. Reiss 1995, 131 (quickly removed), 131, 143, 94 (spirited away), 126, 128 (strategic weapons).

26. Reiss 1995, 128–29 (Ukraine), 136, 138 (Belarus), 149–50 (Kazakhstan).

27. Solingen 2007, 89, 112. Jacob 2008.

28. Solingen 2007, 98, 116.

29. Solingen 2007, 91.

30. Takeyh 2001, 63.

31. Isolated, national security: Simon 2001, 196–97. Qaddafi rhetoric: Wills 2003, 194. Donkeys: Solingen 2007, 219. In 1983, the Organization of African Unity unhelpfully and absurdly pronounced that Libya possessed "the ability to deploy nuclear weapons" (Solingen 2007, 340n4).

32. Enhanced Qaddafi: Takeyh 2001, 64. Continued program: Solingen 2007, 221. Ambitions: Solingen 2007, 226. Shultz: Simon 2001, 200. Although there is considerable reason to believe Iran and Syria were also involved in the Lockerbie bombing, they remained, and remain, unpunished. Simon 2001, 233–34.

33. New wind: Takeyh 2001, 63–67. Domestic opposition: Solingen 2007, 222–26, 228.

34. Indyk 2004; see also Stevenson 2004, 11; Jentleson and Whytock 2005/06; Solingen 2007, 227–28.

35. Hymans 2008, 275, 281. Crates: Sanger and Broad 2004. ElBaradei: *BBC Newsnight,* 3 March 2004. I am grateful to Jacques Hymans for supplying some of this information.

36. Solingen 2007, 223–24.

37. Waltz in Sagan and Waltz 2003, 43.

CHAPTER 10: COSTS OF THE PROLIFERATION FIXATION

1. Supreme: G. Allison 2004, ch. 7. Number one: Cirincione 2007b, 15. Duty: Feinstein and Slaughter 2004; in 2009, Slaughter became Director of Policy Planning in the Barack Obama administration.

2. On some of these issues, see also Hymans 2006, 209, 226.

3. Deaths in the Iraq War: Fischer 2008. For critical prewar examinations of the assumption that Iraq, however armed, posed much of a threat, see Mearsheimer and Walt 2003; J. Mueller (in debate with Lindsey) 2003; Mueller and Mueller 1999, 52–53; 2000, 177–80. For a detailed discussion of threat exaggeration in the run-up to the Iraq War, see Kaufmann 2004. See also Record 2003, 13–19; Record 2004. For broad-scaled examinations of the exaggeration of foreign security threats, see Johnson 1994, J. Mueller 2006.

4. Pollack 2002, xiv (costs; added to these, he suggests, would be another $5 to $10 billion over the first three years for rebuilding: 397); 335 (hegemon); 413 (oil); 418 (predicting).

5. Bush: Reiss 2004, 11; see also G. Allison 2004, 137. McCain: Senate speech, 10 October 2002. Panic: Rice 2000. Mushroom (Rice): http://transcripts.cnn.com/ TRANSCRIPTS/0209/08/le.00.html. Mushroom (Bush): Address to the Nation, 7 October 2002. Wolfowitz: http://transcripts.cnn.com/TRANSCRIPTS/0305/30/se.08.html. Rove: Stein 2008. "Simply stated," the nation was assured by the vice president in a speech to the Veterans of Foreign Wars National Convention on August 26, 2002, "there is no doubt that Saddam Hussein now has weapons of mass destruction." See also Cirincione 2007a, 150; Perle 2009.

6. Perle 2009, 42–43. Fukuyama 2005. On this issue, see also J. Mueller 2009b; Jervis 2006, 8; and, for a different perspective, Bobbitt 2008, 492–93.

7. Weisberg 2008; also Easterbrook 2002, 25. On this issue, see also Arkin 2006b; Jervis 2006, 6; and especially Hymans 2004.

8. Hymans 2004.

9. For assessments of Iraq's rather pathetic efforts to create nuclear weapons, see Hymans 2007; 2008, 275.

10. Jervis 2006, 44.

11. Weiner 1999a, 1999b; Lippman and Gellman 1999. See also Jervis 2006, 43.

12. Last man: J. Mueller 1995, 102. Ammunition: Fallows 2005, 72. Heavy weapons: O'Kane 1998. Even war advocate Richard Perle had written a few years earlier that "Saddam's grip on the regular army...has always been tenuous" (2000, 109). For an extended discussion of Saddam's obsessive worries about a military coup, see Gordon and Trainor 2006, 55–66, 505. War advocates often claimed that "containment" wasn't working because Iraq was able partly to evade some of the sanctions and engage in some modest rearmament (e.g., Pollack 2002, ch. 7). This is a bizarre redefinition of the concept. In the cold war, containment meant keeping the enemy from expanding, not keeping it from developing economically or militarily or from conducting trade. See also Mearsheimer and Walt 2003, 56–59.

13. Garfield 1999. United Nations 1999. Cockburn and Cockburn 1999, ch. 5. Gordon 1999. Mueller and Mueller 2000. Baram 2000. Welch 2002. Ali et al. 2003. Lopez and Cortwright 2004. Welch 2002. Pollack 2002, 138–39.

14. 10 percent levels: Garfield 1997, 182. Material for rebuilding: Loeb 1998; Melby 1998, 121. Syringes: Sweeney 1998. Chlorine: Stahl 1996; Cockburn and Cockburn 1999, 131. World War I: F. Brown 1968, 4, 38. Cancer: Sikora 1999, 203. Radioactive particles, plastic bags: O'Kane 1998b. Fertilizers and insecticides: O'Kane 1998a. Cotton: Borger 1998.

15. Gates: Cockburn and Cockburn 1999, 43. Albright: Stahl 1996.

16. Albright 2003, 275.

17. Middle East: Cockburn and Cockburn 1999, 263. Bin Laden: Wright 2006, 259–60. The benign public acceptance of the sanctions, despite their human costs, is quite impressive, because the American public was strongly disinclined to blame the Iraqi people—unlike, say, the Japanese in World War II—for the policies of the country's leadership. J. Mueller 1994, 79; 2002b, 160.

18. Polls: J. Mueller 1994, 118. Very far from bomb: Hymans 2007. Uprisings: J. Mueller 1995b.

19. Oberdorfer 2001, 314. Harden 2009.

20. Oberdorfer 2001, 307. Sigal 1998, ch. 4. Harrison 2002, 213.

21. Go to war: Oberdorfer 2001, 308, 316; on this issue, see also Fallows 1994/95. Sanctions: Oberdorfer 2001, 318. Paranoid: Oberdorfer 2001, 329; see also Smith 2006, 70–71. Cost of war: Oberdorfer 2001, 324; see also Harrison 2002, 117–18.

22. Extortion: Eberstadt 1999; Oberdorfer 2001, 305, 336. Pay attention: Arkin 2006a; Wiseman 2009. Carter visit: Oberdorfer 2001, 327; see also Harrison 2002, 217. Deal: Sigal 1998, chs. 6–7; Harrison 2002, ch. 18. Promises: Harrison 2002; Kaplan 2006.

23. Famine: Oberdorfer 2001, 399; Natsios 2001, 215. Aid: Natsios 2001, 147–48.

24. Allison and Simes 2006, 13. A somewhat similar process took place with respect to policy toward General Pervez Musharraf's unpopular authoritarian regime in Pakistan. When bothered by outside criticism of his political repression, Musharraf would sometimes suggest that perhaps he would stop cooperating on the terrorism front, and this threat had an effect even though he was substantially beholden to foreign aid and even though he had an intense incentive to bring terrorists and other extremists to heel, since he was one of their primary targets (Grare 2007). An additional cost, as the prominent Pakistani journalist Ahmed Rashid has pointed out, was that millions of middle-class Pakistanis turned "very anti-American" because when they protested against Musharraf's rule, advocating a return to civilian rule, all they saw coming out of the United States was a "continuous barrage of statements in favor of Musharraf, nothing in favor of the democratic movement" (*Weekend Edition*, NPR, 14 July 2007). See also Cole 2009a, 164.

25. Reiss 1995, 327.

26. There was also a strong perception in Israel that the United States might like to see the Arabs win some ground, something that might help compel Israel to negotiate a peace treaty later. The result of Israel's atomic gambit seems to have undercut support for that approach to the degree that it existed. On these issues, see Hersh 1991, 40, 139, 226–39; Paul 2009, 127–28.

27. Liberman 2001, 62. See also Reiss 1995, 15, 28.

28. Betts 2000, 70 n. Top antiproliferator Graham Allison is among those advocating the cartelization of nuclear fuel. He further suggests that nuclear states guarantee to sell the nonnuclear ones all the nuclear fuel they need (presumably in perpetuity) at less than half price, but does not attempt to calculate the price tag for this (G. Allison 2004, 156–65). The 2008 Graham Commission, of which Allison was a member, repeats this demand, though it suggests that nuclear fuel be made available at market prices "to the extent possible." It, too, eschews cost considerations (Graham 2008, xx). There is, however, a glimmer of evidence that the economic cost of hampering the nuclear industry has been considered at least in passing by some dedicated antiproliferators. In a 2007 plea that the world be made free of nuclear weapons, four former top policy officials insisted that the use of highly enriched uranium be phased out from civil commerce and that it be removed from all the research facilities in the entire world, a costly demand that was not repeated in their 2008 version (Shultz et al. 2007, 2008).

29. Schelling 2005, 369. Lasers: Anderson 2008.

30. On this issue, see especially Weart 1988.

31. For alarmed concern on this issue, see in particular W. Allison 2006, 317.

32. Garwin and Charpak 2001, 144–45.

33. Chertoff 2008. A similar process has taken place in the academy, and perhaps for similar reasons. As Bruce Hoffman laments, "Many academic terrorism analyses are self-limited to mostly lurid hypotheses of worst-case scenarios, almost exclusively involving CBRN (chemical, biological, radiological, or nuclear) weapons, as opposed to trying to understand why—with the exception of September 11—terrorists have only rarely realized their true killing potential" (2002, 311–12). For various calculations about the damage caused by international terrorism, to which Chertoff was explicitly responding, see pp. 220–29 below.

34. Larsen 2007, 99. False alarms: Fessler 2007, also Borger 2008. No terrorist interest: Shapiro 2007, 4, 15–16; see also de Rugy 2007.

35. *Charlie Rose*, PBS, March 27, 2009. This issue is considered more fully in chapter 15 below.

CHAPTER 11: RECONSIDERING PROLIFERATION POLICY

1. Hymans 2006, 225.

2. Hymans 2006, 222 (causal link), 209–11 (threat matrix). As noted in chapter 8, Hymans puts prime emphasis on ego, with the added proviso that only when the ego in charge has a conception of national identity that can be considered to be what he calls of the "oppositional nationalist" variety will the country really try to get nuclear weapons. Hymans 2006, ch. 2.

3. Lewis and Xue 1988, 34. Bundy 1988, 531. See also Holloway 1994, 355.

4. Arkin 2006b, 45. Actually, the American threat under Bush, particularly with respect to the Middle East, was considerably broader. Bush may have happened to specify three regimes, but many of his prominent supporters, particularly in the neoconservative camp, went quite a bit farther. In an article in the fall of 2004, Charles Krauthammer urged taking "the risky but imperative course of trying to reorder the Arab world," with a "targeted, focused" effort on "that Islamic crescent stretching from North Africa to Afghanistan" (2004b, 23, 17). And in a speech in late 2006, he championed what he calls "the only plausible answer," an amazingly ambitious undertaking that would involve "changing the culture of that area, no matter how slow and how difficult the process. It starts in Iraq and Lebanon, and must be allowed to proceed." In their 2003 book *The War over Iraq,* Lawrence Kaplan and William Kristol stress that "The mission begins in Baghdad, but does not end there.... War in Iraq represents but the first installment...Duly armed, the United States can act to secure its safety and to advance the cause of liberty—in Baghdad and beyond" (2003, 124–25). Richard Perle suggested at the time that "a short message" should be delivered to other hostile regimes in the area: "You're next" (Mearsheimer and Walt 2006, 274; see also Perle 2009, 42). Most interesting is a call issued in the run-up to the war by neoconservatism's champion guru, Norman Podhoretz. He strongly advocated expanding Bush's axis of evil "at a minimum" to embrace Syria, Lebanon, Libya, Egypt, the Palestinian Authority, and the Saudi royal family, stressing that "it will be necessary for the United States to *impose* a new political culture on the defeated parties" (2002, 28, emphasis in the original). These men did not, of course, directly run the Bush administration. However, given the important role people like that have had in its intellectual development and military deployment, the designated target regimes would be foolish in the extreme not to take such existential threats very seriously indeed. See also Mueller 2009b.

5. PostGlobal Global Power Barometer (http://voices.washingtonpost.com/postglobal/drg/): "A unique perspective on Iran; an interview with Kaveh Afrasiabi; Posted August 8/9, 2007." See also Solingen 2007, ch. 8; D. Smith 2006.

6. Warrick 2007. Cirincione 2008.

7. Hymans 2007, 2008.

8. Solingen 2007, 178, 180, 182, 281 (Pasdaran), 275–97 (internationalize). See also Dueck and Takeyh 2007, 194–98, 202.

9. Hymans 2009. Muller 2998, 35.

10. Downes 1988. See also Sharrock 1999; Mueller and Mueller 2000, 170–76. For sanctions to be effective at shaking up a regime, it is axiomatic that they must weaken, rather than strengthen, the ties of the leader's core support group. For an excellent discussion of this key proposition, see Kirshner 1997.

11. Reiss 2004, 12.

12. Reiter 2005, 362, 365; 2006, 4–6. Betts 2006. Reed and Stillman 2009, 278–79. See also Solingen 2007, 143. Moreover, the reactor the Israelis bombed was essentially incapable of producing sufficient quantities of weapons-grade fissile material because of the conditions under which it was built and operated. Reiter 2005, 357–61.

13. Gavin 2004/05, 115.

14. Hymans forthcoming.

15. For a discussion, see Hymans forthcoming.

16. G. Allison 2004, 166 (50 to 70), 165–71 (launch attack), 169 (initiating).

17. For commentary about the rather pathetic nature of this test, see Hymans 2008, 276; Reed and Stillman 2009, 262.

18. G. Allison 2004, 166. Bobbitt 2008, 529.

19. Clinton: CNN, 6 June 2007. G. Allison 2004, 164. Obama: Cole 2009a, 208. Kay 2008, 18. Political scientist Amitai Etzioni, writing in 2007 after North Korea (more or less) got its bomb, gives that country a pass: since it has apparently already entered the nuclear club, it is too late to do much, and it will have to be "deterred from using its arms via the old-fashioned, Cold War method of threatening nuclear retaliation for any nuclear attack." Now, however, "an unambiguous declaration by all the nuclear powers must be made that North Korea is the *last* new member. No more such powers will be tolerated" (2007, 241–42, emphasis in the original). North Korea would likely be quite happy to join that particular chorus. Curiously, although Etzioni believes North Korea can be deterred using "old-fashioned" methods, he seems mysteriously to believe that Iran cannot. Accordingly, since he insists that the "highest priority" must be given to "neutralizing" the supposed threat presented by proliferation, especially involving terrorists, he is led to declare that a war must be waged against Iran and other potential proliferators (Japan? South Korea? Turkey? Sweden?) if lesser measures fail to halt any potential bids to join the exclusive nuclear club (2007, 242). Interestingly, Etzioni begins his book by extolling a principle he calls the "primacy of life."

20. Morris 2008; see also Boudreaux 2007; Goldberg 2008; G. Allison 2004, 164; Lustick 2008, 48–49; Halevi and Oren 2007. According to Halevi and Oren, "Senior army commanders, who likely once regarded Holocaust analogies with the Middle East conflict as an affront to Zionist empowerment, now routinely speak of a 'second Holocaust.' Op-eds, written by left-wing as well as right-wing commentators, compare these times to the 1930s [when] the international community reacted with indifference as a massively armed nation declared war against the Jewish people." Halevi and Oren suggest that an Iranian nuclear threat would embolden Hezbollah and Hamas, limit Israeli military options, prevent any Arab country from making concessions in negotiations, deter investors from the Jewish state, and drive Israeli elites with opportunities abroad to leave the country. If the West cannot be convinced to prevent Iran from going nuclear by the middle of 2008, say Halevi and Oren, Israel will have to strike Iran militarily, anticipating an all-out conventional war with Iran and other Middle Eastern states if this occurs.

21. A danger for Israel in all this arises not so much from Iran's capacity or potential capacity to do harm—though judicious and balanced concerns about that danger

are, of course, justified—as from the consequences of the hype, at once apoplectic and apocalyptic, on the issue. A concern would be that, if the hysteria persists, a considerable, and increasing, number of Israelis may be led to conclude that, since there is no way really to guarantee that Iran will never be able to obtain a bomb, the situation is hopeless, Israel is ultimately doomed, and it is best to live elsewhere, in a place where one can bring up children free from nuclear fears. For some speculations on this issue, see Mueller and Lustick 2008.

22. Ben-Ami and Parsi 2008; Reed and Stillman 2009, 299. Indeed, the Israelis seem to be fully aware of this: at best, an Israeli assault could only delay Iran's nuclear program, particularly because Israel could not sustain an air campaign against remote targets (Halevi and Oren 2007).

23. Hymans 2008; Reed and Stillman 2009, 262; Muller 2008, 35, 44, 138. More generally, see also Hymans 2007.

24. Harden 2009.

25. Jacques Hymans suggests an additional potential problem in the routine hysteria evoked internationally whenever North Korea tests an atomic device or missile. In the eyes of the regime, this reaction can vindicate its efforts. By contrast, if the international community treated these technologically pathetic achievements with due contempt, the regime, always on the lookout for international recognition, might well dismiss its scientific team, replacing it with even less competent people and therefore delaying progress even more (personal communication).

26. Cole 2009a, 208–09.

27. Garwin 2008, 41. Jervis 2006, 7. Finn 2009. By contrast, Israeli intelligence was reportedly predicting a finished Iranian bomb by 2009. Indeed, observe Yossi Klein Halevi and Michael Oren (2007), "Military men suddenly sound like theologians when explaining the Iranian threat," and some of the ponderings can become downright spooky: "Ahmadinejad's pronouncements about the imminent return of the Hidden Imam and the imminent destruction of Israel aren't regarded as merely calculated for domestic consumption; they are seen as glimpses into an apocalyptic game plan. Ahmadinejad has reportedly told his Cabinet that the Hidden Imam will reappear in 2009—precisely the date when Israel estimates Iran will go nuclear."

28. Garwin 2008, 40.

29. For a discussion of the "map" issue, see Bronner 2006; Steele 2006; Cole 2009a, 201–02. On the misunderstanding of Khrushchev's provocative and somewhat comparable "we will bury you" comment during the cold war, see Fursenko and Naftali 2006, 232.

30. On this issue, see J. Mueller 2006, 100–10. See also Zakaria 2007.

31. Dueck and Takeyh 2007, 195, 205. Powers 2008. According to one observer, participants at a conference on "A Nuclear Iran" held at Hebrew University in Jerusalem grouped themselves into two camps. One, mostly made up of scholars of Iran and of the current regime there, argued that a nuclear Iran, while hostile, would pursue a policy that would of necessity be pragmatic and risk-averse. The other, mostly comprised of nonspecialists, insisted that any pragmatism would somehow be overthrown as soon as Iran obtained the bomb, which they would then use directly or indirectly against Israel. Aronson 2008. As Juan Cole points out, Iran "has not launched an aggressive war of conquest against a neighbor for at least 150 years" (2009a, 199).

32. Schelling 2005, 374.

33. When Jeffrey Goldberg asked Israel's prime minister, Benjamin Netanyahu, "if he believed Iran would risk its own nuclear annihilation at the hands of Israel or America," the response was, "I'm not going to get into that" (2009).

34. Kay 2008, 18–19. In Israel, report Halevi and Oren, "nearly everyone agrees," apparently almost completely without examination, that "Israel cannot live with a nuclear Iran" (2007).

35. Dueck and Takeyh 2007, 201 (effect of strikes); 195, 204–05 (use by Iran); 203 (military action). See also Feinstein and Slaughter 2004.

36. Cirincione 2007b, 16–17; 2007a, 152. Bush: Zakaria 2007.

37. Kay 2008, 18–19. On this issue, see also Mueller and Mueller 1999, 52–53; 2000, 178–80.

38. Hymans 2006, 225.

CHAPTER 12: TASK

1. Failure of imagination: Kean 2004, ch. 11. Commentators: G. Allison 2004, 6; Krauthammer 2004a. Giuliani: CNN, 22 July 2005. See also Benjamin and Simon 2005, 115. For an early suggestion that 9/11 might fail to inspire a sequel of that magnitude, see J. Mueller 2002a, 2002b. Krauthammer apparently missed these items although they appeared in publications he regularly writes for. See also J. Mueller 2003; Seitz 2004. On expert prediction on such matters more generally, see Tetlock 2005.

2. Jenkins 1975, 33. Group: Zenko 2006, 94–95.

3. McPhee 1974, 7 (immediate, easy), 225 (simple), 195–97 (probabilities).

4. Keller 2002. Jenkins 2008, 250–51. Since no weapons more complicated than box cutters were employed on September 11, it would seem that the experience ought to be taken to suggest that the scenario most to be feared is not the acquisition by terrorists of devices of mass destructiveness, but one in which terrorists are once again able, through skill, careful planning, suicidal dedication, and great luck, to massively destroy with ordinary, extant devices. In addition, the potential for destruction on that magnitude is hardly new: a tiny band of fanatical, well-trained, and lucky terrorists could have sunk or scuttled the *Titanic* and killed thousands. K. Mueller 2006, 156.

5. Keller 2002. Gates: Graham 2008, 43.

6. Bunn 2007, vi. See also Langewiesche 2007, 20; Kamp 1996, 33; Bunn 2006, 115; Bunn and Wier 2006, 137; Jenkins 2008, 198; Pollack 2002, 180. For an excellent discussion of nuclear forensics, see Levi 2007a, 127–33. The goal, according to one scientist, is to develop techniques that would "determine the size of a detonation within one hour; the sophistication of the bomb design within six hours; how the fuel was enriched within 72 hours; and the peculiar details of national design . . . within a week" (Vartabedian 2008). See also Schelling 2004; Frost 2005, 64–66; Bunn 2007, 163; Sheets 2008.

7. The result was, says Mir, that when the interview was published in Urdu in *Ausaf,* the sentence was censored. When it later appeared in the English-language newspaper *Dawn,* however, it was not: www.maldivesculture.com/maldives_osama_bin_laden.html. For the variant texts, see Lawrence 2005, 142.

8. Tenet and Harlow 2007, 266.

9. Frost 2005, 64. Jenkins 2008, 143.

10. Oberdorfer 2005; see also Pillar 2003, xxi; Hymans 2008. State assistance: Broad 2008, Kroenig 2009. Soviet nuclear weapons were brought to Cuba at the time of the crisis there in 1962, but at no point was control of them turned over to the Cubans.

11. Closed down: Langewiesche 2007, 169–72. Levi 2007a, 24. See also Tenet and Harlow 2007, 261.

12. Observer: Bergen 2007, 19. Relations with Taliban: Burke 2003, 150, 164–65; Wright 2006, 230–31, 287–88; Cullison 2004. Taliban distancing: Robertson 2008; also comments by Douglas Saunders of Canada's *Globe and Mail* on PRI's *To the Point* on May 14, 2009: "I've talked to a lot of commanders and field officers with the U.S. and Britain and Canada and other countries fighting there. Most agree that al-Qaeda is very unlikely to establish a base even if any of the major groupings of what we together call the Taliban are able to retake Afghanistan and seize power. The groups that are best poised to do so, including Mullah Omar's original Taliban, are very much opposed to Arab and foreign forces such as al-Qaeda. The Taliban grouping that is most friendly to al-Qaeda is very unlikely to be able to take power."

13. Deny: Badkhen 2004. Center for Nonproliferation Studies 2002, 4, 12; see also Smith and Hoffman 1997; Langewiesche 2007, 19; Jenkins 2008, 149–50; McPhee 1974, 145–46. Jenkins 2008, 171. No loose nukes: Pluta and Zimmerman 2006, 56. See also Frost 2005, 17–23; Younger 2009, 152. Graham Allison characterizes Lebed's recantation as "retreating to the Russian line." He also chooses to end his discussion of this issue with a provocative comment by an unidentified American intelligence officer, "We don't know with any confidence what has gone missing, and neither do they" (2004, 10, 43–46).

14. Younger 2007, 93. See also Kamp 1996, 22; Milhollin 2002, 47–48; Younger 2009, 152–53. On Chechnya: Cameron 2004, 84.

15. Linzer 2004a. See also Levi 2007a, 97, 126.

16. Trigger: Jenkins 2008, 141. Reporter: Linzer 2004a. Disassembled: Reiss 1995, 11, 13; Warrick 2007. Younger 2009, 153–54. See also Kamp 1996, 34; Wirz and Egger 2005, 502; Langewiesche 2007, 19; Levi 2007a, 125.

17. Pakistan disassembled: Warrick 2007. Taliban takeover a stretch: Cole 2009a, 158; 2009b. For a discussion of the failed state scenario, including useful suggestions for making it even less likely, see Levi 2007a, 133–38.

18. Wirz and Egger 2005, 502. See also Levi 2007a, 125.

19. Levi 2007a, 26; Lugar 2005, 17. See also Ferguson and Potter 2005, chs. 3–4.

20. Kamp 1996, 33; Garwin and Charpak 2001, 314; Keller 2002; Milhollin 2002, 46–47; Rees 2003, 44–45; Linzer 2004a; G. Allison 2004, 96–97; Goldstein 2004, 131–32; Cameron 2004, 84; Wirz and Egger 2005, 500; Frost 2005, 27–28; Bunn and Wier 2006, 135; Langewiesche 2007, 21–23; Levi 2007a, 73–81; Younger 2009, 142–43. By contrast, Frank Barnaby tends to conclude that terrorists would work with plutonium—though this might result in a bomb much smaller than the one dropped on Nagasaki—because HEU is easily secured, while plutonium is more generally available (2004, 110–17). However, as Langewiesche and many others stress, working with, and transporting, plutonium is far more complicated and dangerous. See also McPhee 1974, 152. Still in the experimental stage, a technique known as laser isotope separation might conceivably make the laborious process feasible for small groups sometime in the future: Anderson 2008.

21. On gun type: see Garwin and Charpak 2001, 350; G. Allison 2004, 95–96; Cirincione 2007a, 11. G. Allison 2004, 97. See also Bunn and Wier 2006, 139; Pluta and Zimmerman 2006, 61.

22. Linzer 2004a.

23. Industrial scale: Milhollin 2002, 45–46; G. Allison 2004; Cameron 2004, 83; Bunn and Wier 2006, 136–37; Langewiesche 2007, 20; Perry et al. 2007; Levi 2007a, 15; Muller 2008, 132. Unlikely to be supplied by state: Bunn 2007, 17–18; Jenkins 2008, 142.

24. Pakistan: Milhollin 2002, 47. Guards: Langewiesche 2007, 46–47.

25. Langewiesche 2007, 33–48.

26. See also Levi 2007a, 29, 32–33.

27. Langewiesche 2007, 75–76.

28. Levi 2007a, ch. 5.

29. Jenkins 2008, 140 (incentive), 152–53 (no case).

30. Known thefts: Linzer 2004a. 100 pounds: Garwin and Charpak 2001, 314, 350; Bernstein 2008, 258. This is equivalent to a thousand tons of TNT, much smaller than the Hiroshima bomb, but far greater than the largest conventional bombs, which have yields of some 11 tons. Actually, some scientists maintain that the amount of fissile material required would be larger—"certainly several, and possibly ten times the so-called formula quantities" (Mark et al. 1987, 60). "As a rule," notes Karl-Heinz Kamp, "the more basic the design of a nuclear weapon, the more fissile material required" (1996, 33). See also Frost 2005, 28–29; Levi 2007a, 29.

31. Jenkins 2008, 55, 152.

32. No buyers lined up: Linzer 2004a; see also Cameron 2004, 83–84; Frost 2005, 11–17; Pluta and Zimmerman 2006, 60; Younger 2007, 87; Levi 2007a, 25, 66. Frost 2005, 9; see also Jenkins 2008, 150–51.

33. Bunn and Wier 2006, 137; Tenet and Harlow 2007, 276–77; Bunn 2007, 24.

34. Jenkins 2008, 146–47.

35. Levi 2007a, 140. Lugar 2005, 16.

36. "Assault on Pelindaba," *60 Minutes,* 23 November 2008. See also the comments by David Albright in Warrick 2007. Earlier attempt: Zenko 2007.

37. Langewiesche 2007, 48–50.

38. Langewiesche 2007, 54–65. On the need to use, and rely on, criminals and corrupt officials at all stages of procuring and making off with the purloined HEU, see Pluta and Zimmerman 2006, 58.

39. Good managers: Keller 2002. Muller 2008, 35; see also Hymans 2008.

40. Pearl and LeVine 2001.

41. Easy: G. Allison et al. 1996, 12; however, Bunn and Wier, who hail from Allison's own Center at Harvard, do more recently acknowledge that "it is not easy to make a nuclear bomb" even after "essential ingredients are in hand" (2006, 134). Child's play: Edwards 2001b. Langewiesche 2007, 49. Wirz and Egger 2005, 499–502.

42. Mark et al. 1987, 58 (detailed design; Pluta and Zimmerman suggest that the drawing preparation, at least, can now be aided by "modern computer-aided design software": 2006, 63), 64–65 (experimenting), 62 (to a close, emphasis added; see also Pluta and Zimmerman 2006, 64). Milhollin 2002, 48.

43. Younger 2007, 86 (wrong), 93 (concerned), 88 (exceptionally difficult). Younger is appalled at the activities of "scaremongers from our nuclear weapons laboratories," and he cites the way "one fast-talking scientist" from the Lawrence Livermore National Laboratory managed in 2004 to convince some members of Congress that North Korea might be able to launch a nuclear device capable of emitting a high-altitude electromagnetic pulse that could burn out computers and other equipment over a wide area. When he queried a man he considers to be "perhaps the most knowledgeable person in the world about such designs" (and who "was never asked to testify"), the response was: "I don't think the *United States* could do that sort of thing today. To say that the North Koreans could do it, and without doing any testing, is simply ridiculous." Nevertheless, concludes Younger acidly, "rumors are passed from one person to another,

growing at every repetition, backed by flimsy or nonexistent intelligence and the repu-
tations of those who are better at talking than doing" (2007, 91–92, emphasis in the
original).

44. Very simple: Bunn and Wier 2006, 140. Tolerances: Younger 2007, 89; see also
Levi 2007a, 39–49; Younger 2009, 144. Far-fetched: Younger 2009, 146.

45. Not able to test: Linzer 2004a; Mark et al. 1987, 64. G. Allison 2007. Levi 2007b;
see also Younger 2009, 144–45. The atomic bombs fabricated by the South Africans were
also never tested. However, they were planning to do so if the project ever came to light
and they needed to use them (Reiss 1995, 16–17).

46. Levi 2007a, 41.

47. Months: Pluta and Zimmerman 2006, 62. Milhollin 2002, 48. Detection equipment: Mark et al. 1987, 60.

48. Curiosity: Langewiesche 2007, 65–69. Steve Coll reports that few among a group
of around 60 Los Alamos National Laboratory scientists were willing to set the probability of a "nuclear fission bomb attack on U.S. soil during the next several decades"
(presumably by states *or* by terrorists) at less than 5 percent. But some of them did joke
about the unlikelihood of a scenario requiring that "half a dozen tenured, ornery and
egotistical physicists cooperate with each other on a demanding project" (2005).

49. The Los Alamos scientists suggest that the process of bomb building could be
speeded up if the team were able to spend "a considerable number of weeks (or, more
probably, months)" preparing and practicing for the assembly using natural—that is,
unenriched—uranium as a stand-in (Mark et al. 1987, 59). This would still not solve the
problem of curious locals, of course. Moreover, it seems to be rather impractical, since,
given the difficulties of securing adequate quantities of fissile material, the team might
spend years, even decades, waiting around for the stuff to arrive.

50. Mark et al. 1987, 55, 60; Bunn and Wier 2006, 142.

51. On this issue, see in particular Levi 2007a, 88, 95.

52. Zimmerman and Lewis 2006. For an additional critique of this article, see
Waterman 2006.

53. Keller 2002.

CHAPTER 13: LIKELIHOOD

1. G. Allison 2004, 15. Kristof 2004. G. Allison 2006, 39. G. Allison 1995. In support
of his 2004 prediction, Allison cites the "world's most successful investor" and "legendary oddsmaker," Warren Buffett, as declaring a nuclear terrorist attack to be inevitable
(2004, 14–15; 2006, 39). Contacted by the *Wall Street Journal*, however, Buffett says he
was worrying about any nuclear explosion, not just one set off by terrorists, and that he
was talking about something that might come about over the next century, not within a
ten-year period (Bialik 2005), something that seems clear in the source Allison uses for
his claim: Serwer and Boorstin 2002.

2. Negroponte: www.globalsecurity.org/security/library/report/2003/n0335167.pdf.
Lugar 2005, 14–15. Garwin: G. Allison 2007.

3. Commission: Graham 2008, vii (current state), xv (more likely than not).
Tauscher: Grossman 2008.

4. Critic: Bergen 2008. Rockford: Lawson 2008; on this definitional issue, see also
Mueller and Mueller 2009.

5. The C-SPAN talk was recorded in Seattle on May 24, 2007, and telecast in June. NPR: *Morning Edition,* 15 May 2007. Langewiesche 2007, 17, 69. None too surprisingly, blurb writers, convinced it is hysteria, not reassurance, that sells, proclaim on the jacket flap for Langewiesche's book that it "examines in dramatic and tangible detail the chances of such weapons being manufactured and deployed by terrorists," an accurate description, but one that deftly avoids revealing the author's conclusion as to what those chances actually happen to be. And when the *Atlantic* (purveyor last decade of cheery cover screeds about "The Crisis of Public Order," "The Drift Toward Disaster," "The Coming Anarchy," and "The Coming Plague") published the relevant chapter from Langewiesche's book in December 2006, it chose to accentuate the negative on its wrap-around grabber: "The Nuclear Nightmare: How a Terrorist Could [not even the slightly more circumspect "Might"] Get a Bomb," and the article itself was provocatively and misleadingly entitled, "How to Get a Nuclear Bomb." Many have taken that to be the Langewiesche's message: for example, the appreciative review of the book in the *Los Angeles Times* (Winslow 2007).

6. For example, Bunn and Wier 2004, 10–30. In the end, the authors rather unhelpfully conclude that the "most fundamental answer" to the question as to why there had been no terrorist nuclear attack by the time of publication "is that the world has been lucky" (p. 27).

7. Bunn and Wier 2006, 133–34, 147. Tenet and Harlow 2007, 266, 279. Levi 2007b, 7 (must succeed); 9–10, 141, 149 (scenarios); 8 (Murphy's); 3 (genuine possibility); 152 (tilt).

8. Actually, maybe it is: monkeys do not invent at random, but rather repeat and generate habits, and therefore might never get around to Shakespeare.

9. Perhaps this last scenario is not quite as bizarre as it sounds. Now residing in a maximum security prison, the notorious Islamic terrorist Ramzi Yousef has let it be known that he has converted to Christianity (*60 Minutes,* 14 October 2007).

10. Gilmore 1999, 31, emphasis in the original.

11. Intractable: Levi 2007b, 9. Study: Bunn 2006, discussed in note 17 below. Himself: Levi 2007a.

12. For an assessment of the damage possible by the detonation of a 10-KT device within a shipping container that had been unloaded onto a pier, see Meade and Molander 2006. Terror even if the bomb fails: see Levi 2007b, 14. However, it may be relevant that the failed effort by terrorists to destroy the World Trade Center in 1993 hardly evoked anywhere near the reaction caused by its actual destruction in 2001; nor did the failed attack on the London subway of July 21, 2005, prove to be remotely as horrifying as the successful one of two weeks earlier.

13. Garwin and Charpak 2001, 343.

14. Levi 2007a. Jenkins 2008, 299–300.

15. G. Allison 2004, 29–42. He cites a 2001 newspaper account of a UN report supposedly suggesting that there were 130 terrorist groups "capable of developing a homemade atomic bomb" if they obtained sufficient fissile material (G. Allison 2006, 38). Actually, however, the account later says that the number comes from a list created by the State Department identifying organizations considered to pose "a nuclear, chemical or biological threat" (Edwards 2001a).

16. This exercise is perhaps problematic because of murkiness about what a "concerted" or "determined" or "dedicated" attempt actually is. For example, it presumably would have to be considerably more than googling "HEU" and "sources" on the Internet,

but it would be difficult to define its precise dimensions. In a brilliant satire of the enterprise entitled "Terrorist Has No Idea What to Do With All This Plutonium," *The Onion* (30 November 2005) imagines a terrorist puzzled over what to do with the quarter kilogram of plutonium he recently acquired: "I drew a circle to represent the plutonium. Then I drew a line pointing to it, and beside it wrote 'plutonium.' After that, I just hit a wall." And: "A friend of mine at university studied metallurgy. I have his e-mail address, but I can't just write him and say, 'Oh, hello, Suleymann, long time no see. Say, I'm a terrorist now, and I was wondering: How do you go about building a nuclear bomb?'" (www.theonion.com/content/node/43012). For dark suspicions drawn from the fact that a couple of apparent jihadists studied physics and agronomy at the University of Arizona in the 1980s, see Tenet and Harlow 2007, 270–71.

17. In all this, of course, everything depends on the plausibility of the probability estimates. Matthew Bunn has gone through a somewhat similar exercise and assigns probabilities that I consider to be wildly favorable to the terrorists (2006). In his model, for example, he assumes terrorists stand a 40 percent chance of overcoming *everything* arrayed in barriers 8 through 15 of Table 13.1, and a monumental 70 percent chance of overcoming everything in barriers 16 through 20. This is comparable to assuming a nearly 90 percent chance of overcoming each of the barriers in the first instance and a chance of well over 90 percent for each in the second. He also posits a 30 percent chance that any attempt to steal fissile material using insiders (that is, everything in barriers 1 through 5) will succeed. With parameters like that and with some additional considerations, he is able to conclude that there is a 29 percent chance of a terrorist atomic bomb being successfully detonated in the next decade.

18. Sheets 2008.

19. Frost 2005, 17–23; Lugar 2005, 2; Pluta and Zimmerman 2006, 257; Bunn 2007, 13–14, 25–25, 36–37; Keller 2002; Ferguson and Potter, 145; Langewiesche 2007, 27–33.

20. Zimmerman and Lewis 2006, 39. See also Brodie 1966, 59; Taleb 2007.

21. On the "aberration" issue, see J. Mueller 2002b, 2002c, 2003; Seitz 2004.

22. Finel 2009; see also Kenney 2009. Environment: P. Smith 2007; see also Schneier 2003, 123–24, 247–48; J. Mueller 2006, 4. Chechens: Kramer 2004/05, 58. Muller 2008, 21–22. See also Jenkins 2008, 299.

23. One of the reasons the Americans were surprised at Pearl Harbor was that they realized the fleet there would never have been able to cramp Japan's style in its key military effort at the time. As historian Samuel Eliot Morison stresses, "The Pacific Fleet was too weak…to go tearing into waters covered by enemy land-based air power.…Even at the most optimistic the Japanese could have conquered everything they wanted in the Philippines and Malaya by leaving Pearl Harbor alone and relying on submarines and aircraft in the Mandates to deal with our Pacific Fleet." Therefore, concludes Morison, "the surprise attack on Pearl Harbor, far from being a 'strategic necessity,' as the Japanese claimed even after the war, was a strategic imbecility." Indeed, one war-plans officer recalled, "I did not think they would attack at Pearl Harbor because I did not think it was necessary for them to do so." Because of many deficiencies, "we could not have materially affected their control of the waters they wanted to control whether or not the battleships were sunk at Pearl Harbor." Some people have argued that there was luck on the other side as well. Admiral Chester W. Nimitz concluded that "It was God's mercy that our fleet was in Pearl Harbor on December 7." If the commander in Hawaii had "had advance notice that the Japanese were coming, he most probably would have tried to intercept them," and, with the difference in speed

between the American and the Japanese ships, the Americans "would have lost many ships in deep water and also thousands more in lives." Because of Pearl Harbor's shallow waters, sunken and damaged ships ended up resting on the bottom, where repair efforts soon revived almost all of them. For a discussion of these issues, see J. Mueller 1995a, ch. 7.

24. Willmott 1983, 515. Willmott 1982, 91.

25. G. Allison et al. 1996, G. Allison 2004. See also Garwin and Charpak 2001, 325–26; Krepon 2009.

26. Need to plan: Perry et al. 2007. Gaming: see, for example, Jenkins 2008, ch. 17.

27. For an analysis of protection measures more generally, see J. Mueller 2010.

28. Nuclear engineer: Rockwell 2003. Fischoff 2005; see also Glanz and Revkin 2002; G. Allison 2004, 8, 59, 220; Linzer 2004b. Other specialists: Ferguson and Potter 2005, 335.

29. Finn 2005. Henriksen and Maillie 2003, 112. Loof 2005.

30. Damaging fears: Henriksen and Maillie 2003, 149. Billions: Jones 2000. This is illustrated well in a study that seeks to estimate the economic costs of a 10-kiloton nuclear explosion of a device unloaded onto a pier in the Port of Long Beach, California. It estimates a cost of $1 trillion, but the bulk of that arises from assuming that wide areas would have to be evacuated because they would become contaminated under current safety standards. Meade and Molander 2006. For an excellent discussion of the cleanup issue, see Eraker 2004. See also W. Allison 2006, 317.

31. Wald 2005; see also Wald 2006.

32. See, in particular, Slovic 2000.

33. G. Allison 2007. On this issue much more broadly, see Posner 2005.

34. Sunstein 2006, 32.

35. Tenet and Harlow 2007, 264. See also Suskind 2006, 61–62.

CHAPTER 14: PROGRESS AND INTEREST

1. Carle 2008.

2. Gerges 2005, 1–3, 27–28, also 161–62. See also Scheuer 2002, 169–77.

3. Kean 2004, 380. See also G. Allison 2006, 37.

4. Kean 2004, 116.

5. Kean 2004, 60. See also Tenet and Harlow 2007, 261.

6. Wright 2006, 197 (walked), 5 (lied). Rogue: Mayer 2006. For Fadl's testimony on the issue, see Bergen 2006, 338–39; Emerson 2001. While under protective custody, Fadl won a prize in the New Jersey Lottery (Wright 2006, 197). The prize, however, was small, and his unamused FBI handlers wouldn't let him keep it anyway (Mayer 2006). Information about the "al Qaeda representative" who made the crack about how easy it is to kill people with uranium also comes from Fadl during court testimony in early 2001 in the *United States v. bin Laden* case.

7. Wright 2006, 191. Contrary to the implication of the 9/11 Commission report, however, Wright also says that bin Laden paid only $10,000 for the material before he found out it was bogus (2006, 191). In his discussion of the episode, Graham Allison (2004, 26–27) neglects to mention that the material was bogus, although his source specifically concludes, "It seems likely either that the material was not useful for a weapon or that it was one of many scams that have been perpetrated involving the sale of supposed

nuclear material" (Benjamin and Simon 2002, 129). Allison also says Fadl "could not confirm whether the uranium actually changed hands," implying that there really was uranium up for sale. Additionally, he asserts that the material was "weapons-usable," although his source nowhere uses such language. In contrast, see the discussion based on the same source in Goldstein 2004, 134.

8. Wright 2006, 194–97. However, Wright does indicate that by the time bin Laden left Sudan in 1996, he had invested some $20 or $30 million in the country overall—and was left with very little (2006, 222 n).

9. Wright 2006, 411–12.

10. Key inspiration: Wright 2006, 282; see also Coll 2004; Clarke 2004, 145–47. Investigators: Silberman and Robb 2005, 271. Leitenberg 2005, 35. Half of pharmaceuticals: Wright 2006, 282. Deaths: the German ambassador to Sudan at the time, Werner Daum, suggests as a "reasonable guess" that "several tens of thousands" of people "died as a result of the destruction" (2001, 19). William Cohen, defense secretary at the time, has admitted that information was so inadequate that policy makers did not know that the plant was producing medicine at all (Stern 1998–99, 178–79). The United States has thus far refused to apologize or offer compensation and has still not ruled out the possibility that the plant did have some "link" to the production of chemical weapons (Lacey 2005). President Bill Clinton claims that Fadl "testified that bin Laden had a chemical weapons operation" in Sudan (2004, 805). The testimony is hardly that definitive. Fadl reported conversions in which he was told al-Qaeda was willing to help the Sudan government make chemical weapons for use against a rebellion in the south of the country: Emerson 2001, 86. On the episode, see also Benjamin and Simon 2002, 259–62, 351–70.

11. Scheuer on *60 Minutes*, CBS-TV, 14 November 2004. There are also suggestions that a founding member of al-Qaeda, Mamdouh Mahmud Salim, expressed interest in obtaining, or sought to obtain, uranium in late 1993. However, he was arrested in Germany in 1998. Bergen 2006, 339.

12. Gerges 2005, 56–60, and personal communication with Gerges. The al-Qaeda diarist is Abu al-Walid al-Masri. See also Bergen 2006, 341–44; Stenersen 2009, 29–31.

13. G. Allison 2004, 20–24. Source: Khan and Moore 2001. See also Tenet and Harlow 2007, 264–68.

14. G. Allison 2004, 23–24.

15. Academic: Khan and Moore 2001; see also Baker 2002.

16. Access: Khan and Moore 2001. Scams in the area: Bergen 2006, 343–45. Son: Baker 2002. Allison puts the radiological material issue more provocatively: the scientists were told that "Al Qaeda had succeeded in acquiring nuclear material for a bomb" (2004, 23). Philip Bobbitt goes much further: at the interrogation, he says, Mahmood reportedly disclosed "that bin Laden insisted that he already had sufficient fissile material to build a bomb, having obtained it from former Soviet stockpiles through a militant Islamic group" in Uzbekistan (2008, 120).

17. Resign: Albright and Higgins 2003, 50. Mystic: Fielding et al. 2002; Albright and Higgins 2003, 51; in quoting Mahmood's list of calamities, Allison sharpens it for his purposes by leaving out hunger, disease, and street violence (2004, 21). Economist: Albright and Higgins 2003, 53. Madman: Tenet and Harlow 2007, 262.

18. Kahn 2001.

19. Officials stressed: Khan and Moore 2001; see also Albright and Higgins 2003, 49, 51; Baker 2002. Princeton scientist: Baker 2002. G. Allison 2004, 24; according to Tenet,

Mahmood had shown his interrogators "a hand-drawn rough bomb design" (Tenet and Harlow 2007, 268), hardly anything that could credibly be labeled a "blueprint." Tenet quotes a Libyan intelligence official who reports that the relief organization Mahmood and Majid were part of had sought to peddle its nuclear expertise to Libya and had even "tried to sell us a nuclear weapon," but were turned down (Tenet and Harlow 2007, 263). Since the organization actually seems to have had no weapons to sell, the story, if true, suggests the Libyans were exhibiting sound business acumen, at least in the weapon issue.

20. Internet: Jenkins 2008, 27. Official report: Silberman and Robb 2005, 272.

21. Beyond theory: Stenersen 2008, 38. Report: Albright 2002. See also Jenkins 2008, 90.

22. Venzke and Ibrahim characterize it this way: "a 25-page document filled with information about nuclear weapons, including the design for one" (2003, 52).

23. Duelfer: Testimony before the Senate Select Committee on Intelligence, 6 October 2004; see also the discussion on this issue in chapter 12. On the post-9/11 cutoff of contact, see Albright and Higgins 2003, 54–55; Suskind 2006, 69–70, 122.

24. Visits: Khan and Moore 2001. Khan: Langewiesche 2007, chs. 3–4. Fingar: Priest and White 2005; however, this same source also reports alarmist, if vague, testimony at the same time from CIA Director Porter Goss that "It may be only a matter of time before al Qaeda or another group attempts to use chemical, biological, radiological and nuclear materials," and from James Loy, acting deputy secretary of homeland security, that "any attack of any kind could occur at any time." Stenersen 2008, 35–36.

25. Albright 2002. By contrast, Bunn and Wier interpret Albright to mean al-Qaeda's nuclear program "could still succeed elsewhere" (2006, 146).

26. Wright 2006, 222 n.

27. On these reports, including source references, see Richardson 2006, 161. See also Scheuer 2002, 191–92. For the suggestion that the Chechen story "has the ring of plausibility, perhaps even echoes of truth," see Scheuer 2002, 192. Very much in the game is the London *Times,* which also suggested that bin Laden had already collected a set of tactical nuclear weapons by 1998 (Binyon 1998).

28. Jenkins 2008, 258–66. For questions about whether there ever were any loose nukes, particularly "suitcase bombs," in Russia, see pp. 165–66 above.

29. Williams 2005, 205.

30. G. Allison 2004, 27. Port and Smith 2001.

31. Richardson 2006, 162. Jenkins 2008, 274.

32. G. Allison 2004, 28.

33. Garwin and Charpak 2001, 324.

34. This was the version published in the English language Karachi newspaper, *Dawn* (Lawrence 2005, 142 n). In the Urdu version in *Ausaf,* the statement was rendered, "If the United States uses chemical or nuclear weapons against us, we will not perish" (Lawrence 2005, 142). For Mir's explanation for this discrepancy, see p. 164.

35. Denton 2004. Graham Allison also reports the Zawahiri claim (2004, 27). As he acknowledges in a note, Allison found this quote in a *San Francisco Chronicle* article that is entitled, "Al Qaeda bluffing about having suitcase nukes, experts say; Russians claim terrorists couldn't have bought them." The portion of that article that apparently did not interest Allison notes, as discussed in chapter 12, that both Russian nuclear officials and experts on the Russian nuclear programs "adamantly" deny that al-Qaeda or other terrorist groups could have bought Soviet-made suitcase nukes (Badken 2004).

36. Bluff: see also Bergen 2006, 349. Previous lies: Wright 2006, 188–89, 245. Face value: Albright 2002; Goldstein 2004, 13. "Interview with Mullah Omar," news.bbc. co.uk/2/hi/south_asia/1657368.stm. It may also be worthwhile to consider the credibility of Mir. In a 2002 interview, discussing the circumstances of the interview, he says, contradicting the published transcript of the interview, that bin Laden told him he had bought a nuclear bomb from a Russian scientist and "had it in a suitcase." He does not mention meeting Zawahiri at all. In conversation with Andrew Denton of Australian television in 2004, Mir says bin Laden "never allowed me to probe his claim that he has nuclear weapons," but that Zawahiri, who Mir thinks is "the real brain behind bin Laden" and "the real strategist," told him about purchasing the Russian suitcase bombs. In a 2006 interview, Mir made a number of assertions relying "on my own investigations," not simply "on claims by al-Qaeda," that 1) Iran is supporting al-Qaeda; 2) Russia is supporting the Taliban insurgents in Afghanistan; 3) al-Qaeda smuggled three suitcase nuclear weapons into Europe in 2000 destined for London, Paris, and California, as well as many kilos of enriched uranium into the United States for dirty bomb projects; 4) it tested at least one dirty bomb in Afghanistan in 2000; 5) before 9/11, 42 trained fighters entered the United States, leaving 23 still "sleeping" there; 6) al-Qaeda can make anthrax. And in a 2007 interview, Mir contended that al-Qaeda operatives had smuggled tactical nuclear weapons into the United States from Mexico before September 11, 2001, and that a nuclear attack on seven to ten cities would take place in 2008, but could occur sooner. Mir says he is writing a biography of bin Laden, and in the 2002 interview maintained he was "finishing the book" and would be "trying to publish it soon." In the 2006 interview he revealed that he was "putting some finishing touches on the manuscript," that his publisher had not authorized him to "disclose the name of the book," that it would reveal bin Laden's "future plans and details of his nuclear designs," and that he was "planning to publish the book this year." In 2007, he claimed it would be out in time for Christmas. 2002: www.maldivesculture.com/maldives_osama_bin_laden.html. 2004: Denton 2004. 2006: www.canadafreepress.com/2006/mauro052506.htm. 2007: Williams 2007. For a further extended questioning of Mir's credibility, see Jenkins 2008, 251–55, 263–66, 271. See also Richardson 2007, 276n65.

37. See fas.org/irp/news/2000/12/irp-001205-afgzss2.htm.

38. For example, G. Allison 2004, 19, Venzke and Ibrahim 2003, 52; Bobbitt 2008, 59. See also Hoffman 2006, 273.

39. Bergen 2006, 339–40.

40. We believe: Richardson 2006, 160–61. Shabby: Lawrence 2005, 72. Worn-out: Venzke and Ibrahim 2003, 54. Supported: Lawrence 2005, 72.

41. jya.com/bin-laden-abc.htm.

42. Richardson 2006, 162. See also Martin 2009; Stenersen 2008, 31.

43. Tenet and Harlow 2007, 261.

44. Tenet and Harlow 2007, 268–69. Levi 2007b.

45. Stream: Tenet and Harlow 2006, 272. Wright 2006, 222, 232, 270. Thwarted: Tenet and Harlow 2006, 273.

46. Ghaith statement: Bergen 2006, 346–47. Tenet and Harlow 2007, 269–70. See also G. Allison 2004, 12; Bobbitt 2008, 119. For a critique, see Lustick 2006, 128–29.

47. Tenet and Harlow 2007, 274. Scheuer on *60 Minutes,* 14 November 2004.

48. Stenersen 2008, 39.

CHAPTER 15: CAPACITY

1. Bergen 2007.

2. Hoffman 2006, 290.

3. Short-lived: BBC News, "The New Threats from 'Bin Laden,'" 6 October 2002, news.bbc.co.uk/2/hi/middle_east/2304569.stm (accessed September 8, 2008). Leave us alone: "Full Text: Bin Laden's 'Letter to America,'" 24 November 2002, www.guardian.co.uk/world/2002/nov/24/the observer

4. Stevenson 2004, 7.

5. Hoffman 2006, 283.

6. www.globalsecurity.org/security/profiles/adam_gadahn_2004_video.htm (accessed September 8, 2008).

7. timesonline, "Extracts from the Zawahiri Tape," 4 August 2005, www.timesonline.co.uk/tol/news/uk/article551518.ece (accessed September 8, 2008)

8. BBC News, "Text: Bin-Laden Tape," 19 January 2006. news.bbc.co.uk/2/hi/middle_east/4628932.stm (accessed September 8, 2008)

9. Kosko 2004. Jenkins 2008, 307. Chertoff: Harris and Taylor 2008. On the "internalization" issue, see J. Mueller 2008. See also J. Mueller 2006, Lustick 2006, Chapman and Harris 2002, Seitz 2004, Fallows 2006, Furedi 2007.

10. See J. Mueller 2006, chs. 3–6; Johnson 1994.

11. This discussion stems from Sageman 2008, from conversations with Sageman, and from a talk on the book he gave in Washington as televised on C-SPAN in early 2008 (ably summarized in Ignatius 2008).

12. On this point, see also Hoffman 2006, 271–72.

13. Gerges 2005 and personal communication.

14. Egyptian, American: Wright 2008. As many as 2,000: Mazzetti and Rohde 2008.

15. Bergen 2007.

16. Unable to uncover: Ross 2005; Isikoff and Hosenball 2007. In 2005, FBI Director Robert Mueller testified that his top concern was "the threat from covert operatives who may be inside the U.S." and considered finding them to be his top priority; however, they had been unable to find any (Priest and White 2005). In 2007, the officer who drafted that year's National Intelligence Estimate testified that "we do not see" al-Qaeda operatives functioning inside the United States (Gertz 2007). In distinct contrast, intelligence officials were estimating in 2002 that there were as many as 5,000 al-Qaeda terrorists and supporters at large in the country (Gertz 2002). Foreigners admitted legally: during 2008, for example, nonimmigrant admissions to the United States alone totaled 175 million (Monger and Barr 2009). Not all of these, of course, enter at international airports; the total includes people repeatedly going back and forth across the borders with Canada and Mexico.

17. Lawson 2008. Sprintering analogy: Karl Mueller, personal communication.

18. Kenney 2009. Other study: Eilstrup-Sangiovanni and Jones 2009.

19. Cordesman 2005, 29–31. Jenkins 2006, 179–84. "Jihadi Attack Kill Statistics," IntelCenter, 17 August 2007, 11 (www.intelcenter.com).

20. Mack 2008; see also Zakaria 2008a. Another perspective on the extent of the terrorist threat comes from astronomer Alan Harris. Using State Department figures, he estimates a worldwide death rate from international terrorism outside of war zones of 1,000 per year—that is, he assumes in his estimate that there would be another 9/11 somewhere in the world every several years. Over an 80-year period under those conditions, some 80,000 deaths would occur, which would mean that the probability that

a resident of the globe will die at the hands of international terrorists is about one in 75,000 (6 billion divided by 80,000). In comparison, an American's chance of dying in an auto accident over the same time interval is about one in 88. If there are no repeats of 9/11, the probability of being killed by an international terrorist becomes more like one in 120,000.

21. Gerges 2005, 252–53, 256–59. Bergen and Cruickshank 2007.

22. Uncomfortable hosts: Burke 2003, 150, 164–65; Wright 2006, 230–31, 287–88; Cullison 2004. No foreign fighters: B. Williams 2008. Extensive study: Jones 2008. Distanced: see Robertson 2008 and note 12 on p. 265.

23. Libicki et al. 2007, 67, 70. The authors suggest an attack in Taba, Egypt in October 2004 may have been run by al-Qaeda, but, as they note (p. 46), Egyptian officials have ruled that out based on confessions and evidence at the scene.

24. Porter 2009, 300. Turned many: Bergen and Cruickshank 2008; Wright 2008.

25. Taxi drivers: Gerges 2008b, 70–71. Rejection: Gerges 2005, 27, 228, 233, also 270; Gerges 2008b, 71.

26. Gerges 2005, 232, and, for a tally of policing activity, 318–19; see also Pillar 2003, xxviii–xxix; Lynch 2006, 54–55; Sageman 2008, 149; Cole 2009a, 163. For an able discussion of the Taliban-Pakistan connections before 9/11, see Rashid 2000. As noted in chapter 14, contacts between Pakistani scientists and al-Qaeda were abruptly broken off after 9/11 (Albright and Higgins 2003, 54–55; Suskind 2006, 69–70, 122).

27. Gerges 2005, 153; Sageman 2004, 47. For a discussion of a similar phenomenon during the war in Algeria during the 1990s, see Botha 2006. On the generally counterproductive effects for terrorists of targeting civilians, see Abrahms 2006, Mack 2008.

28. Indonesia: Sageman 2004, 53, 142, 173. Saudi Arabia: Gerges 2005, 249; Sageman 2004, 53, 144; Meyer 2006. Morocco: Sageman 2004, 53–54. Jordan polls: Pew Global Attitudes Project, "The Great Divide: How Westerners and Muslims View Each Other," 22 June 2006, http://pewglobal.org/reports/display.php?ReportID=253; see also Lynch 2006, 54–55. Religious grounds: Gerges 2008, 75. In sum, says Gerges, although al-Qaeda may retain local affiliates in Saudi Arabia, Yemen, Jordan, Pakistan, and elsewhere, "they are shrinking by the hour and bleeding profusely from the blows of the security services with substantial logistical support from the United States" (2005, 249). See also Pillar 2003, xxiv.

29. Enemies list: Bergen 2007, 19. Porter 2009, 298.

30. Warrick 2008. See also Gerges 2005, ch. 5.

31. Zawahiri: Mack 2008, 15. Mindless brutalities: Woodward 2008. Iraq polls: Mack 2008, 15–17. Grenier: Warrick 2008. See also Bergen and Cruickshank 2007; Jenkins 2008, 191.

32. Lipton 2005.

33. Porter 2009, 300. See also Kenney 2009.

34. Chlorine: Bergen 2008; Stenersen 2008, 42–43. Aum: Linzer 2004a; Frost 2005, 38–40.

35. Laqueur 1996. Waste time: Whitlock 2007. Smith 2004. See also Parachini 2003, 44–46; Stenersen 2008.

36. Weapons they know: Rapoport 1999, 51; Gilmore 1999, 37; Schneier 2003, 236. Jenkins 2008, 189. Suicide: Pape 2005; Bloom 2005.

37. On February 11, 2003, he assured a Senate committee that, although his agency had yet to actually identify an al-Qaeda cell in the United States, such unidentified (or imagined) entities nonetheless presented "the greatest threat," had "developed a support infrastructure" in the country, and had achieved "the ability and the intent to inflict

significant casualties in the US with little warning." On February 16, 2005, at a time when the FBI admitted it *still* had been unable to unearth a single true al-Qaeda cell, Mueller continued his dire I-think-therefore-they-are projections: "I remain very concerned about what we are not seeing," he ominously ruminated. Testimony by Mueller can be found through www.fbi.gov/congress/congress.htm.

38. Carle 2008. Hoffmann 2006, 271.

39. Bergen and Cruickshank 2008. On this consideration, see also Seitz 2004. The al-Qaeda attack on an American ship, the *Cole,* also took place after this conversation. However, Bergen says that Benotman certainly thinks the reference was to 9/11 (personal communication).

40. Parachini 2003, 43–46. Martin 2009.

41. Sageman 2008, 149. For similar sentiments, see Porter 2009; Bacevich 2009, 96. On the "self-limiting" nature of jihadism, see also Gerges 2008. See also Zakaria 2008a.

42. Tenet: *New York Times,* 18 October 2002, A12. Marshaling: Hoffman 2007. Other adherents: Hoffman 2006, 282–95; Bergen 2007; Riedel 2007; Bergen and Cruickshank 2008; Mazzetti and Rohde 2008; Hoffman 2008.

43. Rice 2002. Survival: Scheuer 2004, 160, 177, 226, 241, 242, 250, 252, 263. Time is short: Scheuer 2006, 20. On the Democrats and McCain, see also Zakaria 2008b. For a "subcatastrophic" assessment of the issue, see Posner 2004, 74–75.

44. Jenkins 2008, 284. Gilmore 1999, 37. See also Byman 2003, 163; Posner 2004, 71–75.

45. Jenkins 2008, 377. Arkin 2006b.

46. Jenkins 2008, 283. See also Porter 2009.

47. Jenkins 2008, 291; Porter 2009, 300. As Max Abrahms points out, however, in terrorist groups there is often a sort of self-perpetuating acceptance of the technique arising from the appeal of group solidarity, and many terrorists cannot coherently explain what they are fighting for and how terrorism will help them achieve it (2008; see also Sageman 2008). This is similar to the conclusion from combat studies that soldiers fight much more for their comrades than for any sort of cause. For a discussion of such motivations, see J. Mueller 2004, 9–15.

48. Bin Laden: J. Mueller 2006, 3; on the problems of overreaction to terrorism more broadly, see J. Mueller 2006. Martin 2009.

49. Sageman 2008, 149. See also Porter 2009, 303.

50. See also Arkin 2006, 43; Jenkins 2008, 215. On Katrina, see in particular Cooper and Block 2006.

51. Leitenberg 2005, 35; Bergen 2006, 343; see also Pillar 2003, 21.

EPILOGUE AND AN INVENTORY OF PROPOSITIONS

1. Brodie 1946, 52.

2. Brodie 1946, 76. He also concluded that "if the atomic bomb can be used without fear of substantial retaliation in kind, it will clearly encourage aggression" (1946, 75).

3. For a discussion of this important intellectual development, see Kaplan 1983, 339–40.

4. Worst-case: Brodie 1978, 68. Playing with words: Kaplan 1983, 342.

5. Brodie 1966, 93.

References

Abrahms, Max. 2006. "Why Terrorism Does Not Work." *International Security* 31(2) Fall: 42–78.

———. 2008. "What Terrorists Really Want: Terrorist Motives and Counterterrorism Strategy." *International Security* 32(4) Spring: 78–105.

Albright, David. 2002. *Al Qaeda's Nuclear Program: Through the Window of Seized Documents.* Nautilus Institute Special Forum 47. www.nautilus. org/archives/fora/Special-Policy-Forum/47_Albright.html

Albright, David, and Holly Higgins. 2003. "A Bomb for the Ummah." *Bulletin of the Atomic Scientists* March/April: 49–55.

Albright, Madeleine. 2003. *Madam Secretary.* New York: Miramax.

Ali, Mohamed M., John Blacker, and Gareth Jones. 2003. "Annual Mortality Rates and Excess Deaths of Children under Five in Iraq, 1991–1998." *Population Studies* 57(2): 217–26.

Allison, Graham T. 1971. *Essence of Decision: Explaining the Cuban Missile Crisis.* Boston: Little, Brown.

———. 1995. "Must We Wait for the Nuclear Morning After?" *Washington Post* 30 April: C7.

———. 2004. *Nuclear Terrorism: The Ultimate Preventable Catastrophe.* New York: Times Books.

———. 2006. "The Ongoing Failure of Imagination." *Bulletin of the Atomic Scientists* September/October: 36–41.

Allison, Graham T. (in debate with Michael A. Levi). 2007. "How Likely Is a Nuclear Terrorist Attack on the United States?" New York: Council on Foreign Relations, April. www.cfr.org/publication/13097/how_likely_is_a_nuclear_attack_on_the_united_states.html

Allison, Graham T., Albert Carnesale, and Joseph S. Nye, Jr. 1985. "Analytic Conclusions." In *Hawks, Doves, and Owls: An Agenda for Avoiding Nuclear War.* New York: Norton.

Allison, Graham T., Owen R. Coté, Jr., Richard A. Falkenrath, and Steven E. Miller. 1996. *Avoiding Nuclear Anarchy: Containing the Threat of Loose Russian Nuclear Weapons and Fissile Material*. Cambridge, MA: MIT Press.

Allison, Graham T., and Dimitri K. Simes. 2006. "Churchill, Not Quite." *National Interest* Sept./Oct.: 10–16.

Allison, Wade. 2006. *Fundamental Physics for Probing and Imaging*. New York: Oxford University Press.

Alperovitz, Gar. 1965. *Atomic Diplomacy: Hiroshima and Potsdam. The Use of the Atomic Bomb and the American Confrontation with Soviet Power*. New York: Vintage.

Ambrose, Stephen E. 1990. "Secrets of the Cold War." *New York Times* 27 December: A19.

Anderson, Mark. 2008. "Beware New Nukes." *Wired* October: 182.

Arkin, William M. 1994. "The Sky-Is-Still-Falling Profession." *Bulletin of the Atomic Scientists* April: 64.

———. 2006a. "What to Do about North Korea." *blogs.washingtonpost.com/early warning* 5 July.

———. 2006b. "The Continuing Misuses of Fear." *Bulletin of the Atomic Scientists* September/October: 42–45.

Aronson, Shlomo. 2008. "Iran's Nuclear Program: A Framework for Analysis." Paper presented at the Annual Convention of the International Studies Association. San Francisco, CA, 26–29 March.

Art, Robert J., and Kenneth N. Waltz. 1983. "Technology, Strategy, and the Uses of Force." In *The Use of Force*. Lanham, MD: University Press of America, 1–32.

Bacevich, Andrew J. 2009. "Raising Jihad." *National Interest* March/April: 91–96.

Badkhen, Anna. 2004. "Al Qaeda Bluffing About Having Suitcase Nukes, Experts Say; Russians Claim Terrorists Couldn't Have Bought Them." *San Francisco Chronicle* 23 March: A8.

Baker, Peter. 2002. "Pakistani Scientist Who Met Bin Laden Failed Polygraphs, Renewing Suspicions." *Washington Post* 3 March: A1.

Baram, Amatzia. 2000. "The Effect of Iraqi Sanctions: Statistical Pitfalls and Responsibility." *Middle East Journal* 54(2) Spring: 194–223.

Barnaby, Frank. 2004. *How to Build a Nuclear Bomb and Other Weapons of Mass Destruction*. New York: Nation Books.

Baum, Geraldine. 2008. "France to Cut Back Nuclear Arsenal." *Los Angeles Times* 22 March: A3.

Beaton, Leonard, and John Maddox. 1962. *The Spread of Nuclear Weapons*. London: Chatto & Windus, for the Institute for Strategic Studies.

Ben-Ami, Shlomo, and Trita Parsi. 2008. "The Alternative to an Israeli Attack on Iran: Serious Diplomacy, not Military Action, Will Bring Regional Security." *Christian Science Monitor* 2 July.

Benjamin, Daniel, and Steven Simon. 2002. *The Age of Sacred Terror*. New York: Random House.

———. 2005. *The Next Attack: The Failure of the War on Terror and a Strategy for Getting It Right*. New York: Times Books.

Bergen, Peter. 2006. *The Osama Bin Laden I Know: An Oral History of al Qaeda's Leader*. New York: Free Press.

———. 2007. "Where You Bin? The Return of Al Qaeda." *New Republic* 29 January: 16–19.

———. 2008. "WMD Terrorism Fears Are Overblown." *cnn.com* 5 December.

Bergen, Peter, and Paul Cruickshank. 2007. "Self-Fulfilling Prophecy." *Mother Jones* November/December.

———. 2008. "The Unraveling: The Jihadist Revolt Against Bin Laden." *New Republic* 11 June.

Berger, Thomas U. 1993. "From Sword to Chrysanthemum: Japan's Culture of Anti-Militarism." *International Security* 17(4) Spring: 119–50.

Berkowitz, Bruce D. 1987. *Calculated Risks.* New York: Simon & Schuster.

Bernstein, Barton J. 1995a. "The Atomic Bombings Reconsidered." *Foreign Affairs* Jan–Feb.

———. 1995b. "Compelling Japan's Surrender without the A-Bomb, Soviet Entry, or Invasion: Reconsidering the U.S. Bombing Survey's Early-Surrender Conclusions." *Journal of Strategic Studies* 18(2) June: 101–48.

Bernstein, Richard. 1987. "Meeting Sheds New Light on Cuban Missile Crisis." *New York Times* 14 October: A10.

Betts, Richard K. 1987. *Nuclear Blackmail and Nuclear Balance.* Washington, DC: Brookings.

———. 1998. "The New Threat of Mass Destruction." *Foreign Affairs* 77(1) January/February: 26–41.

———. 2000. "Universal Deterrence of Conceptual Collapse? Liberal Pessimism and Utopian Realism." In *The Coming Crisis: Nuclear Proliferation, U.S. Interests, and World Order,* ed. Victor A. Utgoff. Cambridge, MA: MIT Press, 51–85.

Bialer, Uri. 1980. *Shadow of the Bomber: The Fear of Air Attack and British Politics, 1932–1939.* London: Royal Historical Society.

Bialik, Carl. 2005. "The Numbers Guy: Pondering the Chances of a Nuclear Attack." *Wall Street Journal* 17 July.

Billman, Larry. 1997. *Fred Astaire: A Bio-Bibliography.* Westport, CT: Greenwood.

Binder, David. 1988. "Soviet and Allies Shift on Doctrine: Guiding Terminology Changes—'Class Struggle' Is Out, 'Struggle for Peace' In." *New York Times* 25 May: A13.

Binyon, Michael. 1998. "Bin Laden 'Now Has Nuclear Arsenal.'" *Times* (London) 7 October.

Bird, Kai, and Martin Sherwin. 2005. *American Prometheus: The Triumph and Tragedy of J. Robert Oppenheimer.* New York: Knopf.

Blacker, Coit D. 1987. *Reluctant Warriors.* New York: Freeman.

Blainey, Geoffrey. 1973. *The Causes of Wars.* New York: Free Press.

Blair, Bruce G. 2003. "We Keep Building Nukes For All the Wrong Reasons." *Washington Post* 25 May: B1.

Blight, James G., Joseph S. Nye, Jr., and David A. Welch. 1987. "The Cuban Missile Crisis Revisited." *Foreign Affairs* 66(1) Fall: 170–88.

Bloom, Mia. 2005. *Dying to Kill: The Allure of Suicide Terror.* New York: Columbia University Press.

Bobbitt, Phillip. 2008. *Terror and Consent: The Wars for the Twenty-First Century.* New York: Knopf.

Bohlen, Avis. 2009. Arms Control in the Cold War. *www.fpri.org* May.

Borger, Julian. 1998. "Iraq Élite Rides High Despite Sanctions." *Guardian Weekly* 8 March: 4.

———. 2008. "A Team of Experts is Battling to Retrieve Tons of Nuclear Material Before Terrorists Do. But Time's Running Out." *Daily Mail* 6 September: 42.

Botha, Anneli. 2006. "Terrorism in Algeria: The Role of the Community in Combating Terrorism." In *Countering Terrorism and WMD: Creating a Global Counter-Terrorism Network,* ed. Peter Katona, Michael D. Intriligator, and John P. Sullivan. London and New York: Routledge, 144–57.

Boudreaux, Richard. 2007. "Israel Sounds Alarm on Iran's Nuclear Efforts; The Jewish State Warns of a Second Holocaust If Nations Fail to Prevent Tehran from Acquiring the Bomb." *Los Angeles Times* 7 February: A1.

Boulding, Kenneth E. 1978. *Stable Peace.* Austin: University of Texas Press.

Boyer, Paul. 1985. *By the Bomb's Early Light: American Thought and Culture at the Dawn of the Atomic Age.* New York: Pantheon.

Boyle, Francis Anthony. 1985. *World Politics and International Law.* Durham, NC: Duke University Press.

Bracken, Paul. 1983. *The Command and Control of Nuclear Forces.* New Haven, CT: Yale University Press.

Bradley, Omar. 1949. "This Way Lies Peace (as Told to Beverly Smith)." *Saturday Evening Post* 15 October: 33 ff.

Brines, Russell. 1944. *Until They Eat Stones.* Philadelphia: Lippincott.

Broad, William J. 2008. "Hidden Travels of the Bomb." *New York Times* 9 December: D1.

Brodie, Bernard, ed. 1946. *The Absolute Weapon: Atomic Power and the World Order.* New York: Harcourt, Brace.

Brodie, Bernard. 1959. *Strategy in the Missile Age.* Princeton, NJ: Princeton University Press.

———. 1966. *Escalation and the Nuclear Option.* Princeton, NJ: Princeton University Press.

———. 1973. *War and Politics.* New York: Macmillan.

———. 1978. "The Development of Nuclear Strategy." *International Security* 2(4) Spring: 65–83.

Bronner, Ethan. 2006. "Just How Far Did They Go, Those Words against Israel?" *New York Times* 11 June: 4–4.

Brown, Frederic J. 1968. *Chemical Warfare: A Study in Restraints.* Princeton, NJ: Princeton University Press.

Bueno de Mesquita, Bruce, and William H. Riker. 1982. "An Assessment of the Merits of Selective Nuclear Proliferation." *Journal of Conflict Resolution* 26(2) June: 283–306.

Bundy, McGeorge. 1984. "The Unimpressive Record of Atomic Diplomacy." In *The Nuclear Crisis Reader,* ed. Gwyn Prins. New York: Vantage, 42–54.

———. 1988. *Danger and Survival: Choices about the Bomb in the First Fifty Years.* New York: Random House.

Bunn, Matthew. 2006. "A Mathematical Model of the Risk of Nuclear Terrorism." *Annals of the American Academy of Political and Social Science* September: 103–20.

———. 2007. *Securing the Bomb 2007.* Cambridge, MA: Project on Managing the Atom, Belfer Center for Science and International Affairs, John F. Kennedy School of Government, Harvard University.

Bunn, Matthew, and Anthony Wier. 2006. "Terrorist Nuclear Weapon Construction: How Difficult?" *Annals of the American Academy of Political and Social Science* September: 133–49.

Burin, Frederic S. 1963. "The Communist Doctrine of the Inevitability of War." *American Political Science Review* 57(2) June: 334–54.

Burke, Jason. 2003. *Al-Qaeda: Casting a Shadow of Terror.* New York: Tauris.

Burr, William, and Jeffrey T. Richelson. 2000/01. "Whether to 'Strangle the Baby in the Cradle.'" *International Security* 25(1) Winter: 54–99.

Bush, George H. W. 1990. *Public Papers of the Presidents of the United States: George Bush, 1989.* Washington, DC: United States Government Printing Office.

Butow, Robert J. C. 1954. *Japan's Decision to Surrender.* Stanford, CA: Stanford University Press.

Byman, Daniel L. 2003. "Al-Qaeda as an Adversary: Do We Understand Our Enemy?" *World Politics* 56(1) October: 139–63.

Callahan, David. 1990. *Dangerous Capabilities: Paul Nitze and the Cold War.* New York: HarperCollins.

Cameron, Gavin. 2004. "Weapons of Mass Destruction Terrorism Research: Past and Future." In *Terrorism: Trends, Achievements and Failures,* ed. Andres Silke. London: Frank Cass, 72–90.

Campbell, Kurt M., and Robert J. Einhorn. 2004. "Avoiding the Tipping Point: Concluding Observations." In *The Nuclear Tipping Point: Why States Reconsider Their Nuclear Choices,* ed. Kurt M. Campbell, Robert J. Einhorn, and Mitchell B. Reiss. Washington, DC: Brookings Institution Press, 317–48.

Campbell, Kurt M., and Tsuyoshi Sunohara. 2004. "Japan: Thinking the Unthinkable." In *The Nuclear Tipping Point: Why States Reconsider Their Nuclear Choices,* ed. Kurt M. Campbell, Robert J. Einhorn, and Mitchell B. Reiss. Washington, DC: Brookings Institution Press, 218–53.

Carle, Glenn L. 2008. "Overstating Our Fears." *Washington Post* 13 July: B7.

Carlucci, Frank C. 1989. "Is the Cold War Over: No Time to Change U.S. Defense Policy." *New York Times* 27 January.

Carrington, Lord. 1988. "East-West Relations: A Time of Far-Reaching Change." *NATO Review* June.

Carus, W. Seth. 2006. *Defining "Weapons of Mass Destruction."* Washington, DC: National Defense University Press. Center for the Study of Weapons of Mass Destruction Occasional Paper 4.

Center for Nonproliferation Studies. 2002. *"Suitcase Nukes": A Reassessment.* Monterey, CA: Monterey Institute of International Studies, 22 September. cns.miis.edu/pubs/week/020923.htm

Chapman, Clark R, and Alan W. Harris. 2002. "A Skeptical Look at September 11th: How We Can Defeat Terrorism by Reacting to It More Rationally." *Skeptical Inquirer* September/October: 29–34.

Chertoff, Michael. 2008. "Security Efforts Well Worth Cost." *Phildelphia Inquirer* 4 January.

Cho, Il Hyun. 2009. "Does a Nuclear Neighbor Provoke a Regional Nuclear Arms Race? Explaining Nuclear Restraint in East Asia." Paper presented at the Annual Convention of the International Studies Association. New York, NY, 15–18 February.

Choi, Jong Kun. 2006. "Predictions of Tragedy vs. Tragedy of Predictions in Northeast Asian Security." *Korean Journal of Defense Analysis* 18(1) Spring: 7–33.

Churchill, Winston S. 1932. *Amid These Storms: Thoughts and Adventures.* New York: Scribner's.

——. 1951. *In the Balance: Speeches 1949 and 1950.* Boston: Houghton Mifflin.

Cirincione, Joseph. 2007a. *Bomb Scare: The History and Future of Nuclear Weapons.* New York: Columbia University Press.

——. 2007b. Cassandra's Conundrum. *National Interest* Nov./Dec.: 15–17.

——. 2008. "The Greatest Threat to Us All." *New York Review of Books* 6 March.

Clarke, I. F. 1966. *Voices Prophesying War, 1763–1984*. London: Oxford University Press.

Clarke, Richard A. 2004. *Against All Enemies: Inside America's War on Terror*. New York: Free Press.

Clinton, Bill. 2004. *My Life*. New York: Knopf.

Cockburn, Andrew. 1983. *The Threat: Inside the Soviet Military Machine*. New York: Random House.

Coffey, Thomas M. 1970. *Imperial Tragedy: Japan in World War II, The First Days and the Last*. New York: World.

Cole, Juan. 2009a. *Engaging the Muslim World*. New York: Palgrave Macmillan.

———. 2009b. "Obama's domino theory." Salon.com (30 March). www.salon.com/opinion/feature/2009/03/30/afghanistan

Coll, Steve. 2004. *Ghost Wars: The Secret History of the CIA, Afghanistan, and Bin Laden, from the Soviet Invasion to September 10, 2001*. New York: Penguin.

———. 2005. "What Bin Laden Sees in Hiroshima." *Washington Post* 6 February: B1.

Colton, Timothy J. 1986. *The Dilemma of Reform in the Soviet Union*. Rev. ed. New York: Council on Foreign Relations.

Committee for the Compilation of Materials on Damage Caused by the Atomic Bombs in Hiroshima and Nagasaki. 1981. *Hiroshima and Nagasaki: The Physical, Medical, and Social Effects of the Atomic Bombings*. New York: Basic Books.

Compton, Arthur H. 1956. *Atomic Quest*. New York: Oxford.

Cooper, Christopher, and Robert Block. 2006. *Disaster: Hurricane Katrina and the Failure of Homeland Security*. New York: Times Books.

Cordesman, Anthony H. 2005. *The Challenge of Biological Weapons*. Washington, DC: Center for Strategic and International Studies.

Craig, William. 1967. *The Fall of Japan*. New York: Dial.

Cullison, Alan. 2004. "Inside al-Qaeda's Hard Drive." *Atlantic* September.

Cushman, John F., Jr. 1992. "Senate Endorses Pact to Reduce Strategic Arms." *New York Times* 2 October: A1.

Daalder, Ivo, and Jan Lodal. 2008. "The Logic of Zero." *Foreign Affairs* 87(6) November/December.

Darlin, Damon. 1990. "And the New Champ in 1-Finger Chin-Ups Is Korea's Mr. Kim." *Wall Street Journal* 17 May: A1.

Dart, Bob. 2005. "Leak Plugged: Toll Estimate Rises as Water Begins to Fall." *Atlanta Journal-Constitution* 6 September: 1A.

Daum, Werner. 2001. "Universalism and the West: An Agenda for Understanding." *Harvard International Review* 23(2) Summer: 19–23.

de Rugy, Veronique. 2007. "Is Port Security Funding Making Us Safer?" *Audit of the Conventional Wisdom (Center for International Studies, MIT)* November.

de Seversky, Alexander P. 1946. "Atomic Bomb Hysteria." *Reader's Digest* February: 121–26.

———. 1950. *Air Power: Key to Survival*. New York: Simon and Schuster.

Deane, John R. 1947. *The Strange Alliance*. New York: Viking.

DeBoer, Connie. 1985. "The Polls: The European Peace Movement and Development of Nuclear Missiles." *Public Opinion Quarterly* 49 Spring: 119–32.

De Gaulle, Charles. 1968. "The Thoughts of Charles De Gaulle." *New York Times Magazine* 12 May: 102–03.

Denton, Andrew. 2004. *Enough Rope with Andrew Denton*: "Hamid Mir." Australian Broadcasting Company 22 March. www.abc.net.au/tv/enoughrope/transcripts/s1071804.htm

Djilas, Milovan. 1962. *Conversations with Stalin*. New York: Harcourt, Brace.

Dower, John W. 1986. *War without Mercy: Race and Power in the Pacific War*. New York: Pantheon.

Downes, Richard. 1998. "Saddam's Men Use Sanctions to Secure Their Grip." *Independent* (London) 12 December: 17.

Dueck, Colin, and Ray Takeyh. 2007. "Iran's Nuclear Challenge." *Political Science Quarterly* 122(2) Summer: 189–205.

Dupuy, R. Ernest, and George Fielding Eliot. 1937. *If War Comes*. New York: Macmillan.

Easterbrook, Gregg. 2002. "Term Limits: The Meaninglessness of 'WMD.'" *New Republic* 7 October: 22–25.

Eberstadt, Nicholas. 1999. "The Most Dangerous Country." *National Interest* Fall: 45–54.

Eden, Lynn. 2004. *Whole World on Fire: Organizations, Knowledge, and Nuclear Weapons Devastation*. Ithaca, NY: Cornell University Press.

Edwards, Rob. 2001. "Your Worst Fears: Once Terrorists Have Nuclear Fuel, Building a Bomb is Child's Play." *New Scientist* 2 June.

Eilstrup-Sangiovanni, Mette, and Calvert Jones. 2009. "Assessing the Dangers of Illicit Networks: Why al-Qaida May Be Less Dangerous Than Many Think." *International Security* 33(2) Fall: 7–44.

Einstein, Albert. 1960. *Einstein on Peace*, ed. Otto Nathan and Heinz Norden. New York: Simon & Schuster.

Emerson, Steven. 2001. "Trying Usama Bin Ladin in Absentia." *Middle East Quarterly* 8(2) Spring: 84–94.

Enthoven, Alain C., and K. Wayne Smith. 1971. *How Much Is Enough? Shaping the Defense Program 1961–1969*. New York: Harper Colophon.

Eraker, Elizabeth. 2004. "Cleanup After a Radiological Attack: U.S. Prepares Guidance." *Nonproliferation Review* 11(3) Fall/Winter: 167–85.

Etzioni, Amitai. 2007. *Security First: For a Muscular, Moral Foreign Policy*. New Haven, CT: Yale University Press.

Evangelista, Matthew A. 1982/83. "Stalin's Postwar Army Reappraised." *International Security* 7(3) Winter: 110–38.

Falk, Stanley L. 1961. "Disarmament on the Great Lakes: Myth or Reality?" *U.S. Naval Institute Proceedings* 87(2) December: 69–73.

Falkenrath, Richard A., Robert D. Newman, and Bradley A. Thayer. 1998. *America's Achilles' Heel: Nuclear, Biological, and Chemical Terrorism and Covert Attack*. Cambridge, MA: MIT Press.

Fallows, James. 1994/95. "The Panic Gap: Reactions to North Korea's Bomb." *National Interest* Winter: 40–45.

———. 2005. "Why Iraq Has No Army." *Atlantic* December: 60–77.

———. 2006. "Declaring Victory." *Atlantic* September: 60–73.

Feinstein, Lee, and Anne-Marie Slaughter. 2004. "A Duty to Protect." *Foreign Affairs* 83(1) January/February.

Ferguson, Charles D., Tahseen Kazi, and Judith Perera. 2003. *Commercial Radioactive Sources: Surveying the Security Risks*. Monterey, CA: Center for Nonproliferation Studies, Monterey Institute of International Studies.

Ferguson, Charles D., and William C. Potter. 2005. *The Four Faces of Nuclear Terrorism: Threats and Responses*. New York: Routledge.

Fessler, Pam. 2007. "Auditors, DHS Disagree on Radiation Detectors." *Morning Edition*, National Public Radio, 19 September.

Fielding, Nick, Joe Laurier, and Gareth Walsh. 2002. "Bin Laden 'Almost Had Uranium Bomb.'" *Sunday Times* (London) 3 March.

Finel, Bernard I. 2009. "Counterterrorism and Military Occupation." *smallwarsjournal. com* 20 April.

Finn, Peter. 2005. "Chernobyl's Harm Was Far Less Than Predicted, U.N. Report Says." *Washington Post* 6 September: A22.

———. 2009. "U.S., Israel Disagree on Iran Arms Threat." *Washington Post* 11 March: A4.

Fischer, Hannah. 2008. Iraqi Civilian Death Estimates. *CRS Report for Congress, RS22537* 27 August. www.fas.org/sgp/crs/mideast/RS22537.pdf

Fischoff, Baruch. 2005. "A Hero in Every Seat." *New York Times* 7 August: 4–13.

Freedman, Lawrence, and Saki Dockrill. 1994. "Hiroshima: A Strategy of Shock." In *From Pearl Harbor to Hiroshima: The Second World War in Asia and the Pacific, 1941–45*, ed. Saki Dockrill. New York: St. Martin's.

Freud, Sigmund. 1930. *Civilization and Its Discontents*. London: Hogarth.

Frost, Robin M. 2005. *Nuclear Terrorism after 9/11*. London: International Institute for Strategic Studies, Adelphi Paper 378.

Fukuyama, Francis. 1987. "Patterns of Soviet Third World Policy." *Problems of Communism* 36(5) September–October: 1–13.

———. 2004. "The Neoconservative Moment." *National Interest* Summer: 57–68.

———. 2005. "America's Parties and Their Foreign Policy Masquerade." *Financial Times* 8 March: 21.

Furedi, Frank. 2007. *Invitation to Terror: The Expanding Empire of the Unknown*. London: Continuum.

Fursenko, Aleksandr, and Timothy Naftali. 2006. *Khrushchev's Cold War: The Inside Story of an American Adversary*. New York: Norton.

Gaddis, John Lewis. 1974. "Was the Truman Doctrine a Real Turning Point?" *Foreign Affairs* 52(2) January: 386–401.

———. 1982. *Strategies of Containment*. New York: Oxford University Press.

———. 1987. *The Long Peace: Inquiries Into the History of the Cold War*. New York: Oxford University Press.

———. 1992. *The United States and the Cold War: Implications, Reconsiderations, Provocations*. New York: Oxford University Press.

———. 1997. *We Now Know: Rethinking Cold War History*. New York: Oxford University Press.

———. 1999. Conclusion. In *Cold War Statesmen Confront the Bomb: Nuclear Diplomacy Since 1945*, ed. John Lewis Gaddis, Philip H. Gordon, Ernest R. May, and Jonathan Rosenberg. Oxford, UK: Oxford University Press, 260–71.

Gaddis, John Lewis, Philip H. Gordon, Ernest R. May, and Jonathan Rosenberg, eds. 1999. *Cold War Statesmen Confront the Bomb: Nuclear Diplomacy Since 1945*. Oxford, UK: Oxford University Press.

Gallucci, Robert L. 2008. "Terror in Extremis." *National Interest* November/December: 74–79.

Garfield, Richard. 1997. "The Impact of Economic Embargoes on the Health of Women and Children." *JAMWA* 52(4) Fall: 181–85.

———. 1999. *Morbidity and Mortality among Iraqi Children from 1990 to 1998*. South Bend, IN: Kroc Institute for International Peace Studies, University of Notre Dame.

Garthoff, Raymond L. 1987. *Reflections on the Cuban Missile Crisis*. Washington, DC: Brookings.

————. 1994. *The Great Transition: American-Soviet Relations and the End of the Cold War*. Washington, DC: Brookings.

Garwin, Richard L. 2008. "Evaluating Iran's Missile Threat." *Bulletin of the Atomic Scientists* May/June: 40–42.

Garwin, Richard L., and Georges Charpak. 2001. *Megawatts and Megatons: A Turning Point in the Nuclear Age?* New York: Knopf.

Gavin, Francis J. 2004/05. "Blasts from the Past: Proliferation Lessons from the 1960s." *International Security* 29(3) Winter: 100–35.

George, Alexander L., and Richard Smoke. 1974. *Deterrence in American Foreign Policy: Theory and Practice*. New York: Columbia University Press.

Gerges, Fawaz. 2005. *The Far Enemy: Why Jihad Went Global*. New York: Cambridge University Press.

————. 2008a. "Taking On Al-Qaeda." *Washington Post* 17 June: C8.

————. 2008b. "Word on the Street." *Democracy Journal* (Summer): 69–76. Available at www.democracyjournal.org/article.php?ID=6622

Gertz, Bill. 2002. "5,000 in U.S. Suspected of Ties to al Qaeda; Groups Nationwide under Surveillance." *Washington Times* 11 July: A1.

————. 2007. "Al Qaeda Seen in Search of Nukes: Defense Official Warns U.S. Still Group's Target." *Washington Times* 26 July: 4.

Gilchrist, H. L. 1928. *A Comparative Study of World War Casualties from Gas and Other Weapons*. Edgewood Arsenal, MD: Chemical Warfare School.

Gilmore Commission (Advisory Panel to Assess Domestic Response Capabilities for Terrorism Involving Weapons of Mass Destruction). 1999. *First Annual Report: Assessing the Threat*, 15 December. www.rand.org/nsrd/terrpanel

Gilpatric, Roswell, Chair. 1965. *A Report to the President by the Committee on Nuclear Proliferation*. www.gwu.edu/nsarchiv/NSAEBB/NSAEBB1/nhch7_1.htm

Gilpin, Robert. 1981. *War and Change in World Politics*. New York: Cambridge University Press.

Glanz, James, and Andrew C. Revkin. 2002. "Some See Panic as Main Effect Of Dirty Bombs." *New York Times* 7 March: A1.

Goldberg, Jeffrey. 2008. "Unforgiven." *Atlantic* May: 32–51.

Goldstein, Joshua S. 2004. *The Real Price of War: How You Pay for the War on Terror*. New York: New York University Press.

Gordon, Michael R., and Bernard E. Trainor. 2006. *Cobra II: The Inside Story of the Invasion and Occupation of Iraq*. New York: Pantheon.

Graham, Bob, Chairman. 2008. *World at Risk: The Report of the Commission on the Prevention of WMD Proliferation and Terrorism*. New York: Vintage.

Grare, Frederic. 2007. "Musharraf in the Twilight." *washingtonpost.com's Think Tank Town* 10 July.

Green, Stanley, and Burt Goldblatt. 1973. *Starring Fred Astaire*. New York: Dodd, Mead.

Greenhouse, Steven. 1993. "New Tally of World's Economies Catapults China into Third Place." *New York Times* 20 May: A1.

Grodzins, Morton, and Eugene Rabinowitch, eds. 1963. *The Atomic Age: Scientists in National and World Affairs*. New York: Basic Books.

Grossman, Elaine M. 2008. "Analyst Takes Issue with Estimate of WMD Risk." Global Security Newswire 4 December. Available at gsn.nti.org/gsn/ts_20081204_3626.php

Gwertzman, Bernard. 1981. "Allied Contingency Plan Envisions a Warning Shot, Says Haig." *New York Times* 5 November: A1.

Haber, L. F. 1986. *The Poisonous Cloud: Chemical Warfare in the First World War.* Oxford, UK: Clarendon.

Hackett, John. 1979. *The Third World War: August 1985.* New York: Macmillan.

Halevi, Yossi Klein, and Michael B. Oren. 2007. "Contra Iran." *New Republic* 5 February: 15–19.

Halperin, Morton H. 1987. *Nuclear Fallacy: Dispelling the Myth of Nuclear Strategy.* Cambridge, MA: Ballinger.

Harden, Blaine. 2009. "At the Heart of North Korea's Troubles, an Intractable Hunger Crisis." *Washington Post* 6 March: A1.

Harris, Robert, and Jeremy Paxman. 1982. *A Higher Form of Killing: The Secret Story of Chemical and Biological Warfare.* New York: Hill & Wang.

Harris, Shane, and Stuart Taylor Jr. 2008. "Homeland Security Chief Looks Back, and Forward." Government Executive.com 17 March. www.govexec.com/story_page_pf.cfm?articleid=39539

Harrison, Selig S. 2002. *Korean Endgame: A Strategy for Reunification and U.S. Disengagement.* Princeton, NJ: Princeton University Press.

Hasegawa, Tsuyoshi. 2005. *Racing the Enemy: Stalin, Truman, and the Surrender of Japan.* Cambridge, MA: Harvard University Press.

Hasegawa, Tsuyoshi, ed. 2007. *The End of the Pacific War: Reappraisals.* Stanford, CA: Stanford University Press.

Healey, Denis. 1960. *The Race against the H-Bomb.* London: Fabian Tract 322.

Henriksen, Thormod, and H. David Maillie. 2003. *Radiation and Health.* New York: Taylor & Francis.

Hersh, Seymour M. 1991. *The Samson Option: Israel's Nuclear Arsenal and American Foreign Policy.* New York: Random House.

Hilsman, Roger. 1967. *To Move a Nation: The Politics of Foreign Policy in the Administration of John F. Kennedy.* New York: Delta.

Hoffman, Bruce. 2002. "Rethinking Terrorism and Counterterrorism since 9/11." *Studies in Conflict and Terrorism* 25: 303–16.

———. 2006. *Inside Terrorism.* Rev. ed. New York: Columbia University Press.

———. 2007. "Scarier Than Bin Laden." *Washington Post* 9 September: B1.

———. 2008. "The Myth of Grass-Roots Terrorism: Why Osama Bin Laden Still Matters." *Foreign Affairs* May/June.

Holloway, David. 1994. *Stalin and the Bomb: The Soviet Union and Atomic Energy, 1939–1956.* New Haven, CT: Yale University Press.

Holmes, Robert L. 1989. *On War and Morality.* Princeton, NJ: Princeton University Press.

Holsti, Kalevi J. 1991. *Peace and War: Armed Conflicts and International Order 1648–1989.* Cambridge, UK: Cambridge University Press.

Hosmer, Stephen T., and Thomas W. Wolfe. 1983. *Soviet Policy and Practice toward Third World Countries.* Lexington, MA: Lexington.

Hoyt, Edwin P. 1986. *Japan's War: The Great Pacific Conflict 1853 to 1952.* New York: McGraw-Hill.

Hughes, Llewelyn. 2007. "Why Japan Will Not Go Nuclear (Yet): International and Domestic Constraints on the Nuclearization of Japan." *International Security* 31(4) Spring: 67–96.

Human Rights Watch/Middle East. 1995. *Iraq's Crime of Genocide: The Anfal Campaign Against the Kurds.* New Haven, CT: Yale University Press.

Huntington, Samuel P. 1961. *The Common Defense.* New York: Columbia University Press.

Huth, Paul, and Bruce Russett. 1990. "Testing Deterrence Theory: Rigor Makes a Difference." *World Politics* 42(4) July: 466–501.

Hymans, Jacques E. C. 2004. "The Roots of the Washington Threat Consensus." In *Striking First: The Preventive War Doctrine and the Reshaping of U.S. Foreign Policy,* ed. Betty Glad and Chris J. Dolan. New York: Palgrave Macmillan, 33–45.

———. 2006. *The Psychology of Nuclear Proliferation: Identity, Emotions, and Foreign Policy.* New York: Cambridge University Press.

———. 2007. *Nuclear Weapons Capacity as a Function of State Structure.* University of Southern California: School of International Relations.

———. 2008. "Assessing North Korean Intentions and Capacities: A New Approach." *Journal of East Asian Studies* 8: 259–92.

———. 2009. "Proliferation Implications of Atoms for Peace: A Case Study of the Yugoslav Experience." Paper presented at the Nobel Symposium on Peace, stability and nuclear order. Oscarborg, Drøbak, Norway, 25–27 June.

———. forthcoming. "When Does a State Become a 'Nuclear Weapons State?' An Exercise in Measurement Validation." In *Forecasting Nuclear Proliferation,* ed. William C. Potter. Monterey, CA: James Martin Center for Nonproliferation Studies, Monterey Institute of International Studies.

Ienaga, Saburo. 1978. *The Pacific War: World War II and the Japanese, 1931–1945.* New York: Pantheon.

Ignatieff, Michael. 2004a. Lesser Evils: "What It Will Cost Us to Succeed in the War on Terror." *New York Times Magazine* 2 May: 44 ff.

———. 2004b. *The Lesser Evil: Political Ethics in an Age of Terror.* Princeton, NJ: Princeton University Press.

Ignatius, David. 2008. "The Fading Jihadists." *Washington Post* 28 February: A17.

Indyk, Martin. 2004. "The Iraq War Did Not Force Gadaffi's Hand." *Financial Times* 9 March: 21.

Isikoff, Michael, and Mark Hosenball. 2007. "The Flip Side of the NIE." Newsweek.com 15 August. Available at www.newsweek.com/id/32962

Jacob, Neerada. 2008. "The Sanctions Impact on Nuclear Reversal: A Case Study of Taiwan." Paper presented at the Annual Convention of the International Studies Association. San Francisco, CA, 26–29 March.

Jenkins, Brian Michael. 1975. "International Terrorism: A New Mode of Conflict." In *International Terrorism and World Security,* ed. David Carlton and Carolo Schaerf. New York: Wiley, 13–49.

———. 2006. *Unconquerable Nation: Knowing Our Enemy and Strengthening Ourselves.* Santa Monica, CA: RAND Corporation.

———. 2008. *Will Terrorists Go Nuclear?* Amherst, NY: Prometheus.

Jentleson, Bruce W., and Christopher A. Whytock. 2005/06. "Who 'Won' Libya? The Force-Diplomacy Debate and Its Implications for Theory and Policy." *International Security* 30(3) Winter: 47–86.

Jervis, Robert. 1979. "Deterrence Theory Revisited." *World Politics* 31(2) January: 289–324.

———. 1980. "The Impact of the Korean War on the Cold War." *Journal of Conflict Resolution* 24(4) December: 563–92.

Jervis, Robert. 1984. *The Illogic of American Nuclear Strategy*. Ithaca, NY: Cornell University Press.

———. 1988. "The Political Effects of Nuclear Weapons." *International Security* 13(2) Fall: 28–38.

———. 1989. *The Meaning of the Nuclear Revolution: Statecraft and the Prospect of Armageddon*. Ithaca, NY: Cornell University Press.

———. 2001. "Was the Cold War a Security Dilemma?" *Journal of Cold War Studies* 3(1) Winter: 36–60.

———. 2006. "Reports, Politics, and Intelligence Failures: The Case of Iraq." *Journal of Strategic Studies* 29(1) February: 3–52.

Joffe, Josef. 1987. "Peace and Populism: Why the European Anti-Nuclear Movement Failed." *International Security* 11(4) Spring: 3–40.

Johnson, Robert H. 1994. *Improbable Dangers: U.S. Conceptions of Threat in the Cold War and After*. New York: St. Martin's.

Jones, Ms. Gary L. 2000. *Radiation Standards: Scientific Basis Inconclusive, and EPA and NRC Disagreement Continues*. GAO testimony before the Subcommittee on Energy and Environment, Committee on Science. Washington, DC: U.S. House of Representatives.

Jones, Robert Huhn. 1969. *The Roads to Russia*. Norman: University of Oklahoma Press.

Jones, Seth G. 2008. "The Rise of Afghanistan's Insurgency: State Failure and Jihad." *International Security* 32(4) Spring: 7–40.

Kagan, Donald. 1987. "World War I, World War II, World War III." *Commentary* March: 21–40.

Kahn, Herman. 1960. *On Thermonuclear War*. Princeton, NJ: Princeton University Press.

———. 1970. *The Emerging Japanese Superstate: Challenge and Response*. Englewood Cliffs, N.J.: Prentice-Hall.

Kamp, Karl-Heinz. 1996. "An Overrated Nightmare." *Bulletin of the Atomic Scientists* July/August: 30–34.

Kaplan, Fred. 1983. *The Wizards of Armageddon*. New York: Simon & Schuster.

———. 2006. "The Slime Talk Express." Slate.com 11 October. www.slate.com/id/2151354/

Kaplan, Lawrence F., and William Kristol. 2003. *The War over Iraq: Saddam's Tyranny and America's Mission*. San Francisco: Encounter Books.

Kase, Toshikazu. 1950. *Journey to the Missouri*. New Haven, CT: Yale.

Katzenstein, Peter J., and Nobuo Okawara. 1993. "Japan's National Security: Structures, Norms, and Policies." *International Security* 17(4) Spring: 84–118.

Kaufmann, Chaim. 2004. "Threat Inflation and the Failure of the Marketplace of Ideas: The Selling of the Iraq War." *International Security* 29(1) Summer: 5–48.

Kay, David. 2008. "The Iranian Fallout." *National Interest* Sept./Oct.: 11–19.

Kaysen, Carl. 1990. "Is War Obsolete?" *International Security* 14(4) Spring: 42–64.

Kaysen, Carl, Robert S. McNamara, and George W. Rathjens. 1991. "Nuclear Weapons After the Cold War." *Foreign Affairs* 70(4) Fall: 95–110.

Kean, Thomas H., Chair. 2004. *The 9/11 Commission Report: Final Report of the National Commission on Terrorist Attacks Upon the United States*. Washington, DC: U.S. Government Printing Office.

Keatley, Robert. 1989. "Gorbachev Peace Offensive Jars the West." *Wall Street Journal* 20 January: A18.

Keller, Bill. 2002. "Nuclear Nightmares." *New York Times Magazine* 26 May.

Kennan, George F. 1987. "Containment Then and Now." *Foreign Affairs* 65(4) Spring: 885–90.

Kennedy, John F. 1961. "Text of President Kennedy's Address to the United Nations General Assembly." *New York Times* 26 September: 14.

Kennedy, Paul. 1983. *Strategy and Diplomacy: 1870–1945.* London: Allen and Unwin.

Kennedy, Robert F. 1971. *Thirteen Days: A Memoir of the Cuban Missile Crisis.* New York: Norton.

Kenney, Michael. 2009. *Organizational Learning and Islamic Militancy.* Washington, D.C.: U.S. Department of Justice, National Institute of Justice, May. www.ncjrs.gov/pdffiles1/nij/grants/226808.pdf

Kerr, Jennifer C. 2003. "Terror Threat Level Raised to Orange." Associated Press 21 December.

Kessler, Ronald. 2007. *The Terrorist Watch: Inside the Desperate Race to Stop the Next Attack.* New York: Crown.

Khan, Kamran. 2001. "Pakistan Releases Nuclear Scientists for Ramadan's End." *Washington Post* 16 December: A27.

Khan, Kamran, and Molly Moore. 2001. "2 Nuclear Experts Briefed Bin Laden, Pakistanis Say." *Washington Post* 11 December: A1.

Khrushchev, Nikita. 1970. *Khrushchev Remembers,* ed. Edward Crankshaw and Strobe Talbott. Boston: Little, Brown.

———. 1974. *Khrushchev Remembers: The Last Testament,* ed. Strobe Talbott. Boston: Little, Brown.

Kirshner, Jonathan. 1997. "The Microfoundations of Economic Sanctions." *Security Studies* 6(3) Spring: 32–64.

Kissinger, Henry A. 1979. *White House Years.* Boston: Little, Brown.

Knorr, Klaus. 1985. "Controlling Nuclear War." *International Security* 9(4) Spring: 79–98.

Knox, MacGregor. 1984. "Conquest, Foreign and Domestic, in Fascist Italy and Nazi Germany." *Journal of Modern History* 56 March: 1–57.

Kolata, Gina. 2001. "For Radiation, How Much Is Too Much?" *New York Times* 27 November: F1.

Kosko, Bart. 2004. "Terror Threat May Be Mostly a Big Bluff." *Los Angeles Times* 13 September: B11.

Kramer, Mark. 2004/05. "The Perils of Counterinsurgency: Russia's War in Chechnya." *International Security* 29(3) Winter: 5–63.

Kraus, Sidney, ed. 1962. *The Great Debates: Kennedy vs. Nixon, 1960.* Bloomington: University of Indiana Press.

Krauthammer, Charles. 2004a. "Blixful Amnesia." *Washington Post* 9 July: A19.

———. 2004b. "In Defense of Democratic Realism." *National Interest* Fall: 15–25.

———. 2006. "Past the Apogee: America under Pressure." Foreign Policy Research Institute December. Available at www.fpri.org/enotes/20061213.krauthammer.pastapogee.html

Krepon, Michael. 2009. "The Mushroom Cloud That Wasn't." *Foreign Affairs* 88(3) May/June: 2–6.

Kristof, Nicholas. 1995. "The Bomb." *New York Times* 6 August: 1.

———. 2004. "An American Hiroshima." *New York Times* 11 August.

Kroenig, Matthew. 2008. "The Differential Effects of Nuclear Proliferation." Paper presented at the Annual Meeting of the American Political Science Association. San Francisco, CA, 28–31 August.

———. 2009. "Exporting the Bomb: Why States Provide Sensitive Nuclear Assistance." *American Political Science Review* 103(1) February: 113–33.

Kurth, James. 1988. "Inside the Cave: The Banality of I.R. Studies." *National Interest* Fall.

Lacey, Marc. 2005. "Look at the Place! Sudan Says, 'Say Sorry,' but U.S. Won't." *New York Times* 20 October: A4.

Lambeth, Benjamin S. 1972. "Deterrence in the MIRV Era." *World Politics* 24(2) January: 221–41.

Langer, Gary. 2002. "Trust in Government…to Do What?" *Public Perspective* July/August: 7–10.

Langewiesche, William. 2007. *The Atomic Bazaar: The Rise of the Nuclear Poor*. New York: Farrar, Straus and Giroux.

Lapp, Ralph E. 1949. *Must We Hide?* Cambridge, MA: Addison-Wesley.

Laqueur, Walter. 1996. "Postmodern Terrorism: New Rules for an Old Game." *Foreign Affairs* September/October.

Larsen, Randall. 2007. *Our Own Worst Enemy*. New York: Grand Central Publishing.

Lawrence, Bruce, ed. 2005. *Messages to the World: The Statements of Osama bin Laden*. London: Verso.

Lawson, Guy. 2008. "The Fear Factory." *Rolling Stone* 7 February: 60–65.

Layne, Christopher. 1993. "The Unipolar Illusion: Why New Great Powers Will Rise." *International Security* 17(4) Spring: 5–51.

Lebow, Richard Ned, and Janice Gross Stein. 1994. *We All Lost the Cold War*. Princeton, NJ: Princeton University Press.

Leffler, Melvyn P. 2007. *For the Soul of Mankind: The United States, the Soviet Union, and the Cold War*. New York: Hill & Wang.

Leitenberg, Milton. 2004. *The Problem of Biological Weapons*. Stockholm, Sweden: Swedish National Defence College.

———. 2005. *Assessing the Biological Weapons and Bioterrorism Threat*. Carlisle, PA: Strategic Studies Institute, U.S. Army War College.

Leites, Nathan. 1953. *A Study of Bolshevism*. Glencoe, IL: Free Press.

Levi, Michael A. 2007a. *On Nuclear Terrorism*. Cambridge, MA: Harvard University Press.

Levi, Michael A. (in debate with Graham T. Allison). 2007b. "How Likely Is a Nuclear Terrorist Attack on the United States?" New York: Council on Foreign Relations, April. www.cfr.org/publication/13097/how_likely_is_a_nuclear_attack_on_the_united_states.html

Levi, Michael A., and Henry C. Kelly. 2002. "Weapons of Mass Disruption." *Scientific American* November.

Lewis, John Wilson, and Litai Xue. 1988. *China Builds the Bomb*. Stanford, CA: Stanford University Press.

Liberman, Peter. 2001. "The Rise and Fall of the South African Bomb." *International Security* 26(2) Fall: 45–86.

Libicki, Martin C., Peter Chalk, and Melanie Sisson. 2007. *Exploring Terrorist Targeting Preferences*. Santa Monica, CA: RAND.

Lieber, Keir A., and Daryl P. Press. 2006. "The End of MAD? The Nuclear Dimension of U.S. Primacy." *International Security* 30(4) Spring: 7–44.

Lingeman, Richard R. 1970. *Don't You Know There's a War On? The American Home Front, 1941–1945*. New York: Putnam's Sons.

Linzer, Dafna. 2004a. "Nuclear Capabilities May Elude Terrorists, Experts Say." *Washington Post* 29 December: A1.

———. 2004b. "Attack With Dirty Bomb More Likely, Officials Say." *Washington Post* 29 December: A6.

Lippman, Thomas W., and Barton Gellman. 1999. "U.N. 'Helped U.S. to Spy on Saddam.'" *Guardian Weekly* 17 January: 17.

Lipton, Eric. 2001. "The Toll: Numbers Vary in Tallies of the Victims." *New York Times* 25 October: B2.

———. 2005. "Homeland Report Says Threat from Terror-List Nations Is Declining." *New York Times* 31 March: A5.

Littell, Robert. 1946. "What the Atomic Bomb Would Do to Us." *Reader's Digest* May: 125–28.

Loeb, Vernon. 1998. "Oil-for-Food Program Continues as Key Facet of U.S. Policy on Iraq." *Washington Post* 14 November: A16.

Loof, Susanna. 2005. "False Information Said Worsened Chernobyl." Associated Press, 6 September.

Lopez, George A., and David Cortright. 2004. "Containing Iraq: Sanctions Worked." *Foreign Affairs* 83(4) July/August: 90–113.

Luard, Evan. 1986. *War in International Society.* New Haven, CT: Yale University Press.

———. 1988. *The Blunted Sword: The Erosion of Military Power in Modern World Politics.* London: I.B. Tauris.

Lugar, Richard G. 2005. *The Lugar Study on Proliferation Threats and Responses.* Washington, DC: Senate Foreign Relations Committee.

Lustick, Ian S. 2006. *Trapped in the War on Terror.* Philadelphia: University of Pennsylvania Press.

———. 2008. "Abandoning the Iron Wall: Israel and 'the Middle Eastern Muck.'" *Middle East Policy* 15(3) Fall: 30–56.

Luttwak, Edward N. 1983. "Of Bombs and Men." *Commentary* August: 77–82.

Lynch, Marc. 2006. "Al-Qaeda's Media Strategies." *National Interest* Spring: 50–56.

Mack, Andrew. 2008. "Dying to Lose: Explaining the Decline in Global Terrorism." In *Human Security Brief 2007.* Vancouver, BC: Human Security Report Project, School for International Studies, Simon Fraser University, 8–21.

Mackby, Jenifer, and Walter B. Slocombe. 2004. "Germany: The Model Case, a Historical Imperative." In *The Nuclear Tipping Point: Why States Reconsider Their Nuclear Choices,* ed. Kurt M. Campbell, Robert J. Einhorn, and Mitchell B. Reiss. Washington, DC: Brookings Institution Press, 175–217.

Mandelbaum, Michael. 1981. *The Nuclear Revolution.* Cambridge: Cambridge University Press.

Mark, J. Carson, Theodore Taylor, Eugene Eyster, William Maraman, and Jacob Wechsler. 1987. "Can Terrorists Build Nuclear Weapons?" In *Preventing Nuclear Terrorism: The Report and Papers of the International Task Force on Prevention of Nuclear Terrorism,* ed. Paul Leventhal and Yonah Alexander. Lexington, MA: Heath, 55–65. Available at www.nci.org/k-m/makeab.htm

Martin, Susan B. 2009. "The Threat of Nuclear Terrorism Is Overblown." In *Debating Terrorism and Counterterrorism,* ed. Stuart Gottlieb. Washington, DC: CQ Press.

May, Ernest R. 1984. "The Cold War." In *The Making of America's Soviet Policy,* ed. Joseph S. Nye, Jr. New Haven, CT: Yale University Press, 209–30.

———. 1999. "Introduction." In *Cold War Statesmen Confront the Bomb: Nuclear Diplomacy Since 1945,* ed. John Lewis Gaddis, Philip H. Gordon, Ernest R. May and Jonathan Rosenberg. Oxford, UK: Oxford University Press, 1–11.

May, Michael. 1985. "The U.S.-Soviet Approach to Nuclear Weapons." *International Security* 9(4) Spring.

Mayer, Jane. 2006. "Junior: The Clandestine Life of America's Top Al Qaeda Source." *New Yorker* 11 September.

Mazzetti, Mark, and David Rohde. 2008. "Amid U.S. Policy Disputes, Qaeda Grows in Pakistan." *New York Times* 30 June: A1.

MccGwire, Michael. 1985. "Deterrence: The Problem, Not the Solution." *SAIS Review* 5(2) Summer–Fall: 105–24.

McGlen, Nancy E. 1986. *The Sources of Support of the Freeze Movement*. Niagara University, New York: Department of Political Science.

McNaugher, Thomas L. 1990. "Ballistic Missiles and Chemical Weapons: The Legacy of the Iran-Iraq War." *International Security* 15(2) Fall: 5–34.

McNeill, William H. 1982. *The Pursuit of Power: Technology, Armed Force, and Society since A.D. 1000*. Chicago: University of Chicago Press.

McPhee, John. 1974. *The Curve of Binding Energy*. New York: Farrar, Straus & Giroux.

Meade, Charles, and Roger C. Molander. 2006. *Considering the Effects of a Catastrophic Terrorist Attack*. Santa Monica, CA: RAND Corporation.

Mearsheimer, John J. 1983. *Conventional Deterrence*. Ithaca, NY: Cornell University Press.

———. 1984/85. "Nuclear Weapons and Deterrence in Europe." *International Security* 9(3) Winter: 19–47.

———. 1988. *Liddell Hart and the Weight of History*. Ithaca, NY: Cornell University Press.

———. 1990. "Back to the Future: Instability in Europe after the Cold War." *International Security* 15(1) Summer: 5–56.

———. 1993. "The Case for a Ukrainian Nuclear Deterrent." *Foreign Affairs* 72(3) Summer: 50–80.

Mearsheimer, John J., and Stephen M. Walt. 2003. "Iraq: An Unnecessary War." *Foreign Policy* January/February: 50–59.

———. 2007. *The Israel Lobby and U.S. Foreign Policy*. New York: Farrar, Straus and Giroux.

Medvedev, Roy. 1983. *Khrushchev*. Garden City, NY: Doubleday.

Melby, Eric D. K. 1998. "Iraq." In *Economic Sanctions and American Diplomacy*, ed. Richard N. Haass. New York: Council on Foreign Relations Press.

Meselson, Matthew. 1991. "The Myth of Chemical Superweapons." *Bulletin of the Atomic Scientists* April: 12–15.

———. 1995. "How Serious is the Biological Weapons Threat?" Massachusetts Institute of Technology: Defense & Arms Control Studies Program Seminar, 29 November.

Meyer, Josh. 2006. "U.S. Faults Saudi Efforts on Terrorism." *Los Angeles Times* 15 January: A1.

Meyer, Stephen M. 1984. *The Dynamics of Nuclear Proliferation*. Chicago: University of Chicago Press.

Michel, Lou, and Dan Herbeck. 2001. *American Terrorist: Timothy McVeigh and the Oklahoma City Bombing*. New York: ReganBooks.

Milhollin, Gary. 2002. "Can Terrorists Get the Bomb?" *Commentary* February: 45–49.

Milward, Alan S. 1977. *War, Economy and Society, 1939–1945*. Berkeley: University of California Press.

Mlakar, Paul F. Sr., W. Gene Corley, Mete A. Sozen, and Charles H. Thornton. 1998. "The Oklahoma City Bombing: Analysis of Blast Damage to the Murrah Building." *Journal of Performance of Constructed Facilities* 12(3) August: 113–19.

Morgan, Patrick. 1977. *Deterrence: A Conceptual Analysis.* Beverly Hills, CA: Sage.

Morgenthau, Hans J. 1948. *Politics among Nations: The Struggle for Power and Peace.* New York: Knopf.

Monger, Randall, and Macreadie Barr. 2009. *Nonimmigrant Admissions to the United States: 2008.* Washington, DC: Department of Homeland Security, Office of Immigration Statistics, Annual Flow Report, April.

Morris, Benny. 2008. "Israel's Unhappy Birthday." *Los Angeles Times* 11 May: M7–M8.

Mueller, Harold, and Thomas Risse-Kappen. 1987. "Origins of Estrangement: The Peace Movement and the Changed Image of America in West Germany." *International Security* 12(1) Summer: 52–88.

Mueller, John. 1967. "Incentives for Restraint: Canada as a Nonnuclear Power." *Orbis* 11(3) Fall: 864–84.

———. 1979. "Public Expectations of War during the Cold War." *American Journal of Political Science* 23(2) May: 301–29.

———. 1985. "The Bomb's Pretense as Peacemaker." *Wall Street Journal* 4 June: 32.

———. 1986. "Containment and the Decline of the Soviet Empire: Some Tentative Reflections on the End of the World as We Know It." Paper presented at the Annual Convention of the International Studies Association. Anaheim, CA, 25–29 March.

———. 1988. "The Essential Irrelevance of Nuclear Weapons: Stability in the Postwar World." *International Security* 13(2) Fall: 55–79.

———. 1989. *Retreat from Doomsday: The Obsolescence of Major War.* New York: Basic Books.

———. 1994. *Policy and Opinion in the Gulf War.* Chicago: University of Chicago Press.

———. 1995a. *Quiet Cataclysm: Reflections on the Recent Transformation of World Politics.* New York: HarperCollins.

———. 1995b. "The Perfect Enemy: Assessing the Gulf War." *Security Studies* 5(1) Autumn: 77–117.

———. 2002a. "American Foreign Policy and Public Opinion in a New Era: Eleven Propositions." In *Understanding Public Opinion,* ed. Barbara Norrander and Clyde Wilcox. Washington, DC: CQ Press, 149–72.

———. 2002b. "Harbinger or Aberration? A 9/11 Provocation." *National Interest* Fall: 45–50.

———. 2002c. "False Alarms." *Washington Post* 29 September: B7.

———. 2003. "Blip or Step Function?" Paper presented at the Annual Convention of the International Studies Association. Portland, OR, 27 February.

———. 2004. *The Remnants of War.* Ithaca, NY: Cornell University Press.

———. 2004–05. "What Was the Cold War About? Evidence from Its Ending." *Political Science Quarterly* 119(4) Winter: 609–31.

———. 2006. *Overblown: How Politicians and the Terrorism Industry Inflate National Security Threats, and Why We Believe Them.* New York: Free Press.

———. 2008. "Terrorphobia: Our False Sense of Insecurity." *American Interest* May/June: 6–13.

Mueller, John. 2009a. "War Has Almost Ceased to Exist: An Assessment." *Political Science Quarterly* 124(2) Summer: 297–321.

———. 2009b. "Faulty Correlation, Foolish Consistency, and Fatal Consequence: Democracy, Peace, and Theory in the Middle East." In *Democratic Peace and Promotion: Critical Perspectives,* ed. Steven H. Hook. Kent, OH: Kent State University Press.

———. 2010. "Assessing Measures Designed to Protect the Homeland. *Policy Studies Journal.*

Mueller, John (in debate with Brink Lindsey). 2003. "Should We Invade Iraq?" *Reason* January: 40–48. Also at www.reason.com/0301/fe.jm.should.shtml

Mueller, John, and Ian S. Lustick. 2008. "Israel's Fight-or-Flight Response." *National Interest* November/December: 68–73.

Mueller, John, and Karl P. Mueller. 1999. "Sanctions of Mass Destruction." *Foreign Affairs* 78(3) May/June: 43–53.

———. 2000. "The Methodology of Mass Destruction: Assessing Threats in the New World Order." In *Preventing the Use of Weapons of Mass Destruction,* ed. Eric Herring. London: Frank Cass, 163–87. Also in *Journal of Strategic Studies* 23(1) March 2000.

———. 2009. "The Rockets' Red Glare: Just What Are 'Weapons of Mass Destruction,' Anyway?" *Foreign Policy* 7 July. http://www.foreignpolicy.com/articles/2009/07/07/the_rockets_red_glare

Mueller, Karl P. 1991. "Strategy, Asymmetric Deterrence, and Accommodation: Middle Powers and Security in Modern Europe." PhD diss., Princeton University.

———. 2006. "The Paradox of Liberal Hegemony: Globalization and U.S. National Security." In *Globalization and National Security,* ed. Jonathan Kirshner. New York: Routledge, 143–69.

Muller, Richard A. 2008. *Physics for Future Presidents: The Science behind the Headlines.* New York: Norton.

Mulley, F. W. 1962. *The Politics of Western Defense.* New York: Praeger.

National Planning Association. 1958. *1970 without Arms Control.* Washington, DC: National Planning Association.

———. 1960. *The Nth Country and Arms Control.* Washington, DC: National Planning Association.

Natsios, Andrew S. 2001. *The Great North Korean Famine.* Washington, DC: United States Institute of Peace Press.

Neufeld, Michael. 1995. *The Rocket and the Reich: Peenemünde and the Coming of the Ballistic Missile Era.* New York: Free Press.

Nevins, Allan. 1946. "How We Felt About the War." In *While You Were Gone: A Report on Wartime Life in the United States,* ed. Jack Goodman. New York: Simon & Schuster, 3–27.

Nye, Joseph S., Jr. 1987. "Nuclear Learning and U.S.-Soviet Security Regimes." *International Organization* 41(3) Summer: 371–402.

Oberdorfer, Don. 1992. *The Turn: From the Cold War to a New Era.* New York: Touchstone.

———. 2001. *The Two Koreas: A Contemporary History.* Rev. ed. New York: Basic.

———. 2005. "Dealing with the North Korean Nuclear Threat." Philadelphia, PA: Foreign Policy Research Institute (www.fpri.org).

Office of Technology Assessment (OTA). 1979. *The Effects of Nuclear War.* Washington, DC: Congress of the United States, OTA-NS-89.

———. 1993. *Proliferation of Weapons of Mass Destruction: Assessing the Risks, OTA-559, August.* Washington, DC: U.S. Government Printing Office.

Osgood, Charles E. 1962. *An Alternative to War or Surrender.* Urbana: University of Illinois Press.

O'Kane, Maggie. 1998a. "Sick and Dying in Their Hospital Beds, the Pitiful Victims of Sanctions and Saddam." *Guardian* 19 February: 1.

———. 1998b. "Iraqi Rich Make Mockery of Sanctions." *Guardian* 21 November: 18.

———. 1998c. "Saddam Wields Terror—and Feigns Respect." *Guardian* 25 November: 3.

Paarlberg, Rob. 1973. "Forgetting About the Unthinkable." *Foreign Policy* Spring: 132–40.

Pape, Robert A. 2005. *Dying to Win: The Strategic Logic of Suicide Terrorism*. New York: Random House.

Parachini, John, 2003. "Putting WMD Terrorism into Perspective." *Washington Quarterly* 26(4) Autumn: 37–50.

Paul, T. V. 1994. *Asymmetric Conflicts: War Initiation by Weaker Powers*. New York: Cambridge University Press.

———. 2000. *Power Versus Prudence: Why Nations Forgo Nuclear Weapons*. Montreal, ON: McGill-Queen's University Press.

———. 2009. *The Tradition of Non-Use of Nuclear Weapons*. Stanford, CA: Stanford University Press.

Payne, Keith B. 2009. "On Nuclear Deterrence and Assurance." *Strategic Studies Quarterly* 3(1) Spring: 43–80.

Perle, Richard N. 2000. "Iraq: Saddam Unbound." In *Present Dangers: Crisis and Opportunity in American Foreign and Defense Policy*, ed. Robert Kagan and William Kristol. San Francisco: Encounter Books, 99–110.

———. 2009. "Ambushed on the Potomac." *National Journal* January/February: 35–44.

Perry, William J., Ashton B. Carter, and Michael M. May. 2007. "After the Bomb." *New York Times* 12 June.

Pillar, Paul R. 2003. *Terrorism and U.S. Foreign Policy*. Washington, DC: Brookings Institution Press.

Pincus, Walter. 2008. "Panel Cites 'Tipping Point' On Nuclear Proliferation." *Washington Post* 16 December: A17.

Pipes, Richard. 1984. *Survival Is Not Enough*. New York: Simon and Schuster.

Pluta, Anna M., and Peter D. Zimmerman. 2006. "Nuclear Terrorism: A Disheartening Dissent." *Survival* 48(2) Summer: 55–70.

Podhoretz, Norman. 2002. "In Praise of the Bush Doctrine." *Commentary* 114(2) September: 19–28.

Pollack, Kenneth M. 2002. *The Threatening Storm: The Case for Invading Iraq*. New York: Random House.

Port, Bob, and Greg B. Smith. 2001. "'Suitcase Bomb' Allegedly Sought: Bin Laden Eyes Russian Stockpile." *Seattle Times* 3 October: A3.

Porter, Patrick. 2009. "Long wars and long telegrams: containing Al-Qaeda." *International Affairs* 85(2) March: 285–305.

Posen, Barry R. 1984/85. "Measuring the European Conventional Balance." *International Security* 9(3) Winter: 47–88.

Posner, Richard A. 2005. *Catastrophe: Risk and Response*. New York: Oxford University Press.

Potter, William C. 1995. *The Politics of Nuclear Renunciation: The Cases of Belarus, Kazakhstan, and Ukraine*. Washington, DC: Henry L. Stimson Center.

Potter, William C., and Gaukhar Mukhatzhanova. 2008. "Divining Nuclear Intentions: A Review Essay." *International Security* 33(1) Summer: 139–69.

Powell, Colin L., and Joseph E. Persico. 1995. *My American Journey*. New York: Random House.

Powers, Thomas. 2008. "Iran: The Threat." *New York Review of Books* 17 July.

Priest, Dana, and Josh White. 2005. "War Helps Recruit Terrorists, Hill Told; Intelligence Officials Talk Of Growing Insurgency." *Washington Post* 17 February: A1.

Rapoport, David C. 1999. "Terrorists and Weapons of the Apocalypse." *National Security Studies Quarterly* 5(1) Summer: 49–67.

Rappard, William E. 1940. *The Quest for Peace since the World War*. Cambridge, MA: Harvard University Press.

Rashid, Ahmed. 2000. *Taliban: Militant Islam, Oil and Fundamentalism in Central Asia*. New Haven, CT: Yale University Press.

Ray, James Lee. 1989. "The Abolition of Slavery and the End of International War." *International Organization* 43(3) Summer: 405–39.

Record, Jeffrey. 2003. *Bounding the Global War on Terrorism*. Carlisle, PA: Strategic Studies Institute, U.S. Army War College, December.

Reed, Thomas C., and Danny B. Stillman. 2009. *The Nuclear Express: A Political History of the Bomb and Its Proliferation*. Minneapolis, MN: Zenith Press.

Rees, Martin. 2003. *Our Final Hour*. New York: Basic Books.

Reiss, Mitchell B. 2004. "The Nuclear Tipping Point: Prospects for a World of Many Nuclear Weapons States." In *The Nuclear Tipping Point: Why States Reconsider Their Nuclear Choices*, ed. Kurt M. Campbell, Robert J. Einhorn and Mitchell B. Reiss. Washington, DC: Brookings Institution Press, 3–17.

Revzin, Philip. 1987. "Italy Boasts It Deserves Britain's Place in Rich Nations' Club." *Wall Street Journal* 27 February: 42.

Rhodes, Richard. 2007. *Arsenals of Folly: The Making of the Nuclear Arms Race*. New York: Knopf.

Rice, Condoleezza. 2000. "Promoting the National Interest." *Foreign Affairs* 79(1) January/February: 45–62.

———. 2002. "Dr. Condoleezza Rice Discusses President's National Security Strategy." Washington, DC: Office of the Press Secretary, White House, 1 October. www.whitehouse.gov/news/releases/2002/10/20021001-6.html

Rich, Norman. 1973. *Hitler's War Aims: Ideology, the Nazi State, and the Course of Expansion*. New York: Norton.

Richardson, Louise. 2006. *What Terrorists Want: Understanding the Enemy, Containing the Threat*. New York: Random House.

Richelson, Jeffrey T. 2006. *Spying on the Bomb: American Nuclear Intelligence from Nazi Germany to Iran and North Korea*. New York: Norton.

Riedel, Bruce. 2007. "Al Qaeda Strikes Back." *Foreign Affairs* May/June.

Robbins, Carla. 2008. "Thinking the Unthinkable: A World without Nuclear Weapons." *New York Times* 30 June: A22.

Robertson, Nic. 2008. "Sources: Taliban split with al Qaeda, seek peace." *cnn.com* 6 October. edition.cnn.com/2008/WORLD/asiapcf/10/06/afghan.saudi.talks/index.html

Rockwell, Theodore. 2003. "Radiation Chicken Little." *Washington Post* 16 September: A19.

Ropeik, David, and George Gray. 2002. *Risk: A Practical Guide for Deciding What's Really Safe and What's Really Dangerous in the World Around You*. Boston: Houghton Mifflin.

Rosecrance, Richard. 1964. "International Stability and Nuclear Diffusion." In *The Dispersion of Nuclear Weapons: Strategy and Politics*, ed. Richard Rosecrance. New York: Columbia University Press, 293–314.

———. 1975. *Strategic Deterrence Reconsidered*. London: International Institute for Strategic Studies, Adelphi Paper No. 116 (Spring).

———. 1986. *The Rise of the Trading State: Conquest and Commerce in the Modern World*. New York: Basic Books.

Rosenberg, David Alan. 1994. "The History of World War III, 1945–1990: A Conceptual Framework." In *On Cultural Ground: Essays in International History,* ed. Robert David Johnson. Chicago: Imprint Publications, 197–235.

Ross, Brian. 2005. "Secret FBI Report Questions Al Qaeda Capabilities: No 'True' Al Qaeda Sleeper Agents Have Been Found in U.S." *ABC News* 9 March. abcnews. go.com/WNT/Investigation/story?id=566425&page=1

Rothgeb, John M., Jr. 1993. *Defining Power: Influence and Force in the Contemporary International System.* New York: St. Martin's.

Ruppe, David. 2003. "United States I: Former Bush Official Advocates Low-Yield Weapon Research." Global Security Newswire 11 June. www.nti.org/d%5Fnewswire/issues/2003/6/11/6s.html

———. 2005. "Threat-Mongering?" *National Journal* 23 April: 1218–25.

Rush, Myron. 1993. "Fortune and Fate." *National Interest* Spring: 19–25.

Sagan, Scott D. 1993. *The Limits of Safety: Organizations, Accidents, and Nuclear Weapons.* Princeton, NJ: Princeton University Press.

Sagan, Scott D., and Kenneth N. Waltz. 2003. *The Spread of Nuclear Weapons: A Debate Renewed.* New York: Norton.

Sageman, Marc. 2004. *Understanding Terror Networks.* Philadelphia: University of Pennsylvania Press.

———. 2008. *Leaderless Jihad.* Philadelphia: University of Pennsylvania Press.

Sanders, Eli. 2005. "Judge Delays Terrorist's Sentencing, Hoping for Cooperation." *New York Times* 28 April.

Sanger, David E., and William J. Broad. 2004. "Pakistani's Nuclear Earnings: $100 Million." *New York Times* 16 March: A12.

Schell, Jonathan. 1982. *The Fate of the Earth.* New York: Knopf.

———. 2003. *The Unconquerable World: Power, Nonviolence, and the Will of the People.* New York: Metropolitan Books.

Schelling, Thomas C. 2004. "Deterring Nuclear Terrorists." *Issues in Science and Technology* 20(4) Summer: 11–12.

———. 2005. Nobel Prize Lecture: "An Astonishing Sixty Years: The Legacy of Hiroshima." Nobelprize.org, 8 December. nobelprize.org/nobel_prizes/economics/laureates/2005/schelling-lecture. html

Scheuer, Michael. 2002. *Through Our Enemies' Eyes: Osama Bin Laden, Radical Islam, and the Future of America.* Washington, DC: Brassey's.

———. 2004. *Imperial Hubris: Why the West Is Losing the War on Terror.* Dulles, VA: Brassey's.

———. 2006. "Courting Catastrophe: America Five Years After 9/11." *National Interest* September/October: 20–23.

Schilling, Warner R. 1961. "The H-Bomb Decision." *Political Science Quarterly* 76(1) March: 24–46.

Schlesinger, James. 1967. *On Relating Non-Technical Elements to Systems Studies.* Santa Monica, CA: RAND Corporation, P-3545 (February).

Schneier, Bruce. 2003. *Beyond Fear: Thinking Sensibly About Security in an Uncertain World.* New York: Copernicus.

Schroeder, Paul W. 2006. "The Life and Death of a Long Peace, 1763–1914." In *The Waning of Major War: Theories and Debates,* ed. Raimo Väyryen. New York: Routledge, 33–63.

Schuman, Howard, Jacob Ludwig, and Jon A. Krosnick. 1986. "The Perceived Threat of Nuclear War, Salience, and Open Questions." *Public Opinion Quarterly* 50(4) Winter: 519–36.

Seitz, Russell. 2004. "Weaker Than We Think." *American Conservative* 6 December.

Serwer, Andy, and Julia Boorstin. 2002. "The Oracle of Everything." *Fortune* 11 November.

Shanken, Marvin R. 2003. "General Tommy Franks: An Exclusive Interview with America's Top General in the War on Terrorism." *Cigar Aficionado* December.

Shapiro, Jeremy. 2007. *Managing Homeland Security: Develop a Threat-Based Strategy.* Washington, DC: Brookings Institution, Opportunity 08 paper.

Sharrock, David. 1999. "Iraq Is Falling Apart, We Are Doomed." *Guardian* 24 April: 14.

Sheets, Lawrence Scott. 2008. "A Smuggler's Story." *Atlantic* April: 60–70.

Shevchenko, Arkady N. 1985. *Breaking with Moscow.* New York: Knopf.

Shlaes, Amity. 1988. "Talk Turns to Triple Zero in West Germany." *Wall Street Journal* 9 December: A22.

Shultz, George P., William J. Perry, Henry A. Kissinger, and Sam Nunn. 2007. "A World Free of Nuclear Weapons." *Wall Street Journal* 4 January.

———. 2008. "Toward a Nuclear-Free World." *Wall Street Journal* 15 January.

Sigal, Leon V. 1998. *Disarming Strangers: Nuclear Diplomacy with North Korea.* Princeton, NJ: Princeton University Press.

Sikora, Karol. 1999. "Cancer Services Are Suffering in Iraq." *BMJ* 16 January.

Silberman, Laurence H., and Charles S. Robb. 2005. *Report to the President of the United States of the Commission on the Intelligence Capabilities of the United States Regarding Weapons of Mass Destruction,* 31 March. Available at govinfo.library.unt.edu/wmd/report/index.html

Simon, Jeffrey D. 2001. *The Terrorist Trap: America's Experience with Terrorism.* 2nd ed. Bloomington, IN: Indiana University Press.

Singer, J. David. 1962. *Deterrence, Arms Control, and Disarmament.* Columbus, Ohio: Ohio State University Press.

Slovic, Paul. 2000. "Perception of Risk from Radiation." In *The Perception of Risk,* ed. Paul Slovic. London: Earthscan, 264–74.

Smith, Derek D. 2006. *Deterring America: Rogue States and the Proliferation of Weapons of Mass Destruction.* Cambridge, UK: Cambridge University Press.

Smith, Patrick. 2007. "The Airport Security Follies." nytimes.com 28 December. jetlagged.blogs.nytimes.com/author/psmith/2007/12/28/

Smith, R. Jeffrey, and David Hoffman. 1997. "No Support Found for Report of Lost Russian Suitcase-Sized Nuclear Weapons." *Washington Post* 5 September: A19.

Smoke, Richard. 1993. *National Security and the Nuclear Dilemma: An Introduction to the American Experience in the Cold War.* 3rd ed. New York: McGraw-Hill.

Snow, C. P. 1961. "The Moral Un-Neutrality of Science." *Science* 27 January: 255–59.

Snyder, Glenn H. 1961. *Deterrence and Defense.* Princeton: Princeton University Press.

Solingen, Etel. 2007. *Nuclear Logics: Contrasting Paths in East Asia and the Middle East.* Princeton, NJ: Princeton University Press.

Spector, Ronald H. 1985. *Eagle against the Sun: The American War with Japan.* New York: Vintage.

Stahl, Leslie. 1996. "Punishing Saddam; Sanctions against Iraq Not Hurting Leaders of the Country, But the Children Are Suffering and Dying." *60 Minutes,* CBS Television, 12 May.

Steele, Jonathan. 2006. "Lost in Translation." *Guardian* Comment is free 14 June. commentisfree.guardian.co.uk/jonathan_steele/2006/06/post_155.html

Stein, Sam. 2008. "Rove: We Wouldn't Have Invaded Iraq If We Knew the Truth about WMDs." Huffington Post.com (2 December).

Stenersen, Anne. 2008. *Al-Qaida's Quest for Weapons of Mass Destruction: The History behind the Hype.* Saarbrücken, Germany: VDM Verlag Dr. Müller. Shorter and more accessible version: www.mil.no/multimedia/archive/00114/The_Military_Power__114876a.pdf

Stern, Jessica. 1998–99. "Apocalypse Never, but the Threat Is Real." *Survival* 40(4) Winter: 176–79.

Stevenson, Jonathan, ed. 2004. *Strategic Survey 2003/4: An Evaluation and Forecast of World Affairs.* London: Oxford University Press for the International Institute for Strategic Studies.

Stockton, Richard. 1932. *Inevitable War.* New York: Perth.

Stueck, William. 2002. *Rethinking the Korean War: A New Diplomatic and Strategic History.* Princeton, NJ: Princeton University Press.

Sunstein, Cass R. 2006. "The Case for Fear." *New Republic* 11 December: 29–33.

Suskind, Ron. 2006. *The One Percent Doctrine: Deep Inside America's Pursuit of Its Enemies Since 9/11.* New York: Simon & Schuster.

———. 2008. *The Way of the World: A Story of Truth and Hope in an Age of Extremism.* New York: HarperCollins.

Sweeney, John. 1998. "The Truth About Iraq's Dying Babies." *Guardian Weekly* 15 March: 7.

Takeyh, Ray. 2001. "The Rogue Who Came in from the Cold." *Foreign Affairs* 80(3) May/June: 62–72.

Taleb, Nassim Nicholas. 2007. *The Black Swan: The Impact of the Highly Improbable.* New York: Random House.

Tannenwald, Nina. 2007. *The Nuclear Taboo: The United States and the Non-Use of Nuclear Weapons Since 1945.* New York: Cambridge University Press.

Taubman, William. 1982. *Stalin's American Policy.* New York: Norton.

Tenet, George, and Bill Harlow. 2007. *At the Center of the Storm: My Years at the CIA.* New York: HarperCollins.

Tetlock, Philip E. 2005. *Expert Political Judgment: How Good Is It? How Can We Know?* Princeton, NJ: Princeton University Press.

Thomas, Hugh. 1986. *Armed Truce: The Beginnings of the Cold War, 1945–46.* New York: Atheneum.

Thorpe, James A. 1978. "Truman's Ultimatum to Stalin on the 1946 Azerbaijan Crisis: The Making of a Myth." *Journal of Politics* 40(1) February: 188–95.

Toynbee, Arnold J. 1950. *War and Civilization.* New York: Oxford University Press.

Trachtenberg, Marc. 1985. "Nuclear Weapons and the Cuban Missile Crisis." *International Security* 10(1) Summer: 156–63.

———. 1999. *A Constructed Peace: The Making of the European Settlement, 1945–1963.* Princeton, NJ: Princeton University Press.

Tucker, Jonathan B., and Amy Sands. 1999. "An Unlikely Threat." *Bulletin of Atomic Scientists* July/August: 46–52.

U.S. Army, Manhattan Engineer District. 1946. *The Atomic Bombings of Hiroshima and Nagasaki.* Washington, DC: United States Army.

Ulam, Adam S. 1968. *Expansion and Coexistence.* New York: Praeger.

———. 1971. *The Rivals: America and Russia since World War II.* New York: Penguin.

United Nations. 1999. *Report of the Second Panel Established Pursuant to the Note by the President of the Security Council of 30 January 1999 (S/1999/100), Concerning the Current Humanitarian Situation in Iraq*. New York: United Nations, 30 March. www.un.org/Depts/oip/panelrep.html.

USSBS (United States Strategic Bombing Survey). 1946. *Japan's Struggle to End the War*. New York: Garland.

Valentino, Benjamin. 2004. *Final Solutions: Mass Killing and Genocide in the 20th Century*. Ithaca, NY: Cornell University Press.

van Creveld, Martin. 1999. *The Rise and Decline of the State*. Cambridge, UK: Cambridge University Press.

———. 2006. "The Waning of Major War." In *The Waning of Major War: Theories and Debates,* ed. Raimo Väyryen. New York: Routledge, 97–112.

Vartabedian, Ralph. 2008. "How the U.S. Seeks to Avert Nuclear Terror." *Los Angeles Times* 6 January.

Vasquez, John A. 1991. "The Deterrence Myth: Nuclear Weapons and the Prevention of Nuclear War." In *The Long Postwar Peace: Contending Explanations and Projections,* ed. Charles W. Kegley, Jr. New York: HarperCollins, 205–23.

———. 1998. *The Power of Power Politics: From Classical Realism to Neotraditionalism*. Cambridge, UK: Cambridge University Press.

Venzke, Ben, and Aimee Ibrahim. 2003. *The al-Qaeda Threat: An Analytical Guide to al-Qaeda's Tactics & Targets*. Alexandria, VA: Tempest Publishing.

Voslensky, Michael. 1984. *Nomenklatura: The New Soviet Ruling Class*. Garden City, NY: Doubleday.

Wagar, W. Warren. 1961. *H. G. Wells and the World State*. New Haven, CT: Yale University Press.

Wald, Matthew L. 2005. "Agency Seeks Broad Standard for 'Dirty Bomb' Exposure." *New York Times* 8 November: A20.

———. 2006. "Proposal on 'Dirty Bomb' Attack Would Accept Higher Exposure." *New York Times* 5 January: A15.

Walt, Stephen M. 2000. "Containing Rogues and Renegades: Coalition Strategies and Counterproliferation." In *The Coming Crisis: Nuclear Proliferation, U.S. Interests, and World Order,* ed. Victor A. Utgoff. Cambridge, MA: MIT Press, 191–226.

Waltz, Kenneth N. 1979. *Theory of International Politics*. Reading, MA: Addison-Wesley.

———. 1988. "The Origins of War in Neorealist Theory." *Journal of Interdisciplinary History* 18(4) Spring: 615–28.

———. 1990. "Nuclear Myths and Political Realities." *American Political Science Review* 84(3) September: 731–45.

Warrick, Joby. 2007. "Pakistan Nuclear Security Questioned: Lack of Knowledge About Arsenal May Limit U.S. Options." *Washington Post* 11 November: A1.

———. 2008. "U.S. Cites Big Gains Against Al-Qaeda." *Washington Post* 30 May: A1.

Waterman, Shaun. 2006. "Analysis: No Real Terror A-Bomb Threat." *UPI* 6 November.

Weart, Spencer R. 1988. *Nuclear Fear: A History of Images*. Cambridge, MA: Harvard University Press.

Weiner, Tim. 1999a. "U.S. Spied on Iraq Under U.N. Cover, Officials Now Say." *New York Times* 7 January: A1.

———. 1999b. "U.S. Used U.N. Team to Place Spy Device in Iraq, Aides Say." *New York Times* 8 January: A1.

Weisberg, Jacob. 2008. "How Did I Get Iraq Wrong?" Slate.com. www.slate.com/id/2187105/

Welch, David A., and James G. Blight. 1987/88. "The Eleventh Hour of the Cuban Missile Crisis: An Introduction to the ExComm Transcripts." *International Security* 12(3) Winter: 5–29.

Welch, Larry D. 2000. Foreword. In *The Coming Crisis: Nuclear Proliferation, U.S. Interests, and World Order.* Cambridge, MA: MIT Press, vii–ix.

Welch, Matt. 2002. "The Politics of Dead Children." *Reason* 2 March: 53–58.

Wells, H. G. 1914. *The War That Will End War.* New York: Duffield.

———. 1968. *The Last Books of H. G. Wells.* London: H. G. Wells Society.

Werth, Alexander. 1964. *Russia at War, 1941–1945.* New York: Dutton.

Will, George. 2004. "Global Warming? Hot Air." *Washington Post* 23 December: A23.

Williams, Brian Glyn. 2008. "Return of the Arabs: Al-Qa'ida's Current Military Role in the Afghan Insurgency." *CTC Sentinel* 1(3) February: 22–25.

Williams, Paul L. 2005. *The Al Qaeda Connection: International Terrorism, Organized Crime, and the Coming Apocalypse.* Amherst, NY: Prometheus Books.

———. 2007. "Bin Laden Biographer: American Media Altered Bin Laden's Latest Message." *New Media Journal* 8 August. www.newmediajournal.us/staff/p_williams/09122007.htm

Willmott, H. P. 1982. *Empires in the Balance.* Annapolis, MD: Naval Institute Press.

———. 1983. *The Barrier and the Javelin: Japanese and Allied Pacific Strategies, February to June 1942.* Annapolis, MD: Naval Institute Press.

Wills, David C. 2003. *The First War on Terrorism: Counter-Terrorism Policy during the Reagan Administration.* Lanham, MD: Rowman & Littlefield.

Wilson, Ward. 2007. "The Winning Weapon? Rethinking Nuclear Weapons in Light of Hiroshima." *International Security* 31(4) Spring: 162–79.

———. 2008. "The Myth of Nuclear Deterrence." *Nonproliferation Review* 15(3) November: 421–39.

Winslow, Art. 2007. "Chain Reactions." Review of *The Atomic Bazaar*, by William Langewiesche. *Los Angeles Times* 20 May.

Wirz, Christoph, and Emmanuel Egger. 2005. "Use of Nuclear and Radiological Weapons by Terrorists?" *International Review of the Red Cross* 87(859) September: 497–510. www.icrc.org/Web/eng/siteeng0.nsf/htmlall/review-859-p497/$File/irrc_859_Egger_Wirz.pdf

Wiseman, Paul. 2009. "Upstaging Clinton, N. Korea again exerts influence." *USA Today* 18 February: 8A.

Wolfenstein, Martha. 1957. *Disaster: A Psychological Study.* London: Routledge and Kegan Paul.

Wolfsthal, Jon B. 2005. "The Next Nuclear Wave." *Foreign Affairs* January/February.

Woodward, Bob. 2008. "Why Did Violence Plummet? It Wasn't Just the Surge." *Washington Post* 8 September: A9.

Woolsey, R. James, Jr. 1993. Testimony before the Senate Intelligence Committee, 2 February.

Wright, Lawrence. 2006. *The Looming Tower: Al-Qaeda and the Road to 9/11.* New York: Knopf. Page references are to the hardcover edition.

WuDunn, Sheryl. 1993. "Beijing Goes All Out to Get Olympics in 2000." *New York Times* 11 March: A12.

Younger, Stephen M. 2007. *Endangered Species: How We Can Avoid Mass Destruction and Build a Lasting Peace.* New York: Ecco.

Younger, Stephen M. 2009. *The Bomb: A New History*. New York: Ecco.

Yusuf, Moeed. 2009. *Predicting Proliferation: The History of the Future of Nuclear Weapons*. Washington, DC: Brookings Institution.

Zakaria, Fareed. 2007. "Stalin, Mao and...Ahmadinejad?" *Newsweek* 29 October.

———. 2008a. "The Only Thing We Have to Fear." *Newsweek* 24 May.

———. 2008b. "True or False: We Need a Wartime President." WashingtonPost.com *PostGlobal* 6 July.

Zarate, Robert, and Henry Sokolski, eds. 2009. *Nuclear Heuristics: Selected Writings of Albert and Roberta Wohlstetter*. Carlisle Barracks, PA: Strategic Studies Institute, U.S. Army War College.

Zenko, Micah. 2006. "Intelligence Estimates of Nuclear Terrorism." *Annals of the American Academy of Political and Social Science* September: 87–102.

———. 2007. "A Nuclear Site Is Breached: South African Attack Should Sound Alarms." *Washington Post* 20 December: A29.

Zimmerman, Peter D., and Jeffrey G. Lewis. 2006. "The Bomb in the Backyard." *Foreign Policy* November/December: 32–39.

Zimmerman, Peter D., and Cheryl Loeb. 2004. "Dirty Bombs: The Threat Revisited." *Defense Horizons* January: 1–11.

Index

About the Author

John Mueller is Professor of Political Science at Ohio State University. His books, several of which have won prizes, include *War, Presidents and Public Opinion* (1973), *Astaire Dancing: The Musical Films* (1985), *Retreat from Doomsday: The Obsolescence of Major War* (1989), *Policy and Opinion in the Gulf War* (1994), *Quiet Cataclysm* (1995), *Capitalism, Democracy, and Ralph's Pretty Good Grocery* (1999), *The Remnants of War* (2004), *Overblown* (2006), *War and Ideas* (2011), and *Terror, Security, and Money* (2011). He has also published numerous articles in scholarly journals and general magazines and newspapers, is a member of the American Academy of Arts and Sciences, and has been a John Simon Guggenheim Fellow. Mueller has also received several teaching prizes, and in 2009 received the International Studies Association's Susan Strange Award that "recognizes a person whose singular intellect, assertiveness, and insight most challenge conventional wisdom and intellectual and organizational complacency in the international studies community."

polisci.osu.edu/faculty/jmueller